SIR FRANCIS BACON

A BIOGRAPHY

BY THE SAME AUTHOR

Biographies and Studies

MADELEINE
THE STARR AFFAIR
DOUBLE WEBS
HOROSCOPE FOR A DOUBLE AGENT
THE MAGICAL DILEMMA OF VICTOR NEUBURG
SHELLEY, A BIOGRAPHY
SWINBURNE, A BIOGRAPHY
NOOR-UN-NISA INAYAT KHAN (MADELEINE)
THE GERMAN PENETRATION OF S.O.E.
THE COMTE DE SAINT-GERMAIN
DERICOURT, THE CHEQUERED SPY
BLATAVSKY AND HER TEACHERS
SICKERT AND THE RIPPER CRIMES
CATS AND OTHER IMMORTALS

Verse

VENUS PROTECTED
CARTHAGE AND THE MIDNIGHT SUN
AFRICAN VIOLETS
THE SUN'S CART
SILVER PLANET
DARUN AND PITAR
GILBY
TINTAGEL
CONVERSATIONS WITH A CAPTOR
THE NORN
PROPHECY FROM HELEN
THE GREAT ADVENTURE OF THE MUCH TRAVELLED LITTLE OAK TREE
THE MYSTICAL TALE OF TWO HENS
THE NEW ARRIVAL
THE NIGHTINGALE
BAMBINA, THE THANKSGIVING PICTURE
THE PASSING OF BAMBINA AND THE COMING OF CHALCEDONY
CHALCEDONY'S KITTENS
LEO AND AMERICA
CATS AND BURGLARS

Verse in translation

SHIVA'S DANCE
(from the French of Hélène Bouvard)
THAT THE GODS MAY REMEMBER
(from the French of Hélène Bouvard)
THE PROPHET
(from the Russian of Alexander Pushkin)

JEAN OVERTON FULLER

Sir Francis Bacon

A BIOGRAPHY

GEORGE MANN of MAIDSTONE

SIR FRANCIS BACON
A Biography

First published under the title *Francis Bacon*
by East-West Publications, 1981

This revised edition first published by George Mann 1994

ISBN 0 7041 0256 0

Printed and bound in Great Britain
by Antony Rowe Ltd
of Chippenham, Wiltshire
and published by
George Mann Books, PO Box 22, Maidstone
in the English County of Kent

About the Author

JEAN Overton Fuller has a well-earned high reputation for painstaking research — evinced in her notable biographies *Swinburne* and *Shelley* as well as in the best-selling *Madeleine* and other investigative books on the wartime activities of the French Section of the Special Operations Executive (S.O.E.), whose gross ineptitude sent many brave young people to their deaths at the hands of the Germans in World War II.

She spent some years on the professional stage, has produced books of poetry much broadcast by the BBC, and is an accomplished painter. This present book — *Sir Francis Bacon* — took her seventeen years to research and to write.

Contents

List of Illustrations

11. St Michael's, Gorhambury. Oil by the author. *(Photo: Martin Booth)*

12. Canonbury Tower. Oil by the author. *(Photo: Martin Booth)*

13. The Veiled and Feathered Sunburst. *(The Marquis of Northampton – Canonbury Tower. Photo: Basil Martin)*

14. Headpiece to the title-page of *Venus and Adonis*, 1594. *(Bodleian Library, Oxford)*

15. Headpiece to the *Sonnets*, 1609. *(Bodleian Library, Oxford)*

16. Headpiece to the title-page of *Manes Verulamiani*, 1626. *(Bodleian Library, Oxford)*

17. The title-page to *Cryptomenytices*.

18. The title-page to a Dutch edition of Bacon's *Henry VII* (the Latin text).

19. The title-page to a Dutch edition of Bacon's *Advancement of Learning* (the Latin text).

20. Frontispiece from *The History of the Royal Society*.

Cover Portrait of Bacon by Van Somer *(Royal Society)*.

Acknowledgements

My first acknowledgement must be to Sir Edmund and Lady Bacon, who received me at Raveningham with the utmost kindness and did everything they could to be helpful.

At Gorhambury, the Countess of Verulam lent what aid she could, whilst I am indebted to the Verulam's secretary, Mrs. Norah King, for answering my many queries.

At Alnwick Castle, the Duke of Northumberland graciously received me, laid out the Northumberland Manuscript for me and turned its pages with me.

At Rousham, Mr. and Mrs. Cotrill-Dormer received me and laid out for me the letters of their forbear, the Countess of Southampton, and other papers.

The Marquess of Northampton took the pains to read 'The Veiled and Feathered Sunburst', my chapter relating to his curious London property, Canonbury Tower, and approved it.

Professor Brisco Ford, F.R.S., Fellow of All Souls and Emeritus Professor of Genetics at Oxford, gave me invaluable help on Genetics.

Dr. Margaret Little, M.B., Ch.B, M.R.C.Psych., helped on a miscellany of points, from hereditary ailments to poisons.

Baroness Ward of North Tyneside, C.H., D.B.E., a friend of more than twenty years, looked up the Parliamentary records concerning Bacon, and took me to have a close look at the Woolsack.[1]

Mr. Douglas Matthews of the London Library has rendered so much assistance above and beyond the exigencies of duty, I do not know what I should have done without him.

Miss P.M. Baker, Sterling Librarian of the University of London, allowed me to take home precious volumes from the Durning-Lawrence Library.

At the Bodleian, I should like to acknowledge courtesy of Mr. R.J. Roberts, Keeper of Printed Books; at Trinity College, Cambridge, of Mr. T. Kaye, Librarian; at Corpus Christi, Cambridge, of Mr. G.H.S. Bushnell, Fellow in Charge of Pictures; at the Victoria and Albert Museum, of Dr. Roy Strong, Director; at the National Portrait Gallery of Mr. Robin Gibson, Assistant Keeper, and Miss Sarah Wimbush; at the Ashmolean of Mr. David Piper, Director; at Lambeth Palace of Mr. E.G.W. Bill, Librarian; at the British Museum of Miss Olorenshaw of the Manuscript Department and Mr. T.G.H. James, Keeper of Egyptian Antiquities; in the State Papers Department, to Mr. M.E. Goldrick; at St. Albans School, of Mr. F.I. Kilvington, Headmaster; at Westminster Abbey of Mr. Howard M. Nixon, Librarian; at Gray's Inn of Mr. P.C. Bedingham, Librarian; at the College of Arms of Mr. T.D. Matthews, Windsor Herald, and

---

1. Baroness Ward passed away after this book had been given to the printer. As I began my researches for it in November, 1967, some of the others whose help is acknowledged may also have died.

Mr. F.S. Andrus, Lancaster Herald; at the Royal Academy of Music of Mrs. Elizabeth Wells, Curator, and Miss Celia Clark, Assistant Curator; at the National Maritime Museum at Greenwich of Mr. N.E. Upham, Curator of Models, Mr. Christopher Tyrrel, Director Hydrography and Mr. Roger Quam, Department of Pictures; at the Royal Botanic Gardens, Kew, Miss Rosemary Angel; at the British Astronomical Association of Mr. J.L. White, F.R.A.S.; at Dulwich College of Mr. A.C.L. Hall, Librarian, and Mr. D.C. Banwell; at the Public Record Office of Miss Alice Prochaska; at Hatfield House of Mr. R.H. Harcourt Williams, Librarian; at the House of Lords Record Office of Mr. H.S. Cobb; at the House of Commons of Mr. John Palmer, Librarian; at the Royal Philatelic Association of Mr. A.G. Lee, President; at the Bible Society of Mr. Allan S. Jesson, Librarian; at the Lord Chamberlain's Office of Mr. Geoffrey de Bellaign and Miss J. Brown; at St. Peter's, Titchfield, of the Rev. Norman A. Miller; at Titchfield Abbey of Mr. Cleeve-Evans, Custodian; at Thorton of the Rev. C.J.R. Armstrong, Priest-in-Charge; at Westminster City Library of Mr. K.C. Harrison, Librarian, and Miss S. Swarbrick; at Islington Public Library of Mr. C.A. Elliot, Librarian, and Mr. E.A. Willats; at Richmond Public Library of Mr. Gilbert Turner; at Nottingham Public Library of Mr. Paul Sykes; at Walesby of Mr. Walter Parker; at Lewes Public Library of Miss Christine Connelly, Librarian; at Stratford-on-Avon Public Library of Mr. G.D. Hall; at the Hertfordshire County Records Office of Mr. Peter Walner, County Archivist; at the Hampshire Record Office of Mrs. Eleanor Cottrill, County Archivist, and Miss M.H. Varco; at the City of Southampton Records Office of Mr. S.D. Thomson, City Archivist; at the Linguaphone Institute, Miss Sally Walker, Head of Studio Services; at the Bibliothèque Nationale, Paris, of M. Marcel Thomas, Conservateur en Chef; at the Archives du Nord, Lille, of M. René Robinet, Conservateur en Chef; at the Koninklijke Bibliotheek, The Hague, of Mr. Douwes Dekker; at Thoresby of Mr. R.P.H. McFerran; at the Nottinghamshire Record Office of Mr. A.J.M. Henstock and Mr. Reginald Brocklesby.

Scholars who have given me of their special knowledge are Professor Arthur Child, Professor of Philosophy, University of California; Mr. J.C. Maxwell, of Balliol College, Oxford; Mr. R.H. Hill, Oxford; Dr. Phil. Gerhard Endress, Professor an der Johann-Wolfgang Goethe Universitaet, Frankfurt; Dr. P.M. Coulon, Department of Romance Languages, McMaster University, Ontario; Mr. Roger Hughfield, Librarian, Merton College, Oxford; and Professor A.C. Gimson, Principal of the Department of Phonetics and Linguistics, University College London (once my tutor, under his predecessor in office, my old friend Professor Daniel Jones).

Amongst fellow writers on the period, the one to whom I am most indebted is Mr. Ivor Cook, who gave me prints of photographs he had taken of the signatures of a number of members of the Hervey family. Moreover, in spite of great divergence in our views, he lent me much unpublished work of his own in preparation.

Dr. Neville Williams gave me the source references for several matters mentioned in his books, Elizabeth Jenkins one and Dr. A.L. Rowse one. Mr. Robert Lacey gave me a reply with courtesy, and the late Sir John Neale gave me an opinion.

Mr. Martin Booth gave me an opinion of Bacon's translation of the Psalms and photographed my paintings.

The Francis Bacon Society was welcoming, particularly Commander Martin Pares, R.N., President; Mr. Noel Fermour, Chairman; Mr. T.D. Bokenham, Vice-Chairman; Mrs. D. Brameld, Secretary, Mr. Austin Hatt-Arnold, Mr. Ewen MacDuff, Professor Henrion, the late Dr. Joachim Gerstenberg and Mr. Basil Martin.

Madame Hélène Bouvard, a friend of more than thirty years standing, offered several inspirational suggestions, which I followed up with fruit.

I have left to the last my friend, Mr. Timothy d'Arch Smith. His knowledge of bibliography has at all times been at my disposal, but of course the help he has rendered has not been limited to bibliography. I would be hard put to it to list the ways in which his assistance has been prompt. As usual, he read my proofs, and is affectionately thanked.

JEAN OVERTON FULLER

Chronology

Bacon's Life		Principal publications	Other	
			1533 June 24	Leicester born
			Sept. 7	Queen Elizabeth born
			1558 Nov. 17	Queen Mary dies Queen Elizabeth succeeds
1561 Jan. 22	Born			
			1566 Nov. 10	Essex born
			1572	St. Bartholomew's Night; Massacre of the Huguenots
1573 June 10	Matriculated Trinity College, Cambridge			
1576 June 27	Admitted *de societate magistrorum*, at Gray's Inn			
1576 Sept. 25	Lands in France			
			1577	Marguerite de Valois's tour of Brabant
			1578 Oct. 2	Marguerite de Valois rejoins Henry of Navarre at Casteras
			1579 Feb. 4	Conference at Nerac opens
			Feb. 20	Death of Sir Nicholas Bacon
1579 March 20	Arrives back in England Begins to keep terms at Gray's Inn			
1582 June 27	Admitted Utter Barrister at Gray's Inn			
1584	M.P. for Melcombe, Dorsetshire			
1586	M.P. for Taunton, Somersetshire			
1586	Admitted Bencher at Gray's Inn			
1587	Involved with Gray's Inn Revels			
1588	M.P. for Liverpool		1588	The Spanish Armada
			Sept. 7	Death of Leicester
			1594 May 2	Marriage of the

Bacon's Life		Principal publications	Other	
				Countess of Southampton and Sir Thomas Heneage
1596 Oct. 4	Warns Essex against putting the Queen in fear of him or seeking post of Earl Martial			
1597	M.P. for Southampton	1597 *Essays* (1st small edition)		
	M.P. for Ipswich, Suffolk	1597 *The Colours of Good and Evil*	1597	Marriage of the Countess of Southampton with Sir William Hervey
		1597 *Meditationes Sacrae*		
			Dec.	Essex becomes Earl Marshal
			1599 March 27	Essex and Southampton set out for Ireland
			Sept. 7	Essex parleys with Tyrone
			Sept. 20	Essex bursts into Queen's chamber at Nonsuch; held in custody
			1600 June 5	Essex heard informally at York House; and released within the month
			1601 Feb. 8	Essex and Southampton attempt *coup*; arrested
			Feb. 11	Essex and Southampton tried and sentenced
			Feb. 25	Essex beheaded
			May	Death of Anthony Bacon
			1603 March 24	Queen Elizabeth dies King James succeeds
1603 July 23	Knighted			
		1605 *Advancement of Learning*	1605 Nov. 5	Gunpowder Plot discovered
1606 May 10	Married			
1607 June 25	Becomes Solicitor-General			
1609 May	Becomes Councillor of, and adventurer in, the Virginia Company	1609 *De Sapientiae Veterum (The Wisdom of the Ancients)*	1609 May 23	Virginia Company Charter, with list of adventurers
			June 2	The *Sea Venture* sails from Plymouth, subsequently wrecked

Bacon's Life	Principal publications	Other	
		1610 July 10	Strachey writes a letter to Lady Waldon
		Aug. 27	Lady Bacon dies
		1612 May 24	Salisbury (Robert Cecil) dies
		May	Engagement of Princess Elizabeth to the Elector Palatine
		Oct.	Elector Palatine arrives in England
		Nov. 4	Prince Henry dies Prince Charles left as heir to throne
		1613 Feb. 14	Marriage of Princess Elizabeth and Elector Palatine
		April 25	Elector and Electress sail from Margate
1613 Oct. 26	Becomes Attorney-General		
		1615	King James begins to favour Villiers
1616	Leases Canonbury Manor		
June 9	Becomes Privy Councillor		
1617 March 3	Becomes Lord Keeper		
1618 Jan. 4	Becomes Lord High Chancellor		
July 12	Made Baron Verulam of Verulam		
		1619 August	Elector Palatine offered Crown of Bohemia
		Nov.	Frederick and Elizabeth crowned in Prague
	1620 *Novum Organum*	1620 Nov.	Frederick and Elizabeth flee from Prague
1621 Jan. 27	Created Viscount St. Alban		
Jan. 30	New Parliament opened		
March 14	Attack launched against him		
May 3	Sentenced		
Oct. 12	Pardoned		
	1622 *History of the Reign of King Henry VII*		
1622 Spring	Forced out of York House		
	1622 *Historia Ventorum (Study of Winds)*		

Bacon's Life	Principal publications	Other
	1623 *De Augmentis Scientiarum (The Advancement of Learning* translated and expanded)	
	1623 *Historia Vitae et Mortis (Study of Life and Death)*	
		1625 March 27 King James dies King Charles succeeds
	1625 *Essays* (3rd and final edition)	
	1625 *Apothegms Old and New*	
	1625 *Translation of Certaine Psalms into English Verse*	
1626 April 9 Passes away		
	Fragments and brief pieces posthumously published	
	1627 *New Atlantis* and *Sylva Sylvanum*	
	1653 *Cogitationes de Natura Rerum (Cogitations on Nature* published by Isaac Grutter) *De Fluxu et Refluxu Maris* (Of the Ebb and Flow of Tides)	
	1658 *Historia Densi et Rari (Study of Density and Rarity* published by Rawley)	
	1661 Further *Apothegms* (published by Rawley in *Resuscitatio*)	
	1673 Additional *Apothegms,* (published by Tenison in *Baconiana*)	
	1734 *Valerius Terminus or The Interpretation of Nature* (published by Robert Stephens)	
	1861 *Promus* (published by Spedding)	

Sundry Notes

SPELLING is generally modernised, excepting in verse quotations and a few places where orthography could be evidential.

Dates are given Old Style, excepting that for those falling between January 1st and March 25th, then the start of the year, the year date as it would be given today is added after a slash.

Spedding means *The Works, Life and Letters of Francis Bacon,* edited by James Spedding (Longman, 1858–74) in fourteen volumes.

Note on the pronunciation of Bacon's name

ON this, I consulted Professor A.C. Gimson, Principal of the Department of Phonetics and Linguistics, University College, London.

With regard to Bacon's Christian name, he advised me that the group of words for which there was a variant spelling, with a *u*, dance/daunce, chance/chaunce, France/Fraunce, Francis/Frauncis, is the subject of controversy. The evidence with regard to the pronunciation in that day is complicated, and arguments have been put forward for the sound which is sometimes written with a joined æ as in today's Received Pronunciation of *fan, ran*, etc.), but long; for the sound heard in today's Received Pronunciation of *Francis*, but long; or for the sound heard further towards that known by phoneticians as Cardinal 4, long. Some speakers, even in London, will have pronounced it with the short *a* heard today in Northern England *ran* etc. But generally all speakers, by about 1600, kept the sound separate from that heard in *gaunt, flaunt* etc.

The *a* in Bacon will have been pronounced as the first element of the diphthong heard in today's Received Pronunciation of *air, hare, bare*, etc., but drawn out long; that is phoneticians' Vowel 3, the sound represented by the phonetic symbol shaped like a 3 in reverse, followed by a colon.

Lord Bacon was the greatest genius that England (or perhaps any other country) has ever produced.

ALEXANDER POPE

*The world to Bacon does not only owe
Its present knowledge, but its future too.*

JOHN DRYDEN

Lord Bacon was a poet.

SHELLEY

CHAPTER 1

Infancy

FRANCIS Bacon was born in London, in one of the great houses over-looking the Thames, two years after Queen Elizabeth's accession to the throne. In the baptismal register of St. Martin's-in-the-Fields is entered

Jan 25 Franciscus Bacon (filius D Nicho Bacon, Magni Anglie Sigilli Custodie)[1]

The year was 1560/61, that is 1560 Old Style, 1561 New Style. The number of the year changed then not on January 1st but March 25th. It is Dr. Rawley, his chaplain, who in his biographical introduction to Bacon's works tells us his birthday was on January 22nd. But the calendar then used was the Julian, ten days behind the Gregorian, which we use today. Bacon would have said he was born on January 22nd, 1560, but that is February 1st, 1561, in our terms.[2]

By his first marriage, Sir Nicholas Bacon had Nicholas, Nathaniel, Edward and three daughters, and by Ann, his second wife, Anthony, two years older than Francis. They seem to have been an agreeable family but between Francis and Anthony was a particularly close link.

Within three days of her accession to the throne, Elizabeth had appointed as her Treasurer William Cecil, later created Lord Burghley. Oddly, it was he who recommended for the office above his own brother-in-law and old political friend, Nicholas Bacon. There is something anomalous here. In those days, when there was no Prime Minister and the Lords were more powerful than the Commons, it was the Lord Chancellor who was, as it is expressed in Maitland's *Constitutional History of England,* "First Secretary of State for all departments . . . Prime Minister." Nicholas Bacon, son of a sheep-reeve and grandson of a yeoman sheep-farmer, from near Stowmarket and Bury St. Edmunds, was a man of high legal attainment, but a commoner. When Elizabeth appointed him to the office, she gave him a knighthood but not a peerage. As in promoting a commoner to the office she had done a new thing, she created a new title for it. He was to be called Lord Keeper of the Great Seal of England.

His income was £1,300 in official emoluments, with about £2,500 in fees and perquisites. Elizabethan figures tend to be meaningless to modern readers, as their value has so changed. Yet perhaps we can establish a scale. The Master of Stratford-on-Avon Grammar School, who probably had one master junior to him, received a salary of £20 a year — a one hundred and ninetieth part of Nicholas Bacon's approximate total annual emoluments. Today, in today's money, such a head teacher with one assistant in a small village school would receive at least £25,000 a year and if we multiply this sum by one hundred and ninety we can guesstimate Nicholas Bacon's total approximate gross annual income to have been something in the region of £4,750,000 in today's coin.

No reliable comparisons can be made as regards to purchasing power, however, because the purchasing preoccupations of those times and today are so totally different. As is taxation. Summing up, let us simply say that by any estimation — of his time or of our own — Nicholas Bacon was seriously rich.

The two highest offices in the land being held by the husbands of two sisters, daughters of Sir Anthony Cooke, tutor to Edward VI, it is obvious they formed a close and trusted block, near to the Queen, to whom Lady Bacon was chief lady-in-waiting. She was a highly educated woman, and like the Queen read Latin and Greek. She had translated from the Latin Bishop Jewel's *Apology for the Church of England,* and her translation was printed by order of the Archbishop of Canterbury.

Archbishop Heath, who had been Chancellor to Queen Mary, now vacated York House and leased it to Sir Nicholas as his successor.

An imposing, turreted building, York House stood on the Strand, which was not yet a street. The back steps went down to the river, which was shallower and wider then, and commanded a view of what is now the National Theatre, the water probably lapping up over what is now the open air theatre in the gardens below the water-gate.

The river carried a more elegant traffic than now, since as the streets, narrow and pavementless were evil smelling from want of plumbing, those in the great houses along the river went by water. From the steps of York House, Francis could watch the Queen ascending and descending the steps to her barge; for Whitehall Palace, her residence when in London, was next door to York House.

1. The register preserved in the City of Westminster District Library is not the original paper register but the noble parchment copy of 1598. A caret mark appears before Franciscus, and above it "Mr." One cannot tell whether this was transcribed from the original. The ink looks old, but the pen looks to me to have been another than that which wrote the whole entry. "Mr.", standing for Master, was by later Elizabethan times used as a courtesy title for a gentleman, but I know of no instance of its being used as early as this save for a Master of Arts, a Ship's Master, or in titles such as the Master of the Rolls, or courtesy titles, as Mr. Secretary, Mr. Solicitor.

2. The astrologer, William Lily, gives the hour of Francis' birth as 7.00 a.m. *(Peace or No Peace,* 1643 II, p.168) and casts a map showing: Ascendant Aquarius 5, Sun Aquarius 12, Moon Aries 19, Mercury Aquarius 6 Ret., Venus Pisces 9, Mars Sagittarius 6, Jupiter Aries 19, Saturn Gemini 14 Ret.; to which it is possible by retrospective computation to add: Uranus Scorpio 24, Neptune Taurus 28 and Pluto Pisces 9.

CHAPTER 2

"If he is illegitimate, who is he?"

THE dissimilarity in the faces of Sir Francis Bacon and Sir Nicholas Bacon, stated to be his father, is such as to strike the most casual stroller through the National Portrait Gallery. Sir Francis, in his Chancellor's robes, has dark brown eyes, dark curly hair, and a long, lean face. Sir Nicholas' wisps of greying hair seem once to have been fair, his eyes are grey, his face square and heavy jowled, his lower lip protruding, his nose a high-bridged Roman beak (which Francis has not), his forehead broad but slightly receding, whereas Francis (one can see this better in the unhatted miniature, at Belvoir Castle) has a high and domed forehead.

Neither is the mystery lessened when one goes out to Gorhambury. In the painting of Francis there, from which the one in the National Portrait Gallery was copied, the eyes are almost black. That is probably from the way the oil has affected ageing, dark-brown paint. His face is paler than in the replica, but his bone structure is still long and thin. Sir Nicholas is present again, in a painted terracotta bust and in an oil painting. Though the latter was copied from the one in the National Portrait Gallery, there are stronger traces of a carroty colour in the hair, so perhaps the copyist was told by the family what it used to be like before the colour faded. The eyes are grey. In the bust, much of the paint has flaked off, leaving dark patches, invading the eyes, so it is fortunate the 5th Earl of Verulam thought to have it photographed, before it suffered this damage. Though the picture is in black and white, one can see from the reproduction in his booklet, *The Bacon Family* (St. Albans, 1961) that the irides are light, having practically the same tonal values as the flesh of his face. Bust like portrait confirms the square and heavy structure of the bones.

Of his second wife, Lady Bacon, born Anne Cooke, there is also both a terracotta bust and a painting in oils. Both show her with a wide, round face, high, broad forehead, knotted rather than domed, and small, round nose, whereas Francis' nose is long. The whole modelling is different from that of Francis. Her hair is fair, her eyes shown as light grey, or blue-grey, which may mean that they were blue.[1]

There is also the terracotta bust of a child, with face shaped much like the mother's. There is no name on it, and many have taken it for Francis. However, Dr. Roy Strong, formerly Director of the National Portrait Gallery, now Director of the Victoria and Albert Museum, in his book *Tudor and Jacobean Portraits* (HMSO, 1969), gives his opinion it represents Anthony Bacon, the couple's elder son. This he grounds on the style of the clothing, which coincides with the fashion at the age of the child if he has Anthony's birth-date. To this I would add that if only one son was to be sculpted, it would surely be their first. But there is a deeper reason why I think as Dr. Strong. The child's eyes are light grey, perhaps one should say blue-grey. Francis', in the miniature depicting him at eighteen, by Nicholas Hilliard, in Belvoir Castle, as in all portraits of him as an adult, are dark brown. His physician, Sir William Hervey, is cited by Aubrey for a description of them as ''Hazel''.

'I consulted my medical friend, Dr. Margaret Little, as to Mendel's Law concerning the transmission of characteristics from parents to children, and she replied that it is very rare for two people with light coloured eyes, blue or grey, to have a child with dark eyes, hazel, or brown, for two people with light hair to have one with dark, for two people with straight hair to have one with curly, or for two people with adherent ear-lobes to have one with free. (The converse of these propositions does not apply; two people with dark eyes can have one with light, and so on).

As there seemed to be in the case of Bacon an exception to Mendel's Law with regard to eye colour (more important than hair colour), Dr. Little consulted two eminent geneticists as to what was known of exceptions, before explaining that the effect of Mendel's Law on any particular trait depends on the chemical make-up of that trait and whether it is dominant or recessive. There are scattered through the population a few mutant genes, which behave in the opposite way from the majority producing the same trait. Dark eyes are nearly always dominant and light eyes nearly always recessive, but in the odd family it is the other way about. Where there is an apparent exception to Mendel's Law there is an abnormal light-eye gene. But a gene that has this abnormality is likely to manifest it more than once. If two light eyed people have only one child, and that dark eyed, there is no ''control''. But if they go on to have a large family of children, of whom an impressive number are dark eyed, that would be consistent with the presence in one or other of the spouses of such an abnormal light-eye gene. What has to be sought is a consistent pattern of irregularity, after its own fashion regular. It would be worth trying to discover the colouring of all Sir Nicholas' children even by his first marriage.

One of these latter, Nathaniel, was an amateur artist, several of whose paintings hang at Gorhambury. His self-portraits show him as having auburn hair with grey eyes. I knew nothing of the others.

I made two other expeditions. One was to London, to the Royal Society, to see what Dr. Roy Strong believes to be the original of the pattern of Francis in his Chancellor's robes, sometimes attributed to Van Somer. They had to take me down to the cellars to see it. It used, they assured me, to hang proudly over the main staircase, till it was noticed the central heating was affecting it. The wooden board on which it was painted had warped so badly that one corner had curled right out of the frame. Nevertheless, it was the most beautiful picture, the flesh tones more natural than in either the pallid Gorhambury or florid National Portrait Gallery versions, the hair thick and curling, dark on the head, slightly less so on the beard, the eyes a deep, dark brown. If I had had with me paints, with which to try to match the tint, I think I would have started from the Van Dyke brown.

And I went to Corpus Christi College, Cambridge, where they have two portraits of Sir Nicholas Bacon. In the one in their hall, painted in 1579, I saw the eyes were light grey, very light. What appeared of the hair was grizzling. Their 1562 one has the grey eyes and also plenty of hair, fair to light red.

From the National Portrait Gallery I had obtained the address of Sir Edmund Bacon, Bart. I wrote to him, saying I was writing a book on Sir Francis Bacon and had seen several portraits of him, including, at Trinity College, Cambridge, a copy of the one by William Larkin, the original of which, I read in Dr. Roy Strong's book, was in his private possession. Would he be kind enough to allow me to come to Raveningham to see it? I would at the same time be interested to see any other portraits of members of his family, of that period, which he might have. He replied agreeably. As it would be a long journey for me, he and his wife hoped that after looking at the pictures I would stay to lunch.

Raveningham, the home of Sir Edmund Bacon, Lord Lieutenant of Norfolk, proved to be a stately residence in the deep countryside, off Beccles, on the Norfolk-Suffolk border.

Sir Edmund was a considerable collector of paintings, and the original works of well-known artists adorned hall, staircase and various rooms. He conducted me straight into the sitting-room, where Francis hung, in pride of place, over the fireplace. It was painted when he was already Lord Keeper but not yet Lord Chancellor. The eyes were deep, dark brown. Sir Edmund had also a smaller head and shoulders by Van Somer of Francis, with the eyes deep brown, and another of Sir Nicholas, eyes light grey.

Sir Edmund was the direct lineal descendant of Sir Nicholas, Queen Elizabeth's Lord Keeper, through his eldest son, Sir Nicholas, the 1st Baronet. "There he is!" From high on the wall I saw looking down on me a man, better looking than the Lord Keeper and so like my host, that it was as if either my host had been painted in Elizabethan garb or the subject of the painting had stepped out of it to dress in modern clothes and walk about, showing me the type in very flesh. "Only your eyes are blue." The eyes of the first Baronet were grey.

On the staircase they showed me the Tree of Jesse, depicting the descendants of Sir Nicholas, the Lord Keeper, for many generations. The figures were too small for their eye-colour to be discerned, but the whole clan was represented as golden haired or auburn.

I asked Sir Edmund Bacon whether he saw any likeness between Sir Francis and any other member of his family. The drift of this question was not lost upon my host. Quick as a flash, across the luncheon table, Sir Edmund asked, "If he is illegitimate, who is he?"

Of course he had heard that old tale, that Francis was the Queen's son, by the Earl of Leicester, who had been fostered on to their family. But what he had always said against it was, "If she was his mother, wouldn't she have been nicer to him? She should have been pushing him forward all the time, but she kept him back and back."

I knew of the legend that Francis Bacon, and also the Earl of Essex, were sons of Elizabeth and Leicester. I reflected that Queen Victoria did not push Edward VII forward as Prince of Wales, while Catherine the Great kept her son back to the point of usurping his throne.

Why, I asked Sir Edmund, did he think Sir Nicholas, the Lord Keeper, had left Francis nothing in his will? Sir Edmund did find that perplexing.

The Queen, on the other hand, had granted Francis the reversion of Twickenham Lodge, so that he could never lack a home . . .

In the portraits of Queen Elizabeth, her eyes show as brown, black-brown or black. In the Ditchley, accorded the greatest authority by Dr. Strong, as showing a degree of realism not elsewhere permitted, they are black, therein matching a contemporary eye-witness cited by Dr. Strong, "a good skin although swarthy . . . her eyes are small, yet black and pleasant." The Windsor portrait of her as a young girl shows her hair as auburn and straight. Henry VIII had auburn, straight hair, but with blue eyes. Her dark eyes she would have got from her mother. The beautiful portrait of Anne Boleyn in the National Portrait Gallery shows dark brown, straight hair, with deep, dark brown eyes. Wyatt called her "Brunet" (Egerton MS.95), and Dr. Strong had found an eye-witness description of her as having a "swarthy complexion . . . eyes which are black and beautiful". Her descent was part Irish.

Leicester's hair is, in all his portraits, even to old age, profusely curling, and the one in the Wallace Collection, which may show him before he was out of his twenties (the date being 156 . . . , the last figure illegible) shows it as dark brown, as to the head, a little lighter on the beard, as it is also with Francis. His eyes are brown, though not so dark as Elizabeth's. His own father had brown eyes with brown straight hair.

Elizabeth and Leicester had, therefore, between them the characteristics needed to produce a child with dark brown curly hair and dark brown eyes. This of course does not prove they did so, only that in respect of Mendel's law they had the genetic capability Sir Nicholas and Lady Bacon lacked. With regard to features, Leicester has Francis' nobly curving brows and he has Francis' eyebrows. His nose, however, is short and straight. Elizabeth's nose is long, like that of Francis, but somewhat thinner and certainly more pointed at the tip. There is a nose which exactly replicates Francis', long but with a slight bulging of flesh at the tip, and that may be seen in Holbein's portrait of Henry VIII.

But contemplation of Henry VIII brought up another question. It used to be asserted he died of syphilis, though the eminent medical opinions gathered by Frederick Chamberlain, in *The Private Life of Henry VIII* (Lane, 1932) and the more recent *Henry VIII*, J.J. Scarisbrick (Eyre and Spottiswoode, 1968) are against it. In case he had it all the same, I wrote to Dr. Little asking whether the grandson of a syphilitic man need show syphilitic symptoms. She sent me a recent paper, *Henry VIII: A Medical Study*, J.F.D. Shrewsbury (Department of Bacteriology, University of Birmingham), the burden of which was that Henry was not syphilitic. Even if after reading this one still felt there was room for doubt, women had greater resistance than men to inherited syphilis, so that, supposing he did have it, after all, it would be quite orderly that Edward VI and the Duke of Richmond died in their teens whereas Queen Mary and Queen Elizabeth survived. Elizabeth's face showed no stigmata of syphilis, and her quick intelligence was much against it. If she did have it, none the less, it must have been very slightly, in which case there was no need for her son to have it at all. A better test, Dr. Little suggested, might be gout, which ran very strongly in families. If there was gout to be found in one pair of suggested parents but not in the other, that would be indicative.

Sir Nicholas Bacon, the Lord Keeper, was swollen all over from gout, and Anthony, in a letter to his physician, mentions that he has had it from birth, and that it raged cruelly. Francis did not suffer from gout. In a letter written on June 8th, 1617, by which time he was fifty-six, he mentions that he had been "a little imperfect in my foot", which he attributes to having moved to a Thames-side residence, but he says that if it was gout it did not rage, and has at the time of writing gone away, having only lasted for about a month. The very comprehensive medical study of Queen Elizabeth's ailments in *The Private Character of Queen Elizabeth*, Frederick Chamberlain (Lane, 1922) does not list gout among them (though her father had it). Leicester did not have gout.

Things had reached the point where I felt we should obtain a specialist opinion on the genetic factors at the highest possible level. Dr. Little therefore wrote to Professor Brisco Ford, Fellow of the Royal Society, Fellow of All Souls and Emeritus Professor of Genetics at Oxford, specifying in the first instance only that the particulars she sent him were of a male person, born in the sixteenth century. On the basis of this limited data, he replied:

. . . if two blue (grey) eyed people produce a brown eyed child, the chances are rather heavily against it being their own. How heavily it is impossible to say, at least 1:100 against, I should *think*.

He added:

There is also a very deep brown type which is a sex-linked dominant.

Dr. Little explained to me "It means that a man can only inherit such eyes from his mother, not his father . . . Anne Boleyn may well have had such eyes."

After this I wrote to Professor Ford myself, telling him the subject whose particulars had been sent him was Sir Francis Bacon, that Anthony, the undoubted son of Sir Nicholas and Lady Bacon had, like both of them, grey eyes, and that his half-brothers Nicholas and Nathaniel had grey eyes; that Sir Nicholas came of a yeoman farming stock of a most settled village community, inland in Suffolk, and that Lady Bacon's people came from a neighbouring village in Essex. Might I have permission to quote his comments.

Professor Ford replied:

You can certainly quote me in saying that if Sir Francis Bacon had dark brown eyes and *both* his parents had grey, the chance that he is illegitimate is very high indeed. It would be down to mutation level which, in this case, will be less than 1:100,000.

---

1. In the whole of Shakespeare, the only two references to blue eyes are pejorative: "A blue eye and sunken" *As You Like It*, III, ii, 393, and "the blue-eyed hag", of the witch, in *The Tempest*, I, ii, 269. Pretty girls, when not brunettes, are grey-eyed, thus Olivia in *Twelfth Night*, I, v, 266, Julia and Sylvia, the one a flaxen or a golden blonde, the other a red-head, in *Two Gentlemen of Verona*, V, iv, 196-97. Even the sky is grey, in contexts that suggest not cloudy but clear: "The grey-eyed morn smiles on the frowning night", *Romeo and Juliet*, II, iii, 1, "the sun in the grey vault of Heaven", 2 *King Henry IV*, II, iii, 19. The attitude of mind behind these verbal references seems to spill over into art; it is rare to see a commissioned portrait of the times in which the sitter is shown as blue-eyed. My Shakespearean line references are to the Globe edition of 1891, which is also that of the Bartlett Concordance (Macmillan, 1894), excepting that I have added references to the New Variorum where I have made lengthy quotations from the volumes already issued in that edition.

CHAPTER 3

Elizabeth and Leicester

THOUGH it is but a pretty story of William Camden's they had been born at the same hour of the same day of the same year – Leicester celebrated his birthday on June 24th, whereas the Queen was not born until September 7th, of the same year, 1533 – there is a certain synchronicity in their lives. They had known each other since they were eight years old. They had been imprisoned in the Tower at the same time, during the reign of Mary (1553-1558), he for his part in his father's plot to place Lady Jane Grey on the throne,[1] she for suspected complicity in the plot of Sir Thomas Wyatt to place herself, Elizabeth, on the throne instead of Mary; and after Mary's death, on November 17th, 1558, it was he who rode behind her on a black horse on her triumphal return to the Tower as sovereign.

She made him her Master of the Horse. This does not mean he knew only of horses. Later, she made him Chancellor of Oxford University. The tutor of his boyhood had been Dr. Dee, whose library of philosophic and esoteric works at Mortlake was considered the finest in Europe in private hands. Now he introduced his old tutor to the new Queen, and he chose for her a date and time astrologically apt for her coronation.

Leicester – it is simplest to call him so from the beginning, though he had not his Earldom yet and was simply Lord Robert – was very much with the Queen and it did not escape the eye of the Spanish Ambassador, Count de Feria. On April 18th, 1559, he wrote to his King:[2]

During the last few days Lord Robert has come so much into favour that he does whatever he likes with affairs and it is even said that her Majesty visits him in his chamber day and night. People talk of this so freely that they go so far as to say that his wife has a malady in one of her breasts and the Queen is only waiting for her to die to marry Lord Robert.

His wife, Amy Robsart, was at Cumnor, ill with what according to modern medical opinion must have been a terminal cancer.

De Feria thought it so likely the Queen would marry Leicester that he added it might be wise to approach him on behalf of his King and, promising him help and favour, ''come to terms with him.''

It was of great concern to the King of Spain whom Elizabeth married. He could not marry her himself, having been married to her sister, and his great fear was lest she might make an alliance with France. Her dalliance with Leicester was at least partially agreeable to him, in that it made a French Consort less likely, though it would have suited Spain better if she would marry one of the sons of the Holy Roman Emperor. On April 29th, de Feria wrote to his King that she seemed of divided mind:

she speaks like a woman who will only marry a great prince and then they say she is in love with Lord Robert and will never let him leave her.

De Feria had confidential conversations with Lady Sidney, Leicester's sister, but in November, 1559, reported the Duke of Norfolk had threatened that if Lord Robert would not abandon his pretension to the Queen's hand he would not die in his bed.

In mid-June a woman of Brentwood gossiped that Leicester had given the Queen a petticoat. Another exclaimed, "Thinkst thou it was a petticoat? No, no, he gave her a child, I warrant thee." A Mother Dowe repeated this in another village, expressing it that "Dudley and the Queen had played at legerdemain together and he was the father of her child." Another answered her, "Why, she hath no child yet." Mother Dowe retorted, "No, and if they have not they have put one to the making." The report containing these phrases was sent by Lord Richard Thomas Mildmay to William Cecil (Lord Burghley).[3] For Cecil the affair was alarming, and he always tried to keep Leicester back.

On September 11th, Bishop de Quadra, who had succeeded de Feria, wrote to his King:[4]

She had promised me an answer about her marriage by the third instant and said she was certain to marry, but now she coolly tells me she cannot make up her mind, and will not marry. After this I had an opportunity of talking to Cecil, who I understand was in disgrace, and Robert was trying to turn him out of his place. After making many pledges of strict secrecy he said the Queen was conducting herself in such a way that he thought of retiring . . . he clearly foresaw the ruin of the realm by Robert's intimacy with the Queen, who surrendered all affairs to him and meant to marry him . . . He ended by begging me in God's name to point out to the Queen the effect of her misconduct and persuade her not to abandon business entirely but to look to her realm, and then he repeated twice over to me that Lord Robert would be better in Paradise than here . . .

He ended by saying that Robert was thinking of killing his wife, who was publicly announced to be ill, although she was quite well, and would take very good care they did not poison her . . .

The next day the Queen told me as she returned from hunting that Robert's wife was dead or nearly so, and asked me not to say anything about it. Certainly this business is most shameful and scandalous and withal I am not sure whether she will marry the man at once or even if she will marry at all, as I do not think she has her mind sufficiently fixed . . .

Since writing the above I hear the Queen has published the death of Robert's wife, and said in Italian, ''Que si ha rollo il collo''. (''She broke her neck''.)

Amy had been found at the foot of a staircase, after sending the servants out for the day. Leicester desired there should be an inquest. It was shown he had not been at Cumnor and a verdict of accidental death was recorded. Modern medical research confirms this.[5]

It seems she was suffering from a cancer of the breast with extension into the neck, causing spontaneous fracture of the spine. This would be likeliest to occur while descending stairs, and would be consistent with the absence of damage to her bonnet such as should have been obvious had she been pushed from the top of the staircase. Cecil, therefore, did Leicester wrong, and he was not the only one. Mary Queen of Scots was reported to have said, ''The Queen of England is going to marry her horse-keeper, who has killed his wife to make room for her.'' For Elizabeth to have married Leicester in these circumstances would have further fed scandal. From being everywhere seen with him, now she was hardly seen at all, but withdrew into herself, in Whitehall Palace, for the winter.

Throgmorton, the English Ambassador in Paris, wrote to Cecil on December 31st, 1560 that the Spanish Ambassador had visited him:[6]

who did, amongst other matters, earnestly require me to tell him whether the Queen, my mistress, were secretly married to the Lord Robert; for, said he, I assure you this Court is full of it.

Cecil replied to Throgmorton on January 15th, 1560/61:[7]

What the Queen will determine to be, God only knows.

De Quadra wrote to his King:[8]

. . . on the 13th, Robert and I met in the presence of Sidney, and . . . he besought me, in your Majesty's name, to recommend the Queen to marry him, and he would promise to render your Majesty all the service his brother-in-law had told me . . . he begged me to speak to the Queen at once. I did so two days afterwards, and told her what she already knew, how much your Majesty wished to see her married . . . After much circumlocution, she said she wished to confess to me and tell her secret in confession, which was that she was no angel, and did not deny that she had some affection for Lord Robert for the many good qualities he possessed, but certainly she had never decided to marry him or anyone else, although she daily saw more clearly the necessity for her marriage, and to satisfy the English humour that it was desirable that she should marry an Englishman, and she asked me to tell her what your Majesty would think if she married one of her servitors.

Angels do not eat, excrete or have sexual congress. It looks as though Bishop de Quadra, when Elizabeth confessed to him she was no angel, understood this to mean she was not a virgin. The word ''affection'' had then a hotter sense than now.

On January 22nd, 1560/61, de Quadra wrote to his King that he had received a visit from Sir Henry Sidney. Leicester's brother-in-law:[9]

He said that if I was satisfied about the death of Robert's wife, he saw no other reason why I should hesitate to write the purport of this conversation to your Majesty, as after all, although it was a love affair, yet the object of it was marriage, and that there was nothing illicit about it or such as could not be set right by your

Majesty's authority. As regards the death of the wife he was certain that it was accidental . . .

At the foot, he added some people said the Queen was unhealthy and would never have a child, others that she was a mother already, though this he did not believe.

On the very day de Quadra was writing these words, Francis Bacon was born. Dr. Rawley, who had been his chaplain, begins the first English biography:

> Francis Bacon, the glory of his Age and Nation, the adorner and ornament of learning, was born in York House, or York Place, on the Strand . . .

York Place was the old name for Whitehall Palace, by which, however, it had not been called since Henry VIII seized it from Cardinal Wolsey. Some have felt that Rawley was hinting Francis was born not in York House, next door to it, but in the Palace, implying it was the Queen, not her first lady-in-waiting, who had given him birth.

On June 24th, 1561, Leicester celebrated his birthday with a water-fête on the Thames. The family at York House would have been privileged to a riverside view. Francis was only five months old at the time, but it will later be urged that there is an allusion to it and to the following events in one of his works, and an inference drawn from those allusions and that is why the events of that day and their sequel are related here, at their place in time, as forming eventually a part of his story.

De Quadra wrote to his King:[10]

> In the afternoon we went on board a vessel from which we were to see the rejoicings, and she [the Queen], Robert and I, being alone, on the gallery, they began joking . . . They went so far with their jokes that Lord Robert told her that, if she liked, I could be the Minister to perform the act of marriage, and she nothing loth to hear it, said she was not sure whether I knew enough English. I let them jest for a time and at last spoke to them in earnest, and told them that if they listened to me they could extricate themselves from the tyranny of the councillors who had taken possession of the Queen and her affairs, and could restore to the country the peace and unity so much needed by re-instating religion. If they did this they could effect the marriage they spoke of, and I should be glad, in such a case, to be the minister to perform it.

Half a year later, in January, 1562, that is about the time of Francis' first birthday, we find de Quadra writing to his King that Robert had asked him to request the King of Spain to write to the Queen, advising her to marry him. Shortly after, the Queen herself told him she wished the King of Spain would write her such a letter, so that, should she decide to marry Robert, her people could see that it was upon advice and not to satisfy her own desires.

One recalls that in January of the previous year she had asked de

Quadra how his King would take it if she married Robert in order to satisfy her subject's desire she should marry an Englishman. Now she wanted a letter from the King of Spain advising her to marry Robert, which she could show to her people, as though it were not they who wanted him and she would have to justify such a step. De Quadra, however, told his King he saw no indication that either of them intended to turn Catholic, and in the circumstances he did not see why his Majesty should write the letter they wanted.

In the spring of 1562 some of de Quadra's correspondence was betrayed to the Queen, and he found himself summoned by the Lord Chamberlain to answer a number of charges, particularly:[11]

That I had written to his Majesty that the Queen had been secretly married to Lord Robert at the Earl of Pembroke's house.

Answer: What I wrote to his Majesty about this was the same as I said to the Queen, which was that people were saying all over the town that the wedding had taken place, which at the time neither surprised nor annoyed·her, and she said it was not only people outside of the palace who had thought such a thing, as on her return that afternoon from the Earl's house her own ladies in waiting when she entered the chamber with Lord Robert asked whether they were to kiss his hand as well as hers to which she had told them no and they were not to believe what people said . . . I do not think, considering what others say of the Queen, that I should be doing her any injury in writing to his Majesty that she was married . . .

It is possible the affair came to something of a head at this time, for after it there was a period of estrangement. The Queen gave countenance to the idea she might marry one of the sons of the Holy Roman Emperor, and made the astonishing proposal that Leicester – she now gave him his Earldom – should marry Mary Queen of Scots. She could be unwomanly cerebral at times. Leicester, probably because he felt the rebuff, withdrew to Kenilworth,[12] the great Castle in Warwickshire which the Queen had earlier given him as a present, so that he would not again have been an intimate of Whitehall Palace until Francis was about five.

In March, 1565, the French Ambassador told Gusman de Silva, the new Spanish Ambassador who had replaced de Quadra, that he would see Leicester married to the Queen before his time in England was out, and in September of that year de Silva wrote to his King that Throgmorton had advised Leicester he must, in his own interest, either succeed in marrying the Queen herself or else champion the cause of the Archduke.[13] Otherwise, the English people would regard him as the cause of her continuing to be unmarried. Throgmorton had suggested to Leicester that as the Queen was now flirting with Heneage,[14] Leicester should pay conspicuous attention to some other woman to test whether the Queen was still interested in him. Leicester paid some public courtesies to the Queen's cousin, Lettice.[15] The Queen did, indeed, react, and, de Silva wrote, ''The result of the tiff was both the Queen and Robert shed tears and he returned to his former favour.''[16]

On January 25th, 1565/6, de Silva wrote to his King the English people were divided as to whether the Queen should marry Robert or the Archduke. Those who favoured Leicester's cause wore stripes of purple. Followers of the Duke of Norfolk, being against his candidature, retaliated by wearing stripes of yellow.[17]

The Queen had told him she could not marry a subject, yet her behaviour belied her words. On February 4th, 1565/66, de Silva wrote to his King the Queen had confided to him that if she married Leicester now people would say it was from necessity. Indeed, it appeared to him there was some necessity, if what the French Ambassador had told him was true, ''that he had slept with the Queen on New Year's Night.''[18]

In Stowe's *Historical Memoranda* there is the curious story that on April 12th, 1566, the Queen had agreed to meet Leicester in the morning in a house opposite St. Swithin's Churchyard. She was late, and he gave up waiting. Yet in fact she had set out, accompanied by two of her ladies-in-waiting. However, he met her on the way, and simply rode back with her to Greenwich Palace. Stowe tells it as though a quiet wedding had been intended, but that the Queen had not gone through with it. Again, it is as though frustrations had come to a head, for there was a further withdrawal on his part after this.

If one is interested in the possibility of a pregnancy resulting from intimacy during this period, one needs to look for a birth corresponding to conception between January 1st and the early spring.

A new Parliament was opened on October 2nd. Usually, the Queen made the opening of Parliament the occasion for showing herself to the people. She would leave Whitehall Palace, robed, and be driven through the streets, so that her subjects, thronging the way, could press around her close, to view her. On this one occasion, she cheated them of their accustomed spectacle, slipping out of the Palace from the back, in her usual clothes. She robed when she reached Westminster, but she would have been seen on her excursion only by those aboard her barge, and perhaps by the inhabitants of York House, such as the child Francis, now six years old.

From the steps of York House, he could always see the Queen descending and ascending the steps of the Palace, and her departures and returns by the royal barge.

---

1. Queen Mary, being the daughter of King Henry VIII by his first, Catholic, Queen, Catherine of Aragon, was a Catholic. Lady Jane Grey was the daughter of a different Mary, the sister of Henry VIII, and a Protestant. She was married to Lord Guildford Dudley, the elder brother of Leicester, and the father of these two boys, the Duke of Northumberland, tried to place Jane on the throne instead of Mary. The result was, Lady Jane was beheaded, Northumberland was beheaded and the elder boy, Guilford Dudley was beheaded. The younger one, Robert, who became the Earl of Leicester, was pardoned because of his youth, and merely imprisoned in the Tower.

2. Calendar of State Papers, Spanish, 1558-67, pp.57-58.
3. State Papers Domestic 12/13, folios 55-58.
4. Calendar of State Papers, Spanish, 1558-67, pp.174-76.
5. 'The Death of Amy Robsart', Professor Ian Aird, *English Historical Review*, vol. 71, January 1956.
6. Calendar of State Papers, Foreign, 1560-61, p.475.
7. Calendar of State Papers, Foreign, 1560-61, p.498.
8. Calendar of State Papers, Spanish, 1558-67, p.181.
9. Calendar of State Papers, Spanish, 1558-67, p.178.
10. Calendar of State Papers, Spanish, 1558-67, p.208.
11. Calendar of State Papers, Spanish, 1558-67, p.248.
12. Not far from the modern city of Birmingham.
13. Calendar of State Papers, Spanish 1558-67, p.472
(The Archduke Charles, son of the Holy Roman Emperor of the German Nation.)
14. Later Vice-Chamberlain and Treasurer of her Household.
15. Lettice was the daughter of Mary Boleyn, the sister of Queen Anne Boleyn, mother of Elizabeth (As King Henry VIII had been the lover of Mary before Anne, there has always been some suspicion that Lettice was not only the cousin but the sister of Elizabeth. The father of Lettice (if not Henry VIII) was her mother's husband, Sir Francis Knollys.
16. Calendar of State Papers, Spanish, 1558-67, p.472.
17. Calendar of State Papers, Spanish, 1558-67, p.472.
18. Calendar of State Papers, Spanish, 1558-67, p.511.
19. Calendar of State Papers, Spanish, 1558-67, p.520.

CHAPTER 4

Boyhood

FRANCIS was far from wholly a London child. In the year of his birth, Sir Nicholas had bought and built a Manor in Gorhambury Park, Hertfordshire, about two miles south west of St. Albans. The square tower of the Abbey Church (now Cathedral) could be seen from the grounds, while the as yet un-excavated Roman theatre of Verulamium lay at the gate of the Drive, part of the ancient Watling Street. Close by stood St. Michael's, where the family worshipped.

The Park was notable for its oakwood. Oaks still predominate, though one sees also beech, ash, elm, wych elm, lime, alder, elder, sycamore, maple, hornbeam, whitebeam and hawthorn, with a tangle of wild flowers, stretches of ponds and abundant wildlife. Francis' works are full of the knowledge of trees, plants and creatures; it would have been here his observations had their beginnings. There is also within the grounds a hill, the crest of which, steep and guarded with thorns and nettles, is difficult of access, known as Lord Bacon's Mount. Here he climbed to meditate.

There was a house already, but Sir Nicholas built himself a new one, the Manor, of which practically all that now remains is the three-arched porch, on which one can still read the Bacon family motto, MEDIOCRIA FIRMA; surmounted by the vestiges of figures, believed to have been angels. (See my oil-painting, Plate 10).

Pipes were laid from a reservoir to the house, so that water flowed to every room, which was considered a wonder. But Queen Elizabeth, when she came to visit, said, ''My Lord, what a little house you have gotten!'' Francis says he replied,[1] ''Madam, my house is well, but it is you who have made me too great for my house.''

Personal glimpses of Francis as a boy are lacking, as indeed they are of most of those who lived so long ago. Details of their behaviour come to be recorded only from the time persons of historical note make an impact upon public life, and this, to the regret of the biographer, leaves us without picture of childhood or adolescence, the formative years. All that one can do (if one will avoid fiction) is to indicate what record there is of the circumstances in which one's subject was growing up.

The Grammar School of St. Albans has no record of the pupils going back so far but Sir Nicholas Bacon:[2]

was a man responsible for re-starting this school, and he was instrumental in getting the Queen to grant to the city in 1570 the Wine Charter by which provision was made for the salary of the Masters. He also wrote for us in 1570 our first set of school regulations . . . we have an entry in the first year of our School

Accounts Book, 1587-89, which concerns a gift by Francis Bacon to the school of two books . . . "Imprimis twoo bound faire books in folio well bound and claspt contayning the whole works of Plato set out by Serranus latterly, of the best edition given by Mr. Francis Bacon price whereof vl'',

It looks, therefore, as though Francis would have been a pupil of the school. At the time he would have been attending, the classes were being held within the Abbey, in the Lady Chapel, just behind the shrine. Unless Sir Nicholas sent all the children in a carriage, Francis probably trotted there and back on a pony.

At nine years old, he would not have appreciated any possible relevance to himself, even if he had heard that a man called Marsham had been sentenced to lose both his ears and to pay a fine of £100 (£50,000) for alleging (whilst on trial for his part in the Norfolk rebellion of 1570) that the Earl of Leicester had two children by the Queen.

In April, 1573, when Anthony was fourteen and Francis twelve, they were both sent to Trinity College, Cambridge, where they shared rooms, and had John Whitgift, later Archbishop of Canterbury, for Master.

The scheme of studies, however, Francis found cramping; "liberty of judgement" was discouraged, "For the studies of men in these places are so confined and as it were imprisoned in the writings of certain authors, from whom if any man dissent he is straightway arraigned as a turbulent person and an innovator."[3] What Francis was up against was the universal assumption that man had been at his best in some pre-lapsarian state from which he declined further and further. Hence, the best he could do was to study the authors most ancient, which in practice meant Aristotle, and not as a rule direct, but in potted versions or through the lifeless commentaries of the schoolmen of the Middle Ages and early Renaissance (the authentic Aristotle had a lively and wide-ranging mind, in type very similar to Bacon's own.) Francis felt there must be a better way of approach, and we have no reason to doubt his statement to Rawley, that the idea of his Great Instauration came to him when he was under fifteen.

He had been at Cambridge just over a year when, in August, 1574, the university was closed because of an outbreak of the plague until the following March. The boys then returned, but before Christmas were taken away, having had less than three years at university, and that broken into in the middle.

Continental travel was supposed to polish a young man, and when Sir Amyas Paulet was appointed English Ambassador to France, Francis was sent with him. They landed at Calais on September 25th, 1576 mentioned in the first Life of Bacon written, in 1631, by a Frenchman, Pierre Amboise:[4]

né parmi les pourpres & nourri dedans l'espérance d'une grande fortune . . .
Monsieur Bacon se voulut acquerir cette science qui rendit Ulysse si

recommendable, & lui fit mériter le nom de sage, par sa connaissance des moeurs de tant de nations diverses. Je veux dire qu'il employa dans les voyages quelques années de sa jeunesse, afin de polir son esprit, et façonner son jugement, par le pratique de toute sorte d'estrangers. La France, l'Italie & l'Espagne comme les nations les plus civilisées de tout le monde, furent celles où sa curiosité le porta. Et comme il se voyait destiné pour tenir un iour en ces mains le timon du Royaume, au lieu de considérer seulement le paisage et la diversité des vestemens, comme font la plupart de ceux qui voyagent, il observoit judicieusement les lois et les coustumes des pays où il passoit, remarquoit les diverses formes de gouvernement, les avantages ou les détaux d'un Etat, et tous les autres choses qui peuvent rendre un homme capable de gouverner les peuples.

I translate:

. . . born amidst the purples and nourished in the hope of a great destiny . . . Mr. Bacon thought good to acquire that science which rendered Ulysses so commendable and gained him the name of sage, through his knowledge of the customs of different countries. I mean, he spent several years of his youth in travels, to polish his wit and form his judgement, by reference to the practice of foreigners. France, Italy and Spain, being the countries of highest civilisation, were those to which this curiosity drew him. And, as he saw himself destined to hold in his hands one day the helm of the Kingdom, he did not look only at the scenery and the clothes of the different peoples, as do most tourists, but took note of the different types of government, the advantages and the faults of each, and of all things the understanding of which should fit a man to govern.

Francis has given us no account of his travels, though we shall find him refer to things in Rome, Venice and Madrid as though he had seen them. Mainly, however, he would have been in France, moving with the Court in its progresses through Paris, Blois, Tours, Poitiers, where he mentions having met an exceedingly witty young man, not always kind in his remarks on the effects of age, who became later one of the great men of France. Henri III was on the throne, paederast brother of the weak Charles IX, who had four years previously ordered the massacre of the Huguenots. His mother, the terrible Catherine de Medici, who had persuaded him to it, still lived.

More attractive was her daughter, Marguerite de Valois, who tells us in her *Mémoires* how, unknown to herself, her marriage to the Protestant Henry of Navarre (later Henri IV of France) was used by her mother as the occasion for collecting together, as wedding-guests, those of his faith, to be massacred. She tells how even her own life was risked, by her mother's abstention from warning her not to go to her husband's chamber that night, lest her keeping away should warn others what was pending, and how the first she knew of it was when one of his men burst in, shrieking for protection, to be butchered in her presence. Henry, alone of his religion, was spared, but the couple parted, ''le noce vermeil,'' the bloodstained wedding, unconsummated.

After Marguerite's return from a visit to Flanders, it suited her mother to reunite her to Henry if he was willing. We shall discuss later whether Francis was with the long procession that in August 1578 set out for Casteras, where Catherine handed her daughter to her husband on October 2nd, and continued southward with the couple to Nerac. It will be suggested it may have been there he dreamed as he tells us Gorhambury was draped in black, before a messenger came to tell him Sir Nicholas Bacon has passed away, on February 20th. Francis left at once for home on March 20th, 1578/9.

1. *Apothegms,* 139; Spedding VII, p.144.
2. Letter to myself of June 27th, 1969, from the Headmaster.
3. *Novum Organum,* I, xc; Spedding, IV, p.78.
4. *L'Histoire Naturelle de François Bacon,* Pierre Amboise, Paris 1631. pp.6-8.

CHAPTER 5

The will

SIR Nicholas had died of a chill caught from falling asleep beneath an open window.

His will is a puzzle. What looks like the main part is dated 23rd December, 1578, and what looks like a codicil bears the earlier date of 11th September, 1577, and refers to indentures not attached. At Somerset House[1] what they have is only a copy. The indentures would have been attached to the original will, which is not possessed. What one reads gives nothing to Francis, except in remote or unlikely contingencies, if Anthony should die before the age of twenty-four or Lady Bacon remarry within one year. For the children of his first marriage and for Anthony, there were considerable provisions. For Francis there was only one warming note. After detailing a legacy to his wife, he says, ''I desire her for all the loves that have been between us to see to the well upbringing of my two sons Anthony and Francis (that are left poor orphans without a father).''

Rawley tells us the reason why he left his youngest son unprovided for was that he had set aside a sum with which to purchase land for him, but this ''being unaccomplished at his father's death there came no greater share to him than his single part and portion of the money divisible amongst five brothers.'' (This may mean an automatic right.) It would seem strange that Sir Nicholas, the highest lawyer in the land, should so have bungled things. If Sir Nicholas had accepted Francis as a service to his Queen, he would hardly have considered the obligations he had taken on with regard to him extended to providing for him out of his own estate.

His funeral, which had already taken place when Francis arrived back, was that of a great public figure. Two hundred mourners clothed in black escorted his remains to the tomb prepared for him in St. Paul's Cathedral, while the bells of St. Martins-in-the-Fields tolled all day, at the cost of the estate. The total cost of the funeral was £900 (£450,000 in today's money, by our scale).

1. Where I saw it; the whole collection has now been moved.

CHAPTER 6

The English Circe

WHEN Francis Bacon had a moment to think about anything else, he would have been aware that Jehan de Simier was now in England, suing for the Queen's hand on behalf of the Duc d'Alençon.[1] If we go into this matter a little, it is because although Bacon is not known to have made any public comment on what ensued, we shall later show reason to suppose that it made a deep impression upon him and entered into the composition of a work he was to produce years later.

Simier, sensing that the Queen's reluctance to entertain the suit derived from her attachment to Leicester, disclosed to her, what his spies had found out, that Leicester was married to her cousin Lettice. He had despaired of the Queen's hand and this secret wedding had taken place on September 21st, 1578, which his brother (the Earl of Warwick), his friends Lord North and the Earl of Pembroke, and the bride's father Sir Francis Knollys as witnesses. In this way, he became step-father to the 2nd Earl of Essex.[2]

Elizabeth's fury was such she spoke of sending Leicester to the Tower. The Earl of Sussex persuaded her it would not be fitting, and that "no man should be punished for contracting lawful marriage". In the end she forgave him, but it looked as though she might marry the Duc d'Alençon.

It is in the context of this situation that Professor Greenlaw draws attention to *Mother Hubbard's Tale,* a poem by Edmund Spenser. In the form in which we have it, it was not published until 1591 but he finds indications it was first published, then withdrawn, in 1579, the year in which the French engagement threatened. All persons in the poem are animals. A fox prompts an ape to steal the crown from a sleeping lion, thinking to himself that he, not the ape, will then rule. As Greenlaw points out,[2] "It was a whimsical custom with the Queen to give her admirers the names of animals. Thus. Simier was her ape . . . " He thinks the fox is Burghley, who, although a Catholic marriage should not have pleased a Protestant, was so antagonistic to Leicester that he was backing Simier's courtship of the Queen on behalf of Alençon, and that Spenser, a clerk in Leicester's service, was trying to warn his sleeping master that Burghley aimed to rule England through his dominance of Simier and through him, Alençon and hence, the Queen. With this brilliant analysis I agree, save that the sleeping lion seems to me Elizabeth, as Queen of England, or the English people, rather than Leicester, who, if he was her bear, was also her "Eyes", so called because he had his own very well open. He was not in need of his clerk to tell him what danger threatened, least of all through the medium of a poem published to the public (one may wonder if someone put Spenser up to this). His credit with Elizabeth being precarious since his marriage to Lettice, so little did Leicester welcome being made to appear in her sight as though it were he who had chosen this means to interpose between her and her intended, that he dropped Spenser from his service. That is why one finds Spenser leaving for Ireland with Lord Grey.[3] What I shall later submit worked deep into Bacon's consciousness is the imagery of the animals surrounding Elizabeth, as, in Professor Greenlaw's innocent phrase, ''the English Circe''.

In the end, Elizabeth restored Leicester to her confidence, to the extent that, four years later the virulent pamphlet *Leicester's Commonwealth* (anonymous, but Burghley was master of the art of ''throwing the stone without the hand being seen'')[4] accused him of murdering his wife and whom else he chose, and, by his continuing preoccupation of her person, of being the cause of the Queen's failure to marry.

A particularly strange passage, on folio 81, alleges that Leicester ''tampered'' for a crown:

First by seeking openly to marry with the Queen's Majesty herself and so to draw the crown upon his own head, and to his posterity. Secondly . . . he gave it out . . . that he was privily contracted to her Majesty . . . remember now also, the spectacle he secretly made for the persuading of a subject and Counsellor of great honour in the same cause [the Earl of Pembroke *in margin*] to the end that if her Majesty should by any way have miscarried, then he might have entitled ---- own brood (whereof he hath store in many places as is known) to the ---- of the Crown under cover of the privy and secret marriage ---- by her Majesty whereof he will want no witness to depose what he will.

Loss of words by burning of the edges of the page is represented by ----. Spedding supposes the words lost before ''of the Crown'' to have been ''lawful succession''. The meaning is clear, that Leicester tried to get some kind of statute passed, by which, if the Queen had bastards, they could succeed to the throne.

---

1. D'Alençon was a son of Catherine de Medici, brother to Marguerite de Valois, to the Charles IX who had ordered the massacre of the Huguenots and to the reigning French King Henri III.
2. *Spenser and the Earl of Leicester,* Edwin A. Greenlaw (*Modern Languages Association of America,* 1910).
3. Lord Grey was sent by the Queen to suppress rebellion in Ireland.
4. *Elizabeth and Leicester,* Milton Waldman (Collins, 1944), p.167.

CHAPTER 7

Gray's Inn

FRANCIS entered Gray's Inn in 1579, at the age of eighteen; and it is from here he wrote to Burghley:[1]

My singular good Lord,
    . . . my letter hath no further errand than to commend unto your Lordship remembrance of my suit . . . whether it also pleased your Lordship to give me good hearing so far forth as to promise to tender it to her Majesty, and withal to add in the behalf of it . . . that although it must be confessed the request is rare and unaccustomed, yet if it be observed how few there be which fall in with the study of the common laws, either being well left or friended, or at their own free election, or forsaking likely access in other studies of more delight and no less preferment, or setting hand thereunto without waste of years; upon such survey made, it may be my cause may not seem ordinary, no more than my suit, and so more beseeming unto it . . . From G.Inn, this 16 of September, 1580,
                                Your most dutiful and bounded nephew,
                                                            B.Fra.

The suit must have been for some favour or post which, if granted, would bring him nearer to the Queen, for two days later we find him writing to Burghley again:[2]

My singular good Lord,
    Your Lordship's comfortable relation of her Majesty's gracious opinion and meaning towards me . . . entereth and striketh so much more deeply into me as both my nature and duty presseth me to return some speech of thankfulness. It must be an exceeding comfort and encouragement to me, setting forth and putting myself in way towards her Majesty's service, to encounter with an example so private and domestical of her Majesty's gracious goodness and benignity; being made good and verified in my father so far as it extendeth to his blessing unto us all in our degree, to follow him afar off, and to dedicate unto her Majesty's service both the use and spending of our lives . . . From G.Inn, this 18 Oct.1580.
                                Your Lordship's dutiful and bounden nephew,
                                                            B.Fra.

But if the Queen had seemed to be about to grant something of what he asked, it yet stopped short of his hopes.

---

1. British Museum, Lansdowne MSS, 31 f.14.
2. British Museum, Lansdowne MSS, 31 f.16.

CHAPTER 8

Parliament

IN 1584, on October 12th, a new Parliament was called, and Francis sat for the first time. He had been elected for Melcome, Dorsetshire. That does not mean that he had been required to fight a contested election, for there were no political parties. The local gentry would discuss who should represent them. If there was no one outstanding within their district, they might ask some great person to recommend them, perhaps, a young man, who would welcome the opportunity to show what he could do. There were advantages to having a ''foreigner'', for he did not have to be paid. In this case, it was Burghley who had recommended Francis.

The sittings at Westminster were in St. Stevens Chapel, from eight until eleven in the morning, the hours the law-courts sat. Though it was nearly three hundred years since Parliament had emerged from the judiciary in 1295, there was still much similarity of tone, and a high proportion of the Members were lawyers.

If there was committee business, this would be done still earlier in the morning, between six and eight. One rose early in those days. Tea and coffee had not yet been discovered, and it was usual to breakfast on beer, fruit-juice or whey, though Francis found these chilled the stomach and preferred hot herbal infusions.

If one arrived late, or if one rose before the sitting ended, one was expected to place a voluntary offering of 4d in a box for wounded and retired soldiers, and the poor. There was no civil list, and though Parliament was called chiefly in order that it might vote the monarch a subsidy, this was hardly large enough to enable Elizabeth to pay pensions, or even to pay her judges and other officers of state salaries sufficient to keep them in the life-style expected; they would make up what they needed in fees and perquisites, of which more later.

The main meal of the day was taken by most people at eleven in the morning, and was called dinner. Since the law-courts and Parliament sat until that hour, dinner would be taken a little later, perhaps nearer to twelve. If sittings had to be resumed in the afternoon, it was regarded as all-night sittings are today. Five, half-past five or six were the usual hours for supper; soon after which, unless the company was convivial, one went to bed (reading by lamp-light tiring the eyes).

This Parliament had more than the subsidy to consider. Ever since Mary Stuart's flight to England sixteen years before (May 15th, 1568), she had been a centre of Catholic conspiracies. The recent Throgmorton plot,[1] and abroad the assassination of William of Orange,[2] had brought home to everyone how vulnerable was Elizabeth, and on November 23rd Sir Christopher Hatton told the Commons it was because of concern for her safety they were met. A Bill was drawn up excluding from the succession any claimant who had been a party to an attempt on her life.

Mid-February produced a shock, when one of the Members, William Parry, was charged with having conspired with Catholics against her Majesty's life. He was executed, and the Bill expedited.

It was against this background Francis wrote to the Queen:[3]

Most gracious Sovereign
    and most worthy to be a Sovereign,
    Care, one of the natural and true-bred children of unfeigned affection awaked with these late and wicked and barbarous attempts, would needs exercise my pen unto your sacred Majesty . . .
    . . . the happiness of your present estate can no way be encumbered but by your strong factious subjects and your foreign enemies. Your strong factious subjects be the Papists: strong I count them, because both in number they are (at the least) able to make a great army, and by their mutual confidence and intelligence may soon bring to pass an uniting: factious I call them, because they are discontented:- of whom in all reason of state your Majesty must determine, if you suffer them to be strong, to make them better content, or if you will discontent them, to make them weaker; for what the mixture of strength and discontentment engender, needs no syllogism to prove.
    To suffer them to be strong, with hope that with reason they will be contented, carries with it in my opinion but a fair enamelling of a terrible danger . . .
    Again, to make them contented absolutely, I do not see how your Majesty either in conscience will do it or in policy may do it, since you cannot thoroughly content them but that you must of necessity discontent your faithful subjects; and to fasten a reconciled love with the losing of a certain, is to build houses with sale of lands.
    They must not be martyred, which would but increase their numbers; but should be weakened through the weakening of their discontent. They should not be required to take the oath binding themselves to take arms, if need be, even against the Pope or else be considered traitors to Her Majesty, for such an oath must, by obliging them to chose between shame and martyrdom, make them desperate; and desperate persons may perform desperate acts, such attempts on her Majesty's life.

One sees how shrewd, as well as human, is his advice. For her own safety, Elizabeth must make life bearable for the Catholics.

He turns to foreign enemies. Scotland is not strong enough to cause much annoyance. As for France, he sees no reason why it should be an enemy:

But Spain, Spain it is which, as I conceive, all causes do concur to a just alarm to your excellent judgement.

1. Francis Throgmorton, a nephew of Sir Thomas Throgmorton, Elizabeth's Minister, had conspired with Catholics on the Continent to dethrone Queen Elizabeth and replace her with Mary Stuart.

2. William of Orange, the Dutch Protestant prince and founder of the Netherlands, assassinated in July 1584.

3. British Museum, Harleian MSS, 6867, f.42.

CHAPTER 9

The Armada and the death of Leicester

1588 brought proof of Francis' warning concerning danger from Spain. When the Armada was sighted sailing up the Channel, Elizabeth wanted to go down to the coast. Leicester, as chief of the land forces, wrote her a very sensible letter, saying that to see her exposed to real danger would distress rather than hearten her troops, and that his love would not permit her to hazard her person further than Tilbury.

Shortly after Drake's great victory at sea, Leicester and the Queen dined together, and Leicester mentioned his health. She suggested he should take the baths at Buxton, and on August 27th he wrote to tell her he was setting out. On his way to the spa on September 7th, 1588, her birthday, he died, of fever.

Elizabeth's reaction to the shock was violent. She shut herself up in her room for the whole of the day, night and following day, admitting no one, even to bring food. In the end Burghley ordered the door to be broken down.

After her own death, Leicester's letter of August 27th was found, marked on the outside in her hand: *His last letter.* It was in the casket inset with jewels which she kept beside her bed.

CHAPTER 10

Beginnings of influence

FRANCIS was becoming restive. He had been elected for Taunton in the previous year, but it is obvious from a letter he wrote to Walsingham that delay in reply to his suit was hindering him from going into practice as a lawyer, as he must do if it failed.

He was, in fact, in an unofficial manner becoming her councillor. We saw him advising toleration for Catholics. In 1589, when it was the extremists of the reformed church who were causing trouble, Francis wrote for her perusal *An Advertisement Touching the Controversies of the Church of England.* Basically, he thought they required rest. "If we did not know the virtue of silence and slowness to speak, commended by St. James; our controversies of themselves would close up and grow together." He thought a church should be a house of prayer, rather than of preaching, especially when tending to undermine faith by doctrinal hair-splitting. Nevertheless, the low church preference for simplicity of forms should be respected, and its ministers should not be troubled for praying for her Majesty without her style, bearing in mind, "the very form of prayer in the book of common prayer hath *Thy servant Elizabeth,* and no more."

There appears to be a significant sequel, a letter from Francis to Whitgift, now Archbishop of Canterbury, concerning a letter he had composed as from the Queen or her Secretary, setting forth her policy in religion. Apparently he had wished the Archbishop to run his eye over it. Spedding thinks the letter referred to must be that which went out over the signature of Walsingham to a Monsieur Citroy, the Secretary of France, later printed by Bacon as his own. The text explains it was the Pope's issuing of a Bull of excommunication against her Majesty, absolving her subjects from allegiance to her, which drove her to require of her Catholic subjects an oath placing first their loyalty to her; which oath she has now modified, so as not to make her Catholic subjects desperate. Her Majesty, "not liking to make windows into men's hearts and secret thoughts" does not persecute her subjects for their beliefs, so long as these do not result in acts which endanger her realm.

So, a phrase of Elizabeth, justly famed for its enlightenment, turns out to have been composed by Francis Bacon.

CHAPTER 11

The return of Anthony

ANTHONY Bacon was accustomed to send Walsingham intelligence from the continent, and on one occasion used as his messenger a man called Lawson, suspected of being a Catholic. His mother, whose fear of Catholics was becoming obsessional, prevailed upon Burghley to detain Lawson. Anthony then sent another messenger, Francis Allen, to procure the liberation of the first. Burghley he found reasonable, also Francis Bacon, who desired Lawson should be released; but when he went to Gorhambury, to see Lady Bacon, Allen found her a fury. He wrote to Anthony:[1]

. . . she let not to say that you are a traitor to God and your country; you have undone her; you seek her death . . . She is resolved to procure her Majesty's letter to force you to return; and when that should be, if her Majesty give you your right desert, she should clap you in prison . . . She saith you are hated of all . . . cursed of God in all your actions, since Mr. Lawson's being with you. She had rather you made wars with the King of Navarre than to have stayed so long idle in Montaubon . . . tears in her eyes . . . she wished . . . you had been fairly buried, provided you had died in the Lord. In my simple judgement, she spoke it in passion and repented immediately her words.

These are the strains of religious mania, but in truth Anthony had been in trouble in Montaubon. He had been charged with sodomy; punishable by burning to death. He was saved by Henry of Navarre, who wrote to the King's Councillor of Montaubon begging a clement and expeditious hearing of his appeal, for ''We have great obligations to the Queen, his sovereign.'' Walsingham was asked to recall him. Whether Walsingham knew the reason, we do not know.

Dame Daphne du Maurier, who discovered the papers in the archives of Montaubon, believes that Anthony was by nature homosexual but that the charge was false. A letter he wrote later in life (when thirty-eight) to his physician says a trouble from which he suffered could not be a venereal disease as he had never had carnal contact. He would not, she thinks, have lied to his doctor.[2]

What we cannot know is whether Francis was informed of what had happened in Montaubon.

In February 1591/2, Anthony came home at last, and moved into Gray's Inn, to share rooms with Francis. From this time on, we have a stream of letters from Lady Bacon to Anthony, agitated lest Lawson get in touch with him again, reproaching him for using the coach, which might make people think they were better off than they were, concerned about his health. It does not appear she wrote to Francis directly, though there are messages for him:[3]

Procure rest in convenient time. It helpeth much the digestion. I verily think your brother's weak stomach to digest hath been caused and confirmed by untimely going to bed, and then musing *nescio quid* when he should sleep, and then in consequent by late rising and long lying in bed: whereby his men are made slothful and himself continueth sickly.

Francis had been a Bencher for nearly five years and a Reader for nearly three, but it does not appear he had been getting practice. This may have been because he was not interested in becoming a practising lawyer; but the services he had been rendering to the Queen are not known to have been paid. He wrote somewhat bitterly to Burghley:[4]

My Lord,

 . . . I wax now somewhat ancient; one and thirty years is a great deal of sand in the hour-glass. My health, I thank God, I find confirmed; and I do not fear that action shall impair it, because I count my ordinary course of study and meditation to be more painful than most parts of action are. I ever bear a mind (in some middle place that I could discharge) to serve her Majesty; not as a man born under Sol, that loveth honour; nor under Jupiter, that loveth business (for the contemplative planet carrieth me away wholly); but as a man born under an excellent Sovereign, that deserveth the dedication of all men's abilities . . . Again, the meanness of my estate doth somewhat move me: for though I cannot accuse myself that I am either prodigal or slothful, yet my health is not to spend nor my course to get. Lastly I confess that I have vast contemplative ends, as I have moderate civil ends: for I have taken all knowledge to be my province; and if I could purge it of two sorts of rovers, whereof the one with frivolous disputations, confrontations and verbosities, the other with blind experiments and auricular traditional impostures, both committed to so many spoils, I hope I should bring in industrious observations, grounded conclusions and profitable inventions and discoveries . . . And if your Lordship will not carry me on, I will not do as Anaxagoras did, who reduced himself with contemplation into voluntary poverty: but this I will do; I will sell the inheritance that I have, and purchase some lease of quick revenue, or some office of gain that shall be executed by deputy, and become some sorry book-maker, or a true pioneer in that mine of truth, which (he said) lay so deep . . . from my lodging at Gray's Inn . . .

The contemplative planet is Saturn.

Perhaps Lady Bacon was not well off, for we find him writing:[5]

Madam,

Alderman Haywood died this night; his eldest son is fallen ward. My Lord Treasurer doth not for the most part hastily dispose of wards. It were worth the obtaining . . . Your Ladyship hath never had a ward of my Lord . . . From my lodging, this 18th of February, 1591.

Wardships, a source of income, were for Burghley to give out.

Lady Bacon writes to Anthony:

I am sorry your brother and you charge yourselves with superfluous horses. The wise will but laugh at you both; being but trouble, besides your debts, long journeys and private persons. Earls be Earls.

This is probably a reference to the Earl of Essex, and his lifestyle, with which they should not try to keep up, despite having come to associate with him. For Francis, despairing of Burghley, had taken Essex for his patron, and introduced Anthony to him.

1. Lambeth MSS, 637, f.111.
2. *Golden Lads,* Daphne du Maurier (Gollancz, 1975), pp. 65-9, 196-98.
3. Lambeth MSS, 648, f.106.
4. *Resuscitatio,* p.95.
5. Lambeth MSS, 648 f.5.

CHAPTER 12

Essex

WHO was Essex? What were the circumstances of his birth, and do they exhibit anything suspicious?

There is a manuscript horoscope for him in the British Museum, calculated for 9.45 a.m., November 10th, 1566.[1] On the same sheet of paper is drawn a chart for his son, calculated for 8.0 p.m., January 11th 1591. In the centre of the son's chart is written "Filius Essex", not his name. This suggests that the horoscope was cast at the request of the father, between his son's birth and christening, and that the father had his own done at the same time. The supposition that it was Essex himself who supplied the data is supported by his having been able to tell the astrologer the hour of his birth and also the dates of a number of very minor accidents, such as falls from horseback, which probably only he would have known, which are noted below the chart, and by the absence of such notes concerning any events in his life later than his son's birth. The horoscope is, then, of the highest authenticity.

Since the date it reveals would suit the thesis that he was the fruit of a period of intimacy between Elizabeth and Leicester beginning on January 1st and continuing until the early spring of 1566, we should next consider whether there is any mystery as to the place in which he was born. Walter Bouchier Devereux, in his *Lives of the Earls of Essex,* 1853, tells us that the traditional place of his birth is the family property at Netherwood, Herefordshire, but that although the baptismal register of St. Olaf's, Thornbury, goes back far enough, there is no appropriate entry. Although Essex was supposed to have been born there, his baptism was not entered in the baptismal register.

On the horoscope, the place of birth is not stated; but a horoscope has to be calculated not only for a particular date and hour but for a particular Latitude and Longtitude. The time being given, the place can therefore be deduced. The place for which the horoscope is cast is not in Herefordshire. As I have worked it out (see Appendix), the chart is set for a latitude slightly south of London (whereas for Herefordshire it should be north) and only very slightly to the west (not nearly so far to the west as Herefordshire). The nearest stately residence to the point at which the coordinates meet is Nonsuch Palace. Essex must have told the astrologer that this was where he was born. The church registers for the district do not, unfortunately, go back so far, but Nonsuch belonged to the Queen and was one of her favourite resorts. I have not been able to discover

record of the Queen's whereabouts on the date in question, since neither
the State Papers Domestic nor Nicholls Progresses have anything to tell
us; but it is highly unlikely Lettice went there, for a lying in.

What about Essex' supposed father, the 1st Earl? Is anything known of
his attitude to his supposed son, that could help us? Let us look back. On
September 20th, 1576, he had written the Queen a strange letter from his
death-bed, in Dublin:[2]

> My hard estate, most gracious Sovereign, having by great attempt long ebbed,
> even to the low water mark, made me hope much of your abundance, which,
> when I saw were not in mine own opinion more plentifully poured out upon me,
> drave me to what I dare not call plainness . . . Mine eldest son, upon whom the
> continuance of my house remaineth, shall lead a life far unworthy his calling and
> most obscurely, if it be not holpen by your Majesty's bounty . . . I dare not wish
> him mine office of Earl Marshal here, lest your Majesty should not think him
> worthy . . . But he is my son, and may more fit in his life than his unfortunate
> father hath in his possession at his death.

On the face of it, there might seem to be here a refutation of the thesis
Robert was not his son, yet the letter reads strangely against its historic
context. The 1st Earl had failed in an expedition to Ireland, for which he
had persuaded the Queen to advance him £10,000 (£5,000,000 in
today's money). It was, therefore, the Queen who was displeased her
money had been lost. Why, therefore, should he appear to think he had a
grievance against her? He seems to be saying, in effect, "I have lost a vast
sum of your money, and I must therefore ask you to provide for my eldest
son." Why should he feel it was for her to provide for the upkeep of his
eldest son? Was this not a tactful way of reminding her of a different
situation, in which he might certainly expect this boy to be provided for
by her? Letters could be intercepted, especially in the days before the
creation of a Post Office. The bearer might prove inquisitive. In any case,
it would hardly have been politic to write, "Your Majesty's bastard,
fathered upon us, is a burden daily more resented."

The 1st Earl of Essex had brown eyes and brown hair, straight. Robert,
the 2nd Earl, had brown eyes and brown hair but curly. For him to be the
child of a man with straight hair, his mother should have had curly, but
we cannot say whether there are grounds to perform a Mendelian
exclusion as we have no certain portrait of Lettice. At Longleat there is
what used to be considered the only authentic portrait of her, but the
recent discovery of a panel in every way similar to the Longleat portrait
carries an inscription identifying the sitter as her sister, Cecilia.[3] We
cannot, therefore, consider the Longleat picture as evidence and the
portrait at Sion House is deemed even less reliable. Neither have we
portraits of the undoubted children of the couple, Walter, Penelope[4] and
Dorothy. In *Astrophel and Stella* XCI Sidney tells us that "Stella"
(Penelope) combined dark eyes with amber hair, but omits to mention

whether the latter was curly or straight.

Genetically, one can say no more than that the known laws would permit the 2nd Earl to be a child of Elizabeth and Leicester.

What one can see, however, is that in facial structure, as also in the delicacy of his hands, he bears a strong resemblance to the Queen, whilst he looks so very much like the brother of Francis Bacon that the sight of them together could engender suspicion.

Why was he called Robert? That was Leicester's Christian name, not his supposed father's, which was Walter. It was his second son who was christened Walter, and in this context it is interesting to read what Sir Henry Wotton, later secretary to the young 2nd Earl, writes:[5]

I must not smother what I have received by constant information, that his own father died with a very cold conceit of him, some say through the affection to his second son, Walter Devereux . . .

If he had been obliged to take Robert off the Queen's hands, it may have galled him that having to appear as his father made it impossible for his own son, Walter, to inherit his Earldom. His letter to the Queen could represent a last attempt to get the cuckoo out of the nest.

Wotton continues his life of the 2nd Earl:

The said Earl of Leicester bewrayed a meaning to plant him in the Queen's favour; which was diversely interpreted by such as thought that great Artisan of Court to do nothing by chance . . . Yet I am not ignorant there was some good while a very stiff aversation in my Lord of Essex from applying himself to the Earl of Leicester, for whatever conceit I know not, but howsoever that humour was mollified by time; and by his Mother, and to the Court he came under his lee.

In May, 1587, Leicester had asked the Queen to let Essex succeed him as Master of the Horse, an office worth £1,500, or, in today's money, £750,000, a year, which involved walking at her bridle rein when she rode in state. She had demurred, saying she had at that moment no office to which she could raise Leicester, in order to make his present one vacant for Essex. Leicester had replied that he had no thought of a higher office for himself, but merely wished to renounce his post in favour of Essex. He was certainly doing as much for him as if he was his own son.

The letter from one Anthony Paget to his father from which we have this, adds that the Queen sat up playing cards with Essex until the birds began to sing in the morning. It will be noticed he does not suggest they went to bed together. The popular fancy which weaves a romance around Elizabeth and Essex ignores the fact that she was thirty-three years his senior. When Leicester first presented him to her, Essex was seventeen and she was fifty.

There is no doubt that after Leicester's death, Essex became the apple of her eye, but G.B. Harrison may have written more truly than he knew, of her attachment to Essex, "It had something of the jealous love of a widow towards her only son."[6]

1. This information is new. Until now, there has been uncertainty even as to the year of Essex' birth.

As to read this ancient horoscope correctly, and to work back from the figures presented to the day and hour at which the Sun, Moon, planets and Ascendant would have been in the positions shown, and, from the relation of the Ascendant to the Medium Coeli shown, to deduce the latitude, requires considerable knowledge of astrology, and even the exposition of my workings may tax the inexperienced reader's power to follow, I have, in order to avoid holding up the narrative, placed them in an appendix.

2. British Museum, Harleian MSS, 6922, f.28.

3. Letters to myself, in 1977, from Dr. Roy Strong, Director of the Victoria and Albert Museum, former Director of the National Portrait Gallery, and Mr. Robin Gibson, his successor in the latter post.

4. The Van Dyke anachronistically called 'Lady Penelope Rich' must be of somebody else.

5. *Reliquiae Wottonianae* (1615), p.173.

6. *Robert Devereux, Earl of Essex*, G.B. Harrison (Cassell, 1937), pp.28-29.

CHAPTER 13

Quarrel with the Queen

INTELLIGENCE came in that a new Spanish Armada was being built and that certain Scottish nobles would receive the Spanish forces. To meet the emergency, a parliament was called for February 19th, 1592/3, in despite of an outbreak of plague, that closed the Globe Theatre. The business was to vote a subsidy sufficient for the defence of the realm. It was the custom for the Commons to recommend the amount and for the Lords to confirm. There was precedent for a double subsidy; but on this occasion the Lords, in the person of Lord Burghley, intimated to the Commons that only a triple subsidy would suffice, and offered to join them in their conference. He may have been prompted by the Queen, who wanted as much as possible, quickly. Francis, however, saw the proposal as a threat to the status of the Commons, and feared lest under pressure of emergency, rights be given away which could not easily be recovered. With great courage, therefore, he rose as soon as Robert Cecil, after reading his father's proposition, had sat down.

He agreed that an exceptional subsidy was needed, but "misliked" that the Upper House should be joined with them in their deliberations. He thought the Commons should stand upon their privilege of deliberating first, apart. The Commons were impressed, and despite the protestations of Cecil a vote was taken by which it was decided by 227 to 128 "That no such conference be had." The Lords did not receive this well, but after some further exchange of messages, sank back.

But Francis had not finished. A contemporary record states:

Mr. Frauncis Bacon assented to three subsidies, but not to the payment under six years; and to this propounded three reasons, which he desired might be answered.
1. Impossibility or difficulty.
2. Danger and discontent.
3. A better manner of supply than subsidy.
For impossibility, the poor man's rent is such they are not able to pay so much upon the present. The gentlemen must sell their plate and the farmers their brass pots ere this will be paid . . .

In this he did not prevail. Moreover, he had offended the Queen.

CHAPTER 14

Hope disappointed

BURGHLEY must have told Francis, who wrote to him:[1]

It may please your Lordship,

I was very sorry to find by your Lordship's speech yesterday that my last speech in Parliament, delivered in discharge of my conscience and duty to God and her Majesty and my country was offensive. If it were misreported, I would be glad to attend your Lordship to disavow anything I said not. If it were misconstrued, I would be glad to expound my words, to exclude any sense I meant not. If my heart be misjudged by imputation of popularity or opposition by any devious or officious informer, I have great wrong; and the greater because the manner of my speech did most evidently show that I spake simply, and only to satisfy my conscience, and not with any advantage or policy to sway the cause, and my terms carried all signification of duty and zeal towards her Majesty and her service. It is true, that from the beginning whatsoever was above a double subsidy, I did wish might (for precedent's sake) appear to be extraordinary, and (for discontent's sake) ought not have been levied upon the poorer sort, though otherwise, I wished it as rising, as I think this will prove, and more. This was my mind, I confess it. And therefore I most humbly pray your good Lordship, first to continue me in your own good opinion, and then to perform the part of an honest friend towards your poor servant and ally, in drawing your Majesty to accept of the sincerity and simplicity of my heart, and to bear with the rest, and restore me to her Majesty's favour.

The Queen, not appeased, forbade him her presence.

Nevertheless, Essex proposed Francis' name to her when the office of Attorney-General fell vacant. The other candidate was Edward Coke, already Solicitor-General and nine years Francis' senior. Francis was interested in the framing of laws, but had never conducted a case in the courts. Coke had spent his life in the courts, but was not interested in the making of laws; neither had he any experience of Parliament.

The Queen did not instantly reject Francis' candidature, though she continued to refuse him the accustomed access. Perhaps she was waiting for him to apologise for having crossed the Cecils (herself behind them) in Parliament. That appears to have been the opinion of Cecil, who wrote to him that he could do nothing for him, as by asking his father's intercession; the first step was for Francis to regain his former welcome to her society. Cecil's letter, dated May 7th, 1593, is signed, ''Your loving cousin and friend,'' but Francis was beginning to doubt whether the Cecils, father or son, were friends to him. Burghley, sensitive no doubt to his son's slight hunchback, was not anxious to forward a brilliant nephew who might eclipse him, neither was the son eager.

Eventually Francis, realising he must break the stalemate, wrote to the Queen:[2]

Madam,

Remembering that your Majesty had been gracious to me both in countenancing me and conferring upon me the reversion of a good place, and perceiving your Majesty had taken some displeasure towards me, both these were arguments to move me to offer unto your Majesty my service, to the end to have means to deserve your benefit and to repair my error . . . Thus I most humbly crave pardon of my boldness and plainness. God preserve your Majesty.

He has not owned to knowing it was his speech in Parliament that vexed her, but this was sufficient to procure his renewed access to her presence, and on June 2nd, 1593, he went again to Twickenham, to be near her court at Richmond.

Yet she still did not make up her mind who she wished for Attorney and Francis' finances were running low. Francis had borrowed £30 (£15,000 by our scale) from a certain "Harvy", who, from his distinctive signature, is identifiable with Sir George Hervey, the Lieutenant of the Tower, and was being pressed to return it. Anthony reminded his mother she had once offered to bestow on Francis the interest in a property called Marks, which, if she would do it now, would enable him to pay off Hervey. She replied:[3]

For your brotherly care of your brother Francis' state you are to be well liked, and so do I as a Christian mother that loveth you both as the children of God: but . . . the state of you both doth much disquiet me . . . I have been too ready for you both till nothing is left. And surely though I pity your brother, yet so long as he pitieth not himself but keepeth that bloody Percy, as I told him then, yea as a coach companion and bed companion – a proud profane fellow, whose being about him I verily fear the Lord God doth mislike and doth less bless your brother in credit and otherwise in his health – surely I am utterly discouraged and make a conscience further to undo myself to maintain such wretches as he is. That Jones never loved your brother indeed, but for his own credit, living upon your brother, and thankless though bragging. But your brother will be blind to his own hurt . . . The Lord in his mercy remove them from him and evil from you both. It is most certain till first Enney [?], a filthy wasteful knave, and his Welshmen one after another – for take one and they will swarm ill-favouredly – did so lead him as in a train, he was a towardly young gentleman and a son of much good hope in godliness. But seeing he hath nourished most sinful proud villains wilfully, I know not what other answer to make.

. . . Gorham. 17 Apr [1593]

A.Bacon

This letter has been taken by some to imply sexual relations between Francis and Percy, but the term bed companion was used by Elizabethans innocently. Privacy is modern. Not only did most bedrooms then lead out of one another but beds were wider, meant for occupation by several. If one was a house-guest for the week-end, one might be interested to discover on arrival who one's host had arranged should be one's bed-fellow or fellows. A single woman living alone would have her gentlewoman, and a gentleman would have his gentleman of the bed-chamber. (Queen Elizabeth's enormous gift to Leicester's has been seen as a tip for absenting himself when she paid nocturnal visits.) Catherine Drinker Bowen has pointed out that Percy was the surname of a great Catholic family. If the Henry Percy remembered in Francis' will was a member of it, what would have been worrying Lady Bacon was that Francis had a Catholic as his attendant.

She added a postscript:

If your brother desire a relase to Mr. Hervey, let him require it himself, and but upon this condition by his own hand and bond I will not; that is, that he make and give me a true note of all his debts, and leave to me the whole order and receipt of all his money and his land, to Hervey, and the just payment of all his debts thereby. And by the mercy and grace of God it shall be performed by me to his quiet discharge without cumbering him and to his credit. For I will not have his cormorant seducers and instruments of Satan to him committing foul sin by his countenance, to the displeasing of God and his godly true fear. Otherwise I will not *pro certo.*
                                                                                              A.B.

In other words, she will not give or lend Francis money, but if he will send her all his unpaid bills, and papers relating to moneys owing to him, she will get these in and pay his creditors. She seems not to realise that if Francis, an applicant for a post in which he would be handling the affairs of the nation, acceded to this proposition, it would make him a laughing stock.

Francis' reply to this has not been preserved, but we have her next to Anthony:[4]

I send you herein your brother's letter. Construe the interpretation. I do not understand his enigmatical folded writing. O that by not harkening to wholesome and careful and good counsel, and by continuing still the means of his own hindrance, he had not procured his own early discredit; but had joined with God that hath bestowed on him good gifts of natural wit and understanding. But the same good God that hath given them to him will I trust and heartily pray to sanctify his heart by the right use of them to glorify the giver of them to his own inward comfort. The scope of my so called by him circumstance, which I am sure he must understand, was not to use him as a ward – a remote phrase to my plain motherly meaning – and yet, I thank the Lord and the hearing of his word preached, not void of judgement and conceiving. My plain proposition was and is to do him good. But seeing so manifestly that he is robbed and spoiled wittingly by his base exalted [?] men, which with Welsh wiles pray upon him and yet bear him in hand they have their maintenance, because their bold nature will not acknowledge, I did only desire to receive the money to discharge his debts indeed; and dare not trust such his riotous men with the dealing withal.

The extraordinary word in this passage is "ward". What mother ever said of her own son that she never treated him as a ward? It is true that guardians customarily kept back for themselves some of the money given them to look after wards. Perhaps she thought Francis suspected her of trying to get hold of the little money he had, and wished merely to deny this and protest the purity of her motive. All the same, it is a strange turn of thought, and one may think, not a likely one for a real mother of her real son.

How Francis' debt was settled is not known, though it appears from one of Anthony's letters that it was. Probably it was Anthony who – as usual – paid.

Meanwhile, Francis was kept on tenterhooks with regard to the Queen's decision as to his possible appointment as Attorney. On June 3rd, 1593, Anthony wrote to Lady Bacon that he had understood from Essex that she was "thoroughly appeased and stood only upon the accepting of his years for his present preferment." But two months later, her anger was recrudescent; on August 24th, Essex wrote to Francis:[5]

Sir,

I spoke with the Queen yesterday and on Wednesday. On Wednesday she cut me off short; she being come newly home and making haste to her supper. Yesterday I had a full audience, but with little better success than before. The points I pressed were an absolute αμνηστια and an access as in former times. Against the first she pleaded that you were in more fault than any of the rest in Parliament; and when she did forgive it and manifest her receiving of them into favour that offended her then, she will do it to many that were less in fault as well as to yourself. Your access, she saith, is as much as you can look for. If it had been in the King her father's time, a less offence than that would have made a man be banished his presence for ever. But you did come to Court when you would yourself and she should precipitate too much from being highly displeased with you to give you near access, such as she shows only to those that she favours extraordinarily. I told her that I sought for you was not so much your good, though it were a thing I would ask seek extremely and please myself in obtaining, as for her honour, that those excellent translations of hers might be known to them that could best judge of them. Besides, my desire was that you should neither be stranger to her person nor to her service; the one for your own satisfaction, the other for her Majesty's own sake, who if she did not employ you should lose the use of the ablest gentleman to do her service . . . Her humour is still to delay . . .

Essex

This summer found Anthony in the process of selling an estate called Barly. As it was entailed, nothing could be done without the agreement of his eldest half-brother, Sir Nicholas Bacon. The legal considerations were complex, and Francis drafted a letter for Anthony to send to Nicholas. He also wrote two letters to the person who was buying Barly, Alderman John Spencer. Later, we shall speak of Spencer further. What is of interest here to note is that Bacon must have known him already, and well, for on August 26th, 1593, he signs himself to him, "Your very loving friend."

To a certain Robert Kemp, lawyer of Gray's Inn, Francis wrote on November 4th, 1593:[6]

For my fortune (to speak court) it is very slow, if anything can be slow to him that is certain of the event. In short, nothing is done in that.

Christmas passed, and on January 18th, 1593/4, Essex told Francis nothing would be decided before Easter.

On January 25th, Francis conducted his first case, before the King's Bench, thus removing the objection he had never practised.

Anthony now wrote to tell his mother Burghley had urged the Queen to nominate Coke. By the end of March it came to be thought that Coke would be the new Attorney-General and that Bacon would get the Solicitorship vacated by Coke. For this he would have no rival, and Burghley added his support to that of Essex. Yet Essex wrote to Francis:[7]

I find the Queen very reserved, staying herself from giving any kind of hope, yet not passionate against you till I grew passionate for you. Then she said that none thought you fit for the place but my Lord Treasurer and myself . . . She said she neither was persuaded nor would hear of it till Easter, when she might advise with her Council, who were now all absent; and therefore in passion bade me go to bed, if I would talk of nothing else.

Francis replied bitterly:[8]

I must confess this very delay hath gone so near me, as it hath almost overthrown my health. For when I revolve . . . the honourable testimony of so many counsellors, the commendation laboured and in sort offered by my Lords the Judges and the Master of the Rolls elect; that I was voiced with great expectation, and . . . with the wishes of most men, to the higher place . . . when . . . I revolve all this, I cannot but conclude with myself that no man ever received a more exquisite disgrace. And therefore truly, my Lord, I was determined, and am determined, if her Majesty reject me, this to do. My nature can take no evil ply; but I will by God's assistance, with this disgrace of my fortune, and yet with that comfort of the good opinion of so many honourable and worthy persons, retire myself with a couple of men to Cambridge, and there spend my life in my studies and contemplations, without looking back.

1. British Museum, Additional MSS. 5503, f.1.
2. Lambeth MSS. 649, f.315.
3. Lambeth MSS. 653, f.175.
4. Lambeth MSS. 653, f.165.
5. Lambeth MSS. 649, f.165.
6. Lambeth MSS. 646, f.281.
7. Lambeth MSS. 650, f.90.
8. Lambeth MSS. 650, f.62.

CHAPTER 15

Tower employment

IF Francis was serious in his idea of giving up waiting for possible office and retiring to Cambridge to devote himself to a life of letters, his resolution was undermined by events.

The turn of the year 1593/4 had found Essex engrossed in the investigation of a conspiracy amongst the Portuguese refugees in London, against, he was certain, the Queen's life. The Queen at first refused to believe his allegations that Dr. Lopez, her Portuguese physician, had accepted pay from King Philip of Spain to poison her. The Cecils likewise scorned Essex' allegation of a such conspiracy. Essex, humiliated that what he set forth was not taken seriously, retired to his chamber for two days, refusing to come out. Later, however the Cecils came round to Essex's point of view. Modern scholarship tends to doubt whether Lopez intended anything against the Queen, but grants that he was involved in plotting something against his own prince, Antonio, the exiled pretender to the Portuguese throne, enjoying the hospitality of England; perhaps to poison him. Bacon had no doubt of his guilt; it is not known whether he was present at any of the interrogations, which were undertaken by Essex, but he was present at the trial (which resulted in conviction and execution after the hideous manner of the day) and wrote a Report of the affair for the public. It is not known whether the Queen commanded this or whether he did it simply for Essex.

Hardly had Lopez and his confederates been put to death when, in the early summer of 1594, a new plot was discovered, this time certainly to poison the Queen. Though it seemed to have the same prime movers as before, the executives were English, from the north of England. Two, Henry Walpole and Edward Lyngen, were brought to the Tower, and on June 13th the name of Francis Bacon appears amongst the examiners.

Again, one cannot know if this was at the command of the Queen or merely at the request of Essex, but if Francis took a part in the interrogation to help Essex, surely the Queen must have at least passively consented. It is as if, her life being in danger, her displeasure with him was gone.

Four days later, Francis received a letter from Fulke Greville which sounded most encouraging: her Majesty, he said, spoke "with very exceeding gracious inclination towards you . . . So I will lay £100 to £50 that you shall be her Solicitor . . ."

It looks as though either this sudden favour and use of him did not carry with it any payment for his new service or there was a delay in getting his name on to the lists for payment, for about a fortnight later Francis was having to borrow money in order to go to the north of England upon the Queen's business, that is to pursue enquiries in the locality where the conspiracy had been nursed. To help him fulfil this important mission, Anthony pledged part of his own estate as security for a loan.

He set out on the 18th or 19th July, but was held up by illness. Whether he ever reached the north we do not know, but on the 27th, in Cambridge, he received his M.A. degree, and by the end of the month he was back in London. He now composed a paper concerning the Queen's safety, of which only a fragment has been preserved. In this he urges not only that measures be taken but that they be seen to be taken. As he has observed that where watch booths are set up, no thieving takes place, so he would advise the spreading of a rumour that her Majesty's intelligence service is very much augmented, and that there be everywhere agents feigning to join with the conspirators, only to betray them to her Majesty. Such fear as this report would instil might give her Majesty some respite from these attempts on her life; he would also be disposed to try whether any good might be done by writing to the King of Spain, who was certainly behind these plots, pointing out that it was contrary to the law of nations and the sacred dignity of kings that persons known to have conspired to assassinate her Majesty should be given refuge in his kingdom.

Francis went briefly to Gorhambury, to see Lady Bacon, and when he returned to Gray's Inn she sent after him some pigeons, for his dinner, and a letter ending:[2]

I do not write to my Lord Treasurer because you liked to stay. Let this letter be unseen. Look very well to your health. Sup not nor sit not up late. Surely I think your drinking to bedwards hindreth your and your brother's digestion very much. I never knew any but sickly that used it; besides ill for head and eyes. Observe well yet in time. 20 Aug. Gorh.   In Christo,
                                                                                    A. Bacon.

On the same date as this was written, one of the prisoners now in the Tower made a confession before three examiners: W.G. Waad, Nicholas Blount and Francis Bacon. The Queen was to have been killed with poisoned weapons and the crown offered to the Earl of Derby.

Meanwhile, Francis was apparently still receiving nothing from the Queen for his pains; his means were as straitened as ever and his future uncertain. On August 24th, 1594, we find him writing to the Lord Keeper, now Sir John Puckering, rather pathetically, asking him to ''remember her Majesty of a Solicitor''.[3] In a further note to the Lord Keeper written the following day, he said, ''I cannot bear myself as I should till I be settled.'' Yet the appointment of a new Solicitor was still delayed, and Francis wrote to Anthony:[4] "Brother . . . I hear nothing from the Court in mine own business." Anthony had now moved to a house in Bishopsgate, near the Bull Inn. This disturbed Lady Bacon, as plays were staged in it, and the theatre, for her, was sin.

On August 27th another of the prisoners in the Tower, Williams, confessed before examiners, including Francis; on the 31st they questioned him further, and afterwards Francis drew up for the guidance of the other examiners a list of points on which enquiry should be made of one Sheldon, whom he had implicated.

The prisoners could not be brought to trial until a new Solicitor had been appointed, and Francis seems to have taken his having been used in the preliminary enquiry as an earnest he would receive the post. However, possibly because the Earl of Derby had been mentioned, the Queen decided they were not to be brought to trial, and still delayed the appointment of a Solicitor.

Francis had a case to argue on October 25th, but otherwise nothing to do and was reduced to a great dependence on Anthony. Anthony's accounts show that he lent money to Francis in 1593 on September 11th, £20; September 21st, £5; October 30th, £1; October 31st, £23; November 18th, £5; in 1594 on May 6th, £10; July 11th, £60; August 31st, £100; September 9th, £50; January 29th (94/5), £30; March 8th (94/5), £10; in 1595 on April 14th, £44. Neither was this sum to be the last. To obtain present values, all figures should be multiplied by 500.

It was not that Anthony had money to spare; to raise it for Francis, he mortgaged part of his own estate.

1. See *Elizabeth and Essex,* Lytton Strachey (Chatto, 1968). Chapter 6.
2. Lambeth MSS. 650, f. 171.
3. British Museum, Harleian MSS. 6996, f. 196.
4. Lambeth MSS. 650, f. 168.

CHAPTER 16

Gray's Inn revels

ON December 5th, 1594, Lady Bacon wrote to Anthony, "I trust they will not mum nor mask nor sinfully revel at Gray's Inn." Gray's Inn had formerly been famous for its Christmas Revels. For some years they had not been celebrated, but this year it had been decided to hold them again. An unusually full account of the revels for 1594 is given in the *Gesta Grayorum*[1] (Gray's Inn Revels). The author's name does not appear on it, but Spedding, always a conservative authority, considered Bacon's connection with it "sufficiently obvious"[2] and ascribed to him the composition of the more sober parts.

Over the holiday, Gray's Inn became a pantomime kingdom, with its own sovereign and parliament. The sovereign was the Prince of Portpool or Purpoole, from the ancient Manor of Portpool, on the sight of which the Inn was built. The Prince for 1594 was a member of Gray's Inn named Henry Helmes, and his pantomime Knights were therefore called the Order of the Helmet. Some Baconians believe the pantomime Order of the Helmet masked a real Order of the Helmet, a brotherhood gathered under the aegis of Pallas Athena, goddess of wisdom, who holds a spear and wears a helmet, symbol of secrecy. I do not see that this can be proven, but it is not impossible. On December 20th the Purpoole Prince proceeded to the great hall of Gray's Inn and took his seat on the throne, his Knight-at-Arms proclaimed his style and titles, the Champion threw down the gauntlet, the pantomime Attorney General made a speech and the pantomime Solicitor General read out a list of his homagers and tributories. Though the formal etiquette was true to the reality, there was an element of burlesque, spiced with mischief and (as Lady Bacon had feared) bawdry: the articles sworn by the Knights included reference to "every maid in his Highness' province of Islington continuing a virgin after the age of fourteen years, contrary to the use and custom in that place always observed". Over the holiday, everyone would comport himself and be addressed according to his pantomime role.

The great night was to be December 28th, when they had invited the Ambassador of the neighbouring kingdom of the Inner Temple. He arrived with a great train, but the stage became so crowded that those who were to have given the entertainment were unable to mount it, and, in a tumult, mysteriously disappeared. The guests had to be contented with "A *Comedy of Errors* (like to Plautus his *Menechmus*)" which "was played by the players . . . so that night was begun and continued to the end, in nothing but confusion and errors; whereupon it was ever afterwards called the *Night of Errors.*'' The narrative does not explain how it was possible to have a new play handy to replace the entertainment which should have been given. That it was felt to be somewhat of a hat-trick is evidenced by the fact that the following night a (pantomime) legal inquiry was held, a (mock) commission of Oyer and Terminer issued and a certain ''sorcerer or conjurer that was supposed to be the cause of that confused inconvenience'' arraigned before a (mock) jury upon several charges, of which the last was ''that he had foisted a company of base and common fellows to make up our disorders with a play of errors and confusions''.

The narrâtor does not tell us the name of the member of Gray's Inn who was the ''sorcerer or conjuror'' arraigned on the charge of having foisted *A Comedy of Errors* upon the ''kingdom''. Shakespearean scholars take the play to be Shakespeare's of that title, its first production, and there is no reason to suppose from the terms of disparagement and mock trial that it was not appreciated. In the topsy-turvydom of the revels, it could as well mean that it was a roaring success.

1. First published 1688.
2. Spedding, VIII, p.325.

CHAPTER 17

The Northumberland manuscript

THE first literary compositions in Bacon's name are some slight pieces for the celebration of one of the anniversaries of the Queen's accession to the throne. Spedding, printing two of them, *Mr. Bacon in Praise of Knowledge* and *Mr. Bacon . . . in Praise of his Sovereign*, gave his opinion they were the last two in a set of four.

In 1867 the Duke of Northumberland became curious about two black boxes at Northumberland House. No one could tell him whence they had come, what they were supposed to contain or how long they had been there. He sent them to the Record Office, where they were opened by John Bruce. They contained papers, mostly concerning the Northumberland family but including a folder full of Bacon scripts, in various hands, twenty-two leaves, unnumbered, laid one upon the other; they had once been secured by a stitch. It is not the scripts but the outer leaf, wrapped around them as a cover (see facsimile, Plate 6) which is important. A ragged pear-shape is caused by its having been burned as are, to a lesser extent, the leaves within. As the original is now so faint that it is doubtful whether it would be legible in photofacsimile if the whole were reduced to the size of a page of this book, I reproduce a part of it, to give an idea of what the original looks like, and for greater clarity, transcribe in print words that can be picked out, this printed transcript descending beyond the limit of the facsimile. It will be seen that although the whole is covered with scribble, there is what begins in the top right-hand corner as an ordered table of contents:

Mr. Frauncis Bacon
of Tribute or giving what is dew
The praise of the worthiest vertue
The praise of the worthiest affection
The praise of the worthiest power
The praise of the worthiest person

Thomas
By Mr. Frauncis   Thomas
By Mr Frauncis Bacon of Gr
Frauncis
turner
Greis Inn   in the
Philipp against monsieur
revealed
Earle of Arundells letter to the Queen
from your service
Speaches for my Lord of Essex at the tylt
Speach for my Lord of Sussex tilt
more than externally
honorificabiletudine   Leycesters Common Wealth   Incerto autore
Dyrmonth
Ley   Adam
Orations at Graies Inne revells
Dyr   Queenes Ma^{te} many
By Mr Frauncis Bacon   Bacon
Earle of A   By Mr
ɟɹɐunɔıs   By Mr
Essaies by the same author
printed
sıɔunɐɹɟ
By Mr Frauncis   William   Shakespeare
Shakespear
Rychard the second
Bacon   Frauncis
Rychard the third
Bacon   Asmund and Cornelia   Thomas
Asmund and Cornelia   Thom   Thom
revealing   Ile of Dogs   frmnt
day through   as your
every crany   by Thomas Nashe   inferior plaiers
peepes and
see   William Shakespeare
Shak   Sh   Sh
Sh   Shak   Shakespeare
Shak
William Shakespeare

William Shakespeare   Wlm   Wlm
Will
Shakspe
William
Shakespe   Shakespear

This has the distinction of being the only document of the period on which the names of Bacon and Shakespeare appear together. Near its edges, where the burning browns the paper, the writing is difficult to read, but I went to Alnwick Castle and, by kind permission of the present Duke, was able to examine the original, I was able to make out a little more than shows on even the best facsimile. I discerned eleven repetitions of the full name, William Shakespeare, descending into the burnt part, not counting starts at it. Some of the writing is upside down, including one "Frauncis" just above "Essaies by the same author".

In the scribble top left, appears first the name "Neville", twice, and near it, twice, "ne vile velis", motto of the family of Nevilles into which married Elizabeth, daughter of Sir Nicholas Bacon by his first marriage; then a possibly related sequence or pattern of words, in which there seems to be some carry-through of thought:

> refusing
> of them
> yourselves
> as in Christ
> refusing of any
> all
> Anthony comfort and consorte
> comft
> the hart
> refreshing
> laden with grief and
> oppression of hart

This group seems to be of a different order from the titles and names on the right. It deals with the expression of a mood or the feeling of a deeply burdened spirit.

This group is connected with the other by "your lovinge friend" which comes just over "honorificabiletudine".

Also top left is a verse in Latin (medieval, not classical, as can be seen from its having beats, not quantities) known to Anthony Bacon, for he quotes it in a letter, though not to Francis; the name "Philipp", and lower down "end of hall".

What is it? Spedding was delighted to find the two earlier "In praise of . . . " pieces he had predicted must exist. He thought the set of four must have been composed for Queen's Day, 1592. Having earlier ascribed to Bacon's composition another set of speeches, for delivery by the Earl of Essex as his own, for Queen's Day, 1595, he found support for this in the presence of the scripts within this folder, though they, like some other minor Bacon works found within, were not included in the table of contents on the wrapper.

To prevent its further deterioration, the front of the wrapper, like the rest of the leaves, had to be pasted down upon firm paper, and it is a pity Spedding did not think to tell us whether, before this was done, there was a bulge in the back sufficient to have accommodated also *Richard II* and *Richard III.* Spedding had been irked by a meeting fourteen years before with a Miss Delia Bacon who told him she thought Bacon wrote Shakespeare, and is reported to have replied that had it been so he would have discovered it – an assertion which might carry greater conviction if he had not failed to discover Bacon had anything to do with the Virginia Company (see below p.210), a matter belonging to the public domain. Spedding, now expressing some dismay at what might be made of the collocation of Bacon's and Shakespeare's names, treats the scribble summarily as the work of someone trying a pen.

Le Marchant Douse suggested the scribble to be exhibition of different styles of handwriting by John Davies of Hereford, writing master to the Earl of Northumberland's children. There is, however, in the British Museum, an example of Davies' hand, a holograph copy of his poem *A Dedicatory and Consolatorie Epistle to the right Honourable Henry Earl of Northumberland.* The hand is very beautiful, but nothing like that of the scribbler.

E.K. Chambers, in his *William Shakespeare,* dismissing a suggestion the scribbler could be Shakespeare, says, ''I take him to have been Adam Dyrmonth.'' He gives no reason, but goes on to prove that since Dermont existed as a name, Dyrmonth could also have existed. This is what is called in Logic an *Ignoratio Elenchi,* the fallacy of proving the wrong conclusion.[1] What requires to be proved is not that somebody really could have borne the name of Dyrmonth, but that, if a real person bore it, he was the author of the scribble. Thomas Nashe indubitably existed, but though his name is also written, Chambers does not suggest he must have been the author. Perhaps Chambers (who does not say he has consulted the manuscript in the original) did not notice Nashe and was merely looking for an alternative to Shakespeare that did not let in Bacon.

One would have thought that if the hand was Bacon's, Spedding would have recognised it. It is a pity those experts on hands of the period, W.W. Greg, A.W. Pollard and Sir Maunde Thomas, who identified as Shakespeare's Hand D in the additions to the manuscript play of *Sir Thomas More,* were not interested to view the Northumberland Manuscript and deliver judgement on the hand that wrote the scribble.

In the absence of expert witness, I can only do the best I can. I have sought for, in Bacon's manuscript, *Promus,* and in his letters, words which occur in the Northumberland scribble, copying out pairs, so as to discover differences or similarities in the way the pen has moved. The way in which Gray's Inn is written in the scribble, particularly in the second instance, is very like the way in which Bacon writes it, as his address.

There is the same failure of the *y* to descend below the line, though in other words (in both hands) it does so. It can hardly be, in either case, that the intention was to write Grais, with an undotted *i*, for both Bacon and the scribbler dot their '*i*'s carefully, close to, and in any case it has two arms. It was probably the frequency of his occasion to write it that caused Bacon's careless treatment of this word. Bacon never signs his Christian name in full, but, shorn of the flourishes which adorn his signature to letters, the way the name is written on the Northumberland Manuscript is very like the way he writes it. All the letters are made in the same basic form, particularly in the first instance, ''Mr. Frauncis Bacon of Tribute or giving what is dew.''

I have found in his letter asking a friend to the funeral of his (supposed) mother, the word ''comfort'', to compare with ''Anthony comfort and consorte'' in the scribble. The letters are made in the same way, and they share a distinctive feature, which is that the second *o* is very small and does not follow the *f*, but is comprised in the backward movement that makes its cross-bar, or rather, cross-circle. If the hand is Bacon's, Anthony may be his brother.

The word ''speech'' occurs three times in *Promus*, f.85r, and three times in the scribble. Most of the word seems to be written in the same way, though the final *h* is written in the scribble more like a reversed figure 3 and in *Promus* more like an 8, that is to say, there has been a leftward movement before the termination.

It looks as though the wrapper had first been intended to contain only the speeches for Queen's Day, and afterwards had been used as a place to stow other things. One cannot say that *Richard II* and *Richard III*, because they figure in the list, must be by Bacon, for he certainly did not write *Leicester's Commonwealth*, noted as of uncertain authorship, or the suppressed play *Isle of Dogs* (Nashe and Jonson). He may have had copies made of vexatious works for his reference. *Asmund and Cornelia*, on analogy with *Romeo and Juliet*, sounds like a play about lovers. If it was a play written but lost, one should have heard of it. Perhaps it was a projected play, never written. But then, who projected it, Bacon? As for the doodling, if the author is Bacon, why did he doodle the name of Shakespeare so many times? ''Honorificabiletudinatibus'' occurs in *Love's Labour's Lost*, but is an old joke word, which can be found in Erasmus – which Bacon did read. ''Revealing day through every cranny peeps'' is practically *The Rape of Lucrece*, 1086, ''Revealing day through every cranny spies.'' The great question is, does the slight difference represent the doodler's inaccurate memory of a work he had read by somebody else, or is it his own first try-out for a poem which he had not completed in final form yet?

There are plenty of reasons why Bacon, if he wished to write plays and poems, should need a pseudonym or cover. A gentleman might write verses for private circulation amongst his friends (as in ancient Rome), but publication in print, of copies for sale to the public, was still a vulgarism and would hardly help his career.

But the Shakespeare authorship question can be approached from another angle.

1. *General Logic,* Ralph M. Eaton (Scribner's, New York, 1931) p.345.

CHAPTER 18

Promus

BACON had by this time begun keeping a notebook.[1] The beginning of it is missing, but the third of the extant folios, which bears the number 83, carries the date: Dec. 5, 1584, and the title, *Promus*. This is Latin for larder, or storehouse, and it seems he used it as a private jotting-place for phrases which had struck him, presumably for storage in case of need for future use.

On f.100, Bacon has written:

Adonis gardens (things of great pleasure but soon fading)

In Shakespeare, we read:

> Thy promises are like Adonis gardens,
> That one day bloomed, and fruitful were the next.
>
> *I King Henry VI, I, vi,* 6-7.

The Dauphin is addressing La Pucelle, and as the play is written from the English point of view, we can be sure the choice of simile was intended by the author to be unlucky. In the next Act, a reverse causes the Dauphin to turn upon La Pucelle, taxing her with having flattered his expectation with a little gain at the beginning, only to lose much more, after.

Adonis Gardens, as Plato makes quite clear in the *Phaedrus*, 276b, were shallow containers, within which the seeds of quick-growing plants could be forced up under the hot sun, beating down upon the roof-tops on which they were placed, for the festival of Adonis, so that within eight days of sowing they would have attained their full development, after which, not being in proper soil, they would die down having had a life as untimely short as Adonis.

Shakespeare is not the only writer of the period to mention Adonis gardens, but in all works by others the sense is different. Spenser introduces them to *The Faerie Queene*, III, vi, 29f, but as pleasure gardens, into which Venus led Amoret, grounds of some extension, with arbours and groves, where myrtles, flowers and fruit-trees grew in the fertile soil. The whole is intended, plainly, to be symbolic of voluptuous pleasure. Admittedly, the scythe of Time will one day cut them down, but this is a moral reflection upon the difference between earthly and heavenly paradise. In *Colin Clout Comes Home Again*, Spenser writes of the mixing of couples by Venus, and then says, 803-04:

Cupid she brought forth
And in the gardens of *Adonis* nurst

Here there is nothing about brevity; solely the idea of erotic coupling, within a garden.

Gabriel Harvey writes about Art beginning to sprout in Greene, Wit to blossom in Pierce Pennilesse "as in the garden of poor Adonis"; both to grow to perfection in Nashe.

Jonson brings them into *Every Man Out of His Humour*, IV, viii, 29 as synonymous with "all the delights of the Hesperides, the Insulae Fortunatae . . ." and again in *Cynthia's Revels*, V, x, 102-13, where Mercury says to Cupid, "Remember thou art not now in Adonis garden, but in Cynthia's presence . . ." Cynthia being meant for Queen Elizabeth, as symbol of virgin chastity, the gardens stand, in his mind, plainly for cupidinous licence. At a later date, one will find Fletcher making the same mistake. It was the brevity of the life of the Adonis Gardens that was their essential characteristic. So it is *Promus* and *I King Henry VI* which pair in getting it right.

To obtain the correct sense, it would not have been necessary to read the *Phaedrus* in Greek. Plato was generally read in the Latin translation by Serranus; but this particular passage is picked out, together with two others bearing upon the subject, Theocritus, *Idylls*, 15, 112f and Plutarch, *Moralia*, 560c, in Erasmus' *Adagia*.[2] The citations are in Greek, but the Latin text makes clear the sense. The latter was probably Bacon's source, for it comes in a part of the *Promus* devoted to a whole series of adages from Erasmus. Professor Baldwin, in his *William Shakespeare's Small Latine and Lesse Greek* (Illinois, 1944) shows us the extent to which school curricula followed the educational precepts of Erasmus, and tells us the *Adagia* were often set as a Grammar School text. In that case, it would appear not impossible Shakespeare read it at Stratford Grammar School. Moreover, as lexicographers, commentators, collectors of sayings and the like, might cite the work, an Englishman might pick just this bit up without having seen Erasmus at all. But if one is going to say that the material was so easily accessible, how comes it that Spenser, Harvey, Jonson and, later, Fletcher, all missed it? In Holland's English translation of Pliny, p.10, will be found the source of their mistake. How is it supposed the Stratford rustic resisted this easy lure, whilst all the others – and all excepting Jonson were Cambridge graduates – fell for it?

What is really interesting here is not to prove that Shakespeare could not have had his own access to the information, but simply to notice that Bacon and Shakespeare alone stand together.

Mrs. Pott, in her edition of the *Promus*, really a concordance to *Promus* and the works of Shakespeare (Longman Green, 1883) lists over 1,200 similarities, but nothing so striking as this, which, surprisingly, she failed to notice. Some of her examples are slight, and one must beware of what may be proverbs, since obviously Bacon collected such things. *Alls Well That Ends Well* sounds like one. Perhaps the same could be said of, "Things doone cannot be undoone", *Promus*, f.103, and "What's done cannot be undone", *Macbeth*, V, i, 75. "Golden sleepe", *Promus*, f.111, may have been a popular phrase, but hardly one Bacon would need to take from the larder for his legal or philosophical works. Where we do find it again is in *Romeo and Juliet*, II, iii, 38. Against its being a fixed phrase are permutations of it, as "The golden dew of sleep", *Richard III*, IV, 84, "golden slumber", *Titus Andronicus*, II, iii, 26 and "golden slumber", *Pericles*, III, ii, 23.

Some of the entries are in foreign languages, for instance, "L'affaire va a quattre roues", *Promus*, f.132. We shall later see a line in *Antony and Cleopatra* which is practically incomprehensible without this key.

There is an entry:

> Several playes or ideas of play. Frank play;
> wary play; venturous, not venturous, quick, slowe
>
> *Promus, f.110*

Here we are in the writer's workshop. The old storehouse of phrases could have been used for:

> And will this brother's wager frankly play
>
> *Hamlet, V, ii, 264*

---

1. British Museum, Harleian MSS, f.7017.
2. The *Adagia* were first published in Paris in 1500, and then in an expanded form in Venice in 1508, under the title *Chiliades adagiorum* (Thousands of sayings). There is a Basel edition of Erasmus' *Works* of 1540, where the *Adagia* are in Vol. II, and 'Adonidis horti' on pp.23-24. Any of these could have been the edition used by Bacon, or any of his contemporaries with the requisite scholarship.

CHAPTER 19

Hall and Marston

THE satirists Joseph Hall and John Marston both write of a contemporary whom they call Labeo, and it is Labeo whom it is important to
identify.

Hall, who first gave tongue, was a churchman, later a Bishop, puritan
and hierarchical. In 1597 he published the first volume of his
Virgidemiarum (bundle of rods), intended as a flail to scourge the bad
morals and immoral writers of the time. He makes passing glances at
Marlowe's *Tamberlaine,* Nashe's *Pierce Pennilesse, his Supplication to
the Deuil* and *The Choice of Valentines,* writers such as Hopkins and
Sternhold, who render sacred scripture into verse, and a popular
compilation called *Mirror for Magistrates,* in which the ghosts – Hall calls
them ''drerie whining ghosts'' – of historical characters, including notably
monarchs' mistresses, come forward to tell the sad stories of their bad
ends. These, however, are but minor targets. Hall's sustained attack is
upon Labeo. In the earlier satires he is not given a name, yet internal
references bind certain passages to the ones concerning Labeo. The first
comes in Book I, Satire iii, and follows on from the jibe at Marlowe,
though the details, we shall see, show that the satirist's aim has shifted to
a different dramatist:

I, iii, 13–44

> Then weeneth he his base drink-drowned spright,
> Rapt to the threefold loft of heauen hight,
> When he conceiues vpon his fained stage
> The stalking steps of his greate personage,
> Graced with hug-cap termes, and thundring threats,
> That his poore hearers hayre quite vpright sets.
> Such some as some braue minded hungrie youth
> Sees fitly frame to his wide-strained mouth,
> He vaunts his voyce vpon an hyred stage,
> With high-set steps and princely carriage;
> Now sooping in side-robes of Royalty,
> That earst did skrub in lowsie brokerie.
> There if he can with terms Italianate,
> Big-sounding sentences, and words of state,
> Faire patch me vp his pure *Iambicke* verse,
> He rauishes the gazing scaffolders:
> Then certes was the famous *Corduban*
> Neuer but halfe so high tragedian.

Now, least such frightful showes of fortunes fall,
And bloudy tyrants rage, should chaunce appall
The dead stroke audience, midst the silent rout,
Comes leaping in a self-misformed lout,
And laughs, and grins, and frames his mimik face,
And iustles straight into the princes place.
Then doth the theatre echo all aloud
With gladsome noyse of that applauding croud.
A goodly *hotch-poch* when vile *russettings*
Are match with monarchs and with mightie kings;
A goodly grace to sober *tragic muse,*
When each base clowne his clumbsie fist doth bruise,
And show his teeth in double rotten-row,
For laughter at his self-resembled show.

"Russettings" meant coarse, rustic dress, usually rust-brown, such as was worn by menials and yokels.

I, iv, 5-12

Some brauer braine in high heroick rimes
Compileth worme-eate stories of olde times;
And he, like some imperious Maronist,
Coniures the Muses that they him assist.
Then striues he to bombast his feeble lines
With farre-fetcht phraise:
And maketh vp his hard-betaken tale,
With strange enchantments . . .

Retain in the memory "coniures the Muses that they his assist". We shall come back to this and show how it fits into a developing pattern. Our next clue, closely related to it, is:

I, ix, 1-6

Enuie ye Múses, at your thriuing mate,
Cupid hath crowned a new laureate:
I saw his statue gayly tyr'd in greene,
As if he had some second Phoebus beene.
His statue trimd with the Venerean tree,
And shrined faire within your sanctuarie.

In the second book, Labeo is named:

II, i, 1-8

For shame, write better *Labeo,* or write none:
Or better write, or *Labeo,* write alone,
Nay, call the Cynick but a wittie foole,
Thence to abiure his handsome drinking bole:
Because the thirstie swaine with hollow hand,
Convey'd the streame to wet his drie weasand.
Write they that can, tho' those that cannot, doe:
But who knowes that, but they that do not know?

II, i, 19-26

> But now men wager who shall blot the most,
> And each man writes: ''There's so much labour lost,
> That's good, that's great; nay much is seldome well,
> Of what is bad, a little is a great deale.
> Better is more: but best is naught at all.
> Lesse is the next, and lesser criminall;
> Little and good, is greatest good save one;
> Then, *Labeo,* or write little or write none.

II, i, 51-64

> Striue they, laugh we; meanwhile the black storie
> Passes new *Strabo,* and new *Straboes Troy,*
> Little for great; and great for good; all one:
> For shame or better write, or, *Labeo,* write none.
> But who coniured this bawdie Poggies ghost,
> From out the stewes of this lewde home-bred coast;
> Or wicked *Rablais* drunken reuellings
> To graue the mis-rule of our tavernings?
> Or who put bayes into blind Cupids fist,
> That he should crowne what laureate him list?
> Whose words are those to remedie the deed,
> That cause men stop their noses when they read.
> Both good things ill, and ill things well; all one?
> For shame! write cleanly, *Labeo,* or write none.

That *Labeo* is Shakespeare was noted, almost in passing, by the Comtesse de Chambrun, in the study of Florio for which she obtained her doctorate from the Sorbonne:[1]

... sous le nom de Labeo (homme aux grosses lèvres) il est accusé par Joseph Hall d'avoir avili l'art tragique, en mettant en scène de bouffons vulgaires à coté des rois malheureux (Richard II et Henri IV). Hall lui fait aussi reproche d'avoir montré l'intérieur des tavernes malfamées et d'avoir été plus loin dans ses déscriptions de la débauche que le méchant Rabelais lui-mème, (Falstaff et la Prince Henri IV).

I translate

... under the name of Labeo (man with big lips) he is accused by Joseph Hall of having vilified the tragic art, by exhibiting on the stage vulgar buffoons in the company of unhappy kings (Richard II and Henry IV). Hall reproaches him also with having set scenes within taverns of ill repute, and of having gone further in his depiction of debauchery than even the evil Rabelais (Falstaff and Prince Henry).

If the ''stew'' of the ''drunken reuellings'' and ''mis-rule of our tauernings'' is Mistress Quickly's tavern, wherein the Prince rubbed shoulders with ''vile russettings'', then the ''self-misformed lout'' (perhaps padded out to monstrous proportions) must be Falstaff, and there should be a scene in which he "leaps" or "iustles straight into the prince's place". Is there? Of course there is. It is *I King Henry IV*, II, iv, where the Prince invites Falstaff to ape his father, the King, examining him on his life, and afterwards they change roles. Hall is telling us with what zest the part was played and with what delight the performance was received by the crowd, perched upon its scaffoldings, or cheaper seats, and banging on them. It is surprising this has not been noticed by Shakespeareans.

The "black storie", II, i, 51, is probably *Titus Andronicus*.

We have to be grateful to the Comtesse de Chambrun for drawing to our attention that Labeo is the author of *King Henry IV*, but there is much more in Hall, which she did not observe. This comes mainly into his second volume, published the following year, 1598:

IV, i, 17-44

> *Labeo* is whip't, and laughs mee in the face:
> Why? for I smite and hide the galled place,
> Gird but the *Cynicks* Helmet on his head,
> Cares he for Talus and his flayle of lead:
> Long as the craftie *Cuttle* lieth sure
> In the black *cloude* of his thicke vomiture;
> Who list complaine of wronged faith or fame
> When he may shift it to anothers name?

IC, iv, 14-15

> Let *Labeo,* or who also list for mee
> Go loose his ears and fall to *Alchemie*

IV, vii, contains a list of things Hall loaths: "I loathe . . .

IV, vii, 7

> Labeos poems

VI, i, 1-4

> *Labeo* reserues a long nayle for the nonce
> To wound my Margent through ten leaues at once,
> Much worse than *Aristarchus* his blacke Pile
> That pierc'd olde *Homers* side.

VI, I, 185-96

> *Labeo* weans it my eternall shame
> To proue I never earnd a poets name

VI, i, 245-80

> Tho *Labeo* reaches right (who can deny?)
> The true straynes of *Heroicke* Poesie
> For he can tell how fury reft his sense
> And *Phoebus* fild him with intelligence,
> He can implore the heathen deities
> To guide his bold and busie enterprise,

Or filch whole pages at a clap for need
From honest Petrarch clad in English weed;
While huge *But ohs* ech stanza can begin,
Whose trunk and tayle sluttish and hartlesse bin;
He knows the grace of that new elegance,
Which sweet *Philisides* fetched late from *France,*
That well beseemed his high-stiled *Arcady,*
Tho others marre it with much liberty,
In epithets to ioyne two words in one,
Forsooth for Adjectives cannot stand alone;
As a great Poet could of Bacchus say,
That he was *Semele-femori-gena.*
Lastly he names the spirit of Astrophel:
Now hath not *Labeo* done wondrous well:
But ere his Muse her weapon learne to wield,
Or dance a sober *Pirricke* in the field,
Or marching wade in blood up to the knees,
Her Arma Virium goes by two degrees,
The sheepcote first hath been her nursery
Where she hath worne her idle infancy,
And in her hy startups walk't the pastur'd plaines
To tend her tasked herd that there remains,
And winded still a pipe of Ote or Brere
Striving, for wages, who the praise shall beare;
As did whilere the homely *Carmelite*
Following Virgil, and he *Theocrite;*
Or else hath beene in *Venus* chamber train'd
To play with *Cupid,* till shee had attain'd
To comment well upon a beauteous face,
Then she was fit for an *Heroike* place . . .

Labeo's verse has the graceful style borrowed by Sidney from the French; this suited Sidney but was marred by other writers, such as Labeo. Labeo's Muse has been "in *Venus* chamber". This straightway suggests *Venus and Adonis,* and the stylistic criticisms are apt. The poem does contain an exceptional number of exclamations of "O", many of them at the head of stanzas, and there are a great many double-barrelled adjectives, though for a treble-barrelled one, it is necessary to go to *The Rape of Lucrece,* line 44. The jibe that Labeo boasts "Phoebus fild him with intelligence" can be applied to the distich from Ovid at the head of the poem.

Possessed with this clue, we can now see that the lines in Hall, I, iv, and I, ix, earlier quoted, also refer to the distich. What has really got under Hall's skin is the idea that the author of an erotic poem about Venus has, as it were, conjured up the god of the highest Art and claimed his inspiration. The work is Cupid got up to be Apollo (Phoebus), or the sun-god's statue inappropriately decked in the green myrtle of Venus. I shall go further into the significance of the distich – which is of crucial importance – later, as it will become more meaningful after further information has been gathered. At this point, it is brought in merely to tie Hall's reference to Labeo's Muse being in ''Venus chamber'' to *Venus and Adonis,* and the passages in Book I, where the name of Labeo is not used, to Labeo and his *Venus and Adonis.*

Before we can come back to the distich from Ovid, however, we have to seek illumination from Marston.

Marston, a lawyer, published in 1598, that is after the appearance of the first volume of Hall's satires but probably before the appearance of the second, a book entitled *The Metamorphosis of Pigmalions Image, and Certain Satires.* To *The Metamorphosis of Pigmalions Image* there is an addendum, entitled 'The AUTHOR in praise of his precedent Poem'. This contains the lines:

> So Labeo did complaine his love was stone,
> Obdurate, flinty, so relentlesse none.

As the Rev. Walter Begley pointed out in his book *Is it Shakespeare* (John Murray, 1904), this is very close to lines 199-200, *Venus and Adonis:*

> Art thou obdurate, flintie, hard as steele,
> Nay, more than flint, for stone at raine relenteth

So, let us turn back and read Marston's poem, *The Metamorphosis of Pigmalions Image.* It is a simple reconstruction of the classic tale of the sculptor who fell in love with the statue of a woman which he had created. But it is in exactly the same verse-form as *Venus and Adonis,* and there are verbal reminiscences. Asking himself what real women are like, the sculptor says,

> Or are they all, like mine, relentless stone?

and in line 191 we find ''flinty hard''. Moreover, when he takes the statue to bed with him, prays to Venus to transform it into living flesh and finds his prayer granted, we find line 202 reads:

> If she, in recompense of his love's labour

This, like ''so much labour lost'' in Hall, II, i, 27, plays upon the title of *Love's Labour's Lost.* It also, perhaps, answers or rebuts Hall, for the sculptor's labour was not lost, on the contrary, it was recompensed. The addendum seems intended as a riposte to ''a barking satirist'', that is, Hall.

The *Certain Satires* which follow seem likewise to be directed at Hall. In II, 73-74, Marston says:

> No Jew, no Turke, would vse a Christian
> So inhumanely as this Puritan.

In III he ridicules Hall's idea that love sonnets do any harm. In IV, *Reactio,* he defends Hall's victims, starting with those who have turned Biblical themes into verse. Because the pagans honoured the gods in verse, must it be impious in Christians to write hymns in verse?

> Pure madness! Peace, cease to be insolent,
> And be not outward sober, inly impudent.
> Fie, inconsiderate! Why should those mirrors seeme
> So vile to thee, which better judgements deeme
> Exquisite then, and in our polish'd times
> May run for senseful tolerable lines?
> What, not *mediocria firma* from thy spight?
> But must thy enuious hungry fangs need light
> On *Magistrates Mirror?* Must thou needs detract
> And striue to work his ancient honours wrack?
> What, shall not *Rosamund* or *Gaveston*
> Ope their sweet lips without detraction?
> And must our modern critics enuious eye
> Seeme thus to quote some grosse deformity,
> Where art, not error, shineth in their style,
> But error, and no art, doth thee beguile?
> For tell mee, critic, is not fiction
> The soul of poesys invention?

Rosemund and Gaveston both came into *Magistrates Mirror,* that ancient compilation by Lydgate and others which had recently been reissued. Gaveston enters also, prominently, into Marlowe's *Edward II.* by this allusion, Marston was, therefore, taking care of the glance made by Hall at Marlowe as well as his attack on the ghosts in the *Mirror.* The "his" before "ancient honours wrack" refers to Lydgate.

Mediocria firma is the motto of the Bacon family. It can still be discerned over the porch which is practically all that remains of the ruins of Gorhambury, and appears over the portrait of Bacon on the title-page of his *Sylva Sylvanum.* The motto is from Seneca, best rendered by the English one, "Safety in moderation". At a first reading, it might appear that a word must be missing from Marston's line, and yet it is not so; *firma* is doing double duty, as part of the Bacon motto and as a substitute for the English word "secure" or "safe" which should follow it. The line means, "What, is not Bacon secure against thy spite?"

Bacon is not mentioned by name by Hall, but neither are any of Hall's victims. Hall's chief victim is Labeo, and Marston does not name Labeo in his defence of Hall's victims. One cannot simply say, Labeo is Shakespeare, *Mediocria firma* is Bacon, therefore Bacon is Shakespeare, without seeing the reply the Stratfordian is going to make. It could be in some other writing, unpreserved, or even by word of mouth, that Hall had attacked Bacon; or it could be that Marston left Labeo undefended, because, though he disliked his attacks on the several whose defence he took up, he agreed with him about Labeo. The question is are these things likely?

Bacon had at the time published nothing under his own name, excepting for the first small collection of *Essaies*. These appeared in the same year as Hall's first volume, and in any case contained nothing which could be the object of puritan censure. It is possible his hand in the *Gesta Grayorum* (Gray's Inn Revels) may have been suspected, but I can find in Hall's first volume no hit at the *Gesta Grayorum*. The construction of Marston's *Reactio* gives the impression it was Hall's *Virgidemiarum*, through which he was working his way, systematically. His reference to "whips" plays upon the title, which means "bundle of rods", and the *Reactio* ends:

159-66:

> Cease, cease at length, to be malevolent
> To fairest blooms of vertues eminent;
> Striue not to soil the freshest hues on earth
> With thy malicious and vpbraiding breath.
> Envy, let pines of Ida rest alone,
> For they will grow in spight of thunderstone;
> Striue not to nibble in their swelling graine
> With toothless gums of thy detracting braine.

The sub-title of *Virgidemiarum* is "toothles satires", and "toothless gums" plays on that, surely confirming that it was in the *Virgidemiarum* the abuse of Bacon took place. Yet even had it taken place elsewhere, the fact remains, he is sandwiched between Lydgate and Marlowe as one whom Hall had criticised in respect of his "poesie".

As to the other "escape", it could not be that Marston of purpose left Labeo undefended because, while resenting the criticism of the others, he agreed with Hall about Labeo, for his Metamorphosis of *Pigmalions Image* is so close modelled upon *Venus and Adonis* as to preclude any possibility he did not admire its author, who as we have seen is Labeo.

One has to consider the whole motive of Marston in publishing. He was not, prior to the appearance of this volume, a professional poet. It looks as though it were admiration for *Venus and Adonis* which had inspired him to attempt something similar. Then, before he had been able to get it into print, there appeared Hall's volume, in which it and its author were attacked. Should he thereby be deterred from publishing his own poem, or proceed in defiance, adding a few satires showing his contempt for Hall's judgement? If this is what he decided to do, then his defences of Hopkins and Sternhold, Lydgate and Marlowe are but incidentals to his defence of Labeo?

Why, then, is the name of Labeo not used, and why do we find, instead, an unexplained *Mediocria firma*? The Stratfordian is going to ask, if

Labeo is the one Marston is ''worked up'' about, how is it that he is not
defended at even comparable length to the others? Here I think one must
be prepared to put oneself in Marston's shoes. Suppose he was a friend of
Bacon, which is not impossible as they were both lawyers, and believed it
was he who had composed *Venus and Adonis,* what should be his course?
He admired the poem but it had been heavily censured by this
churchman. He might want to defend Bacon, but on the other hand, he
might not think he ought to give Bacon's authorship away to those who
did not know it already. A solution would therefore be to trounce Hall all
round, as an uncharitable churchman whose criticisms of literature were
not to be taken seriously, whatever his target, bringing in only edgeways
Mediocria firma, without tying it so inescapably to the authorship of
Venus and Adonis as to give Bacon grounds to reproach him for having
given away what shreds of his alias remained after Hall's attack.

Marston was to publish a second volume of satires, *The Scourge of
Villanie,* in which he parodied Hall's attack on Labeo, II, 19–26:

> What icy Saturnist, what northern pate
> But such gross lewdness would exasperate?
> I think the blind doth see the flame-god rise
> From sisters couch, each morning to the skies,
> Glowing with lust. Walk but in dusky night
> With Lynceus eyes, and to thy piercing sight
> Disguised gods will show, in peasants shape,
> Prest to commit some execrable rape.

This is very close to *The Rape of Lucrece,* 1086–90, where the sun
rises upon Lucrece' rape. Hall is so prurient-puritanical he would see lust
even in the sun.

Further, in *The Scourge of Villanie,* we come to:

IX, 38ff

> My soul adores judicial scholarship;
> But when to servile imitatorship
> Some spruce Athenian pen is prenticed,
> 'Tis worse than apish . . .
>   Fond affection
> Befits an ape and mumpion babion.
> O what a tricksy, learned, nicking strain
> Is this applauded, senseless, modern vein.
> When late I heard it from sage Mutius lips
> How ill, methought, such wanton jigging skips
> Beseemed his graver speech. ''Far fly thy fame,
> Most, most of me beloved! whose silent name
> I ever honour; and, if my loue beguile
> Not much my hopes, then thy unualued worth
> Shall mount fair place, when apes are turned forth.''

I am too mild. Reach me my scourge again
I once did know a tinkling pewterer,
That was the uilest stumbling stutterer
That ever hack'd and hew'd our native tongue,
Yet to the lute if you had heard him sung,
Jesu! how sweet he breathed! You can apply.
O senseless prose, judicial poesie,
How ill you're match'd.

In the beginning, the parody of Hall is still evident, and since what goes before mentions "rhymes" and "poesie", the whole must refer to somebody's poetic style. Whose? Athens, for both Hall and Marston, was Cambridge, therefore the poet in question must have been educated at Cambridge. What is the force of the word "judicial", three times repeated: "judicial scholarship . . . judicial style . . . judicial poesie"? It looks as though the Cambridge man is a lawyer, who, from time to time, abandons his grave judicial style for "wanton jigging skips", such as deal with "fond affection" (foolish passion). Why is he called "Mutius"? Mutius is a character in *Titus Andronicus*. Latin *mutus* means dumb, or mute. Poets are not usually thought of as mutes. The clue is surely given just below, where, between quotation marks, Marston breaks out of his parody of Hall to speak with his own voice, to say something in quite a different vein:

Far fly thy fame,
Most, most of me beloved! whose silent name
I ever honour

From Marston, who is not given to praise, this is a change indeed. Who is this person whom he ever honours, a Cambridge lawyer, reviled by Hall, on account of his poetic compositions, whose name is silent? It must be in his anonymity that Mutius is silent. Is Mutius Labeo? The name, Labeo, itself is interesting. The best known holder of this name was Antistius Labeo, an eminent Roman jurist of the time of Augustus. There was, however, another, Attius Labeo, of the reign of Nero, a minor poet, none of whose work has survived, and of whose very existence we know only from Persius, *Satires,* I, 4, in a passage denouncing his translation of the *Iliad* as wretched, *"Turpe et miserabile"* "shameful and wretched". Hall tells us he read Persius, so he will have seen the name there, yet he could have found a better pseudonym for an erotic poet such as the author of *Venus and Adonis* – why not Ovid, to whom it owes so much? – unless Hall thought that a name which had been borne both by a distinguished legal man and a low poetaster singularly fitted a contemporary, qualified in law and a postulant to the highest legal offices, who forsook his gravity for poetic meandering "in Venus chamber".

Marston gave up his legal career; indeed he may have had to. His

Pigmalion and satires were, with Hall's satires and some other satirical
publications, condemned to be burnt by the Archbishop of Canterbury,
Whitgift, under whom Bacon had studied at Cambridge. Why did
Whitgift intervene? It is rare for an Archbishop to condemn another
churchman's writings, and indeed there was a reprieve for Hall's
Virgidemiarum in as much as it was spared the humiliation of public
burning, the order being softened to suppression of publication. Lawyers,
however, are expected to be of sober behaviour and not to write poems
that get burnt by episcopal decree, and it looks as though Marston's
defence of *Venus and Adonis* and its author cost him his career. Why was
not *Venus and Adonis*, the cause of the trouble, likewise ordered to be
burnt? Had Whitgift a regard for Labeo?

Marston now became a playwright, and through his work we shall find
echoes of the greater poet's *Hamlet, Richard II, Richard III, King Henry
IV, Macbeth, Troilus and Cressida*. In *What You Will* (1607), by title and
by theme related to *Twelfth Night*, there is, in Act II, scene i, a place
where the characters step out of their proper roles to allude to their
author. One says:

> Away idolator! Why, you Don Kinsayder,
> Thou canker eaten rusty cur!

Kinsaider was the pseudonym beneath which Marston had published *The
Metamorphosis of Pigmalions Image and certain Satires and The Scourge
of Villanie*. He is giving the character a Hall-like stance, mocking himself.
We should therefore expect to find in what follows some further allusion
to the situation as it was then. In fact we find (the same character speaking
as before):

> No, sir; should discreet Mastigophoros,
> Or the dear spirit acute Canaidos
> (That Aretine, that most of me beloued
> Who in the rich esteeme I prize his soul
> I terme myself) should these once menace me,
> Or curb my humours with well governed check,
> I should with most industrious regard
> Observe, abstain, and curb my skipping lightness;
> But when an arrogant, odd, impudent,
> A blushless forehead, only out of sense
> Of his own wants, bawls in malignant questing
> At others means of wauing gallantry . . .

So here again we have the intimation there is just one person whom
Marston sincerely reveres and deeply loves. It would be inconceivable the
''most of me beloued'' of this passage is not the ''Most, most beloued of
me'' of *The Scourge of Villanie,* written so long – nine years – before. We
have, then, a relationship running right through Marston's life, as a

source of inspiration and uplift. Had this one dear and respected man reproved him for the levity of his writings, he would have mended his style. Who should this one be, but the greater poet whose lines so haunt his verse? In *The Scourge of Villanie* the beloved was defined as a lawyer, with a Cambridge background, who wrote some wanton poetry, but whose name had to remain silent in connection with it; in *What you will* he is further characterised as an Aretine, implying some of his verse was erotic, one whose memory is brought to mind by the reference to the old controversy with Hall, not merely dear but "acute", therefore a man of high intelligence.

"Canaidos" is a made-up word. It sounds vaguely canine, but probably glances at "Cyned", another made-up word, used by Hall, IV, I, 90-95:

> Those toothless *toyes* that dropt out my mis-hap
> Bee but as lightening to a thunder-clap:
> Shall then that foule infamous *Cyneds* hide
> Laugh at the purple vales of others side?
> But, if he were as neere, as by report,
> The stewes had wont to be to the tenis-court . . .

If this goes back to Latin *cinaedus*, there is no hint of the specific meaning of the Latin, and it seems more likely that having called Labeo a "Cynick", he coined *cyned* out of it, as having something of the same sound combined with overtones of some sickening licence. As we have no information that either Bacon or Shakespeare played tennis, it could be there is a glance at *King Henry V*, where tennis-balls are sent as an insulting present to the young monarch, so newly apparent as a bright and shining character, so lately a visitor, with Falstaff, to Mistress Quickly's "stew".

Marston, in any case, calls his beloved "Canaidos" not to insult him, but to recall the insulting term used of him by Hall.

If this seems to link the beloved lawyer of the silent name to Labeo, author of *Venus and Adonis*, a direct link is made between that poem and *Mediocria firma* in the edition of Hall's *Collected Poems* by A. Davenport (Liverpool University Press, 1949). He has not noticed that *Mediocria firma* is the motto of the Bacon family, and plainly he had neither Bacon nor Shakespeare in his mind. His concern is to show the importance of Hall, for the understanding of Marston, and to this end he is demonstrating how many passages in Marston need to be seen as glances at something in Hall. For instance, he says, the word "fiction", in Marston's *Reactio*, line 82, means some sort of apparition, and is best understood as a glance at the word "enchantments", in Hall, I, iv, 12. But if we look back to the latter, we see that the "enchantments" are in the tale headed by the conjuration of the Muses, and when we took Hall I, iv, 4-12, with Hall, I, ix, 1-6 and Hall, VI, i, 245-80, we saw that the

reference in all these passages was to *Venus and Adonis* and the distich
from Ovid on its title-page, which irritated Hall. Now, the only other
poets mentioned in the *Mediocria firma* passage of Marston's Reactio are
Lydgate, more than a hundred years dead, and Marlowe, more recently
dead, neither of whom published an erotic poem with this couplet from
Ovid at its head. If Davenport is correct in supposing ''fiction'' to glance
at ''enchantments'', it is a member of the Bacon family who is the author
of *Venus and Adonis.*

We have now come to the point at which we can consider the Latin
quotation on the title-page in greater fullness. It is a distich from Ovid,
Amores, I, 15, 35f:

> Vilia miretur vulgus, mihi flauus Apollo
> Pocula Castalia plena ministret aqua.

It is an elegiac couplet, that is a dactylic hexameter followed by a
pentameter; it would be usual slightly to inset the latter, but there is no
indentation as it is set on the title-page of *Venus and Adonis.* The
meaning is, literally:

> Let the crowd marvel at cheap things, to me let yellow [haired] Apollo
> Serve cups full of Castalian water.

Castalia was a spring on Mount Parnassus, sacred to Apollo and the
Muses. To be served with cups of its water would be to have inspiration
granted to one. The verbs are subjunctive, with jussive sense, so it is
really less of a boast than a prayer, though it is obvious Hall took it for a
presumptuous claim:

We need, now, to read again Hall, II, i, 1–6:

> For shame, write better, *Labeo,* or write none:
> Or better write, or *Labeo,* write alone,
> Nay, call the *Cynick* but a wittie foole,
> Thence to abiure his handsome drinking bole:
> Because the thirstie swaine with hollow hand,
> Conueyd the streame to weet his drie weasand.
> *Write they that can, tho they that cannot doe:*
> *But who knowes that, but they that doe not know?*

Davenport says in his editorial notes:

Cynick: Diogenes. This story is derived from Laertius,[2] VI, 37:
θεασάμενός ποτε παιδίον ταῖς χερσὶ πῖνον ἐξέρριψε τῆς πήρας τὴν κοτύλην, εἰπών
«παιδίον με νενίκηκεν εὐτελείᾳ».

But is it? One has to consider the whole meaning of the Greek and the
whole meaning of Hall. Diogenes the Cynic, in his search for the simple
life, was already sleeping in the open streets or in his famous tub or urn,
retaining as his sole possession the bowl he would take to the public

fountain, when he saw a boy drink from his cupped hands. Diogenes realised he retained something superfluous and threw away his drinking bowl.

It is inconceivable the bowl Diogenes threw away would have been handsome. His life being already so austere, this utensil would have been of the meanest, and the water he drank from it was not that from the sacred Castalian spring. Further, Hall would not have mocked the ascetic life, though he might have considered disgusting that Diogenes made a principle of shamelessness in performing all natural functions in the streets, and it may be that this side of Diogenes' life connects the passage with that concerning Rabelais, Labeo and the ''stewes'' in *King Henry IV*. In this case there may be the idea the brothel scenes correspond to a public defecation. But to the bowl!

The Times Literary Supplement of July 11th, 1936, carries a letter signed J. Denham-Parsons, relating the ''handsome drinking bole'' to the poculum from which the poet was served Castalian water, as described in the distich on the title-page of *Venus and Adonis*.

Who, then, is ''the thirstie swaine''? A letter signed A.G. Dent in the following issue says the ''thirstie swaine'' must be one who took the credit for inspiration granted to another. This is not impossible for why should he be thirstie for the water of inspiration, save that he had none of his own. Moreover, the italicised lines:

> *Write they that can, tho' those that cannot doe:*
> *But who knows that, but they that doe not know?*

have a riddling quality. If Hall meant only that some who write do not write well, that is a banality, hardly requiring the italicisation, or appearance of enigmatic hinting. Could the meaning be that the inspiration-dry swain drank from a cup the god gave to another, then pretends to write, although he does not; and those who know this pretend not to?

The word ''swain'' is from Middle English ''swein'', from Norse ''sveinn'', cognate with old English (Anglo-Saxon) ''swan'' (ā long), meaning a swineherd. By Elizabethan times, the specific connection with swine had probably vanished, yet the word preserved rustic and even menial flavour.

In our reception of it we are probably over-influenced by its use in the lyric in *Two Gentlemen of Verona*, ''Who is Sylvia? what is she, that all our swains commend her?'', and insufficiently by ''By my soule, a swaine, a most simple clowne'' (*Love's Labour's Lost*, IV, i, 142), ''the Athenian swaine'' (of Nick Bottom, *A Midsummer Night's Dream*, IV, i, 70), ''You peasant swaine'' (*The Taming of the Shrew*, IV, i, 132), ''a hedge-born swaine'' (*I King Henry IV*, IV, i, 45) and ''As one a king, another some base swaine'' (*Histriomastix*, an anonymous play, attributed to Marston, Scene I, lines unnumbered). The last example is particularly explicit, in that the author is polarising the highest and the lowest.

The person who took at second-hand the inspiration given to another was, then, a man from the country, of modest origins, one whom the more polished might think of as a hedge-born clown. Who is the Cynick who abjured in his favour the cup of inspiration?

Let us look again at that other passage in which the Cynick enters:

IV, i, 37-44

> *Labeo* is whip't, and laughs me in the face:
> Why, for I smite and hide the galled place,
> Gird but the Cynicks helmet on his head,
> Cares he for Talus and his flayle of lead:
> Long as the craftie Cuttle lieth sure
> In the blacke *cloude* of his thicke vomiture:
> Who list complaine of wronged faith or fame
> When he may shift it to anothers name?

Here, again, we must first consider whether there is a reference to Diogenes. Diogenes lived in a tub, like a dog in its kennel, and therefore *was nick-named* ὁ κύων the dog, and those who adopted his philosophy were called οἱ κυνικοί the dog-like ones, which became in Latin *Cynici*, from which we have the English word cynic. In *Lives of the Philosophers*, by Diogenes Laertius, there is in the life of Diogenes an anecdote involving a helmet (VI, 41 and 54):

ἐντρίψαντος αὐτῷ κόνδυλόν τινος «Ἡράκλεις», ἔφη, «οἷον με χρῆμ' ἐλάνθανε τὸ μετὰ περικεφαλαίας περιπατεῖν», and again: ἐρωτηθείς τί θέλοι κονδύλον λαβεῖν, «περικεφαλαίαν», ἔφη.

Literally: (41) When someone hit him a blow of the fist, he said, "Herakles! How did I come to forget to go walking with (ie wearing) a helmet?"

> (54) Asked what he would take (as compensation) for (receiving) a blow of the fist, he said, "A helmet".

"Cynicks helmet" cannot, therefore, refer to the helmet of Diogenes, since the whole point of the story about Diogenes is that he had not got one. Labeo, on the other hand, had a very good one, which apparently not only protected him from the flail of lead but helped to conceal him from view, since there are references to "hiding". This, therefore, is another example of the pseudo classical allusion. As in the story of the bowl and the swain, the introduction of the word "Cynick" leads those who know their classics to think of Diogenes, though to do so will not conduce to the discovery of Hall's meaning. Diogenes is a red herring across the trail.

Certain helmets have a projecting crest affording concealment. The most notable belonged to Hades, and was borrowed by Pallas Athena, who used it to cover the foot-soldiers of a hundred towns. Curiously, in Bacon's Promus, one reads, f.97v:

> Plutoes Helmett; secrecy Invisibility

Pluto was the Romans' name for Hades. In the *Gesta Grayorum,* Prince Purpoole's arms are blazoned with an Imperial Diadem ''guarded by the Helmet of the greatest goddess Pallas, from the violence of Darts, Bullets and Bolts of Saturn''. This sounds like the sort of helmet worn by Labeo, and, lead being the metal of Saturn, could, rather than the need to find a rhyme for ''head'', be the reason Hall changed the ''yron flale'' of Talus to a ''flayle of lead'' (see *The Faerie Queene,* V, i, 12–20). The Knights of the Helmet are a mock Order, whose articles contain bawdry to which Hall would have objected. But why should Hall go to the *Gesta Grayorum* for a helmet as cover for Labeo's unchaste writings, unless Labeo were *Mediocria firma?*

> Gird but the Cynicks Helmet on his head,
> Cares he for *Talus* and his flayle of lead:
> Long as the craftie Cuttle lieth sure
> In the blacke *cloude* of his thicke vomiture . . .

The link between Helmet and Cuttle is that both hide, transitively and intransitively. Labeo, the Cynick, is hiding beneath the Helmet, as the Cuttle hides itself in his own black fluid.

When he says, ''*Labeo* is whip't and laughs me in the face'', Hall must be referring to some retort made after he had first lashed Labeo in his first volume. The whole tenor of IV, i, implies there has been a literary riposte. The opening lines are

> Who dares vpbraid these open lines of mine
> With blindfold *Aquines* or darke *Venusine?*

Aquinum was the birthplace of Juvenal, Venusia of Horace. Both wrote satires, but the latter was probably chosen because the name Venusia suggests affinity with Venus. Hall would appear to be alluding to *The Metamorphosis of Pigmalions Image and Certain Satires.* Hall probably thought Marston was replying on behalf of Labeo.

Labeo can laugh at Hall's denunciation of his erotic writings because, hidden by his Helmet and black cloud, he does not have to receive the blows of criticism himself when he can shift it to another's name.

Labeo is the author of *Venus and Adonis.* If the author is Shakespeare, he did not ''shift it to another's name''. He put his own on it. The poem is not by the person whose name is on it. The same is true of *King Henry IV* etc.

If Labeo is Bacon, he did not have to bear, publicly, responsibility for these works. He had "shifted it" to Shakespeare.

1. *Giovanni Florio,* Longworth Chambrun (Payot, Paris, 1931), p.176.
2. Meaning Diogenes Laertius, a writer who lived probably in the third century A.D., not to be confused with Diogenes the Cynic, c.400–c.325 B.C., one of the people whom he wrote about.

CHAPTER 20

Jonson I

BEN Jonson's *Every Man Out Of His Humour,* 1599, seems to be a somewhat generalised satire on the times, with little plot for a play, and it has been suggested he wrote it in this form to get round the order, made at the time when the Hall and Marston satires were suppressed, forbidding the publication, henceforth, of satires. It may be therefore that there is some carry-through of ideas, and indeed the name of one of the characters, Cinedo, sounds like another conjured out of Hall's "Cyned", though here applied to a follower of Sir Fastidius Briske, who it has been suggested may have been meant for Marston.

More important to us is "Sogliardo, An essential Clowne, brother to Sordido, yet so enamour'd of the name of Gentleman, that he will have it, though it buys it." Sogliardo has just acquired a coat of arms, of many colours (which in heraldry is considered vulgar) and a Motto, *Not without mustard.* Sir E.K. Chambers indicated this as a dig at Shakespeare's *Non sans droit.* If so, Jonson, when he wrote this play, saw the actor from Stratford as an essential clown, and was poking fun at him.

Sogliardo goes out to meet a gentleman called Puntarvolo, at his country house, and Puntarvolo asks him what his crest is. Sogliardo replies, "Marry, sir, it is your Boar without a head rampant." Bacon's crest was a boar.

Puntarvolo is described as "A vainglorious knight, over-Englishing his trauels, and wholly consecrated to singularity; the very Iacobs staffe of compliment: a Sir that hath liu'd to see the revolution of time in most of his apparrel." Could Bacon be seen in this way? Puntarvolo's speech is studded with precious terms, but his chief singularity lies in his obsessive concern with his dog, which recalls nothing so much as Launce in *Two Gentlemen of Verona.* Of Bacon and dogs we know nothing, excepting that he said, "Every gentleman loves a dog," after Coke had turned one off a chair. Yet is it possible the caricature is meant for the creator of Launce?

Puntarvolo's other peculiarity is that he courts his wife as though she were his mistress. This does not fit, as Bacon was not married. Yet there is a scene in which she appears to him at her window above, while he addresses her from below, surely imitated from *Romeo and Juliet.* She promises to descend, he expresses himself astonished, and an eavesdropper comments, "What? with speaking a speech of your own penning?" Is he, then, not merely a character in the scene but the author of it?

The Poetaster, 1601, is set in Rome in the time of Augustus. Horace has always been identified with Jonson himself, Crispinus with Marston and Demetrius with Decker. But who are Ovid and Virgil? The play opens with Ovid discovered. Luscus warns him his father is approaching, and says, "away with your songs and sonnets". The sonnet is not a classical verse-form, but Mediaeval Italian, and (though used by Dante in *La Vita Nuova)* was in England mainly associated with Petrarch. Some people may use the term loosely for any short lyric, but hardly Jonson.

Then, Luscus calls Ovid "castalian mad". This could be said of any person mad on poetry, but what is curious is that the passage declaimed by Ovid immediately afterwards is (in English translation, mainly Marlowe's) that from *Amores* I, xv, containing the couplet:

> *Vilia miretur vulgus mihi flauus Apollo*
> *Pocula Castalia plena ministret aqua*

Let the crowd marvel at cheap things, to me let yellow (haired) Apollo serve cups of castalian water

which had featured on the title-page of *Venus and Adonis,* provoking the many animadversions in Hall's satires. Surely, to most of Jonson's readers, Ovid would have evoked the author of *Venus and Adonis.* In 1598, Francis Meres had written, in his *Palladis Tamia: Witts Treasury:*

As the soul of Euphorbus was thought to live in Pythagoras: so the sweete wittie soule of Ovid lives in mellifluous & honey-tongued *Shakespeare,* witness his *Venus and Adonis,* his *Lucrece.* his sugared Sonnets among his priuate friends.

Could any Elizabethan fail to make the connection, when attending Jonson's play.

But now there enters to Ovid, Ovid's father, a Lawyer, who had wished his son to follow in his footsteps, he is angry to hear him declaiming poetry, and tells him his name will be "scorn'd and contemn'd in the eyes and eares of the best and grauest Romanes":

OVID SE: . . . Are these the fruits of all my trauaile and expenses? Is this the scope and aime of thy studies? are these the hopeful courses, wherewith I haue so long flattered my expectation from thee? verses? *poetrie?* OVID, whom I thought to see the pleader, become OVID the play-maker?

OVID IU: No, sir.

OVID SE: Yes, sir, I heare of a *tragedie* of yours comming foorth for the common players there, call'd MEDEA. By my household-gods, if I come to the acting of it, Ile adde one tragick part, more than is expected, to it: beleeue me when I promise it. What? shall I haue my sonne a stager now? an enghle for players? a gull, a rooke? a shot-clogge? . . .

OVID IU: They wrong mee, sir, and doe abuse you more,
That blow your eares with these vntrue reports.
I am not knowne vnto the open stage,
Nor doe I traffique in their *theatres.*
Indeed, I doe acknowledge, at request
Of some neere friends, and honourable *Romanes,*
I have begun a *poeme* of that nature.

At first glance, this may seem to be closely underpinned by historical reality. The father of the historical Ovid was a lawyer and tried to discourage his son's involvement with poetry, as the latter tells us in the *Tristia.* But that seems to have been because it consumed time which could have been spent profitably. Private poetry readings, at which someone would read his own verses to a group of his friends, were very much a feature of upper class Roman social life. It was these discreet readings that were known as the publication. Now it is possible he would afterwards permit one or two to sit with the manuscript and make their own copies, but not for sale. The publication was not expected to be a money-making enterprise.

Jonson's Ovid senior seems to be taxing his son with something different, writing for the stage. The historical Ovid junior is usually thought of solely as a poet. It is true he did write a play, lost to us, and it was called *Medea.* He refers to it, though without title or clear indication of subject, in *Amores* II, 18, 13f. III, i, 11 and 67. He published the *Amores* in B.C.14, when he was twenty-nine. The play is referred to by name and author in Tacitus, *Dialogus de Oratoribus,* 12.6, and Quintillian, X,1.98, two lines are quoted from it, one by Seneca the elder, *Suasorial,* 3,7, and the other by Quintillian, VIII, 5.7:

> *feror buc illuc: vae, plena deo.*
> I am borne this way and that, alas, full of the god.

and

> *servare potui: Perdere an possim, rogas?*
> I have been able to serve: do you ask if I can lose?

It would seem, then, that copying must have been permitted. Nevertheless, it is more likely publication was by Ovid's reading the play, as though it were a poem, to an invited audience of friends, rather than by performance on the public stage by a company of actors. (It is doubted whether Seneca was staged.)

In the *Tristia,* V, vii, Ovid writes a line, 27, quoted by Herford and Simpson in their edition of Jonson:

> *Nil equidem feci (tu scis hoc ipse) theatris*
> It was indeed (you yourself know this) not for theatres I wrote

but really one needs to take it together with the lines that go before and after, 25-28, and the total situation. Ovid is wretched because he is banished, in middle life, to a cold and desolate place near the mouth of the Danube, devoid of any cultural amenities. A friend has written, telling him, apparently in the endeavour to cheer him, that in Rome his work is still appreciated. It is to this letter Ovid is replying:

> As to your writing that our (e.g. my) songs are danced in the open theatre, and that there is applause for my verses, you yourself know that I, indeed, did nothing for the theatre, nor is my Muse ambitious for applause.

He appears, then, to be rejecting consolation. Perhaps one should take with the above, *Tristia* II, 519-20:

> *Et mea sunt populo saltata poemata saepe,*
> *Saepe oculos etiam detinuere tuos.*
> My poems have often been danced for the people,
> Even your eyes have been diverted by them.

Neither *poemata* nor *carmina* suggest a play, and although the lost *Medea* could have contained songs or odes for the chorus, it seems more likely that it was extracts from the elegiac verse, *Amores, Heroides,* or even the *Metamorphoses,* which had been presented in the theatre as a sort of pantomime with dancing.

In any case, if it was upon the first of the two passages in *Tristia* that Jonson built, he has totally altered both the occasion and the sense of the dissociation between Ovid and the staging of his work. Instead of the exile, fifty and feeling more like seventy because so miserable, refusing to be cheered, Jonson gives us an exuberant young man, at the beginning of his career, who, taxed by his father with having written a play, avoids a direct answer to the charge, sliding out of it with ''I am not known vnto the open stage''. Note that there is a distinct implication Ovid composed more than he actually acknowledged when pressed by close friends. Jonson represents Ovid as a true poet, worthy of respect. Why, then, does he make him so evasive and, indeed, deeply equivocal in his answers, unless he was getting at more than appears?

In Act IV, ix, we have a scene between Ovid and Julia, the daughter of the Emperor, Augustus, in which she appears at her casement, he below. This may be referred to a passage in Sidonius Apollinaris, Carminum xxiii, 158-61, asserting that Ovid's ''Corinna'' was Augustus' daughter Julia. It has been pointed out that dates are against this; Julia was banished for her adulteries in B.C.2, Ovid was exiled only in A.D.8. However, Julia the daughter of the first was banished in A.D.9, like her mother for adulteries, so if Ovid fell with one of the two it would be more likely the latter. It must be said, however, that *Tristia* and *Ex Ponto,* the volumes of letters he wrote home to his wife and friends, give not the slightest support for the theory of his involvement with either. What he says is, it was his misfortune that his innocent eyes accidentally witnessed the commission of a criminal act, which threw him off keel, causing him to commit a folly considered by Augustus as an affront to himself. Could it be that he saw the younger Julia with one of her lovers and was persuaded not to tell Augustus? It may be said it is the dramatist's licence to choose the theory which will afford his play the most effective scenes, but need the balcony scene so closely have resembled that in *Romeo and Juliet*? Even the dialogue is very similar, notably where the lovers keep trying to say good-bye, for fear of discovery, yet lingering. To consider this as mere plagiarism is to reduce Jonson to the level of a very inferior writer; surely it is more likely that he fully intended his audience to think of the author of *Romeo and Juliet*.

Swinburne, in his *Study of Ben Jonson*, remarked there was a constructional fault, in that the play opens with Ovid, who is quickly built up as if to be the chief character, though he is not and vanishes before the last Act. Is it not possible Jonson knew very well what he was doing, and achieved an artistic balance satisfying to himself when, after he has let Ovid disappear, he for the first time brings on Virgil, and lets him dominate the scene until the end?

Jonson's Virgil is immensely grave, close to the ear of Augustus, and his unofficial counsellor. In the trial of the satirists he appears as a kind of judge, directing witnesses to take the oath, asking, "What says the plaintiff?" and finally delivering what seems to be the summing up to the jury. Yet there is no reason to associate the historical Virgil with the law. Virgil's education, like that of all Romans of good family, included the study of rhetoric; construction and delivery of public speeches in courts of law or on other public occasions, but he seems never to have practised, or at the most appeared but once. He knew Augustus and may have been educated with him, but he inherited a farm, in the country, and seems to have gone to live on it and spent most of his time in its husbandry. His *Georgics* is divided into four books, respectively consecrated to agriculture, horticulture, stock-rearing and bee-keeping.

Jonson's Horace says of Virgil:

> His learning labours not the school-like glosse
> That most consists of *echoing* wordes, and terms,
> And sooner wins a man an empty name;
> Nor any longer, or far-fetch'd circumstance,
> Wrapt in the curious generalities of artes:
> But a direct, and *analyticke* summe
> Of all the worth and first effects of artes.
> And for his *poesie*, 'tis so ramm'd with life,
> That it shall gather strength of life, with being,
> And liue hereafter more admir'd than now.

"school-like" sounds like an anachronistic reference to the "School-men", the scholars and philosophers of the Middle Ages. There was just one man, and only one, who made it his whole life's work to get away from their endless glossing and echoing of one another's commentaries on the texts of the long dead, and to make direct and independent observations of the natural world, and that was Bacon. Virgil seems, therefore, to be Bacon, and that would fit, moreover, with his being a judge. Only, it was a forward-looking portrait. Bacon's great philosophic works had yet to appear, and he had yet to become Lord Chancellor, or even Solicitor General. It was, however, plain he aspired to the highest offices of the law, and would with time probably attain to them, and we need not doubt his own statement that even from his years at Cambridge he had had in his mind the idea of what was to become The Great Instauration. Jonson's portrait would seem to be, then, simply a little previous.

Note that he says, "And for his poesie". Why "And"? The historical Virgil was noted for nothing but his poetry. Jonson's Virgil's learned and analytic work is, therefore, not to be found within his poetry, but is a separate body of work, coming before it in importance, the poetry being, apparently, a kind of extra grace. Yet if the character is meant to be Bacon, he not only went beyond the school-man in his analytic work, but wrote "poesie . . . ramm'd with life".

We should look, also, at what another character, Gallvs, says of him:

> And yet so chaste, and tender is his ear,
> In suffering any syllable to passe,
> That, as he thinkes, may become the honour'd name
> Of issue to his so examin'd selfe;
> That all the lasting fruits of his full merit
> In his own *poems* he doth still distaste

There is ample justification for representing Virgil as an unduly severe critic of his own work. He composed slowly (Quintillian, X, iii, 8) and delayed letting Augustus see any part of the *Aeneid,* saying he needed to put more study into it and must have been mad to undertake to write such an epic (Macrobius, I, 24, 11). He was eventually persuaded to read some parts of it to him and to his circle, but when he knew himself to be on the point of death, still not having completed it, he told his friends that as he had not revised it they should burn it, or tried to burn it himself (Donatus, 39–41, Jerome's *Chronicles,* on 16 B.C. and Servius' Commentary on the *Aeneid,* at the beginning). Augustus, however, commanded the publication.

Here then, Jonson's representation is amply true to the historical character. It is only because his earlier anachronistic and inappropriate attributions seems to make of the character a stand-in for Bacon that it is possible to connect this "distaste" for "his own *poems*" with Ovid's denial of his own work in the first Act. It is possible the apparent constructional fault noticed by Swinburne derives from Jonson's use of Ovid and Virgil to represent a single person at different levels?

CHAPTER 21

The Countess of Southampton

THE richest source of biographical information concerning the poet is the *Sonnets*; but before we can approach them we need to look at the history of the Countess of Southampton. The thesis which will be developed is that she is the Dark Lady, but the evidence will emerge only slowly.[1]

She was born c.1553, the daughter of Anthony Browne, the 1st Viscount Montagu, and brought up at Castle Cowdray, near Midhurst, just on the Sussex side of the Sussex-Hampshire border. Mary, as she was christened, was only thirteen when she was married to the 2nd Earl of Southampton. For some unknown reason his mother opposed the match, though the Montagus were a much older family than the Wriothesleys, and so the wedding took place without her presence, in her father's house in London. Both families were Catholics, and Southampton, who had had Queen Mary for a god-mother, involved himself in the Norfolk rising.[2] For this, he suffered a spell of imprisonment. His young wife was, however, permitted to visit him, and it was thus that their son Henry, the future 3rd Earl, was begotten in the Tower. Shortly afterwards the 2nd Earl was released, but on condition of his residing under the roof of his father-in-law. So, the future 3rd Earl was born, at 3 a.m., on October 6th, 1573, at Cowdray.

Restrictions on the 2nd Earl being eventually lifted, he took his wife and child back into Hampshire with him, to live at Titchfield. Before the child was six years old, things had gone wrong between the parents. This we learn from a long letter written by the Countess to her father, in reply to one from him asking for her own account of the situation. She had apparently been expelled from Titchfield to some lesser property, and the Earl was communicating with her only through one of his gentlemen of the bed chamber, Thomas Dymock, whom she detested. She writes to her father:[3]

My Lord sent me word by Dymock the other day that it was not in his meaning to keep me as a prisoner, nor to bar me of my libertie either within doors or without, only he barred me to his board and presence . . . I told the messenger my Lord could lay no greater punishment upon me, neither could I take that but in the highest degree of imprisonment . . . "My Lord (saith Dymock) your Ladyship knoweth is resolute, yet be there means to win him." Would God I knew them, quoth I, they must be told me before I can put them to proof . . .

"Nay, saith he, from my Lord I can say nothing. But what my own opinion is, if it please you to hear it, I will tell you."

Apparently her husband wanted her to procure for him the support of two of her powerful relations, not an aggravation of his troubles through revenge. She had replied that notwithstanding his hard usage of her, she would stir none to be revenged upon him. One of his servants, Pretie, was in prison for misdemeanours against her brother, the heir apparent to Cowdray, and she would not wish her father or his friends to petition for Pretie's release (even, presumably, to procure her own).

Below, she says it is in revenge for his ''lewd servant his just punishment'' she is treated thus. Her husband has said he will not be reconciled to her except upon command of the Queen, who will never speak for her; yet she asks her father to speak to the Queen and does not abandon hope of her intervention:

And truly my Lord by the last speech I had with Dymock (who is the other himself) I find some little hope that she may do that none other can.

She had some support in the county, where certain people offered her their service. She continues:

Did your Lordship see this house, by my troth, I think you would say in your life you never came in the like so wholly bent against their young. Mr. Dymock, as they think not to tell him to his face, it is a pity he liveth to be the beginner and continuer of the dissensions between us . . . This house is not for them that will not honour Dymock as a God. It is a piece of comfort to find that not one servant in this house (Mr. Dymock only set aside and someone that he hath made as himself) but is ready either to depart with me or to deliver me out of this thraldome . . . I beseach your Lordship do not think I would so far disguise myself to you my dear father, that I would, to my own harm, keep anything from your knowledge, whereby I might prevent that extremity that is intended to me. Truly my Lord, if I be charged with more than you are aquainted withal, it is by corruption, and upon no truth. It may be my Lord will unrip old matters, repented and forgotten, long since, if he do, well, he may blame me of folly, but never justly condemn me of fault. And as for the matter charged of Dogmarshfields and [name difficult to read] his coming thither, he shall never prove it as he would, except he win some one to perjure themselves about it, for, by my truth, in my life did I never see him in that house, neither I assure your Lordship since I was by my Lord forbidden his company did I ever come in it. Desire I did to speak with him, I confess, and I told you why, and I wish that the cause, with my meaning, were uttered by the party himself upon his conscience (if he have any) wherefor I coveted to speak with him, and then I trust I shall be acquitted of greater evil than overmuch folly, for desiring or doing that which, being by my enemy mistaken, doth breed this my slander and danger. Neither had I ever done for him as I did, or used him other than [as] a common person of his calling, had I not seen my Lord his liking so extraordinary for him, as warranted me to friend him so far as I might, without evil meaning.

This life have I led these two years, with the bitterness that I have with patience endured, hath been sufficient to satisfy for so much as I have erred in, but . . . it is not my fault but my self he hateth . . . Doylye hath promised to work cunningly to overthrow me, and so did at my coming from London, and put it largely in practice, but I trust in God he shall fail of his purpose.

And now my Lord, with my humble duty to your Lordship and my Lady, with earnest desire for your daily blessings,

Your humble and obedient daughter,

M.S.

The doubtful word following "Dogmarshfield" is transcribed by Charlotte Stopes as "Dowsam" and by Professor Akrigg as "Donsame", while Mr. Cook reads it as "Doylye", which occurs further down, since Doylye and the illegible both seem to be synonyms for Dymock. To me the illegible looks less like "Doylye" than either "Dowsam" or "Donsame" – the third letter could be an *m* – but "Doylye" rhymes with "oily", and it is possible the Countess rang the changes on insulting deformations of Dymock's name. In any case, I agree with Mr. Cook as to the sense: the Earl preferred his servant to herself, she was bitterly humiliated, and to cap it all, this "common person" to whom her husband had taken "liking so extraordinary" had poisoned her own reputation by saying she had made advances to him and had offered him an assignation.

Seeking to touch his heart, she sent her small son with a letter to him; he did not read it, but kept the child, whom she never saw again so long as her husband lived. When he died, on October 4th, 1581, he left a terrible will, making Dymock his son's guardian and forbidding Mary, their daughter, ever to be in the same house as her mother. Dymock was an executor of the will, and none of the other executors, who included the Duke of Northumberland, could do anything without the consent of this servant. Dymock set off in haste to get the will proved, and in her extremity the Countess wrote to the Montagus' most powerful relation, the Earl of Leicester. Leicester laid the matter immediately before the Queen, who had the will quashed. The Countess' daughter was allowed to join her mother at Cowdray, and the young 3rd Earl aged eight was made a ward of Lord Burghley, and therefore spent the rest of his minority at Theobalds, in Hertfordshire, and so became a neighbour of Lady Burghley's sister, Lady Bacon, and her family.

Francis, thirteen years older, was already at Gray's Inn, but seems to have come home in the vacations. One has the impression the children of the Bacon and Burghley households lived on cousinly relations, and the new ward, arriving in circumstances of some scandal, from a difficult Catholic family, would be a likely object of interest in the Protestant stronghold to which he had so unexpectedly been transferred.

The Countess of Southampton wrote to Leicester again:[4]

My good Lord,

. . . The hard dealing of my Lord towards me in his life was not unknown to your

Lordship, and how he hath left me at his death is too apparent to all, making his servant his wife, by giving to him all and to myself nothing that he could put from me. His only daughter is so little preferred in benefit before his man, who surely, my Lord, could never deserve it with aught that is in him, except with feeding my Lord his humour against me to increase his own credit to that hate as now (with dishonour more than enough) it is comen unto. What grief it is to me, I cannot now make known unto your Lordship, the rather for that it is not remediless. It resteth now that by your Lordship's good means and other my friends' there may be that done for the good of the child and surety of that which his father hath left unto him that your authority or credit may afford, that his evil start may not rest at the devotion of Dymock, who hath sufficed in no way to discharge it, and so do mind to deal as I am dealt withall by them. That my little son refuse to hear service is not my fault that hath not seen him almost these two years. I trust your Lordship esteems me to have some more discretion than to forbid him that which his few years cannot judge of. Truly my Lord, if my self had kept him he should in this house have come to it as my Lord my father and all his doth . . .

> from Cowdray this 25th of October, your assured
> friend and cousin,
>
> M.Southampton.

A husband had not the right to leave his wife penniless. She had her widow's third of the estate. What she is trying to tell Leicester about her small son is that, although she and her father are Catholics, she would not have taught him to refuse the Prayer Book service, which is in fact used in her father's house.

The young Southampton was sent to St. John's, the most Puritan college at Cambridge, and then, at the age of fifteen, to Gray's Inn, where, as a new student, he would be somewhat under the protection of Francis Bacon, as Burghley's (supposed) nephew, and a bencher. Across the road, he could see, exactly opposite Gray's Inn, on the south side of Holborn (on the site of the present Southampton Building), his late father's town residence, Southampton House, which would be his when he attained his majority.

The Countess of Southampton was now living at Place (Palace) House, Titchfield, and the likeliest way for Bacon to have met her would be through his accompanying the young Earl, when at last he was allowed to visit his mother. He would there have found her somewhat irked because, even after the quashing of the clauses in her late husband's will most vicious towards her, Titchfield was one of the places over which Dymock retained an executor's powers and stewardship until the 3rd Earl came of age. She must have been obliged to suffer his presence when he wanted to come and oversee the estate.

A guardian had, in those days, the right to arrange the marriage of his ward, and Burghley had arranged the young Earl of Southampton should marry his own granddaughter, Elizabeth Vere, daughter of his daughter, Anne, and the Seventeenth Earl of Oxford. Southampton, however, shrank from the match. This was alarming to the Countess and her father, as if he refused, Burghley had the right to demand compensation, on a scale to hit the family heavily. The Countess told a Sir Thomas Stanhope who visited her,[5] ''I do not find in my son a disposition to be tied as yet''. Viscount Montagu wrote to Burghley on 19th September, 1580, assuring him that both he and his daughter had sought to persuade him, but was obliged to ask on his behalf, ''a further respite of one year, in respect of his young years.''[6]

The first seventeen of the *Sonnets* urge a young man to marry, and Dr. Rowse is probably right in believing they were written at the behest of the mother. *Venus and Adonis,* published in 1593 and dedicated to the young Southampton, plays upon the same theme, Venus, instead of the author in his own voice, endeavouring to persuade a young man of the delights of congress. It is ironic that the poem which so much shocked Hall should have been written not in any erotic spirit, but as an effort to stir a young man to what his mother and her father held to be his duty, and to save the family from a penal fine.

But that the poet should have put his pen to such eloquence to such an end, supposes a very special relationship with the mother. Perhaps he was in love with her.

How long had he known her? Sonnet 98 begins:

> From you I have been absent in the Spring,
> When proud pide Aprill (drest in all his trim)
> Hath put a spirit of youth in euerything;
> That heauie Saturne laught and leapt with him.

Dr. Patricia Thomson has suggested[7] this indicates a conjunction of the sun with Saturn. In such a position, astrologers would expect the heavy influence of the leaden planet to be less, burnt out by the Sun. There were conjunctions of the Sun and Saturn on March 20th, 1585, April 3rd, 1586, April 18th, 1587 and May 2nd, 1588. Astrologers would allow for this influence an ''orb'' of practically a fortnight, either way, and so would a poet. Further down in the poem there is mention of ''lillies whites'', which may be lilies-of-the-valley, which do flower in late April or early May, and of roses, which do not usually open until June, though they might already be exhibiting buds. I think one can take it, therefore, that the relationship had started early enough for the poet to have written these tender lines in the spring of 1588, at the latest.

His reluctance to let *Venus and Adonis* go out under his own name could have had more motives than one. Had it appeared as by Francis Bacon, it would have embarrassed Southampton as a too heavily obvious attempt to get him to marry into the family, and Burghley would not have liked it either, as it might be thought it was he who had put his nephew up to writing a poem to work on his granddaughter's reluctant intended;

these reasons might have weighed with Francis more seriously than possible censure of its erotic content by Puritans such as Hall. As this was the first Shakespearean work to be published, he may in this way have set a precedent for himself in using the name of an actor with whom he had struck up an association and who had taken responsibility for the plays already acted. Obviously, Southampton would have known who was the real author.

John Florio had been engaged as Italian tutor to Southampton, and his *First Fruites* (1591) contains amongst other prefatory matter a sonnet 'Phaeton to his Friend Florio', which both Sir Sidney Lee and Sir E.K. Chambers believed to be by Shakespeare. But Florio's *A World of Wordes* (1598) carried an address ''To the Reader'' in which he refers to one who belittles ''a good sonnet of a gentleman, a friend of mine, that loved better to be a poet, than to be counted so''. Shakespeare could not have been referred to as a gentleman prior to the grant of arms in 1596, and by that time work had been printed in his name. This is difficult for Shakespeareans to explain, but falls into place if Florio, as an intimate of the Titchfield circle, knew the author not only of the 'Phaeton' sonnet but of *Venus and Adonis* and the rest was Bacon.

Mr. Ivor Cook has suggested that Samuel Daniel, Florio's brother-in-law, visited him at Titchfield, wrote to the Countess of Southampton the *Delia* sonnets and is therefore ''the Rival Poet''. It was only by opportunism that twenty-eight of the sonnets from *Delia* were tacked on to Sidney's *Astrophel and Stella* (1591) and therefore dedicated to the Countess of Pembroke. He speaks of having been three years Delia's faithful singer, but three years prior to 1591 he would hardly even have met the Countess of Pembroke. Moreover, the description of the river by which ''Delia hath her seat'' as ''poor in waters'' would insult it, but that Titchfield is on the River Meon, pronounced almost like Mean.

It is not being suggested she slept with Daniel, yet there are hints in the sonnets she had more than one man in her life.

The Countess' eyes in the only portrait are brown. No human eyes, not even those of negroes, are black, literally. The eyes called by licence of language black appear so from the shadow of the lashes upon the balls of the eyes, obscuring the brown irises and the pupil. It is also possible the term ''black'' was used then as we use it today of ''black coffee'' and ''black treacle'', as the simple opposite of coffee with milk or golden treacle. Anne Boleyn's eyes are verbally described as black, though the portrait in the National Gallery shows them brown.

There is also, in 138, the suggestion both she and the poet are embarrassed because they are elderly lovers:

> When my loue swears that she is made of truth,
> I do beleeue her though I know she lyes,

That she might thinke me some vntutered youth,
Vnlearned in the worlds false subtleties.
Thus vainely thinking that she thinkes me young,
Although she knowes my dayes are past the best,
Simply I credit her false speaking tongue,
On both sides thus is simple truth supprest;
But wherefore sayes she not she is vniust?
And wherefore say not I that I am old?
O loues best habit is in seeming truth,
And age in loue, loues not t'haue yeares told.
  Therefor I lye with her, and she with me,
  And in our faults by lyes we flattered be.

On May 2nd, 1594, the Countess married Sir Thomas Heneage. He was sixty, she only about forty-one. But her father had died, in October, 1592, and her brother had, untimely, predeceased him; she may, therefore, have felt she needed the protection of a man who stood well with the Queen. Professor Bullough suggests *A Midsummer Night's Dream* was written for the wedding. When Theseus discovers the lovers in the wood, he says, ''No doubt they rose up early to observe the rites of May.'' It is therefore the early morning of May 1st. They all go back to the palace, where the clowns perform their contribution to the entertainments preceding the wedding. This would accord very well with the celebration of a wedding which actually took place on May 2nd. Theseus and Hippolyta, mature lovers, should then stand for Heneage and the Countess. But if the poet was in love with her himself, the occasion must have been a sad one, and indeed perhaps one can see in the follies of the lovers his wry comment on romantic love.

They are practically interchangeable dummies. But if they lack personality, it may be for the same reason they have none in Heine's poem:

> *Ein Junglein liebt ein Mädchen,*
> *Die hat einen andern erwählt;*
> *Der andre liebt eine andre*
> *Und hat sich mit dieser vermählt*
> . . .

which I render:

> A young man loves a maiden,
> Who has another chosen;
> That other loves another
> To whom he is bespoken.
> . . .

The sense is one of universal comi-tragedy, in which the humans are scarcely more than marionettes moved by the caprice of erotic passion, which, unlike friendly love, based upon mutual regard, hurls its victims at those most unsuited to return it.

Puck, then, is the personification of this wayward Eros, so wantonly destructive of self-possession as it might almost seem malicious. He slightly lessens the responsibility of the lovers for their behaviour. Racine, in his very different treatment of the Theseus legend, his *Phèdre*, uses a comparable device for lifting some of the guilt off his heroine by debiting to the prompting of a servant her worst crime. The French dramatist's need was the greater in that his subject was a Queen; but perhaps there is a Queen involved in this story, too.

1. This identification was first put forward by Mr. Ivor Cook, in a letter to *The Times*, 'Shakespeare's Sonnets and Mr. W.H.' 7th November 1969.

2. Thomas Howard, 4th Duke of Norfolk, was a Catholic who proposed to marry Mary Queen of Scots. Mary Queen of Scots, a Catholic, did not recognise the divorce of Catherine of Aragon and therefore considered the marriage of Henry VIII to Anne Boleyn invalid and Elizabeth a bastard and not entitled to have been crowned Queen. Mary considered herself to be Queen, not of Scotland only but of England also, although she could not reign because Elizabeth was enthroned. Because of these views of Mary, no subject of Queen Elizabeth could propose marriage to her without first obtaining Elizabeth's consent, which in this case was not sought. The plan was plainly for Norfolk to marry Mary and place himself at her side on the English throne as King and Queen of England. This would certainly have meant murdering Elizabeth first. After some fighting, he and some fellow conspirators were captured, tried and executed.

3. British Museum, Cotton MS, Titus B II, 370 r to 372 v.

4. Rousham, Cotrell-Dormer MSS. (I went to Rousham and studied in the original all of the Countess of Southampton's letters there. Rousham, however, is a private residence and I hardly felt I could trespass upon Mr. Cotrell-Dormer's hospitality for so long as it would take to copy all of her letters out, and there were difficulties about photocopying; I therefore accepted his suggestion that with regard to the two letters to Leicester I should use Charlotte Stopes' transcription.)

5. Stanhope to Burghley, July 15th, 1590; Calendar of State Papers Domestic, 1582-90, 680.

6. Calendar of State Papers Domestic, 1580-90, 680.

7. 'The Date Clue in Shakespeare's Sonnet 98', Patricia Thomas *(Neophilologus)* 1966.

CHAPTER 22

Ovid's Circe

IT is a popular belief that Titania, Queen of the Fairies, is, like Spenser's *Faerie Queene,* meant to be Queen Elizabeth. But if so, is Oberon Leicester? They enter quarrelling:

> Ill met by Moone-light,
> Proud *Tytannia.*
>
> *II, i, 60 Var: 63-64*

They have, then, become estranged, each one taxing the other with having become involved with somebody else. This would fit the period when Elizabeth was dallying with d'Alençon whilst Leicester was hardly in a position to protest, his secret marriage to Lettice having just been discovered. Titania says:

> I know
> When thou wast stolne away from Fairy Land,
> And in the shape of *Corin,* sate all day,
> Playing on pipes of *Corne,* and versing loue
> To amorous *Phillida.*
>
> *II, i, 64-68 Var: 68-72*

If Titania is Queen of the Fairies, Fairy Land is the Court. Then, as Corin is a stock name for a shepherd in pastoral poetry, the allegation is that he slipped away from Court to make love to another in the country, which could be referred to what happened in the country between Leicester and Lettice, unknown to Elizabeth. Of great interest is Oberon's speech to Puck:

> thou remembrest
> Since once I sat vpon a promontory,
> And heard a Meare-maide on a Dolphins backe,
> Vttering such dulcet and harmonious breath,
> That the rude sea grew ciuill at her song,
> And certain starres shot madly from their Spheares,
> To heare the Sea-maids musicke.
> PUCK: I remember.
> OBERON: That very time I say [1] (but thou couldst not)
> Flying betweene the cold Moone and the earth,
> CUPID all arm'd; a certaine aime he tooke
> At a fair Vestall, throned by the West,

And loosed his loue-shaft . . .
    the imperiall Votresse passed on,
In maiden meditation, fancy free.

II, i, 148-64 Var: 153-70

Cupid's aim at the fair Vestal has widely been taken as an allusion to Leicester's at Elizabeth's hand. Dover Wilson thought the lines about listening to a mermaid on a dolphin's back must relate to some fête given by Leicester in Elizabeth's honour. He is surely right, only he thinks of the fête of 1575 given at Kenilworth. To me, mermaids and dolphins would seem inappropriate to a place so inland. I think the allusion is to the water-fête which Leicester gave on the Thames on June 24th, 1561. Here it would be much more suitable to have artificial dolphins, escorting the barge in which he entertained the Queen, very likely with "mermaids" riding them and fireworks, which the Queen loved, to soar and descend like shooting stars. This was the day on which Leicester chanced his aim, building up an enchanted atmosphere and then, having so engineered things that Bishop de Quadra, the Queen and he should be alone at the moment when the magic had most worked upon her emotions, simply proposing to de Quadra he should marry them there and then on the barge. Moreover, this attempted *coup* gives the title to the play, *A Midsummer Night's Dream*; June 24th, is near enough to the solstice to count as Midsummer. To capture the hand of the Queen by a bold stroke was Leicester's midsummer night's dream. As in Ibsen's *Ghosts,* the action goes back behind the present setting to an all important past.

The poet seems to be identifying himself with Leicester and his demand for the "little changeling boy" that the Queen had refused him. Who is the "little changeling boy", if not Francis? He was a changeling in that his name and home had been changed to that of the Bacon family, denied to Leicester in that by refusing to marry him she made it impossible for him to acknowledge his son as theirs. Oberon wanted the boy to be his "henchman", that is, his page of honour, to walk in front of him in all processions of state, proudly shown to all the world, trained by him to man's estate. The quarrel was about the child that had been kept from him.

Titania says his mother, who died in giving him birth, was "a Votresse of my Order". What Order? A votaress is a priestess of some cult, as the Vestal Virgins, who spent their lives tending the sacred flame, that must never go out. And indeed this allusion to a Votaress comes in the same scene as the reference to that other Votaress who was a Vestal seated on a throne, always taken for Queen Elizabeth. Are the two not facets of one another? The imperial Vestal Votaress who passed on was the Queen as the world saw her and as she wished to be seen, invincibly Virgin, and another Votaress of the same Order must likewise be a Vestal. Though the child-bearing is removed from the Fairy Queen by being put upon another in her Order, however one may juggle with the concepts, the "changeling boy" was the son of a Vestal Virgin, and would have been her death as such, and entailed her death physically. For the Vestals, Virginity was of primary importance. If one was known to have lain with a man, she was buried alive.

Curiously, the Vestals' favourite beast was the ass.[2] But why, in the play, is Titania made as a punishment to fall in love with a man with an ass's head? Is there not in the author's mind the idea that, having refused a true man, in nature her husband, and with him the legitimisation of their son, it was occultly appropriate she should fall to doting upon a deformed creature, not the chaste Vestals' ass, but an ass which may have something in common with the ass into which Apuleius was turned for his sexual mistakes? Is the reference not to Elizabeth's apparent enchantment with the deformed d'Alençon?

We have seen that Elizabeth called some of her admirers after animals; Hatton was her sheep, Simier her monkey, d'Alençon her frog. In Ovid, Titania is a name of Circe (*Metamorphoses, XIII*, 968 and XIV, 14, 376, 382, 438). Circe turned humans into beasts. Ovid found her in Homer. In Homer, she offers men a cup, which, when they drink from it, turns them into swine. In Ovid's presentation she is encountered with her fawning beasts about her - *ferarum agmen adulantum*[3] - and, for spite, because a man will not love her, turns the loins of the girl he does love into a pack of yelping hounds, forever leaping up her flanks. In both Homer and Ovid one feels a sexual undertow, which was, moreover, not missed in *The Faerie Queene*, Book II, Canto 12, stanzas 84–86, wherein is a description, clearly derived from the Circe legend, of how Guyon, snared in the Bower of Bliss, finds himself in thrall to Acrasia and her throng:

> Said he, These seeming beasts are men indeed,
> Whom this Enchantress hath transformed thus,
> Whylome her louers, which her lusts did feed,
> Now turned into figures hideous . . .

And *The Faerie Queene* comes from the author of *Mother Hubbard's Tale*, wherein symbolic use was made of Elizabeth's zoo to deal with the meance posed by d'Alençon.

It is not being alleged that Elizabeth slept with Simier, d'Alençon or Hatton, or that the poet thought she did. But it does appear the animal appellations irritated him. Perhaps because she should, instead of toying with the fawning circle, have legitimized the union by which she had a child, a strain of resentment within him wanted her to drink of her own medicine and come, herself, to dote on "lion, bear, or wolf or bull, or meddling monkey, or on busy ape . . . ounce, or cat or bear, Pard, or boar with bristled hair . . . ''

There is another consideration. If the poet was the man from Warwickshire, he had no reason for feeling about the Queen in this way. He would not even have known of the situation. De Quadra specifies that Leicester, the Queen and he were alone at the moment when Leicester tried to make him marry them. Only one of the three could have told about it. Not de Quadra; he went back to Spain soon after, and in any case would never have told a British subject (we know only because his letter to his King has now become a document in the Simanca archives); not the Queen: only Leicester would have told. And who would he have told? Not, surely, the actor from Warwickshire, but Francis. He would have wanted him to know who his real parents were and that he had done everything in his power to get him legitimised, only the Queen refused. It means, surely, that Leicester told Francis the whole story.

1. Editors, from Rowe onward, have amended to "saw".
2. Virgil, *Copa*, 26 and depictions on *lararia*.
3. "Her crowd of fawning beasts about her."

CHAPTER 23

The friend

HENEAGE survived the celebration of his wedding to the Countess by only just a year, dying in October, 1595. Notwithstanding the Queen's insistence that his widow return the £12,000 (£600,000) she had advanced him for services to the crown, the Countess (she retained her title after marriage to a commoner) was now secure, and could afford to indulge her inclination in the choice of a new husband. This might have been the moment at which the poet might hope. Sonnet 152 indeed, by saying that in loving him she broke her bed-vow and tore new faith, suggests a physical liaison during the lifetime of Heneage, which she might, now, be glad to regularise. But already another had crossed her path.

It is from Southampton we first hear of a new element in his mother's life. He had preserved his liberty at a cost of £5,000 (£2,500,000 in today's money), exacted by Burghley as the price of not marrying his granddaughter. As soon as he reached his majority he had to go to the money-lenders to pay it. Soon afterwards he became intimate with Elizabeth Vernon, a maid-of-honour of the Queen and a poor relation of the Earl of Essex. He was in France, at the Court of Henri IV, when he learned she was pregnant with his child. He returned, in September, 1597, and, although she had no dowry, married her secretly. We may think this was his noblest act, but Queen Elizabeth took it otherwise. She ordered the new Countess to be kept in the Fleet prison (at Essex' expense) and sent after Southampton, as he was returning to France, commanding him to her presence. He, in fear, made excuses to delay, and when he did come back was in his turn imprisoned in the Fleet (from which his wife had now been released), whether for intimacy with a maid-of-honour or secret marriage is not clear. The situation is not unlike that in *Measure for Measure*, where Claudio is imprisoned for getting with child a girl whom he truly loves and, despite her absence of dowry (recalling the condition of Elizabeth Vernon) is willing honourably to marry. The drama may have been remembered when the play was later written. Wife and mother were both pleading for him, when now he became anxious about a rumour the latter had secretly married Sir William Hervey. He briefed Essex to find out.

Essex saw both, in November, and warned them that if they married they would incur not only her son's displeasure but his own. Probably Southampton feared she would leave Hervey all he hoped to inherit from her, while Essex saw the danger that the young Earl and his penniless bride would, if deprived, come to depend on him. Although they had called the infant daughter with whom she had been brought to bed Penelope, which was ominous.

Nevertheless, on January 31st, 1597/8, the gossip John Chamberlain wrote to Carleton, "Sir William Harvies marriage with the old Countess of Southampton that have lien smothering so long comes now to be published."

Southampton appears, on his release, to have become reconciled to the union, but who was Hervey?

To Mr. Ivor Cook belongs the honour of having discovered the origins of Sir William, later Admiral Hervey, Baron Kidbrook, the Countess' third husband. He might long ago have been recognised as "Mr. W.H.", the Friend of the Sonnets, had not his marriage to Southampton's mother seemed to place him with the older generation. Mr. Cook noticed that he had three sisters and a father of the same names as a William Hervey certified dead on March 3, 1589/90 aged twenty-four. Moreover, both had been Gentlemen Pensioners, a select body of only about fifty, and examination of its Roll showed they had only one William Hervey. It therefore appeared to Mr. Cook, Hervey must have been certified dead when he was not. He went to the Public Record Office and found this to be the case. Hervey had been presumed dead when lost at sea, whereas he was a prisoner in Spain. On his eventual return, he had been obliged to "traverse", that is cancel, the certification of his own decease, with an explanation.

Hervey was, then, born c.1566, and therefore thirteen years younger than the Countess, and only seven years older than her son. His having returned after being presumed drowned at sea, to marry the Countess, made him very like Sebastian in *Twelfth Night*. Mr. Cook, who is very much a "Shakespeare wrote Shakespeare" man, believes *Twelfth Night* to be set in Titchfield, the Countess Olivia to be the Countess of Southampton, Sebastian to be Hervey, Malvolio Dymock, the steward who got above himself and gave out the Countess was making advances to himself, and Aguecheek Shakespeare. I have no objection to Aguecheek's being the actor from Stratford, but if so, he is not in the right relation to the lady; I feel that Orsino is Bacon.

His character is in the opening lines:

> If Musicke be the food of loue, play on;
> Giue me excesse of it, that, surfetting,
> The appetite may sicken, and so dye.
> That straine agen! it had a dying fall:
> O, it came ore my eare like the sweet sound
> That breathes upon a banke of Violets,
> Stealing and giuing odour!

I, i, 1-7 Var: 4-10

Here we have "the melancholy planet" carrying him away, as he himself said that it did.[1] We have his love of music, of scents and of violets. We shall later find him in the *Novum Organum*[2] giving a method for the distillation of scent from violets, though he owns in his *Historia Vitae et Mortis*[3] that the healing property of which he writes elsewhere is not to be found in the scent so preserved, or even in the cut flowers, but must be inhaled from them while they are part of the growing plant. As they grow so low, it would be necessary, in order to bring one's nose to them, practically to lay oneself upon a bank of violets, which would place one in a very "love-melancholy" posture.

The close association of music with odours is also typically Baconian. In *The New Atlantis* we shall find the "sound-houses" followed by the "perfume-houses", while in the essay 'Of Gardens' it becomes so close as to amount to synesthesia:

> And because the breath of flowers is far sweeter in the air (where it comes and goes like the warbling of music) . . .

For anything like it, one has to go right forward to Shelley:

> music so delicate, soft and intense,
> It was felt like an odour within the sense
>
> *The Sensitive Plant*

It may be objected that the "sweet sound" of which Orsino speaks is that of the breeze, rustling the violets, but would so faint a sound be audible? It seems to be a sound special to the bank of violets, an emanation from them, almost a synonym for the scent it carries.

The apparent literary sources of *Twelfth Night* are *Gl'Ingannati*, an Italian play of the Academy of Siena, the various derivatives. Professor Bullough, who credits Shakespeare with the ability to read both Italian and French, thinks he must have read *Gl'Ingannati*, in the original, and also *Gl'Inganni*, made from it by Nicolo Serchi, the Italian prose story made from it by Bandello and the French version of the Bandello by Belleforest in his *Histoires Tragiques*, in addition to two stories by Barnaby Rich.[4] The central idea of a sister's taking her brother's name and sex after his supposed death is carried over from the literary sources. Hervey had no sister to be a consolation to the poet for the lady he had stolen from him, and it may be the delicacy with which the picture of Viola is built up represents a wish-fulfilment, a distillation from Hervey of his feminine side.

How could Bacon have come to know Hervey? Finding, at Lambeth, the signature "Harvy" at the bottom of the letter to Bacon requesting the return of £30,[5] (£1,500) I wrote to Mr. Cook asking him whether, in his research into Hervey, he had come upon documents bearing his signature or signatures of members of his family. He kindly sent me photographs he had taken of a number of documents, on one of which I recognised the "Lambeth" signature. It was that of Sir George Hervey, Lieutenant of the Tower, uncle of Sir William Hervey, the *Mr. W.H.* of the *Sonnets.*

Plainly the poet became attached to the younger man, perhaps building more upon the friendship as the lady became less dependable. How Hervey came to visit Titchfield is less clear; perhaps the poet took him, or even, as in the play, sent him as a messenger, little thinking to be cut out by him. That he had come to think of the young man as a better character than the lady seems evident from his exclamation in 42, "That she hath thee is of my wayling cheefe." To lose the friend was a worse blow than losing the mistress. And yet in 41, "Aye me, and yet thou mightst my seate forbeare" implies he had thought of the relationship as permanent; for "seate" surely means more than the woman's body, nothing so crude as her property as a "seat", yet the sense that it was his settled place of refuge and perhaps the hope she might consent to marry him.

The play upon the name of Will, in 135, "Whoever hast her wish, thou hast thy Will, and Will to boote, and Will in ouer-plus" and in 136, "Make but my name thy loue, and loue that still, And then thou louest me for my name is Will' refers of course to Hervey's Christian name, William, and, in my submission, the poet's use of William Shakespeare's name for his cover. Naturally, the Countess would have been in the know concerning this arrangement. In 135, he seems to envisage keeping a share in her, but resignation is the key-note of *A Lover's Complaint.*

The poem introduces us (stanza 2) to a lady:

> The carkas of a beauty spent and donne.
> Time had not sithed all that youth begun,
> Nor youth all quit, but spight of heavens fell rage,
> Some beauty peept, through lettice of fear'd age.

(Lettice means lattice-work of wrinkles.) This more than bears out the hint in Sonnet 138 that she is no longer in her first youth, though retaining magic for the poet. She tells the "reuerend man" who would comfort her, (11th stanza),

> ... though in me you behold
> The iniury of many a blasting houre;
> Let it not tell your Iudgement I am old ...

Defamed and humiliated by her first husband in his doting on Dymock, she had certainly known "many a blasting houre", though her present distress was of a different order. She is weeping into a river, (5th stanza),

> Her haire nor loose nor ti'd in formall plat
> ... slackly braided in loose negligence.

In these lines are described the Heneage motto, ''Fast but unbound'' and the Heneage knot, slackly tied. (This was drawn to my attention by Mr. Ivor Cook, but I have verified it at the College of Arms).

Mr. Cook further believes that in stanza 6 her dropping her tears into the stream:

> Like vsery applying wet to wet,
> Or Monarches hands that lets not bounty fall,
> Where want cries some, but where excesse begs all

refers to the Queen's peremptory insistance she pay not some of the Heneage debt (money she had advanced him for his duties) but all of it.

At Rousham there is a collection of letters from the Countess to her brother-in-law, Sir John Dormer, which I have never seen printed. They are undated, but one reads:

> Mr. Dormer, careful for my friends and of my own credit I send to intreat your presence the sooner the better. The beginning of November is the time of payment of such money as you know, if by your means I cannot hold it. But a certainty I must be at, and without you I cannot know or do anything in it. I came upon Saturday from Copt Hall where I held health and quiet . . . this 8th October,
>   M.Southampton
> My Sir William salutes you most kindly and hopes to see you very presently

Copt Hall had been left her by Heneage, and the letter appears to concern the Heneage debt. The demand for its repayment came in 1596, but she would hardly have been so unconventional as to refer to Hervey as ''My Sir William'' before she was married to him. As Southampton was in November, 1597, still uncertain whether she had married him secretly, the letter to Dormer may have been written in the following autumn. This narrows to within a couple of years the period within which *A Lover's Complaint* must have been composed (a matter over which scholars have speculated, most making it a very early work, Swinburne a late one. In his emphasis on its maturity, he is proved right).

The young man in the poem must surely be Hervey, though why she should feel betrayed by him is not clear. Perhaps, she only means that there had been intimacy, about which she had misgivings – as she may well have done, before deciding to marry a man so little older than her son and beneath her in station. In that case, the poem has been composed before her third marriage, though after the arrival of the demand for repayment of the Heneage debt, which further narrows the period.

There remains the third person in *A Lover's Complaint,* the ''reverend man'' to consider. Stevens, ed. 1780, took ''his greyned bat'', on which he slid down the bank to sit beside the weeping lady, to be ''his staff, on which the grain of the wood was visible''. This suggests Leicester, with his ''ragged staff'', to whom the Countess had poured out her woes at an earlier period. But he was dead now. Could it be that the poet is here identifying himself with Leicester? Though he was distressed when she preferred his young friend to himself, it would have been like him, on philosophical reflection, to accept the role of confidant.

1. See above, p.
2. Spedding IV, pp.212–13.
3. Spedding V, p.298.
4. *Narrative and Dramatic Sources of Shakespeare*, Geoffrey Bullough (Routledge, 1968), II, Introd. to *Twelfth Night*.
5. See above, p.62.

CHAPTER 24

A retrospect

IT has been pointed out that Rosaline, in *Love's Labour's Lost,* has black eyes, and the suggestion has therefore been made that she is the same person as the Dark Lady of the Sonnets. That may or may not be the case. It is true that there are elements of the Titchfield circle in *Love's Labour's Lost.* Holofernes, with his synonyms: "caelo, the sky, the welkin, the heaven'' IV, ii, 5, is plainly Florio, engaged by the dowager Countess as Italian tutor to the young Earl. His great work was the making of an Italian-English dictionary, and "cielo'', here perhaps contaminated by Latin "caelum'', is Italian for sky. Moth has generally been recognised as Nashe. Doubtless they were intended to come to the performance and enjoy these affectionate caricatures of themselves.

But the play has a double setting. If partly brought into Titchfield, it brings to Titchfield something of another enchanted place. In 1917, Mrs. Bunten discovered that the passports of Anthony Bacon and his train were, when they went to Navarre, signed Biron, Dumain, Longaville and Boyesse. This I verified myself at the British Museum, where they now are. Biron is written in a particularly large and clear, almost copybook, hand, Dumain is also clear. The only one I was in any doubt about was the third, which starts Lomga . . . and ends with a threadlike scrawl. For phonetic reasons, the nasal which preceeds a *g* is not usually *m* but *n*, so it is probably Longa . . . I consulted Miss Olerenshaw of the Manuscript Department, without mentioning the reason why this signature was of interest to me. She thought the threadlike termination probably stood for a syllable which ends French names with extreme frequency, -ville, -ment or -court; as there was no suggestion of a *t,* most likely -ville.

Though never mentioned by Shakespeare scholars, the coincidence of these four names with those of four of the characters in *Love's Labour's Lost,* set in Navarre, surely links the play with Anthony Bacon's visit to that country.

Nevertheless, though the warm relations between Anthony and Francis make it likely Anthony talked of his travels, and so put Francis in mind of his own, almost a decade earlier, there are elements in the play which link it not to Anthony's but to Francis' period on the continent. When Rosaline meets Berowne or Biron, she says, "Did I not dance with you in Brabant once?'' II, i, 114, showing that she had been one of the *esquadrille volant* of beautiful ladies-in-waiting whom Marguerite de Valois took with her wherever she went. When Rosaline says to

Katherine, of Cupid, "'You'll ne'er be friends with him; a' killed your sister'' she refers, surely, to the tragedy of Hélène de Tournon (which we shall relate later, in reference to another play), who died of a broken heart during the Flanders tour. The story would have been on their lips on their return, when Francis could have heard it from them, if indeed he had not already danced with one of them in Brabant once. Francis was on the continent solely to be present at whatever was interesting, lively or colourful. Therefore, when Catherine de Medici escorted her daughter, Marguerite de Valois, south to re-present her to her husband, King Henry of Navarre, in an effort at reconciliation, it is more likely than otherwise that Francis went with the Court, as did everyone with a taste for spectacle and occasion. Marguerite, a beautiful woman, with her chestnut hair and blue-green eyes,[1] rode in a gown of orange-gold upon a white palfrey. It was by no means certain King Henry of Navarre would receive her, but if he did, she was to ask for the cession of Aquitaine to France, as the Princess asks it of the King of Navarre in *Love's Labour's Lost.* Even her passion for hunting, as revealed in the play, accords with what Marguerite tells us in her own *Mémoires,* that up to the moment her brother, King Henri III of France, suggested to her that she should play a political role, she had not a thought in her head save of dancing and hunting. Henry came part of the way to meet her. The joint cavalcade wound its way down to Nerac, where Marguerite was to create a park, and where nobody apparently had anything to do but dance and make love – except that, on February 4th, 1578/9, the Ministers sat down to the conference for the negotiation of the treaty.

If Francis was there – and how could he have stayed away – he must have been called back suddenly when he was informed of Sir Nicholas Bacon's death. This heavy blow, falling upon such a garden-party setting, recalls the death which severs the tentative, teasing relationships in *Love's Labour's Lost.* Only, in the play, it was the father of the Princess who had died. Marguerite's father had been dead for years. The only notable death we know of in February, 1578/79 is that of the Lord Keeper. Artistically, so heavy a blow strikes a discordant note in so light a comedy. We are unprepared for it because nothing has led up to it; the father who had died has been in nobody's thoughts, until these solemn tidings break off all.

Celibacy was not in Henry's nature, and the vows may have a different origin. It is possible Bacon at one time thought that to develop the higher powers of the mind a celibate state was desirable, but later changed his mind, for the reasons Berowne gives.

As for the black eyes of Rosaline, it is not unknown for men to choose for their successive loves women of the same colouring, which may be in some way meaningful for them. Rosaline may have been an earlier love, encountered on the continent in the poet's impressionable 'teens, whose memory was overcome by a love that went deeper, even as was Romeo's first love for Rosaline – the same name – extinguished in his love for Juliet. Juliet was thirteen when plighted by her parents to an old man, the age at which Viscount Montagu's daughter was married to the 2nd Earl of Southampton, who made her so unhappy. There may be a vein of wishful thinking here: if only the poet could have met her when she was that age! The name Montague is from Arthur Brooke's *Romeus and Julietta*, but was the Countess' father's title, while the feud between the Montagues and Capulets finds its parallel in that between the Danvers and the Longs, in which the young 3rd Earl of Southampton involved himself by abetting the escape of one who had killed a member of the other family.

The character of Rosaline in *Love's Labour's Lost* is not that of the Countess as it comes through in Olivia in *Twelfth Night* and in the Countess of Roussillon in *All's Well that Ends Well* (see below p.151); on the other hand, there is a line of these sprightly, delicately teasing, taunting girls that runs from Rosaline in *Love's Labour's Lost*, through Rosalind in *As You Like It* to Beatrice in *Much Ado About Nothing*, and they may have the same inspiration. As to the witty young man, as he appears in Berowne in *Love's Labour's Lost*, as Mercutio in *Romeo and Juliet* and Gratiano in *The Merchant of Venice*, he may be modelled upon that surpassingly witty young man, not always kind, whom Bacon tells us he met while with the French Court at Poitiers. He does not tell us his real name, only that he lived to become eminent.

I cannot, however, leave *Love's Labour's Lost* without a quotation from Dr. Rowse.[2] Referring to the sub-plot involving Moth and Armado, he says, ''The second element was suggested by the furious literary quarrel between Gabriel Harvey and Nashe . . . It was all a quarrel among Cambridge men.'' How then should the actor from Stratford have been concerned with it?

There is another allusion that would have been difficult for the actor from Stratford. In *I King Henry VI*, III, iii, there is a scene in which Joan of Arc tells the Duke of Burgundy he should be ashamed to join the English against his own countrymen. Joan never met the Duke, but she did send him a letter to this effect, dictated and signed with her mark, dated July 17th, 1425. The Duke appears to have kept quiet about it. Eventually it passed with the papers of the Dukes of Burgundy to the *Chambre des Comptes de Lille*, where it still forms part of the *Archives du Nord: B* 300, pièce 23 616. It was not made public until 1780, by Denis-Joseph Godefroy, Keeper of the *Archives de la Chambre des Comptes de Lille*, in *Journal de Litterature et des Arts*, ed. Abbé Grossière, Paris. T.IV, 1780, p.448.

For the author of King Henry VI to have imagined what a disclosure of papers two hundred years later was to prove true, would seem an over-remarkable coincidence. We do not know that Bacon met the Duke or anyone with access to his private papers, but moving on the continent and in high society, he had better chance to do so than the actor from Warwickshire.

Warwickshire allusions canot be pinned down so easily as many Shakespeareans imagine. A certain Richard Davies, Rector of Sapperton, Gloucestershire, in 1659, wrote that Shakespeare was whipped for stealing deer and rabbits from Sir Thomas Lucy and "in revenge turned his armorial luces [pikes] into louses." Nicholas Rowe, re-telling the story, added that the deer were in a park. Sir Lucy had no park at Chalcote and Sir E.K. Chambers, who gave warning concerning the "Mythos", commented, "It has been held that the whole story is nothing but a myth which has grown about the passage in *The Merry Wives of Windsor.*" It cannot then be evidential.

Objects dropped in the Avon from Clopton Bridge will hit a bank and be carried against the flow, as described in *The Rape of Lucrece,* 1667–70, but the like phenomenon will reproduce itself on any river where a bank projects downstream of a bridge.

It is said that Wincot and Burton Heath, in the Induction to *The Taming of the Shrew,* must be Wilmcote and Barton-on-the-Heath. This would fall into line if one were otherwise satisfied the author came from Warwickshire, but is too weak to stand as the sole proof that he did.

Popular biographies of Shakespeare are driven to Michael Drayton for a description of Warwickshire in verse. In the whole of the works, Stratford-on-Avon is not mentioned once. St. Albans is mentioned seventeen times, not counting stage directions and scenes set in or near it. It is true that most of these come in the *King Henry VI* trilogy, and that St. Albans is mentioned in the sources consulted, though the introduction of the Mayor, townsmen and Beadle is the poet's own. But why did the poet choose this king, by no means the most impressive of our sovereigns, to treat at greater length than any other? Today, we see a great series, running from the rift between the houses of Lancaster and York in the tragedy of Richard II to the healing in the accession of Henry VII; but if the author had from the beginning intended this, why did he not start at the beginning, with *Richard II,* instead of in the middle with *King Henry VI*? It has often been observed that an author's first work tends to draw strongly upon either the events of his own life or those of the locality in which he has grown up and with which he identifies himself – witness the concentration in Shelley's juvenilia upon the environs of Horsham and legends of St. Leonard's Forest. The references to St. Albans come thickest in the second part, suggesting this was composed first; and that, though upon other grounds, was the opinion of both Chambers and Dover Wilson.

It is, however, in a later play, *2 King Henry IV* II, ii, 182–85, that we find:

This Doll Tear-sheet

Should be some road.
I warrant you, as common as the way between
St. Albans and London.

Here the reference is quite gratuitous. The great north road was, doubtless, like all other roads out of London, thronged with prostitutes, but who would think of such a simile, save one who had frequent occasion to travel from St. Albans to London? Notice that the journey starts from St. Albans. St. Albans is home.

This comes in a play where there is no historical pretext for the introduction of the town's name.

In *I King Henry IV,* we have a further needless reference to St. Albans, where Falstaff, on a road near Coventry, complaining that his men have but a shirt and a half between them, ornaments his point with, "and the shirt, to say the truth, stolen from my host at St. Albans."

This brings us to something very interesting. Arthur Gray, Master of Jesus College, Cambridge, noticed that Falstaff was required to proceed from London to Shrewsbury, as a matter of urgency, and should therefore have taken the shortest route. The direct route from London to Shrewsbury runs through Stratford-on-Avon, and it seemed to Gray impossible a Stratford man should not know this. He would have thought it more natural to him to take the historically valid occasion for setting a scene there, showing Falstaff and his men surrounded by the good people of Stratford, amongst the features of the town well known to Shakespeare. Instead, he has set a scene in Coventry, which is much too far to the north to be on the route. It came to Gray, Shakespeare could not really be a Stratford man. The descriptions of the countryside in the works related mainly to woodland. The Master of Jesus felt that wherever the poet had been born or baptised, he had grown up amongst woods, whereas the country around Stratford was of a bare, Cotswold type, unlike that with which the poet seemed familiar. Becoming suspicious, Gray now made an inventory of the place-names occurring in the works, and found none at all on the route from Stratford to London, whether one took the road through Oxford or through High Wycombe. He did not think the poet could have travelled that road. But there was a road along which he found place-names. It was the road that entered London from the due north. Starting from the London end this time, the Master of Jesus began plotting all the places named along this road, to see where it would lead. He found Barnet (two references), St. Albans (the greatest cluster), then Stony Stratford, on the Buckinghamshire-Northamptonshire border (one reference), Daventry, in Northamptonshire (one reference) and Sutton Coldfield, in the extreme north of Warwickshire (one reference). He noticed this was not far from Polesworth, in the well wooded northern-most tip of the county where it met with Leicestershire, Staffordshire and Derbyshire, where Michael Drayton had been a page, and suggested

Shakespeare must have been transferred there, likewise to be a page. This notion has not received support, and the Master of Jesus failed to notice he was playing into Baconian hands. He did not think of Bacon, with his home in the oakwood off St. Albans.

Bacon would, of course, have come into London through Barnet, and would have used the northward extension of the road when he wished to go north, as for instance to visit his early constituency at Liverpool, to which it leads in the end.

Also curious among the early historical plays is *King John,* where the King is eclipsed in interest by the Bastard. What drove our poet to create out of the sketchiest historical sources a character at once cynical and loyal, and who gave up his Faulconbridge inheritance to his apparent brother, the legitimate son of the late Sir Robert Faulconbridge, on learning that he himself was the bastard of Richard Coeur de Lion? If Bacon was the son of Elizabeth and Leicester, and that was the reason for Sir Nicholas' leaving him unprovided, the situation is extraordinarily like his own.

1. Portrait by François Clouet, in the Musée Condé.
2. *William Shakespeare,* A.L. Rowse (Macmillan, 1963), p.213.

CHAPTER 25

Fool's garb

WHY should Bacon have wished to ''shift'' his dramatic and poetic work to another's name? In the ages before printing, a book was the treasure of a rich man or of a monastery, each copy being made by hand; slowly, exquisitely. A gentleman might show a few verses in his own hand, but unless he permitted the making of copies, the readership could not go beyond the individuals he favoured with this exposition of his sentiments. Printing made possible the circulation to persons not known. The press was first used for the Bible, in Latin. The first sizeable non-religious book to be printed, on blocks separately cast for each letter, was the *Catholicon* (Mainz, 1460). Since that date, secular printing had gathered momentum, but to place something of one's own personal composition upon some stall so that a copy might be taken up by any person who put down the price marked, that was still felt, even in Elizabethan days, an exposure tantamount to vulgarism. Prefaces of the period tend to be excusatory. The writer had intended the work for private circulation only, but had been urged by others to have it published; or copies had come to be in circulation which misrepresented his thought, and so he was obliged to publish the correct text. Where the theatre was concerned, the vulgarisation was greater, the cheaper seats being within the purchasing power of illiterates.

To write for such an audience might be considered evidence of a levity, such as would go against a man who was a candidate for public office; especially if he allowed himself great freedom:

The purgative Jaques declares his need for disguise:

> I am ambitious for a motley coat.
> . . . I must haue liberty
> Withall, as large a charter as the winde,
> To blow on whom I please . . .
> Inuest me in my motley; giue me leaue
> To speake my mind, and I will through and through
> Cleanse the foule body of th' infected world.
>
> *As You Like It, II, vii, 43-60*
> *Var: 45-63*

But in Jaques our poet seems also to be satirising himself. Orsino suffered from a love melancholy. Jaques avers his is not a love melancholy, nor any other melancholy of known kind, ''but it is a melancholy all of my own, compounded of many simples.'' (IV, i, 15-

1. Sir Francis Bacon as Lord High Chancellor (something is hanging from his collar that cannot be seen). Engraved by Francis Hall after an old print by Simon Pass.

2. Sir Nicholas Bacon. Oil by an unknown artist. *(The Master, Fellows and Scholars of Corpus Christi College, Cambridge)*

3. Lady Bacon (born Anne Cooke). Oil attributed to George Gower. *(Reproduced from The Gorhambury Collection by permission of the Earl of Verulam)*

4. Robert Dudley, Earl of Leicester. Oil by an unknown artist. *(National Portrait Gallery)*

5. Queen Elizabeth. The "Ditchley Portrait", September 1592. Oil by
Michael Gheeraerts the Younger. *(National Portrait Gallery)*

6. Part of the Northumberland manuscript. The word "comfort" is left of the centre, close to the lower bracket. *(Duke of Northumberland – Alnwick Castle)*

7. *(right)* Bacon's letter to Michael Hicks about the funeral of Lady Bacon. The word "comfort" begins on line 12. *(British Museum)*

8. Portrait of Queen Elizabeth by A. van der Werff. *(The Board of Trinity College, Dublin)*

16). Is not this self-mockery? Bacon had avowed the ''melancholy planet'' carried him away from practical affairs. Had he, however, been only Orsino and Jaques, he would have gone under. But perhaps he escapes, also, into Touchstone, the professional fool, who by his down-to-earth wit – the touchstone of reality against which can be seen the extravagancies of the romantics – is obviously a survivor. He, too, is an exile from the Court, unexpectedly contended with his odd little country Muse. Audrey voices what may be his own doubt whether poetry is honest; and he seems to be in some uncertainty whether he wants to be tied to her in such a way as to be unable to escape the connection – she is also involved with a swain, William – but accepts with resignation his destiny to be married to her, ''foul'' and ''an ill-fauoured thing'' – perhaps because writing for the theatre was a foul and ill-favoured thing relative to the proper expectations of one born royal – ''but mine own''. (V, iv. 60).

The main characters of *As You Like It* are all out of the romance *Rosalynde or Euphues' Golden Legacy*, by Thomas Lodge – except that the line

> So holy and so perfect is my love
>
> *III, v, 99*

lent to Silvius, so perfectly translates the beginning of one of the most beautiful of all Dante's poems:[1]

> *Tanto gentile e tanto onesta pare*
> *La donna mia*

as to suggest a reminiscence.

But Jaques, Touchstone, Audrey and William are all our poet's own creations.

---

1. *La Vita Nuova, Sonetto XV, Il Saluto.* Dante's accompanying prose makes plain that by *gentile* and *honesta* he means gracious and holy as the Angels are.

CHAPTER 26

The tooth out

FRANCIS was still waiting for the Queen to make a decision as to the Solicitorship. Even Lady Bacon, often critical of Francis, wrote on January 23rd, 1594/5 to Anthony saying that Francis was "but strangely used . . . ''. She had, she said, obtained an interview with Robert Cecil (Lord Burghley's son) to discuss the matter, travelling from Gorhambury for the purpose, but all the young Cecil had to say was, "Experience teacheth that her Majesty's nature is not to resolve but to delay.'' His only advice, not very helpful, was that Francis should "bear delay as accustomed''.

Francis by this time felt certain Cecil was secretly working against him. Only a few days before Lady Bacon wrote to Anthony, he had written to Anthony himself,[1] "Good brother, Since I saw you this hath passed . . . '' He had been sent for by Cecil as if from the Queen and told she had said she would "seek all England for a solicitor rather than take me'', also that she had said she had "pulled me over the bar (note the words, for they cannot be her own) . . . ''

Presumably, to "pull someone over the bar'' was linguistic jargon, slang of the Inns of Court, with which the Queen would not have been familiar. In short, Francis suspects Cecil is working against him.

There is an undated letter from Francis to Cecil, perhaps written just after this, in which, abruptly, he exposed his suspicions to the suspect:[2]

Sir,

Your Honour knoweth my manner is, though it be not the wisest way, yet taking it for the honestest, to do as Alexander did by his physician, in drinking the medicine and delivering the advertisement of suspicion. So I trust on, and yet do not smother what I hear. I do assure you, Sir, that by a wise friend of mine, and not factious toward your Honour, I was told with asseveration that your Honour was bought by Mr. Coventry for two thousand angels; and that you wrought in a contrary spirit to my Lord your father. And he said further, that from your servants, from your Lady, from some counsellors that hath served you in my business, he knew you wrought underhand against me. The truth of which tale I do not believe. You know the event will show, and God will right. But as I reject this report (though the strangeness of my case might make me credulous), so I admit a conceit that the last messenger my Lord and yourself used dealt ill with your Honours; and that word (*speculation*) which was in the Queen's mouth, rebounded from him as a commendation; for I am not ignorant of those little arts. Therefore I pray, trust not him again in my matter. This was much to write . . .

The reference to "speculation'' is curious. It has been sugggested that the Queen hesitated to appoint Francis because his interest in philosophy made her think he had a speculative rather than a practical mind; it may be Francis is letting Cecil know he thinks it is he who, by referring to him always as a man of philosophical speculation, is teaching her to suppose him unfit to handle practical matters.

In a letter to Burghley[3] written on March 21st he said that he had probably been too credulous of hearsay concerning the younger Cecil. Yet in exposing his suspicions he must, even if all was healed on the surface, have given an affront that would not be forgiven.

To a friend, Fulke Greville, he wrote that the matter of the Solicitorship was still "in endless question." He began to feel that he was like a piece of stuff in a shop that had been bespoken but which the customer now did not want to take. "For to be, as I told you, like a child following a bird, who when he is nearest flieth away and lighteth a little before, and then the child after it again, and so on ad infinitum . . ."[4]

The Easter term reached its end, and Francis went back, as usual in the vacations, to Twickenham.

He thought the trouble was the Queen had never forgiven him that speech in Parliament, and wrote about it to Burghley, asking to put in a word for him with her that would be "a good tide to remove her from that shelf".[5]

To Essex he wrote almost with resignation:[6]

. . . desiring your good Lordship . . . not to conceive out of this my dilligence in soliciting this matter that I am either much in appetite or much in hope. For as for appetite, the waters of Parnassus are not like the waters of the Spaw, that give a stomach, but rather they quench appetite and desires.

The waters of Parnassus are those of inspiration. He must have been writing poetry, a sustained work that took away his appetite for worldly place. Essex, then, must have been one of those who knew about his poetic authorship.

July, August and September passed, and still a Solicitor was not appointed. By the middle of October, Francis must have got wind that a decision had been made, perhaps against him, for he wrote to the Lord Keeper (Sir John Puckering) with philosophy:[7]

It may please your Lordship,

I conceive the end already made, which will I trust be to me a beginning of good fortune, or at least of content. Her Majesty by God's grace shall live and reign long. She is not running away, I may trust her. Or whether she look towards me or no, I remain the same, not altered in my intention. If I had been an ambitious man, it would have overthrown me . . .

From Twickenham Park, this 14th of October . . .

Fr. Bacon

On November 4th, 1595, a new Solicitor was appointed. He was

Serjeant Fleming.

Francis had been kept waiting for two years and nine months.

One person who did not take the disappointment with equanimity was Essex. It was a setback to him, personally, not only because it would have helped him to have Francis in a high place but because, having been a suitor for him to the Queen, her choice of a man other than the one he put forward showed to the world that she was capable of denying something to Essex. As the favourite, it lessened his prestige.

One can let Francis tell in his own words, as he did nine years later, how Essex came to give him the news:[8]

After the Queen had denied me the Solicitor's place, for the which his Lordship had been a long and earnest suitor on my behalf, it pleased him to come from Richmond to Twickenham Park, and brake with me, and said, "Master Bacon, the Queen hath denied me yon place for you, and hath placed another; I know you are the least part of your own matter, but you fare ill because you have chosen me for your mean and dependence; you have spent your time and thoughts in my matters: I die (these were his very words) if I do not somewhat towards your fortune: you shall not deny to accept a piece of land which I will bestow upon you." My answer I remember was, that for my fortune it was no great matter, but that his Lordship's offer made me to call to mind what was wont to be said when I was in France of the Duke of Guise, that he was the greatest usurer in France, because he had turned all his estate into obligations; meaning that he had left himself nothing, but only had bound numbers of persons to him. "Now, my Lord," said I, "I would not have you imitate his course, nor turn your state thus by great gifts into obligations, for you will find many bad debtors." He bade me take no care for that, and pressed it: whereupon I said, "My Lord, I see I must be your homager and hold land of your gift: but do you know the manner of doing homage in law? Always it is with a saving of his faith to the king and his other lords: and therefore, my Lord (said I) I can be no more yours than I was, and it must be with the ancient savings: and if I grow to be a rich man, you will give me leave to give it back to some of your unrewarded followers.

There is a very peculiar, indeed a very sinister implication here. Why should it have been necessary to mention "the ancient savings" concerning loyalty to the sovereign unless something in Essex's words or manner had shown – even at this early date – a half formed wish to spite the Queen?

Francis, in accepting a gift of land in compensation for the time he had been kept waiting, has to make it plain his prime loyalty must always be to the Queen.

The same note of warning is discernible in a letter he wrote to Essex, undated, but thought to have been written a day or two after the conversation described:[9]

It may please your good Lordship,
I pray God her Majesty's weighing be not like the weight of a balance; *gravia*

deorsum, levia sursum. But I am as far from being altered in devotion towards her, as I am from distrust that she will be altered in opinion towards me, when she knoweth me better. For myself, I have lost some opinion, some time, and some means; this is my account; . . . for time, it is true, it goeth and cometh not; but yet I have learned that it may be redeemed.

For means, I value that most; and the rather because I am purposed not to follow the practice of the law (If her Majesty command me in any particular, I shall be ready to do her willing service), and my reason is only, because it drinketh too much time, which I have dedicated to better purposes. But even for that point of estate and means, I partly lean to Thales opinion, that a philosopher may be rich if he will . . . but without any such high conceit, I esteem it like the pulling out of an aching tooth, which, I remember, when I was a child and had little philosophy, I was glad of when it was done. For your Lordship, I do think myself more beholden to you than to any man. And I say, I reckon myself as a *common* (not popular, but *common*) and as much as is lawful to be enclosed of a common, so much your Lordship shall be sure to have.

Your Lordship's, to obey your honourable commands,

(The Latin means "heavy things down, light things up"). What does he mean by "a common"? He can hardly be referring to the enclosure of common lands, a grievance to the common people who had grazed their livestock on them, which had caused some trouble in the reign of Queen Mary and was destined tóbecome, in that of Charles I, one of the causes contributory to the Civil War. Neither can he mean he is a member of the House of Commons; that would be too obvious and too pointless. Surely, he is opposing the notion of common to that of noble or royal, and why should he do that in the context of loyalty to the Queen? This would be pointless unless indeed Francis and Essex are both sons of the Queen. If that is the situation, Francis is resisting an undertow of suggestion in Essex' remarks that they should combine to seize their inheritance. Francis will have none of it. In loyalty to her, he accepts the status of a commoner.

But, if this is the meaning, how long had the secret of their birth been known to both? We have seen that *A Midsummer Night's Dream* shows Leicester must have told Francis. But Essex cannot have known when he wrote an undated letter to the Queen:[10]

Madam – The delights of this place [Croydon] cannot make me unmindful of one in whose secret company I have joyed as much as the happiest man doth in his highe contentment, and if my horse would run as fast as my thoughts do fly, I would as often make mine eyes rich in beholding the treasures of my love, as my desires do triumph when I seem to myself in a strong imagination to conquer your resisting will . . . as humble to do you service as in my love I am ambitious . . .

or when he wrote to her (again undated):[11]

Most dear Lady – Your kind and often sending is able either to preserve a sick man or rather to raise a man that were more than half dead to life again. Since I was first so happy as to know what love meant, I was never one day, nor one hour, free from hope and jealousy . . .

The imagery is lover-like and even sexual.

He would in any case hardly have written in these terms until after Leicester's death. Leicester must, then, have died without telling Essex. He had preferred to tell Francis, despite less ease of access. He was the elder, and therefore, should the Queen ever be persuaded to recognise them, first in line of succession to the throne. Also, he was infinitely the more sensible, self-controlled and discreet. Essex being such a hot-head, Leicester might have thought it better he knew nothing about it, unless circumstances should arise in which Francis deemed it needful to tell him. After Leicester's death, the Queen's increasing devotion to Essex, and Essex' evident misunderstanding of the nature of her love for him, may have made Francis feel acutely uncomfortable. He may have felt he had to tell him, to prevent his assaulting his own mother, unknowingly, like Oedipus.

If this is what happened, Francis must have told Essex between Leicester's death, in 1588, and Essex' marriage, in 1590. Essex may have married on the rebound from an emotional shock. At any rate, Essex must surely have known when he asked the astrologer for a horoscope for his yet unchristened son, born in January, 1591, and for one for himself, at the same time, giving to the astrologer birth-data which Leicester must have obtained from the Queen and given to Francis. Leicester believed in astrology, and therefore would have wished to know both the place and the hour of his second son's arrival.

Mr. Robert Lacey, in his interesting biography of Essex, seeks to discover what went wrong with him, and suggests that his want of judgement and unbalanced behaviour from a certain moment might be attributable to syphilitic dementia, if as Dr. Lopez alleged, he acquired the disease. As he did have promiscuous contacts, this is not impossible; but the sudden disclosure of a deeply Oedipal situation could, by itself or in addition, have thrown him off keel. Francis, having had to cope first with Essex' embarrassing wooing of the Queen, would now be faced with his suddenly exaggerated disaffection for her. He is now saying that his own course will be one of loyalty to her, and that it is with this reservation he accepts the piece of land Essex gives him.

The whereabouts of the piece of land Essex gave him, and which he sold for £1,000, is not known for certain. Essex had property in Herefordshire, Essex, London and Twickenham. The piece of land he gave Francis cannot have been in Twickenham Park, as loosely stated by Bushell, though it may have adjoined it. Twickenham Park, with its lodge,[12] was Crown Property, and it was the Queen who now granted to Francis Bacon the reversion of it, when the present lease, to one Milo

Dodding, should in twenty-one years time run out. It was as a sub-tenant of Milo Dodding that Francis lived in it, paying him a rent of twelve guineas (£6,300) a year. The Queen probably felt that by giving Francis the reversion, she was making it up to him for not having made him Solicitor.[13]

He planted a row of alders, to strengthen the bank. The Lodge was on a pretty bend of the river, almost opposite and just downstream of the royal Palace at Richmond, in which the Queen spent so much of her time – so that, although she appeared unenthusiastic about him, she took this way to keep him near to herself, where their comings and goings could be seen by each other.

He planted a herb garden, where doubtless he built up that practical knowledge of herbs, and their uses, which so liberally transpired through his later philosophical works.

More detailed evidence of Francis' love for gardens can be found at Gray's Inn. Here, the pension book records that in 1598 he persuaded the Fellows that ''our back field'' should become a garden, and that they could afford it. The ''field'' was more extensive then than now. What is today Raymond Buildings stands on a rise. The rise is artificial. Oral tradition says it was Francis Bacon who, considering a completely flat expanse inartistic, directed some sculpting of the ground and, in particular, the creation of this rise, as a bank whereon might be displayed to advantage low-growing flowers, particularly violets. The pension book for 1598 records the amounts spent on gardeners' wages, on tools, and on the purchase of elm trees, birch trees, beech trees, sycamores, oziers and apple trees and privet; on woodbines (honeysuckles), eglantines (single petaled hedge roses); violets, primroses and pinks; to be supplemented in the following year by further trees, eglantines, sweetbriars and red roses (presumably damask). The plants and the numbers of each had been selected by Bacon himself. Already he was beginning the experiments which would give Gray's Inn roses flowering through the winter. Left of a central walk was all flowers, tended by Bacon himself, on the right, a lawn.

On the lawn is still cherished today an elderly, sprawling catalpa tree. It is believed to have grown from a seed, brought from Virginia by Sir Walter Raleigh and planted in Gray's Inn garden by Francis Bacon.

1. Lambeth MSS, 650, f.28.
2. Lambeth MSS, 650, f.31.
3. British Museum Lansdowne MSS, lxxviii, f.74.
4. Rawley's *Resuscitatio*, p.89.
5. British Museum, Additional MSS, 5503, p.1 b.
6. *Resuscitatio*, William Rawley, Supplement P.85; Spedding VIII, p.345.
7. British Museum, Harleian MSS, 6897, F.119.
8. *Apologie* . . . Spedding X, p.143-4.
9. *Resuscitatio*, Supplement, p.111.

10. and 11. *Lives of the Earls of Essex,* Walter Bouchier Devereux, Vol.1, Letters CXXXVII, p.292, and CXLIV, p.495.

12. Nothing remains of Twickenham Lodge. On the site are now only small modern houses with thin gardens, fenced off individually.

13. A number of works carry the incorrect statement that Essex gave Bacon Twickenham Park Lodge.

CHAPTER 27

Warning to Essex

ESSEX wrote violently to the Lord Keeper that Francis was not made for an idle life; he called idle a life not spent in public affairs. He commended the care of his advancement to the Lord Keeper as he himself would be away.

In June he was setting out with the fleet for Spain. The former Henry of Navarre, now Henri IV of France, had asked the English for help as the Spaniards were now attacking Calais; even while men were being mustered, Calais had fallen into Spanish hands. This the English could not accept inactively, for Calais was far too close a jumping-off point for our own white cliffs. Elizabeth sent the English fleet Spainwards to attack the Spanish fleet in its own waters. It defeated the Spanish fleet off Cadiz, a landing was made and Cadiz occupied, largely through the initiative of Essex. He wanted to stay, but it was no part of Elizabeth's plan to have an English garrison permanently stationed upon Spanish soil and she called him home. He obeyed the order to withdraw from Spain, but gave the impression it was reluctantly, as though he felt his wings had been clipped before he had been able to open them to their full span. On the fleet's return, he found himself the hero of Cadiz. Yet some felt that he bore a grudge against the Queen.

It was in these circumstances that Francis wrote him, in the autumn, a very severe warning:[1]

My singular good Lord,
I will no longer dissever part of that which I meant to have said to your Lordship at Barn-Elms from the *exordium*[2] which I then made. Whereunto I will only add this; that I humbly desire your Lordship, before you give access to my poor advice . . . to consider, first, whether I have not reason to think that your fortune comprehendeth mine. Next, whether I shift my counsel . . . Thirdly, whether you have taken hurt at any time by my careful and devoted counsel . . . I suppose you do since believe that it did much attemper a cold malignant humour then growing upon her Majesty towards your Lordship . . . I said to your Lordship last time, *Martha, Martha, attendis ad plurima, unum sufficit,*[3] win the Queen: if this be not the beginning, of any other course I see no end. And I will not speak of favour of affection, but of other correspondence and agreableness . . . But how is it now? A man of a nature not to be ruled; that hath the advantage of my affection, and knoweth it; of an estate not grounded to his greatness; of a popular reputation; of a military dependence; I demand whether there can be a more dangerous image than this represented to any monarch living, much more to a lady, and of her Majesty's apprehension? And is it not more evident than demonstration itself,

that whilst this impression continueth in her Majesty's breast, you can find no other condition than inventions to keep your estate bare and low; crossing and disgracing your actions; extenuating and blasting of your merit; carping with contempt at your nature and fashions; breeding, nourishing and fortifying such instruments as are most factious against you; repulses and scorns of your friends and dependents that are true and steadfast; winning and inveigling away from you such as are flexible and wavering; thrusting you into odious employments and offices, to supplant your reputation; abusing you and feeding you with dalliances and demonstrations, to divert you from descending into serious consideration of your own case; yea and percase venturing you in perilous and desperate enterprises. Herein it may please your Lordship to understand me; for I mean nothing less than that these things should be plotted and intended as in her Majesty's royal mind towards you; I know the excellency of her nature too well. But I say, wheresoever the formerly described impression is taken in any King's breast towards a subject, these other recited inconveniences must, of necessity of politic consequence, follow . . .

For the removing the impression of your nature to be *opiniastre* and not rulable: First and above all things I wish that all matters past, which cannot be revoked, your Lordship would turn altogether upon insatisfaction, and not upon your nature or proper disposition. This string you cannot upon every apt occasion harp upon too much . . . Next, whereas I have noted you to fly and avoid . . . the resemblance or imitation of my Lord of Leicester and my Lord Chancellor Hatton; yet I am persuaded . . . that it will do you much good between the Queen and you, to allege them . . . for authors and patterns. For I do not know a readier mean to make her Majesty think you are in the right way. Thirdly, when at any time your Lordship upon occasion happen to speeches to do her Majesty right, . . . I fear you handle it . . . so that a man may read formality in your countenance; whereas your Lordship should do it familiarly . . . Fourthly, your Lordship should never be without some particulars afoot, which you should seem to pursue with earnestness and affection, and then let them fall, upon taking knowledge of her Majesty's opposition and dislike . . .

The impression of greatest prejudice next, is that of a militar dependence. Wherein I cannot sufficiently wonder at your Lordship's course; that you say, the wars are your occupation . . . For her Majesty loveth peace. Next, she loveth not change. Thirdly, that kind of dependence maketh a suspected greatness. Therefore . . . let that be a sleeping honour awhile, and cure the Queen's mind in that point. Therefore again, whereas I heard your Lordship designing to yourself the Earl Marshal's place, or the place of Master of the Ordnance, I did not in my mind so well like of either; because of their affinity with a martial greatness. But of the places now void, in my judgement and discretion, I would mention the place of the Lord Privy Seal . . . it is a fine honour, quiet place, worth a thousandpound a year . . . And it fits a favourite to carry her Majesty's image in seal, who beareth it best expressed in heart. But my chief reason is that which I first alleged, to divert her Majesty from this impression of a martial greatness . . .

The third impression is of a popular reputation; which because it is a thing good in itself, being obtained as your Lordship obtaineth it . . . is one of the best flowers of your greatness both present and to come; it would be handled tenderly. The only way to quench it is *verbis*[4] and not *rebus*[5] . . .

For the fifth and last, which is of the advantage of a favourite; as, severed from the rest, it cannot hurt; so, joined with then, it maketh her Majesty more fearful and shadowy, as not knowing her own strength. The only remedy to this is, to give way to some other favourite, as in particular you shall find her Majesty inclined . . . And so I rest . . . October 4, 1596.

He is warning Essex he could lose his head.

Anthony was his comfort. At the beginning of February, 1596/7, he dedicated to "Mr. Anthony Bacon, his dear brother" his first, slender published volume of *Essays,* later to be so much expanded.

About the same time, he wrote a fragment, The *Colours of Good and Evil,* commentaries upon certain of Aristotle's dicta.

Shortly afterwards, he published his *Meditationes Sacrae:* whereof, "But if evil overtake your enemy from elsewhere, and you in the innermost recesses of your heart are grieved and distressed, and feel no touch of joy, as thinking that the day of your revenge and redress has come; – this I account to be the summit and exhaltation of Charity."

1. *Resuscitatio,* Supplement, p.106 ff.
2. Introductory part of a speech.
3. Thou art careful and troubled about many things: But one thing is needful (St. Luke, X. 41-42).
4. In words.
5. In deeds.

CHAPTER 28

The return for Southampton

ON September 26th, 1597, Bacon was returned as Member of Parliament for Southampton.

How did this come about? In the archives of Southampton, his name does not even appear in the book of burgess admissions. Whose influence was responsible? Unless a gentleman in the district was so eminent as to need no introducer, it was usually the person of most sway who made a recommendation. This need not be for a local man, though he would usually be invited to come and meet the local gentry at a small and friendly gathering, it was the great person's recommendation which secured the adoption. Who was the great person? Neither Burghley nor Essex had influence in Southampton, and I would think it was the Earl of Southampton.

Three weeks later, on October 18th, Francis was returned as the Member for Ipswich, here his proposer being Essex. Double returns were not unusual, though normally the person elected for two constituencies would have to choose which he would represent. Sir John Neale thought Francis would have chosen Ispwich,[1] but if he gave up Southampton it must have gone unrepresented. In the records of the House of Commons, the Member for Southampton in the Parliament of 1597-98 is Francis Bacon.[2] It looks as if he was allowed to keep both seats.

1. Sir John Neale, letter to myself.
2. Discovered for me by the late Baroness Ward of North Tyneside, C.H., D,B.E , then Dame Irene of the Lower House and confirmed for me by Mr. John Palmer, Research Division of the House of Commons Library, letter to myself.

CHAPTER 29

A lady richly left

THERE is a letter from Francis to Essex, undated, but written, Spedding thinks, in 1597, in which he says:[1]

I brake with your Lordship myself at the Tower, and I take it my brother hath since renewed the same motion, touching a fortune I was in thought to attempt *in genere oeconommico.*[2] *In genere politico*[3] certain winds have blown contrary. My suit to your Lordship is for your several letters to be left with me, dormant, to the gentlewoman and either of her parents . . .

Spedding believes the gentlewoman to have been Lady Hatton, whom the recent death of Sir Christopher had left a glistening prize, for which, on account of her enormous wealth, there was likely to be competition.

It was usual in those days to think of money in connection with marriage. The ideal of the poor girl, burdened with no dowry save of her virtue, is Victorian. In the time of Elizabeth, if a woman brought a fortune, it was important amongst her charms.

That he asked Essex to act for him does not mean he did not know her. Since she was the daughter of Burghley's eldest son Thomas Cecil, it is more likely they had known each other long on cousinly terms. Until far later than Elizabethan days (as readers of Pepys' Diary will recall) it was usual, amongst persons of high rank, to avoid the bluntness of a proposal face to face, with the risk of possible rebuff, by asking a friend or relative first to broach the matter to the parents of the lady. Then, if there was a refusal, or negotiations concerning the financial settlement broke down, there was no reason for the principals to be embarrassed, not having been involved directly.

The next we hear of Francis, he had been arrested for debt. It happened at a most inopportune moment, in more senses than one. There had been another plot to murder the Queen, this time by smearing her saddle with poison. As before when there was a plot against her life, Francis had to go to the Tower to assist in the interrogation of the accused. It was as he was leaving the Tower after one of these sessions that he was arrested.

He wrote at once to Sir Thomas Egerton, who had succeeded Sir Christopher Hatton as Lord Keeper of the Great Seal:[4]

It may please your Lordship,
I am to make humble complaint to your Lordship of some hard dealing offered me by one Sympson, a goldsmith, a man noted much, as I have heard, for extremities and stoutness upon his purse; but yet I could hardly have imagined, he

would have dealt . . . so contemputuously towards her Majesty's service. For this Lombard (pardon me . . . if being admonished by the street he dwells in, I give him that name) having me in bond for £300 principal, and I having the last term confessed the action, and by his full and direct consent respited the satisfaction till the beginning of this term to come, without ever giving me warning either by letter or message, served an execution upon me, having trained me at such time as I came from the Tower, where, Mr. Waad can witness, we attended a service of no mean importance. Neither would he so much as vouchsafe to come and speak with me . . . though I sent for him, diverse times, and his house was just by . . . He would have urged it to have had me in prison, which he had done, had not the sheriff More, to whom I sent, gently recommended me to a handsome house in Coleman Street, where I now am.

And to Robert Cecil, now Secretary of State, he wrote:[5]

It may please your Honour,
I humbly pray you to understand how badly I have been used by the enclosed, a copy of a letter of complaint thereof, which I have written to the Lord Keeper. How sensitive you are of wrongs offered to your blood in my particular, I have had not long since experience. But herein I think your Honour will be doubly sensitive, in tenderness also of the indignity to her Majesty's service. For as for me, Mr. Sympson might have had me every day in London; and therefore to belay me, while he knew I came from the Tower about her Majesty's special service, was to my understanding very bold. And two days before he brags he forbore me, because I dined with sheriff More. So as with Mr. Sympson, examinations at the Tower are not so great a privilege, *eundo et redendo,*[6] as sheriff More's dinner . . .
From Coleman Street, this 24th of September [1598]

Fr. Bacon

The incident can have set him back in the eyes of Lady Hatton. Two months afterwards, on November 7th, 1598, she married Sir Edward Coke, whom the Queen had preferred to Bacon for Attorney General.

The Merchant of Venice, though not printed for another two years, was entered in the Stationer's Register in July, 1598, which is two months before Bacon's arrest but he had obviously been under pressure from Sympson for some time; also, the play may not have reached the form we know by July. The entry may have been to prevent anybody else from using a theme borrowed from Marlowe's *Jew of Malta* at a time when the Lopez affair had given the English an unpleasing image of Jewry. Shakespeare scholars tend to think Shylock was modelled on Lopez, but it was Bacon who had the opportunity to know Lopez at close quarters, since he was one of those who examined him in the Tower. Having had, in 1598, to interrogate in a second case of attempting the Queen's life by poison had probably put him in the mind of the first, and the personality of Sympson may have fused with that of Lopez. There are in *The Merchant of Venice* several elements to be found in Bacon's situation at that moment. There is the ''lady richly left'', the heiress, by marriage to whom Bassanio hopes to redress his fortunes, there is Bassanio's being already in debt, there is the monstrous money-lender, and there is Antonio.

Anthony Bacon had time and time again to advance Francis money or pay his debts; he had even to mortgage part of his own estate to do it. The "pound of flesh" is in Marlowe's *Jew of Malta,* and also in *Il Pecorone,* by Ser Giovanni Fiorentino, which had not been translated into English but which Professor Bullough believes Shakespeare to have consulted in the Italian, and indeed used for his main source.[7] Francis may well have felt it was a pound of flesh Anthony had to mortgage on his behalf. Antonio has one very strange line, not explained by Shakespeare scholars, "I am a tainted wether of the flock, meetest for death", IV, i, 114-15. Why "tainted"? Anthony Bacon had whilst abroad been charged with sodomy, and Dame Daphne du Maurier believes that though not guilty he was by nature homosexual. Such a man, however chastely living, may well have felt himself tainted. In the happy ending, when the other three young men are paired with three girls, only Antonio, after whom the play is named, is unprovided with a wife.

1. *Resuscitatio,* Supplement, p.112.
2. In economic kind.
3. In political kind.
4. *Letters, Speeches* etc of Lord Bacon, Murdin; 1763.
5. Ibid.
6. Going and coming.
7. *Narrative and Dramatic Sources of Shakespeare,* Geoffrey Bullough, I, p.449.

CHAPTER 30

Essex and Southampton leave for Ireland

ESSEX had become Earl Marshal in December, 1597. It was the post Francis had warned him not to seek, lest it made him appear in the Queen's eyes minded to war. It was not only before the Queen he cut such an image. Burghley, now an old man, and his son, the younger Cecil, were both peace-minded, and when Henri IV of France concluded a peace with Spain, they thought Elizabeth could join in the treaty to be signed with Phillip. Essex wanted England to continue the war against Spain. Old Burghley, at almost the last Council meeting he attended, laid his prayer-book before Essex, opening it at the 55th psalm and pointing to the words, "Bloodthirsty and deceitful men shall not live out half their days". The words were meant for Essex.

Essex became only the more high-handed. In Ireland there rose a rebellion, led by the Earl of Tyrone. Essex urged the Queen to send Sir George Carew to quell it. She chose, instead, Sir William Knollys. Essex was furious that she had not accepted his choice. A June day in 1598 witnessed a scene. The Court was at Greenwich. Essex repeated his recommendation she should send Carew. She repeated she would send Knollys. Unbelievably, Essex turned his back on his Sovereign, to walk out of the room. She flew after him, and boxed his ears. He put his hand on his sword as if to draw it on her. Lord Nottingham rushed forward to prevent him, and he dashed from the room, and made for his country house at Wanstead.

It has been suggested that lines in *Much Ado About Nothing,* thought to have been composed during this year, refer to Essex' behaviour at this time:

> the pleached bower
> Where honeysuckles, ripen'd by the sunne,
> Forbid the sunne to enter, like fauourites
> Made proud by princes, that aduance their pride
> Against that power that bred it.
>
> *III, i, 7–11*
> *Var: 9–13*

Julius Caesar, first performed and probably composed in the same year, reads in the context like a warning to Essex not to allow himself to become involved with malcontents, such as Charles Danvers, Christopher Blount and Henry Cuffe, in conspiracy against the Sovereign. They would use his grievance to their own ends, and he could be drawn upon a disastrous course. The analogy was the more exact in that there has always been an idea Brutus was the son of Caesar, who had a relationship with his mother, favoured him and even gave him a command after receiving most deep offence.[1]

Essex' sulking in Wanstead was awkward for the Queen's other advisers. Decisions had to be taken by the Council, so that in his refuge he was holding things up. An anonymous letter thrown in at his window by a well-wisher advised him he was not acting in his own interests by absenting himself, for if he did not come to the Council table decisions would be taken without him.

The Queen's mind was at this moment occupied by Lord Burghley's last illness. When at the end of August he passed away, she was seen to weep.

In the end, she did not send Knollys to Ireland, she sent Essex. Francis tried to dissuade him from going into Ireland, but when the matter was decided wrote him a letter bidding him remember:[2]

that merit is worthier than fame . . . that obedience is better than sacrifice . . . as it is most fit for you to desire convenient liberty of instructions, so it is no less fit for you to observe the due limits . . . that the exceeding of them may not only procure in case of adverse accident a dangerous disavow, but also in case of prosperous success be subject to interpretation, as if all were not referred to the right end.

This is not the vein in which one of the Queen's lesser servants wrote to his patron. It is obvious the real relationship was by this time quite different.

Francis was not alone in feeling apprehensive of the outcome. Sir John Harrington received a letter from a friend at Court saying:[3]

I hear you are to go to Ireland with the Lieutenant, Essex . . . Observe the man who commandeth . . . he goeth not forth to serve the Queen's realm, but to humour his own revenge . . . though the Queen hath granted forgiveness for his late demeanour in her presence, we know not what to think hereof. She hath in all outward semblance placed confidence in the man . . . but I sore fear what may happen hereafter.

When Essex set off, on March 27th, 1599, he took with him the Earl of Southampton, and, against the Queen's express commandment, made him his Captain of the Horse.

---

1. Suetonius, *Caesar*, 50, 2, Plutarch, *Brutus*, 5, Appian, *Civil Wars*, II, 112.
2. British Museum, Additional MSS 5503, f.6.
3. *Nugae Antiquae*, I, 240; Spedding IX, p.133.

CHAPTER 31

Falstaff

WHILE Southampton was away, his young wife (Elizabeth Vernon) went to stay with her sister-in-law, Lady Penelope Rich, at Chartley the Devereux's property in Staffordshire. From there, she wrote Southampton several letters. All beginning ''My deare Lorde and only love of my life,'' they are fond little letters and contain, for the most part, nothing she could ever have imagined to interest any but her husband and herself. She had hoped she was going to have another baby, but her condition is not as she had thought. But there is one, dated June, in which, having come to an end at the foot of the page, she has turned the sheet upside down to add, above the salutation, a postscript:[1]

All the news I can send you that I thinke will make you merry is that I reade in a letter from London that Sir John Falstaffe is by his mrs. dame pintpot made father of a godly milers thumb, a boie thats all heade and veri litel body – but this is a secret.

In *I King Henry IV,* II, iv, 438, Falstaff addresses Mistress Quickly as ''pintpot''. The young Countess' letter, therefore, tells us there were two living persons, known to Southampton and herself by the names of Falstaff and Quickly or ''pintpot''. Taken by itself, the passage would only tell us that Southampton had infected his wife with his enthusiasm for the plays, and that she was sufficiently conversant to know who Falstaff and ''pintpot'' were. It could not tell us who were the persons to whom they had given these nicknames.

But there is a clue, and it is amongst Sir Tobie Matthew's letters to Francis Bacon, of which he was to write many, unfortunately undated, so that we do not know exactly at what date the young son of the Archbishop of York came into Bacon's life. That he was already close enough to the Southamptons to relay gossip about them we know from a letter he wrote to someone before they were married, mentioning Elizabeth Vernon's pregnancy as a thread that would draw the Earl back to her. But it is when writing to Francis about a minor matter he had handled for him, that he says:

As that excellent author Sir John Falstaff, sais, what for your bysiness news, device, foolerie and libertie, I never dealt better since I was a man.

The last phrase is a quotation from *I King Henry IV,* II, iv, 188, where Falstaff, after boasting of his encounter with the ''buckram men'', declares, ''I never dealt better since I was a man.''

This was not missed by Sir Sidney Lee, who made the comment, ''The soubriquet of Sir John Falstaff seems to have been bestowed on Shakespeare''. He draws no inference from this and appears to have been puzzled by it. Indeed, in itself, it gives no inkling why Falstaff should be used as the name for, not a character in the play, but the ''excellent author'' of it.

It is when the two passages, that from Sir Tobie's letter to Bacon and that from the young Countess of Southampton to her husband, are put together, that it leaps to the eye it was William Shakespeare, of Stratford-on-Avon, who had had a son by ''pintpot'', a London tavern hostess who must be the original of Mistress Quickly.

There is more interest to this than merely of gossip. Whether or not Sir William Davenant was telling the truth when he claimed the actor for his sire, chastity during the years of separation from Anne Hathaway has never been claimed amongst his virtues. It would therefore surprise few, and be of minor interest, that he had during the London years a boy by a tavern hostess.

But that he frequented one known to the Earl and Countess of Southampton as ''pintpot'', that is Mistress Quickly, and that the Earl and Countess, Sir Tobie Matthew and Francis Bacon all four said ''Sir John Falstaff' when they meant William Shakespeare, is interesting.

What is the shared joke? It has to be of a literary order. The young Countess of Southampton could not possibly have met ''pintpot'' or entered her bawdy tavern, where Falstaff had recourse to Doll Tearsheet. That the Earl should make her privy to the personalities of such a world is, of itself, extraordinary, and only to be understood in a context that did not involve his own patronage of whores. Only if the joke is a literary one, is it fun they can both enter into. That the Earl receives news of the doings in the tavern from his young Countess means that the letter she had received from London was from one of the other participants in the joke. Why is there the idea of secrecy?

The joke seems to be that the character of Sir John Falstaff is modelled upon that of Shakespeare, who does not see it, though he is made to seem the author of the plays. The words ''that excellent author'' surely carried an irony that escaped Sir Sidney Lee.

It is sometimes innocently remarked that nobody's handwriting changed so often as Bacon's It is more likely he used secretaries. Secretaries existed before typewriters, and shorthand before Pitman. They took down in a kind of abbreviated writing and afterwards fair-copied in longhand. It is significant the only manuscript we have of a literary composition of Bacon's, that contained within the folder of the Northumberland Manuscript (see above p.72) is not in his hand, and the hand it is in changed at easily observable places. Spedding refers to the folios as ''Bacon transcripts''. Why transcripts? This may have been the original form in which it was taken down, and his other manuscripts, if ever found, might be in the same form. If Bacon was an author who dictated, as in the case of *Sylva Sylvarum,* at least, we know,[2] walking up and down, or reclining at ease, it would explain the amount he was able to produce, and be in line with his health warning against long sitting in one position. What I think is that he called upon his friends for this service – in the same spirit that we shall find him asking a friend to save him time by translating the *Advancement of Learning* into Latin for him, though he could not afford to pay for the work and only hoped it might be found of some interest to do. I believe that is the meaning of his reference to ''good pens'' at Twickenham, waiting apparently for a guest to pick up.

Works of philosophy would be best taken down by someone interested, as legal works by a legal friend, but plays could very suitably be taken down by an actor. The works would have to have been in Shakespeare's hand, for John Downes relates a tradition he produced the plays himself, instructing the actors in their parts, and a producer normally notes on his copy ''effects'' such as noises off or changes in lighting. If these were not in the same hand as the text, other members of the company would realise he must have obtained it from elsewhere. The plays had therefore, to be in his hand. I suggest Bacon, having come to know him, dictated the works. Either he formally asked the actor to give them out as his own, or noticing he was inclining to do so, saw in this the solution of what had been a problem to him – ''If a lie may do thee grace, I'll gild it in the happiest terms I have'', *I King Henry IV,* V, iv, 162.

If there is something of Shakespeare in Falstaff, is there anything of Bacon in the Prince? Both were ''waiting in the wings'' till their destiny met them. The historical Henry V was as Prince of Wales riotous, and the Gad's Hill prank would hardly have been in Bacon's line. But to a person of his standing, merely to have met with a play-actor in a bawdy tavern, even if it was only to dictate texts to him, would in itself have been conduct mildly riotous. If ever he came to his greatness, he would be unable to keep up such company. This he would have known from the beginning, and may explain Hal's apparently callous intent to drop Falstaff when he came to the throne. There is a book, *The Player King, a Theme of Shakespeare's Histories,* James Winny (Chatto, 1968), which refers to *King Henry V,* I, ii, 267, the King's line, ''How he comes o'er us with our wilder days, not measuring the use we made of them''. This irks Mr. Winny, because he cannot see he made any use of them. If he meant that as Prince of Wales he had thought it good to mingle with his father's common subjects in order to prepare himself eventually to reign with greater understanding, surely this could have better been done than by patronage of a bawdy tavern. But if it is Bacon, reflecting that he passed the time the Queen kept him waiting largely in the company of a reprobate character, yet gave the world, through him, works that should live, he might well feel the hours spent over a pint had been made into some ''use''. And that may give us the clue to the relationship between them; he was without illusions, and yet he was fond of the scapegrace.

1. Hatfield House, Cecil Papers, 101, 16.
2. See below, p.306 ff.

CHAPTER 32

The sombre tragedy of Essex

FRANCIS had feared Essex would err in Ireland through overshooting the mark, exceeding his instructions by plunging into reckless and showy actions. The contrary appeared to be the case. The Queen's instructions to him were to proceed straight north and attack Tyrone. Instead, he went south, avoiding Tyrone and doing, apparently, nothing at all. In one normally ardent for action, this bred suspicion. The Queen wrote asking why he had not proceeded upon his orders. His replies were evasive, unsatisfactory . . . he was reconnoitering . . . the time was not right. On June 10th she wrote, un-making the knights he created, without her authority and against her instruction not to create knights; and un-making Southampton Master of the Horse. The demotions caused Essex to lose face before his men.

Francis advised her to recall him, ''for'', he said, ''to discontent him as you do and yet to put arms and power into his hands may be a kind of temptation to make him prove cumbersome and unruly.''

Perhaps she was afraid to call him home. Fearing he meant to return leading an army against her, she had already forbidden him to leave Ireland without permission, while putting England under arms, on pretext of preparation against a new Spanish invasion.

G.B. Harrison, in his excellent biography of Essex, reminds us that Chapman dedicated his translation of Homer to him, called him ''Most true Achilles'' and spoke of his ''Achilleian virtues'', and suggests that Achilles in *Troilus and Cressida,* sulking in his tent instead of going out to fight the Trojans, is meant for Essex sulking in Wanstead, in '98, when his presence was needed at the Council table. Professor Bullough comments, if so ''Shakespeare must have blushed to remember his own *Prologue* to Henry V''. But if Bacon is the author, there is not necessarily a reversal of attitude. He had never thought it a good idea Essex should concentrate on the military side, and his departure for Ireland plainly filled him with misgivings. All the same, the die being cast, he would try, for the sake of Essex' public image, to make the best of it, and the compliment in the prologue to Act V would be in line with this, as well as, perhaps, representing a hope against hope. This would have been before Essex' behaviour there reinforced misgivings. Achilles in *Troilus and Cressida* may carry over some reminiscence of Essex sulking in Wanstead the year before, but surely reinforced by the present unsatisfactory behaviour of Essex in Ireland. Dr. Rowse sees something of

Essex and Southampton in ''Achilles and Patroclus . . . sulking in their tent together''.

All's Well that Ends Well would appear to refer to the same situation. O.J. Campbell postulates 1599 as the date of composition, and Professor Akrigg has tabulated the similarities between Bertram and Southampton.[1] Both are royal wards, both resist marriages arranged for them, both go abroad leaving a loving wife, both are there appointed Master of the Horse, and although Bertram is a Count (and in *Much Ado About Nothing* and *Twelfth Night* foreign Counts are called ''Count'') the author twice slips and calls him ''Earl''. His widowed mother, the Countess of Rousillon, would then be the dowager Countess of Southampton, and perhaps Helena has in her something of the young Countess, which would sort with her being of modest position, since Elizabeth Vernon brought no fortune. They have been worked into a story from Boccaccio, except that Parolles is an invention. Who is Parolles? Barnaby Barnes has been suggested, because of his want of courage in the 1591 campaign in Normandy. There could be something of Barnes in the characterisation, Professor Akrigg suggests alternatively two other associates of Southampton, Bowyer Worsley, described as a coward, and Pierce Edmonds. The latter seems particularly apposite since he was in Ireland with Southampton and was later to be described by an informer as a worthless man to whom Southampton showed too much favour, giving him a horse, sharing his tent with him, and being seen to hug and ''play wantonly with him''. It may be that Parolles is a composite portrait, intended to personify Southampton's tendency to attach to himself worthless persons. Like Essex, he was doing no good in Ireland, and would be better home with his loving wife.

Essex, having let the whole of the summer pass in inaction, on September 7th (the Queen's birthday), taking only Southampton with him, rode out at last to meet Tyrone, not on the field of battle, but to hold a parley on horseback in a ford.

On the 20th, suddenly, he was in London, against her order not to return without her permission, and with 200 armed men. Learning in London that the Court was at Nonesuch, he had himself and a supporting party ferried across the Thames. At Lambeth, they took horse again. Another party appeared on the road. It was Lord Grey of Wilton, come to constitute an escort. Overtaking Essex's party from behind, Lord Grey rode up so that he flanked Essex. One of Essex's men drew level and asked to be let pass. Lord Grey refused to let him, saying that he had business ahead, and, moving forward, in fact took the head of the procession. Essex' man, Sir Christopher St. Lawrence, asked if he should kill Lord Grey, and also the Secretary of the Council. Essex said no. Camden, who is the source for this story, tells it as in Essex's favour, because he refused. But, as Spedding pointed out, it really tells against him that it was thought possible such a proposition would suit his interest.

When they arrived, Essex saw that Lord Grey, having spurred ahead, was already in conversation with Robert Cecil. It was ten in the morning and the Queen had not yet descended. Against all convention, Essex rushed upstairs and into her bedroom. Seated at her dressing-table, with only her waiting-women round her, she was in a condition in which she would never, voluntarily, have received anyone. She had not put on her wig, and her grey hair was about her ears. Though startled, she seemed at first reasonably glad to see him; she told him to go and wash, as his face was splashed with mud from riding, while she finished dressing.

Later, coming down fully dressed, she spoke with him briefly, and then he sat down with her while they took mid-day dinner. During this, no essential question was raised. After the meal, they moved into a different room, where he was invited to explain the position to the Queen and to her Privy Council.

He now informed them that he was the one man able to deal with Tyrone: "'with those that have heretofore dealt with him he protested he would not deal in this free manner . . . since he had no confidence that they could procure him that which only would satisfy him . . . '" But Essex had not been sent to deal with Tyrone; he had been sent with an army to reduce him. The Queen and Council listened with what must have been increasingly heavy apprehension as he went on.

Essex proceeded to enumerate twenty-one conditions on which Tyrone would lay down arms. Perhaps the greater number of them embody what today may seem legitimate Irish freedoms, but it must have seemed to Elizabeth and her Council that Essex had come to speak to them as Tyrone's representative; not her Majesty's servant. Was he, by showing he had made a separate peace with the Irish and so got them behind him, trying to blackmail her into offering him a position which would make him almost her equal in power?

When he had finished, she dismissed him, and remained in conference with her Council. At ten in the evening – exactly twelve hours after his precipitate arrival – an order reached him that he was to keep to his room.

Francis Bacon had not been at Nonesuch, but came the next day and both asked for speech with Essex and wrote him a letter. The phrasing was understandably guarded:[2]

Mr Lord,
Conceiving that your Lordship came now up in the person of a good servant to see your sovereign mistress . . . I hope . . . that your Lordship's wisdom and obsequious circumspection and patience will turn all to the best . . .

He was allowed to see Essex privately for a quarter of an hour. He was later to say that he had during his interview given Essex three pieces of advice: not to present his negotiation with Tyrone as a glory, but as a "shuffling" to which he had had resort in order to patch up an admittedly unsatisfactory action; not to represent to the Queen any circumstances by which she should feel forced "as by a coercion or wrench" to send him back to Ireland; and to request further speech with her.

The following day, however, Essex was conveyed under guard to York House, where he was put into the charge of the Lord Keeper, while further examinations were made. His enormous popularity with the ordinary people was a cause for concern, as they would wonder why he was held. It was dangerous to let him be heard publicly, and the Queen thought it would be a solution, on a day when public admonitions were issued from the Star Chamber, to give out an official declaration of the faults laid to Essex' charge. Francis, when she told him, was very much against this tactic, and "told her plainly, that the people would say that my Lord was wounded upon his back, and that justice had her balance taken from her, which ever consisted of an accusation and a defence". As, on the other hand, Essex' oratory invariably won him people's hearts, he further advised her "that my Lord *in foro famae*[3] was too hard for her; and therefore wished her, as I had done before, to wrap it up privately."

One sees the good part which Francis played in all this. To Essex, he never ceased saying that he should be meek before the Queen; but to the Queen he always counselled handling Essex in a way that would not provoke him or the people to violence. To both, he urged conciliation. This was a proper, ethical course for one whose dearest connections had come to be at perilous enmity; but it was also sage, for he knew them both, and saw that it was necessary to lessen the tension if a tragedy were to be averted. After it had been "wrapped up," he suggested the Queen should "restore him to his former attendance, with some addition of honour to take away discontent".

The Queen, however, felt that this would be too soft, and had a proclamation of the charges issued from the Star Chamber on November 29th, 1599. Bacon was absent from the Star Chamber on that day, because he did not wish to be associated with the charge, which was issued as from all present, together. The Queen reproached him for staying away. Excusing himself, he replied:[4]

It may please your excellent Majesty,
I most humbly entreat your Majesty, not to impute my absence to any weakness of mind or unworthiness, But I assure your Majesty I do find envy beating so strongly upon me . . . My life hath been threatened, and my name libelled, which I count an honour . . .

What does he mean? It becomes a little clearer in a letter he wrote at the same time to Lord Henry Howard:[5]

There is shaped a tale in London's forge, that beateth apace at this time, that I should deliver opinion to the Queen in my Lord of Essex cause: first, that it was *praemunire* and now last, that it was high treason . . . But the untruth of this fable God and my sovereign can witness; . . . knowing no more remedy against lies than others do against libels. The root, no question of it is, partly some light-headed envy at my accesses to her Majesty; which being begun and continued since my childhood, as long as her Majesty shall think me worthy of them I scorn those that think the contrary.

Now, one sees the trouble, he has been constantly with the Queen, and the people are being taught by those who envy him or wish him ill to associate this with Essex' confinement. Essex, being adored by the people, they are certain he can have done no wrong. The Queen, being perfect, can do no wrong. Therefore, it must be the person constantly with her who is urging her to harshness.

Essex' dealings had in fact been more disloyal than either she or Francis knew. According to a statement made in 1601 by Sir Charles Danvers, Essex had sent Lord Mountjoy to King James of Scotland to discuss the succession to the English throne which the law forbade to be discussed and to assure him Essex would support his claim to succeed Elizabeth.

James VI was the son of Mary Queen of Scots and could not, naturally, be expected to entertain gentle feelings towards the Queen who had had his mother beheaded. Moreover, Mountjoy's mission was to speak of some step which could lead to recognition of James' claim in Elizabeth's lifetime. Specially sinister was Sir Charles' explanation of the embassy: "He entered into it the rather at that time to serve my Lord of Essex, who by loss of her Majesty was like to run a dangerous fortune, unless he took a course to strengthen himself by that means." If by "loss of her Majesty" he means loss of her favour, in as much as she was certainly not pleased with his performance in Ireland, his present proceeding, as Spedding has pointed out, was certainly not one whereby to regain it, should she learn what he was doing. It is difficult to avoid the conclusion that he intended putting his army in Ireland, with perhaps Tyrone's forces to back it, at the disposal of the Scottish King, for the purpose of exerting pressure on the English Queen.

But the Queen knew nothing of this negotiation, and now appointed Mountjoy to take over what had been Essex' command in Ireland. He, thereupon, recommenced the secret overtures to James VI, and according to Sir Charles Danvers, sent one Harry Leigh to Scotland:[6]

with offer that if the King would enter into the course, my Lord Montjoy would leave the kingdom of Ireland defensively guarded, and with four or five thousand men assist him: which with the party that my Lord of Essex would make head withal, were thought sufficient to bring that to pass that was intended.

James' answer, however, was "dilatory".

On March 20th, 1599/1600, Essex was allowed to return from York

House to Essex House, formerly Leicester House, on the Strand. The Queen had adopted Francis' suggestion that she should "wrap it up privately", or at least have the charges – since they had been made – heard not in the Star Chamber – where if he were found guilty Essex must be sent to the Tower – but at a Council table.

Before the hearing took place, there came to the Queen's knowledge a book entitled *The First Part of the Life and Raigne of King Henrie IIII Extending to the end of the first yeare of his raigne, Written by I.H.* It had been printed that year, 1599, and was dedicated to the Earl of Essex, by John Hayward, in words tending to associate him with the usurping Prince, and so suggesting he might dethrone Elizabeth.

The study is written entirely from the side of the usurper. The vices of Richard II are painted as inordinate and not to be borne; Henry is without improper ambition, at first loth to act upon the urging of the Archbishop of Canterbury, that he should seize the crown and reign in Richard's stead: a perfect hero, moved only by concern for the public good. On pp.66–7, he is supplied with numerous precedents for the deposing of kings.

No sovereign could care for this work, but what made it particularly noxious to Elizabeth was that Essex had accepted the dedication. The very terms of it were ambiguous. Why should "our Henrie" fare better for association with his name? Still worse, why should Henry hide beneath Essex' name as the archer Teucer beneath Ajax's shield? Coupled with the sugggestion that his greatness was to increase, it could almost mean he was to play Henry to her Richard: usurp the throne from her.

She gave it to Francis to read, and asked him whether there was not treason in it.

Francis says:[7]

I remember an answer of mine in a matter which had some affinity with my Lord's cause, which though it grew from me, went after about in others' names. For her Majesty being mightily incensed with that book which was dedicated to my Lord of Essex, being a story of the first year of King Henry the fourth, thinking it a seditious prelude to put into the people's heads boldness and faction, said she had good opinion that there was treason in it, and asked me if I could not find any places in it that might be drawn within case of treason: whereto I answered, for treason surely I find none, but for felony very many. And when her Majesty hastily asked me wherein, I told her that the author had committed very apparent theft, for he had taken most of his sentences of Cornelius Tacitus . . .

This, for Bacon, was an agile way of avoiding an awkward issue. What does he mean by a matter which "though it grew from me, went after about in other's names"? Grew from me, in respect of a book, is an odd phrase. If, as is here submitted, he himself was the author of *Richard II* and 1 and 2 *King Henry IV,* the Queen's questions touched him very nearly, even though it was Hayward's book on the same subject which, being dedicated to Essex, was actually in question. He would feel some responsibility for having initiated work on a theme which went about, first in Shakespeare's name, then in Hayward's prose tale. This he wants to make clear to his correspondent without uncovering himself badly.

The Queen had Hayward committed to the Tower. Nevertheless, she was apparently not certain that in the titular author she had the right man. Francis continues:[8]

And another time, when the Queen would not be persuaded that it was his writing whose name was to it, but that it had some more mischievous author, and said with great indignation that she would have him racked to produce his author, I replied, Nay, Madam, he is a doctor, never rack his person, but rack his style; let him have pen, ink and paper, and help of books, and be enjoined to continue the story where it breaketh off, and I will undertake by collating the styles to judge whether he were the author or no.

What should have given the Queen the idea that Hayward's book about Richard II and Henry IV was not by him whose name was on it, but by someone of greater importance? Was it that she had heard that something that was about Richard II and Henry IV was not by the titular author, and imagined the report to refer to the Hayward? Or was she only pretending to be confused in the hope of provoking Francis to a confession of his own authorship of prior works on the same theme, which, if innocent in their intent, had become vexatious by their consequence? Why did she single out Francis Bacon to question on this matter?

He asked the Queen to be spared the duties of crown counsel in the case against Essex, "out of consideration . . . of my obligation to him". Nevertheless, he was sent for, with four other counsellors, and the Lords arranging presentation of the case informed them they would each deal with one part of the charge against Essex, Bacon with that part concerned with his having given "occasion and countenance to a seditious pamphlet", that is Hayward's book.

Whereupon I replied . . . that it was an old matter, and had no manner of coherence with the rest of the charge, being matters of Ireland, and therefore that I having been wronged by bruits before this would expose me to them more; and it would be said I gave in evidence mine own tales.

But it was not an old matter. If it is the Hayward that is in question, it had only just been published. Surely, Bacon's calling it an "old matter" gives away that what he had in his mind was "Shakespeare's" *Richard II* and *King Henry IV,* and are these not what he means by "mine own tales"? People who know will say that, he, having composed these works himself, is in no position to arraign Essex for having accepted the dedication of another on the same theme. He will be seen as bringing up as evidence against Essex works he himself had composed.

All the same, though it embarrassed him, by putting him in charge of

9. The Pillar between the Oak and the Grotto. Oil by the author. *(Photo: Martin Booth)*

10. Gorhambury – all that remains. Oil by the author. *(Photo: Martin Booth)*

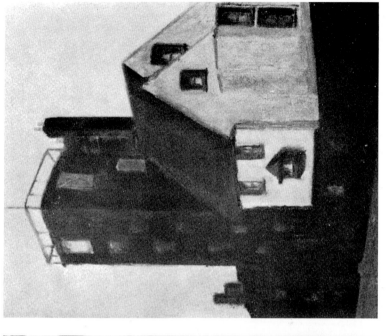

11. St Michael's, Gorhambury. Oil by the author.
(Photo: Martin Booth)

12. Canonbury Tower. Oil by the author.
(Photo: Martin Booth)

13. The Veiled and Feathered Sunburst. *(The Marquis of Northampton – Canonbury Tower. Photo: Basil Martin)*

VENVS

AND ADONIS

Vilia miretur vulgus: mihi flauus Apollo
Pocula Castalia plena ministret aqua.

14. Headpiece to the title-page of *Venus and Adonis,* 1594. *(Bodleian Library, Oxford)*

SHAKE-SPEARES

15. Headpiece to the *Sonnets,* 1609. *(Bodleian Library, Oxford)*

16. Headpiece to the title-page of *Manes Verulamiani,* 1626. *(Bodleian Library, Oxford)*

GUSTAVI SELENI
CRYPTOME-
NYTICES ET CRY
PTOGRAPHIÆ
Libri IX.

In quibus & planiſſima
STEGANOGRAPHIÆ
à
JOHANNE TRITHEMIO,
Abbate Spanheymenſi & Herbipolenſi,
admirandi ingenij Viro, magicè &
ænigmaticè o.im con-
ſcriptæ,
ENODATIO
traditur.
Inſperſis ubiquè Authoris ac
Aliorum, non contemnendis
inventis.

cɪɔ ɪɔ cxxɪɪɪɪ.

17. The title-page to *Cryptomenytices.*

18. (right) The title-page to a Dutch edition of Bacon's *Henry VII* (the Latin text).

19. (far right) The title-page to a Dutch edition of Bacon's *Advancement of Learning* (the Latin text).

20. Frontispiece from *The History of the Royal Society.*

this part of the arraignment, the Queen had given him control over what would be said, and so enabling him to make sure the name of Shakespeare was not uttered nor any mention made of his own plays.

Hayward, in the Tower already, was brought to trial and imprisoned for at least two years. Shakespeare was not even arrested.

Answering Francis' objection to handling this part of the charge their Lordships explained to him that preference of the charge relating to the acceptance of the dedication of the seditious booklet had been allocated to him because:

it was considered how I stood tied to my Lord of Essex, therefore that part was thought fittest for me which did him least hurt . . .

He did not like the role:

yet the conclusion binding upon the Queen's pleasure directly, *volens nolens,* I could not avoid that part that was laid upon me . . .

The hearing of the case was round a Council table at York House, on June 5th, 1600. Sitting were, "four Earls, two Barons, and two judges of the Law, making in the whole a council or court of eighteen persons, who were attended by four of her Majesty's Learned Council [including himself] for charging the Earl, and two Clerks of the Council, the one to read, the other as a register, and an auditory of persons to the number, as I could guess, of two hundred . . . The upper end of the table was left void for the Earl's appearance". The proceedings opened with a historical summary of what had passed in the case since Essex was first confined, after his return from Ireland, and of the reasons why it was now being heard, not in the Star Chamber, but in this place: that it should be seen the Earl received "justice mixed with mercy . . . justice, but with the edge and point taken off and rebated".

This preamble was not spoken all in one. Some of it was spoken by one of her Majesty's Learned Counsel, one may suppose that the last part, concerned with the reasons why it was being heard here, and not as usual, echoing as it does some of the words he had used in persuading the Queen, was spoken by Francis. There was no counsel for the defence in those days, but with one of the crown counsel asking for "justice mixed with mercy", Essex had virtually a defender.

The matters charged against him by the other three Learned Counsel fell into three main groups: that almost from the moment of arrival in Ireland he acted, in numerous particulars, in a manner contrary to the instructions he had received from her Majesty; that he concluded a "dishonourable and dangerous treaty" with Tyrone; and that he left his post, in contempt of her Majesty's order to remain at it. Of the lawyers, only Coke – Bacon's old rival – was really disagreeable to the Earl; who, after being kept for a long while kneeling, at the head of the table, was at length permitted to defend or rather, since he admitted the charges, excuse, himself. The hearing had begun at eight in the morning and lasted until nearly nine at night. At the end, the Council pronounced a censure on him, and he was debarred from holding certain offices, and sentenced by the Lord Keeper ''to return to his own house, there to continue a prisoner as before'' until it should please her Majesty to release him.

The next day, the Queen sent for Francis and asked him for an account of what had happened:[9]

And further she willed me to set down in writing all that passed that day. I obeyed her commandment, and within some few days brought her again the narration, which I did read unto her at two several afternoons: and when I came to that part that set forth my Lord's own answer (which was my principal care), I do well bear in mind that she was extraordinarily moved with it, in kindness and relenting towards my Lord, and told me afterwards (speaking how well I had expressed my Lord's part) that she perceived old love would not easily be forgotten: whereunto I answered suddenly, that I hoped she meant that by herself.

He also advised her not to make public use of the narration he had brought her:[10]

for since your express direction was, there should be no register nor clerk to take this sentence, nor no record or memorial made up of the proceeding, why should you now do that popularly, which you would not admit to be done judicially?

Despite Francis' apparent opinion that his account of the proceedings would be better destroyed, part of it has been preserved.

From the moment Essex was returned to the comfort of his own house, Francis worked indefatigably for his total liberation and restoration to favour. As letters from Essex to herself would be suspected of flattery, Francis took the extraordinary step of composing an exchange of letters between Anthony Bacon and Essex, for them to copy out, wherein the most admirable sentiments were expressed, such as should melt the Queen's heart towards Essex:[11]

I did draw with my Lord's privity and by his appointment two letters, the one written as from my brother, the other as an answer returned from my Lord, both to be by me in secret manner showed to the Queen . . .

The one composed as from Anthony to Essex explained to him how extremely good and kind had been her Majesty's course in having him heard by the Council at York House instead of by the Star Chamber, and suggested that the list of offices which he had been barred from holding was as interesting for its omissions as for its inclusions:[12]

. . . the very distinction which was made in the sentence of sequestration from the places of service in state, and leaving your Lordship the place of Master of the Horse, doth to my understanding . . . point at this, – that her Majesty meant to use your Lordship's attendance in Court, while the exercises of the other places stood suspended.

This was to put the idea into her head, if she had not thought of it. Francis had always thought Essex would be more safely employed in home than in overseas or martial duties.

In the reply, drawn up as from Essex to Anthony, Francis makes him say:[13]

You say the Queen never meant to call me to public censure, which showeth her goodness; but you see I passed it, which showeth others' power. I believe most steadfastly her Majesty never intended to bring my cause to a sentence: and I believe as verily that since the sentence she meant to restore me to attend upon her person. But they that could use occasions, . . . and amplify occasions, and practise occasions, to represent to her Majesty a necessity to bring me to the one, can and will do the like to stop me from the other. You say my errors were my prejudice, and therefore I can mend myself: it is true. But they that know that I can mend myself, and that if ever I recover the Queen, I will never lose her again, will never suffer me to obtain interest in her favour.

It is with imagination that Francis throws himself into the composition of this fictitious correspondence. The Queen, coming, as she thinks by accident, to the sight of letters never intended for her gaze, is to be affected by their touching expressions of loyalty. Of course, Francis never doubted that Essex, having learned his lesson, would now in fact be loyal, and so make good the words given him to copy out. And by suggesting that there are some who would try to prevent her from seeing Essex again, Francis tries to stimulate in her the desire to grant him access.

At the same time as he showed her this ''correspondence'', Francis took every opportunity to appeal to her in conversation. When she exclaimed that some doctors, having given medicines ''to draw out the ill humours'' – purges and the like – did not, as they should, change soon enough to medicines designed to build up positive good health, he seized upon the occasion to draw an analogy:[14]

Good Lord Madam (said I) how wisely and aptly can you speak and discern of physic ministered to the body, and consider not that there is the like occasion of physic ministered to the mind: as now in the case of my Lord of Essex . . . I know you cannot but think that you have drawn the humour sufficiently, and therefore it were more than time . . . that you did apply and minister strength and comfort unto him.

Within a month of the hearing by the Council, she ordered his release. There are turning-points at which one is the master of one's destiny. Essex could now have had before him a free and peaceful life. He did not choose it.

---

1. *Shakespeare and the Earl of Southampton* G.P.V. Akrigg (Hamish Hamilton, 1968), p.256.
2. *Resuscitatio,* Supplement, p.86.
3. In the forum of fame.
4. *Resuscitatio,* Supplement, p.99.

5. *Resuscitatio*, Supplement, p.100.
6. Edinburgh, National Library of Scotland. Advocate MS. 33.1.7 (1) No. 32.
7. *Apologie concerning the Earl of Essex*, Spedding, X, pp.149-50.
8. *Op.cit.*, p.150.
9. *Apologie*, Spedding, X, p.154.
10. *Op cit.*, p.155.
11. *Op. cit.*, p.157.
12. British Museum, Additional MSS. 5503.
13. British Museum, Additional MSS. 5503.
14. *Apologie*, Spedding, X, p.156.

CHAPTER 33

The execution

SHORTLY after Essex was released, Francis wrote to him, assuring him that – subject always to his higher loyalty to the Queen – he was still his friend:[1]

My Lord,
No man can better expound my doings than your Lordship, which maketh me need to say the less. Only I humbly pray you to believe that I aspire to the conscience and commendation first of *bonus civis*,[2] which with us is a good and true servant to the Queen, and next of *bonus vir*,[3] that is an honest man. I desire your Lordship also to think that though I confess I love some things much better than I love your Lordship, as the Queen's service, her quiet and contentment, her honour, her favour, the good of my country, and the like, yet I love few persons better than yourself, both for gratitude's sake, and for your own virtues, which cannot hurt but by accident or abuse. Of which my good affection I was ever and am ready to yield testimony by any good offices but with such reservations as yourself cannot but allow: for as I was ever sorry that your Lordship should fly with waxen wings, doubting Icarus' fortune, so for the growing up of your own feathers, especially the ostrich's, or any other save of a bird of prey, no man shall be more glad. And this is the axletree whereupon I have turned and shall turn; which to signify to you, though I think you are of yourself persuaded as much, is the cause of my writing; and so I commend your Lordship to God's goodness. From Gray's Inn, this 20th day of July, 1600.

Your Lordship's most humbly,

Fr. Bacon

Essex replied with a letter which was the model of tact, and at his request Francis drew up two letters for him to send to the Queen. Francis tells us about this in his own words: "And I drew for him by his appointment some letters to her Majesty; which though I knew well his Lordship's gift and style to be far better than mine own, yet because he required it, alleging that by his long restraint he was grown almost a stranger to the Queen's present conceits, I was ready to perform it".[4] The first of the letters preserved, Francis drew up as if from Essex, for the latter to copy out and sign:

It may please your Majesty,[5]
It were great simplicity in me to look for better, than that your Majesty should cast away my letter as you have done me . . . Neither mought I in reason presume to offer unto your Majesty dead lines, myself being excluded . . . were it not . . . to clear myself in point of duty. Duty, though my state lie buried in the sands, and my favours be cast upon the waters, and my honours be committed to the wind,

yet standeth surely built upon the rock, and hath been, and ever shall be, unforced and unattempted. And therefore, since the world out of error, and your Majesty I fear out of art, is pleased to put upon me . . . this my absence from attendance, I cannot but leave this protestation with your Majesty; that I am and have been merely a patient, and take myself only to obey and execute your Majesty's will. And indeed, Madam, I had never thought it possible that your Majesty could have so disinterested yourself of me; nor that you had been so perfect in the art of forgetting: nor that after a quintessence of wormwood your Majesty would have taken so large a draught of poppy; as to have passed so many summers without all feeling of my sufferings. But the only comfort I have is this, that I know your Majesty taketh delight and contentment in executing this disgrace upon me. And since your Majesty can find no other use for me, . . . I am glad I can serve for that. Thus making my most humble petition to your Majesty, that in justice . . . your Majesty would not touch me in that which is indissoluble; that is point of duty, and that your Majesty will parden this my unwarranted presumption of writing, being to such an end: I cease in all humbleness;

Your Majesty's poor, and never so unworthy servant,

Essex

One may think that this is a very personal letter for Francis to have drawn up for Essex to the Queen; but presumably he knew what kind of letter it would please her to receive from Essex.

The other which has been preserved is couched in the second person, for Essex to transpose into the third:[6]

THE SUBSTANCE OF A LETTER I NOW WISH YOUR LORDSHIP SHOULD WRITE TO HER MAJESTY

That you desire your Majesty to believe *id quod res ipsa loquitor,*[7] that it is not conscience to yourself of any advantage her Majesty hath towards you . . . nor any drift or device to win her Majesty to any point or particular, that moveth you to send her these lines of your own mind; but first and principally gratitude, next a natural desire out of, you will not say the tedious remembrance, for you can hold nothing tedious that hath been derived from her Majesty, but the troubled and pensive remembrance of that which is past, to enjoy better times with her Majesty, such as others have had, and that you have wanted. You cannot impute the difference to the continuance of time, which addeth nothing to her Majesty but increase of virtue, but rather to your own misfortune or errors . . . But that which toucheth to the quick, is that whereas you accounted it the choice fruit of yourself to be a contentment and entertainment to her Majesty's mind, you found many times to the contrary, that you were rather a disquiet to her and a distaste.

Again, whereas in the course of her service, though you confess the weakness of your own judgement . . . you do not doubt of her Majesty's goodness in pardoning and obliterating any your errors or mistakings heretofore, refreshing the memory and contemplation of your poor services or anything that hath been grateful to her Majesty from you . . . For as you have determined your hope in a good hour not willingly to offend her Majesty either in matter of court or state, but to depend absolutely upon her will and pleasure . . .

Therefore your most humble suit to her Majesty is, that she will vouchsafe you that approach to her heart and bosom *et ad screnium pectoris,*[8] plainly, for as much as concerneth yourself, to open and expound her mind towards you, suffering you to see clear what may have bred any dislike in her Majesty, and in what points she would have you to reform yourself, and how she would be served by you. Which done, you do assure her Majesty she shall be both at the beginning and the ending of all that you do, of that regard as you may presume to impart to her Majesty.

And so hoping that this may be an occasion of some further serenity from her Majesty towards you, you refer the rest to your actions, which may verify what you have written, as that you have written may interpret your actions, and the course you shall hereafter take.

Essex was already freed from confinement in his house; on August 20th, he was further freed, to go anywhere that he would, except to Court. He retired for a while to the country, but by October was back at Essex House, voluntarily. He might have hoped for an eventual return to favour, which was what Francis had been trying to procure for him, but to others he appeared to be in a very strange and dangerous state of mind. Sir John Harrington, who was his friend, wrote of him:[9]

It resteth with me in opinion that ambition thwarted in his career doth speedily lead on to madness; . . . who shifteth from sorrow and repentance to rage and rebellion so suddenly as well proveth him devoid of good reason or of right mind. In my last discourse he uttered strange words bordering on such strange designs, that made me hasten forth and leave his presence. Thank heaven I am safe at home, and if I go in such troubles again I deserve the gallows for a meddling fool. His speeches of the Queen become no man who hath *mens sana in corpore sano.*[10]

It got back to the Queen that Essex had spoken of her in a contemptuous manner, and this not only hardened her heart against him but caused her to withdraw from Francis, because of his incessant urging of her to forgive Essex. Francis says simply: "the Queen, by some slackness of my Lord's, as I imagine, liked him worse and worse, and grew more incensed towards him. Then she, remembering belike the continual and incessant and confident speeches and courses that I had held on my Lord's side, became utterly alienated from me, and for the space of at least three months, which was between Michaelmas and New Year's tide following, would not so much as look on me, but turned away from me with express and purposelike discountenance whensoever she saw me''.

Too loyal to Essex, Francis had damaged his own relations with the Queen. He decided to bring matters to a head:[11]

. . . immediately after New Year's tide I desired to speak with her; and being admitted to her, I dealt with her plainly and said, Madam, I see you withdraw your favour from me, and now that I have lost many friends for your sake, I shall lose you too: you have put me like one of those that the Frenchmen call *enfans perdus,*[12] that serve on foot before horsemen, so have you put me into matters of envy without place, or without strength; and I know at chess a pawn before a king is ever much played upon; a great many love me not, because they think I have been against my Lord of Essex; and you love me not, because you know I have been for him: yet I will never repent me, that I have dealt in simplicity of heart towards you both . . . and so, Madam (said I) I am not so simple but that I take a prospect of mine overthrow, only I thought I would tell you so much, that you may know that it was faith and not folly that brought me into it, and so I will pray for you. Upon which speeches of mine uttered with some passion, it is true her Majesty was exceedingly moved, and accumulated a number of kind and gracious words upon me, and willed me to rest upon this, *Gratia mea sufficit*,[13] and a number of other sensible and tender words and demonstrations, such as more could not be; but as touching my Lord of Essex, *ne verbum quidem.*[14] Whereupon I departed, resting then determined to meddle no more in the matter; so that I saw would overthrow me, and not be able to do him any good. And thus I made mine own peace with mine own confidence at that time; and this was the last time I saw her Majesty before the eighth of February, which was the day of my Lord of Essex his misfortune.

''Misfortune'' is a kind word. The eighth of February, 1600/01, was the day of the Essex rebellion. Early that Sunday morning, Essex was observed addressing a crowd of two or three hundred swordsmen in the courtyard before Essex House. As this was only a few steps along the Strand from York House and the palace, it was not long before the Lord Keeper arrived with a commission from the Queen to enquire the cause and purpose of this assembly. With him were the Lord Chief Justice, Sir William Knollys and Lord Worcester. What made them particularly suspicious was that the previous evening Essex had been with a party to a special performance of *Richard II* at the Globe, thought to have been put on at his instigation. The Queen, when she had heard of it, had said, ''Know you not that I am Richard?'' Fearing that Essex was plotting her overthrow, and had the play put on again at this moment to brace his sympathisers to depose a monarch, she had sent him a summons, through her Council, though it was the middle of the night, to present himself at Court. He had sent word that he was ill, which did not appear the case now.

Faced now with this deputation from her Majesty, Essex made as if to receive the Lord Keeper, Sir William Knollys, Lord Worcester and the Lord Chief Justice. He led them into Essex House and into the library. There he locked them in. He then led his army out of the courtyard into the Strand, but instead of proceeding, as had been feared, to Whitehall to surround the palace, they turned the other way and marched up Fleet Street and up Ludgate Hill. They appeared to be making for St. Pauls, it was thought with intent to try to enlist the support of the congregation, and as they went, Essex called out to the staring population to rally behind him, as there was a plot to sell the country to the Infanta of Spain and his own life was in danger; but he and his army were pursued by a sheriff sent by Cecil proclaiming him a traitor. The people did not join Essex, as he had expected and barriers were erected across his way. Seeing that he could not prevail, he took a side street to the river, and, leaving the army, took a boat and returned to Essex House by the watergate. Inside, he found that the four Lords whom he had imprisoned in the library had been let out and were gone. The Earl of Southampton, who had been at his side throughout, was still with him as were some fifty followers. The purpose of their return was to burn some papers. By now Essex House was surrounded by forces of the crown; at first Essex seemed minded to defend the stronghold against siege, and some hours passed, during which another deputation from the Queen arrived and called out to him to surrender. He shouted from the roof that he would do so only on condition of an audience with the Queen. This was denied. Darkness fell. The Lord Admiral sent for gunpowder and gave Essex an hour in which to let his sister and wife, with their gentlewomen, out of Essex House, after which it would be blown up. Kegs were being unloaded on the lawns when Essex and Southampton came out and surrendered their swords.

About ten in the evening they were conveyed to Lambeth Palace, and thence to the Tower. So ended what Francis kindly called "the day of my Lord of Essex's his misfortune".

On Wednesday February 11th, he received a summons from the Council to attend a meeting at which the method of examining the affair would be decided. The Council, probably to Francis' relief, reserved to itself the interrogation of Essex and Southampton; Francis and Coke were detailed to make subsidiary examinations, involving the interrogation of lesser prisoners. Certain of these, seeking to save themselves by turning Queen's evidence, disclosed – and this must have been infinitely distressing for Francis – that plotting had been going on for months, and that the intent had been to take the Queen prisoner and force her to dismiss from the councils Cecil, Sir Walter Raleigh and some others, and "alter the government" to one dominated by Essex.

The case was brought to trial speedily. On February 19th, The Earls of Essex and Southampton were arraigned. Twenty-five peers were seated in judgement; it was the largest jury ever called. There were two charges, the one concerning the plot to surprise her Majesty's person and the other concerning the open rebellion in the City. Essex' having imprisoned in the library the Lord Keeper, the Lord Chief Justice and the other two Lords – all now present – counted against him, for it was not merely in their private persons that they had received the affront of being locked in: they had come as a commission from her Majesty, and their locking in was a defiance of her.

In his defence, Essex said that the imprisonment of the four Lords had been forced upon him by his unruly associates; that he had never intended any hurt to her Majesty's person and that he only desired access to her, for which he had thought to pray the help of the people of the City; and that it was true what he had called out to them: he feared to be assailed by private enemies.

It was this that provoked Francis, present as one of the crown counsel. When it came to his turn to speak (for Coke had already spoken), he said that it sounded to him like the case of Pisistratus, who wounded himself and ran through the streets of Athens shouting that his life was sought, so as to get the people behind him, though his motive was to try to seize control of the government. He did not believe that the Earl of Essex had enemies who sought to destroy him.

It is this which, when Bacon has been judged before the bar of history, has been held against him by those writers who, following Macauley, paint him black: that he spoke these words against his friend. Yet, as those who see Bacon with sympathy have pointed out, he was present as one of the counsel on the Queen's command, and he had to say something. Moreover, it is likely that he spoke under the stress of exasperation. He had done an amazing amount for Essex; and though it is a fact that early in their association Essex had ardently though unsuccessfully endeavoured to help him, the debt had been more than repaid when, at Essex' first trial, he had got him off. It is true that, this time, Francis did not ask for "justice mixed with mercy."

If he had gone even beyond friendship's demands when he framed the letters designed to help Essex restore himself to the Queen's favour, he was held to ransom for it. Essex cried, "I call Mr. Bacon against Mr. Bacon". He then referred to the two letters composed by Bacon, the one as from Anthony Bacon to himself and the other as from himself to Anthony Bacon, for showing to the Queen when they had copied them out, wherein many things were said in his favour and the point was made that some persons were against his seeing the Queen, "For then Mr. Bacon joined with me in mine opinion, and pointed out those to be mine enemies and to hold me in disgrace with her Majesty, whom he seems now to clear of such mind towards me".

This was awkward for Francis, for the Queen was possibly until this moment ignorant of the deception practised upon her. He might easily have lost his keel, but he acknowledged briefly that he did write the letters to which Essex referred, and said that if they could be produced before the Court he "would not blush to be seen for anything that was in them". He added that he had "spent more time in vain in studying how to make the Earl a good servant to the Queen and state, than he had done in anything else". With that, he sat down.

It does not appear that he spoke against Southampton.

The proceedings occupied but a single day. Both the Earls were found guilty and sentenced to death.

. . . between the arraignment and my Lord's suffering, I well remember I was but once with the Queen; at what time, though I durst not deal directly for my Lord as things then stood, yet generally I did both commend her Majesty's mercy . . . and not only so, but I took hardiness to extenuate, not the fact, for that I durst not, but the danger, telling her that if some base or cruel-minded persons had entered into such an action, it might have caused much blood and combustion; but it appeared well they were such as knew not how to play the malefactors . . .

During the day following the trial of Essex and Southampton, the cases of the less important persons charged with conspiracy with them were heard, and Francis assures us it was his "diligence and information touching the offenders" which obtained the discharge of six out of the nine, without their being brought into court. From this one can see how wrong it is to equate the Crown Counsel of those day with the Crown Counsel of today, who presents the case for the prosecution only. But Sir Christopher Blount, the third husband of Lettice, was amongst the few beheaded.

Francis tells us Essex said he would be grateful to her Majesty if his execution might be private, and so it was arranged within the walls of the Tower;[15]

he did use vehement detestation of his offence, desiring God to forgive his great, his bloody, his crying, and his infectious sin: and so died very penitently, but yet with great conflict (as it should seem) for his sins. For he never mentioned nor remembered there wife, children, or friend, nor took particular leave of any that were present, but wholly abstracted and sequestered himself to the state of his conscience and prayer.

1. British Museum: Lansdowne MSS, lxxxvii, f.210.
2. "Good citizen."
3. "Good man."
4. *Apologie*, Spedding X, p.155.
5. *Resuscitatio*, Supplement, p.94.
6. Lambeth MSS, 941.139.
7. That which speaks for itself.
8. And to the tablet of her memory.
9. *Nugae Antiquae*, I, p.179.
10. A healthy mind in a healthy body.
11. *Apologie*, Spedding X, pp. 157-58.
12. Lost children.
13. My thanks suffice.
14. Not even my word.
15. *Some particularities of that which passed after the arraignment*, Spedding, IX, p.205.

CHAPTER 34

Shadows of a closing reign

AFTER the execution, the Queen sent for Francis and commanded him to write a history of the whole affair; ''which I did'', he tells us:[1]

but so as never secretary had more particular and express directions and instructions in every point how to guide my hand in it; and not only so, but after that I had made a first draught thereof, and propounded it to certain principal counsellors, by her Majesty's appointment, it was perused, weighed, censured, altered, and made almost a new writing, according to their Lordships' better consideration . . .

It was then perused again by the Queen and some further alterations made by her appointment, and sent to press. But even this was not the end of the altering, for:

. . . after it was set to print, the Queen, who . . . as she was excellent in great matters, so she was exquisite in small, and noted that I could not forget my ancient respect of my Lord of Essex, in terming him ever My Lord of Essex, My Lord of Essex, in almost every page of the book, which she thought not fit, but would have it made Essex, or the late Earl of Essex: whereupon of force it was printed *de novo*, and the first copies suppressed by her peremptory commandment.

The new title, under which we know it, was:

A Declaration of the Practices and Treasons attempted and committed by ROBERT LATE EARL OF ESSEX and his complices Against Her Majesty and Her Kingdoms, and of the proceedings as well at the arraignments and convictions of the said late Earl, and his adherants, as after: Together with the Very Confessions.

It was printed in 1601, and is our main source.

Southampton remained imprisoned in the Tower.

The next that we hear of Francis, three months after the execution, is of a brush he had with his old rival Coke. On April 24th, 1601, Francis wrote to Robert Cecil to tell him about it. It occurred in the Exchequer, when Francis moved to have a re-seizure of the lands of a relapsed recusant. Apparently Coke, as Attorney-General, felt that Bacon's movement implied a reflection upon the manner in which the case had formerly been handled on the Queen's behalf, for (Francis says):[2]

Mr. Attorney kindled at it, and said, ''Mr. Bacon, if you have any tooth against me, pluck it out; for it will do you more hurt than all the teeth in your head will do you good. I answered coldly in these very words, "Mr. Attorney, I respect you: I fear you not: and the less you speak of your own greatness, the more I will think of it."

He replied, "I think scorn to stand upon terms of greatness towards you, who are less than little; less than the least;" and other such strange light terms he gave me, with that insulting which cannot be expressed.

Herewith stirred, yet I said no more but this: "Mr. Attorney, do not depress me so far; for I have been your better, and may be again, when it please the Queen."

With this he spake, neither I nor himself could tell what, as if he had been born Attorney General; and in the end bade me not meddle with the Queen's business, but with mine own; and that I was unsworn, &c. I told him, sworn or unsworn was all one to an honest man; and that I ever set my service first, and myself second; and wished to God, that he would do the like.

Then he said, it were good to clap a *cap.utlagatum* upon my back! To which I only said he could not; and that he was at a fault; for he hunted upon an old scent.

He gave me a number of disgraceful words besides; which I answered with silence, and shewing that I was not moved with them.

The phrase *cap. utlegatum,* as it everywhere appears in print, has perplexed generations of Bacon scholars, especially those acquainted with Latin, since there is no Latin word *utlegatus.* There is a Latin word *Legatus,* but it means an ambassador or legate, incomprehensible in the context. Spedding, X, p.2, gives as his source *Letters, Speeches, Charges . . .,* Thomas Birch, 1763, and tells us Bacon's letter was found at Hatfield by Murdin, who sent a copy to Birch, who reproduced it in his book, from which latter he, Spedding, copied it. In Birch, also, one reads *utlegatum.* From Spedding's having chosen to copy from Birch, mistake and all, one might suppose Bacon's original letter to have disappeared. I enquired, however, of the Librarian at Hatfield House, Mr. Robin Harcourt Williams,. who produced it for me without difficulty. The reference is *Cecil Papers 86/87.* In Bacon's hand one reads not *utlegatum* but *utlagatum.* This was, in the standardised legal jargon of the time, the short title of a bill of outlawery. *Cap.* is for *Capias* ("Thou mayst seize"); *utlagatus* is the English word "outlaw", not translated but barbarised into Latin, the English word "out" dropping its *o,* as Latin did not have an *ou* diphthong, and the English word "law" changing its *w,* since Latin did not have a *w,* into a *g,* and an accusative form contrived. Latin has no exact equivalent for "outlaw", the nearest Latin terms, *proscriptus* ("proscribed"), or *"relegatus"* ("banished") reflecting different law, hence the barbarising of our English word "outlaw".

Bacon, however, was not an outlaw. Coke may have thought he could pin on him a debt which had in fact been paid.

He wrote at the same time a sharp letter to Coke:[3]

Mr. Attorney;
   I thought best, once and for all, to let you know in plainness what I find with

you, and what you shall find of me. You take to yourself a liberty to disgrace and disable my law, my experience, my discretion. What it pleaseth you I pray, think of me: I am one that knows both mine own wants and other men's; and it may be, perchance, that mine mend, and others stand at a stay. And surely I may not endure in public place to be wronged without repelling the same to my best advantage to right myself. You are great, and therefore have the more enviers; which would be glad to have you paid at another's cost. Since the time I missed the Solicitor's place (the rather I think by your means) I cannot expect that you and I shall ever serve as Attorney and Solicitor together, but either to serve with another upon your remove, or to step into some other course; so as I am more free than ever I was from any occasion of unworthy conforming myself to you, the more general good manners or your particular good usage should provoke. And if you had not been shortsighted in your own fortune (as I think) you might have had more use of me. But that tide is past. I write not this to show my friends what a brave letter I have written to Mr. Attorney; I have none of those humours. But what I have written, is to a good end, that is to the more decent carriage of my mistress' service, and to our particular better understanding of one another.

1. *Apologie,* Spedding, X, p.159.
2. Hatfield House, Cecil Papers, 86/87.
3. British Museum, Additional MSS. 5503, f.36.

CHAPTER 35

The blackness needing eisel

THERE are two sonnets which I suggest relate to this period. One is 36

> . . . those blots that do with me remaine . . .
> I may not euer-more acknowledge thee
> Least my bewailed guilt should do thee shame,
> Nor thou with publike kindnesse honour me,
> Unlesse thou take that honour from thy name . . .

and 111:

> O For my sake doe you with fortune chide . . .
> That did not better for my life prouide,
> Then publick meanes which publick manners breeds.
> Thence comes it that my name receiues a brand,
> And almost thence my nature is subdu'd
> To what it workes in, like the Dyers hand
> . . . I will drink
> Potions of Eysell . . .

What are the ''blots''? There is no kind of sexual scandal in Bacon's life (or Shakespeare's) which could excite language such as this. The ''blots'' could perhaps be the ''bruits'' of which Francis informed the Queen, hideous bruits that it was he who had put her against Essex. If people thought it so, it would shame the dowager Countess of Southampton (now married to Hervey) to receive on terms of friendliness one who was acting against her son's patron. Worse, after the Essex rebellion, Southampton was beside Essex in the dock.

The idea that 111 could relate to the acting profession seems to me grotesque. No actor ever thought of his appearances on the boards as shaming him, and Shakespeare was not forced to take it up; he could have carried on his father's business at Stratford. What I suggest Bacon means is that if the Queen would have acknowledged him as her son, none of this trouble would have happened. As she did not provide for him, he had to earn his livelihood by public means, that is by qualifying as a lawyer, and having become so qualified, he could be called upon by her, *nolens volens*,[1] to conduct a case he would have preferred not, and feels stained by the action in which he has played a part. Eisel was a kind of particularly bitter vinegar, used by dyers to remove the dye from their hands, and it is this that he feels the need to gulp down, to cleanse his whole being. J.Q. Adams noted (M.L.N., 1914, XXIX 2f) that the word occurred also in

Hamlet, V, i, 299, "Woo'd drinke eysell?" as representing something supremely distasteful to do, and suggested the use of this unusual word in both places meant that Sonnet 111 and *Hamlet* were contemporaneous.

Hamlet has seen Ophelia laid in earth, when he cries:

> woo't tear thyself?
> Woo't drink up eisel? eat a crocodile?
> I'll do it.

These are the self-tearing pangs of remorse.

Hamlet is the deepest of all the plays. Even the origins of the tale are lost in the mists. The first we hear of it is from Snaebjorn the Boar, an Icelander writing about 850; and he sets it in "ages long past". Iceland was only settled about that time, so (unless the settlers brought the tale from the mainland) it must have been soon after the settlement that somewhere amongst the glaciers and hot-springs, the sulphur-springs and the bogs, someone called Amleth feigned madness, while plotting how to avenge the murder of his father, by the uncle who had married his mother.

Charlotte Stopes suggested some of the difficulty we experienced with *Hamlet* came from its being a pre-Christian story re-set in Christian times. She was right, but could have gone further. In the Iceland that worshipped Odin and the Norse pantheon, there was no public force for the maintenance of order. It was for each man to protect his own and preserve balance by revenge for any wrong to his family, and this had to be nicely judged, neither too harsh or too soft. One may absorb the atmosphere and the ethos of it by reading the *Njal Saga*. A man who knew his father to have been murdered and did nothing about it would have been spoken of as a coward.

Snaebjorn's story, preserved for us in the *Skaldskaapar-mal* of 1230, by Snorri, another Icelander, passed into the *Historiae Danicae* of Saxo Grammaticus. In this twelfth century work, printed only in 1514, the wicked uncle, Feng, suspects Amleth to be only feigning madness, and sets a foster sister, loved by him, to cross his path in the hope he will betray his sanity by recognition. A foster-brother warns him. Amleth goes to the bedroom of his mother, Queen Gerutha, and tells her only mares couple with the vanquishers of their former mates. Seeing a movement beneath the straw covering the floor, he stabs through it and finds he has killed an eavesdropper. Feng sends him to England with two companions who bear a block of wood, on which is incised a message begging the English king to have Amleth killed. Amleth cuts his own name out and carves theirs. Arriving to a royal welcome, he returns with the King of England's daughter for his bride, kills the wicked uncle and is crowned king of Jutland.

Next, the story was adapted into French by Belleforest, in his *Histoires*

Tragiques. Here, it is the foster-sister who warns Amleth their meetings are watched. For the rest, Saxo is followed, but the details relating to a primitive society are replaced by more elegant counterparts; and so, as it is Belleforest from which our poet worked, it is no surprise that in *Hamlet* the original straw beneath which the eavesdropper was stabbed has become an arras, the block of wood a letter, on paper. New characters are the Ghost, the players, Horatio and Ophelia with her relations. The Ghost is probably borrowed from Kyd, *The Spanish Tragedy.* Polonius is generally recognised as Lord Burghley in his later years, and the Oxfordian, J.T. Looney, has well observed parallelism between the advice given by Polonius to Laertes and that given by Burghley to his son, Robert Cecil, when going abroad, such as to preclude coincidence, and also make it unlikely the actor from Stratford could have been in possession of material that would hardly be known far outside the Cecils' family. Oxford was Robert Cecil's brother-in-law, Bacon his cousin (nominally). It does not follow Ophelia is Anne Cecil.

One does not see the *Mémoires* of Marguerite de Valois cited amongst the sources of *Hamlet,* and indeed they were not published until 1628, but to re-read *Hamlet* after reading the *Mémoires* is, where Hamlet, returning unexpectedly, encounters the funeral procession and learns it is for Ophelia, whom he let down, to experience a sense of *déjà vu.* In the *Mémoires,* XV, is the story of one of Marguerite's ladies-in-waiting, Hélène de Tournon. She loved the young Marquis de Varenbon. He returned her affection, yet seemed not master of his destiny. His powerful elder brother, the Duke of Burgundy, intended him for the church. Her mother, seeing nothing but heartbreak in store for her child through attachment to a man promised to a celibate vocation, forbade further association. But Marguerite, when she visited Flanders in 1577, took Hélène with her, knowing de Varenbon was now there. In Namur they saw him, yet though he saw her he did not look at Hélène. So long as they were in the town, Hélène bore up, but when they moved on she collapsed and died, it was believed of a broken heart. Her funeral, at Liège, was pompous, and a rider was held up by the cortège. It was de Varenbon, come after all to ask for her hand in marriage. Impatient of the delay, he asked whose funeral was passing, and when he was told, fainted.

Even Polonius' warning to Ophelia that Hamlet's high destiny would make marriage between them impossible has something in common with Madame de Tournon's warning to Hélène.

That our dramatist was familiar with the story of the Belgian tour and of Hélène, we have already seen in our study of *Love's Labour's Lost.* Bacon could have heard it from Marguerite or one of her ladies in waiting when he was with the French court in the following year.

The deepest change our author has made in the story is, however, in the character of Hamlet. How has the straightforward Norse hero become so introspective and indecisive?

Sigmund Freud, in an informal letter to William Fliess of 15.10.'97, says he can remember feeling jealous of his father with his mother, and that if this is a general phenomenon of early childhood it would explain the gripping power of *Oedipus Rex*. He adds:[2]

> The idea has passed through my head that the same thing may lie at the root of *Hamlet*. I am not thinking of Shakespeare's conscious intentions, but supposing rather that he was impelled to write it by a real event because his own unconscious understood that of his hero.

This was the genesis of an idea he was to elaborate over the years. Thus, in *An Outline of Psycho-Analysis,* he was to write: Hamlet "came to grief over the task of punishing someone else for what coincided with the substance of his own Oedipus wishes".[3]

Such brief indications were worked out extensively by his disciple Ernest Jones in *Oedipus and Hamlet* (Gollancz, 1940). Here it is pointed out that Hamlet seems less concerned over the murder of his father than the incest of his mother. One does not have to go all the way with Freud and Jones as to the reason for Hamlet's delay in killing his uncle, but Jones makes one very telling point. Hamlet, just before going into his mother's bedchamber, says:

> Now I could drink hot blood.
> And do such bitter business as the day
> Would quake to look on; soft, now to my mother—
> O heart, lose not thy nature, let not ever
> The soul of Nero enter this firm bosom,
> Let me be cruel, not unnatural.
> I will speak daggers to her, but use none.

III, ii, 408-414

Why is Hamlet talking about Nero at all? In Tacitus, XIV, ii, we read that Nero's mother, Agrippina, would come to him at banquets seductively clad and "prepared for incest", and that such lascivious kissings took place that Seneca, seeking to avert sacrilegious intercourse, introduced to him a freed-woman, Acte; but Acte, terrified, declared incest to have been committed already, as was publicly known, from Agrippina's glorying in it, and that the troops would not tolerate a sacrilegious emperor. Nero, therefore, had his mother assassinated.

Jones tells us most cases of matricide go back to a too great carnality in the woman, disturbing the son and causing him to kill her to be rid of the temptation. He does not mention the manner of the assassination in this case. Tacitus tells us, XIV, iii-viii, that Nero arranged for the construction of a boat, such that part, bearing her couch, would come away and go adrift, and invited his mother to the Bay of Baiae, where he saw her and her maid aboard for a midnight excursion. The mechanics proved awkward and the vessel failed to come in half as it should have; the two women were nevertheless tipped into the water, but it was, by mistake, the maidservant who was hit on the head and pushed under. Agrippina swam to a fishing-smack, which took her ashore. Nero, learning, sent troops to her villa, where she had taken refuge. Seeing herself surrounded, she offered (significantly), her womb to the sword.

In Nero's mind, however, the original intent was that she should be drowned, and this, had Jones noticed it, would have strengthened his case, for the drowning has been shifted to Ophelia, on to whom Hamlet has already transferred his resentment against his mother's shamelessness. This would give a deeper meaning to the drowning than the accidental slip of one Katherine Hamlet into the Avon in 1579. It would not be impossible Shakespeare told Bacon of this, but the hero's name, Hamlet, is direct from the Norse Amleth. Icelandic has, like English, conserved the *th* sound from Primitive Germanic. Modern Icelandic still uses the two special symbols for the voiceless and voiced varieties possessed by Old English (Anglo-Saxon). Old Icelandic Amlothi (the "othi" part of it probably corresponding to Modern Icelandic "othur", meaning "mad") was Latinised by Saxo as Amlethus, which English commentators render Amleth. Belleforest changed this to Hamblet, and the name had come to be known in England as Hamlet when, with probable reference to a now lost play by Thomas Kyd, Nashe wrote, in 1589, "hee will affoord you whole Hamlets".[4]

A further point, first noticed by Mr. William Montgomerie,[5] concerns the change of the name of the uncle from Feng to Claudius. This is special to our author. It is not followed, for instance, in a loose English rendering of Belleforest of 1608, where the uncle of "Hamblet" is "Fengon". Claudius is not a Norse name, but it was the name of the uncle of Agrippina, whom she had incestuously married, making him step-father to Nero before she transferred her interest to her son. English readers have not had to wait for Robert Graves to depict Claudius to them as one of the more sympathetic Roman emperors, who murdered no one. A god in Britain, he was always well regarded here. Why, then, has our author made of him the villain, except for his horror of the incest with Nero's mother?

We see now that the time and culture shifts are even more complex than was suspected by Charlotte Stopes. It is not merely that a pre-Christian Norse story has been re-set in Christian times; it is a story of Iceland before the conversion which (after passage through Mediaeval Denmark and Renaissance France) has been shifted even further backwards in time, to the ancient Rome of the reign of Nero, at the moment of his incest and matricide, in order better to reflect the author's feelings about the situation engulfing him in Elizabethan England.

Although Anne Hathaway was older than Shakespeare, his removal

from Stratford to London was much against an abnormally strong
attachment to his mother, and Freud began to look elsewhere. He
reconnoitered the Baconian camp but only briefly (assuredly there is
nothing to suggest an Oedipal attachment of Bacon to Lady Bacon, his
supposed mother, whom he never once mentions excepting upon the
occasion of her funeral) and passed into the Oxfordian, to the extent of
asking Jones to explore whether Oxford's life would show an Oedipal
situation, such as he felt the author of *Hamlet* must have experienced. But
apparently Jones found nothing in Oxford's life either to fit the Oedipal
theory.

One must not seek in the play for an exact analogue to the author's
family situation. Elizabeth did not marry Leicester's brother; it was to
Essex she came so close as to give Francis the feeling of incest. But it is
a fact there was some suspicion Leicester's death was not natural. When
eventually the scurrilous *Leicester's Commonwealth* was reissued, it was
with an addendum, *Leicester's Ghost,* a poem wherein it was alleged that,
Leicester, having got wind of the adultery of Lettice with the young Sir
Christopher Blount, the guilty lovers, fearing he might be revenged upon
them, murdered him, by poison. This story has generally been discounted
by historians on the ground that Leicester's will shows no distrust of
Lettice. Yet Elizabeth Jenkins, who notes that Lettice married Blount
(twenty-four years her junior) remarkably quickly after Leicester's death,
without going into formal mourning for him, believes something of the
story must have reached Elizabeth's ears when she called Lettice "a
whore".[6] Bliss, the editor of Wood's *Athenae Oxoniensis,* tells us he had
seen a manuscript copy of *Leicester's Ghost* wherein the author said it was
from William Haynes, Gentleman of the Bedchamber to Leicester at the
time of his death, that he had the story Lettice joined them on the journey
towards Buxton Spa, and that he saw her administer to Leicester, as he lay
in bed, the glass of what must have been the poison that killed him. If
Francis had seen this, (we cannot know how early it was composed) then
we have the reason for the introduction of the Ghost into the play, who
existed neither in Saxo nor Belleforest; indeed we have an exact parallel to
Hamlet's situation, since it must have set him wondering whether
Leicester's Ghost spoke true and wishing he could interrogate his father's
real departed spirit as to whether he thought he had been poisoned. He had
no practical problem as to whether Blount should be brought to book for
murder, since he had been, by the time *Hamlet* was written, beheaded,
like Essex, for his part in the Essex rebellion, but the character of
Gertrude may be modelled in part on Lettice, though probably more on
the Queen, who having been made into Circe in *A Midsummer Night's
Dream* appears here as Agrippina. I wish to make quite plain I do not
believe impropriety between Elizabeth and Essex took place, but there was
sufficient of the atmosphere of it to disturb Francis. The likeness of

Hamlet's entry to his mother's bedchamber to Essex' intrusion into the Queen's at Nonesuch has been noted before, and it is significant that Jonson in his *Cynthia's Revels,* V, xi, 14-15:

> For so A CTAEON, by presuming farre,
> Did (to our grief) incurre a fatall doome

is seeing the execution of Essex as a punishment not for his treason but for having, by thrusting into her chamber, seen the Queen before she was fully dressed in the morning.

What happened in those moments we can never know. She never saw him after, and if there had been in his movement towards her anything that caused her an immeasurable shock, she may have felt it impossible they should ever meet again. We are in the face not of matricide but filicide.

But I do not think Hamlet is wholly Essex, or yet wholly Francis. He is Essex where he is "the expectancy and rose of the fair state", the popular one, but he is Francis speaking of

> The pangs of disprized loue, the law's delay,
> The insolence of office, and the spurns
> That patient merit of the unworthy takes
>
> *III, i, 72-74*

The insolence of office was surely that he had recently endured from Coke, and the pangs mainly those occasioned by the Countess of Southampton. Had Jones known the real mother to have black eyes, it would have reinforced his diagnosis that behind the Dark Lady stood the author's mother, for whom she was to some extent a substitute in his deeper feelings. The mother sets the pattern sought in the wife.

Hamlet is, I feel sure, Francis in all the respects that suggest a dark midnight of the soul. There had been not only Essex' attempt on his mother, followed by his death on her warrant, there had been the trial, at which Francis had appeared for the Crown and for his mother against his brother. He would have seen, what was veiled, from the public, that Essex' insurrection was a bid for the throne. For Essex' professed concern, merely that the succession should go to King James of Scotland, will not bear examination. Barring some contrary will by the Queen, it would go to him anyway, as her apparent next-of-kin. Why should Essex hazard his own head merely to unseat the Queen in her own lifetime and settle James on her throne prematurely? Coke may have smelled some whiff of the truth, or else spoken more truly than he knew, when at the trial he had exclaimed that Essex would, of an Earldom, be the last, who had thought "of a Kingdom to be Robert the First". These words, generally taken to have been empty ranting, may have had, for Francis, a nasty ring of probable truth. Moreover, the rebellion was not merely against their mother but against him, as the elder brother and first in line of the illegitimate succession, if that be realised. He may, still, never have believed a beheading would be carried out. He may have thought that an inevitable verdict and sentence passed for form's sake, to warn Essex, would be followed by a stay of execution and a pardon. Had the warrant not been acted on so fast, perhaps it might have been. But the total situation, precisely because it was so full of undisclosed undertows, must have given to Francis the sensation of having participated in an act of blackness.

> Woo't drink up eisel? eat crocodile?

Hamlet is Francis in his sense of ineffectuality. This is triggered by the players. He (because he is the author of plays) can bring players on to the scene, write a play for them to perform, create through them, but not act in a direct manner. After hearing the first player declare upon the death of Hecuba, Hamlet exclaims:

> What would he do,
> Had he the motive and the cue for passion
> That I have . . .
> I, a muddy-metaled rascal, peak,
> Like John-o-dreams pregnant of my cause   *II, ii, 586-95*

What cause? Hamlet is not really interested in killing Claudius. Perhaps the author has slipped into speech *in propria persona*. Psychologically, the Queen had died with Essex. For what remained of her life, she was but the shadow of her former self. Sir John Harrington tells us that she would sit at times alone in a darkened room, weeping, he believed, for Essex. Physically, she was failing.

Francis, as he saw her life sinking to its close, must, if he was her son, have known the time was short in which she still could recognise him. If he wanted to reign, for all the good that he could do, he should not let her slip away without doing anything. He should find the roughness to beard her. That he could not do it—"the native hue of resolution . . . sicklied o'er with the pale cast of thought"—was perhaps because he could not bring himself to dash the myth of her virginity, which had contributed so much to her image as Gloriana.

Therefore, he would let the king from the north come in:

> . . . he hath my dying voice.

1. Willy nilly.
2. *The Origins of Psycho-Analysis, Letters to Wilhelm Fliess . . . 1887-1902 . . .* translation by Eric Mosbacher and James Strachey, (Imago, 1954), first English edition.
2. Translation by James Strachey (Hogarth, 1949, p.61.
4. *The Works of Thomas Nashe,* McKerrow, III, p.315.
5. 'More an Antique Roman than a Dane', *Hibbert Journal,* LIX, 1960, pp.67-74.
6. *Elizabeth and Leicester,* Elizabeth Jenkins (Gollancz, 1961) pp.279-80.

CHAPTER 36

Bereavement

IN May, 1601, Anthony died. The date is unknown, but his burial, in St. Olave's Church, Hart Street, was on May 17th. He had left Essex House in March 1600, and Dame Daphne du Maurier, who found the entry in the register, thinks he may have been staying at the nearby home of Lady Walsingham, widow of his first employer and mother of Essex' widow.

The last months cannot have been happy for Anthony, because of two people who were dear to him, Francis and Essex. The latter's growing wildness must have been a matter of acute concern to him, and a letter he wrote him during his first imprisonment, in York House, shows that, deeply feeling for both, he regarded Francis as the wiser, who would do everything he could. That was presuming Essex would be guided by his counsels, and before it became evident his first follies were but the prelude to worse.

Why was not Anthony at Gorhambury when he died? We cannot know. In 1601 there appeared (in *Love's Martyr*) *The Phoenix and the Turtle*. This strangely beautiful dirge has always been difficult to explain. The two birds are represented as both being dead, childless though married, not from incapacity but from "Married chastity". It has sometimes been felt the Phoenix should be Queen Elizabeth, of whom there exists the 'Phoenix' portrait. But in 1601 the Queen, though failing, was still alive, and a dirge could not have been written for her. Moreover the other details do not fit. Some have thought it was for a literally married couple, who died childless, but we do not know of a couple who died in circumstances such as to have been the subject of the poem. And how could the poet have been so intimate with a couple as to know that their childlessness was from "married chastity"? The poem is probably symbolic. Dr. Rowse thinks the death is the death of love; in a sense it may be, but the Dark Lady is hardly one to have inspired thoughts of married chastity. Professor Akrigg, noting how shortly after the death of Essex it appeared, thinks the love must have been that between Essex and his followers, all now dead on the block.

I suggest it may have been written by Francis after the death of Anthony. If Dame Daphne du Maurier is right about his having died a virgin, then, as a sublimated homo-erotic, his friendships will have been very intense; on the Northumberland Manuscript, in which Baconians believe to be Francis' hand, are doodled the words, "Anthony comfort and consort". Here, then, are the elements of "married chastity":

So they loued as loue in twaine,
Had the essence but in one,
Two distincts, Division none,
Number there in loue was slaine
. . .
Either was the others mine
. . .
It was married Chastitie.

Francis was alive, but may well have felt his heart was in the coffin with
Anthony; the only one who had stood by him in all things and never let
him down. The poem, one of the strangest, gravest and most beautiful in
our literature, has an unusual simplicity of diction, such as may speak a
purification of style by the weight of death.

Francis was now very much alone. During 1602 we hear nothing of
him.

On March 24th, 1602/3, the Queen died.

CHAPTER 37

James I

IN the evening of the day on which the Queen died, Cecil, who had been in communication with the Scottish King already, proclaimed him King of England.

It would take a week to bring him from Scotland to London. There was an enormous rush of people northwards to meet him and be the first in favour. Francis hung somewhat back. One reason for this may have been that those in England who had been most loyal to the old sovereign now stood at a disadvantage, with the new; especially Bacon, who had appeared for the Crown against Essex, whom the King was referring to as "my martyr". There may also have been another reason, which may be glimpsed between the lines of a letter he wrote to the incoming king:[1]

It may please your most excellent Majesty,
. . . this royal virtue of access, which nature and judgement have planted in your Majesty's mind . . . could not of itself . . . have animated me to make oblation of myself immediately to your Majesty, had it not been joined with an habit of like liberty, which I enjoyed with my late dear Sovereign Mistress; a Prince happy in all things, but most happy in such a successor. And . . . I was not a little encouraged, not only upon the supposal that unto your Majesty's sacred ears . . . there might perhaps have come some small breath of the good memory of my father, so long a principal counsellor in this your kingdom . . . most high and mighty King, my most dear and dread sovereign lord . . . there is no subject of your Majesty's who loveth this island . . . whose heart is not set on fire, not only to bring you peace-offerings . . . but to sacrifice himself a burnt offering to your Majesty's service . . .

The key-words are "oblation" and "sacrifice himself a burnt offering" (in a copy perhaps made from a different draft the words "or holocaust" are added). An ordinary lawyer, and MP without special position, would in no sense be sacrificing himself by promising loyalty to his King, and the phrases would be but empty verbiage. If, however, Bacon is writing as the bastard son of the late Queen, then he is sacrificing his claim to the throne, for the sake of the unification of the "island", suddenly seen as a geographical and potentially political unit, through the falling together of the two crowns. This, presumably, would have been the consideration which weighed with him in his decision to stand aside. That bastardy would have been no necessary bar can be seen from the number of people who were to support the Duke of Monmouth, the illegitimate son of Charles II, rather than his brother to succeed him.

Again, Bacon's position would not be without danger. For if James knew he was entering a kingdom where there was a bastard, representing an alternative line of succession, he might be asking himself what to do about him: placate him by advancing him, so as to mitigate grievance and put him under a debt of gratitude, or have him put down. Supposing that Francis did not know if James knew, but thought he might have heard the rumour, then the letter would be designed to give him, in such case, all the reassurances he needed, and the bringing in of a reference to Sir Nicholas as his father would carry the message that he was content with the apparent parentage allotted him, and was not a pretender.

It may have been partly with the idea of assuring James that any secret occupations he had were with literature, not aspirations to the throne, that he also wrote to John Davies (later Sir) of the Inner Temple, who had already set out:[2]

Mr. Davies,

Though you went on the sudden . . . I commend myself to your love and to the well using of my name, as well in repressing and answering for me if there be any biting or nibbling at it . . . So, desiring you to be good to concealed poets, I continue,

> Your very assured,
> Fr. Bacon

Davies, then, knew of Bacon as a ''concealed poet''. In 1596, Davies had published a fine poem, *Orchestra,* in which were five stanzas omitted from the later, 1602 edition:

> Oh that I had Homer's abundant vein,
> I would hereof another *Ilias* make
> Or else the man of Mantua'a charmed brain,
> In whose large throat great Jove the thunder spake,
> Oh that I could old Geoffrey's muse awake,
> Or borrow Colin's fair heroic style,
> Or smooth my rhymes with Delia's servant's file.
>
> Oh could I, sweet companion, sing like you,
> Which of a shadow, under a shadow sing!
> . . .

The first four of the poets following Homer are Dante (the Mantuan), Chaucer (Geoffrey), Spenser (Colin) and Daniel (Delia's servant). But who is the next one, the sweet companion who sings under a shadow? Who would be the natural next in such a list? It cannot be Sidney, for ''Astrophel'' follows later. Who is the one missed out? Surely it should be Shakespeare, often said to be ''sweet'', but then why does he sing ''under a shadow''? Also, it would seem unlikely that the actor from Stratford would, rather than other contemporaries, be thought of by the lawyer as a ''companion''. If it is his fellow in the Inns of Court who is the ''concealed poet'' singing under the ''shadow'' of Shakespeare's name, to whom Davies adverts, the passage becomes clear.

Only when King James' southward journey had brought him to Broxbourne, in Hertfordshire, did Francis go forward to meet him.

On April 10th Southampton was released from the Tower. People flocked to congratulate him, If Francis went, he risked a rebuff, and if he did not, it might look as though he grudged his liberation. So he sent him a note saying he would have paid a call had he felt sure it would not be unpleasing.

James was now creating knights, for a price. Coke received a knighthood, at his own request. Francis was arrested for debt. On this occasion it was Robert Cecil who, for the family honour, transferred Francis' indebtedness from the money-lender to himself. Francis, writing to thank him, adds that for this ''almost prostituted title of knighthood'', he would be glad to have it to offset the disgrace, and also because, ''I desire . . . to marry with some convenient advancement . . . I have found an alderman's daughter, an handsome maiden, to my liking.''[3]

This is the first we hear of Alice Barnham. Her father, who had sat in the Parliament of 1597, was now dead, and her mother had married a Sir John Packington. Alice was the second of four daughters, each of whom would inherit £6,000 in land, with an annual £300. She was only eleven, and the marriage would not take place until she reached nubile age.

Francis was knighted, in a troop of 300, at Whitehall Palace, on July 23rd, at a time when most other assemblies were forbidden because of a new outbreak of plague. During two weeks the deaths in London were 2,313. The King was crowned on July 25th, 1603, and the next day a proclamation ordered every man to his home.

Francis now sent the King a paper touching *The Pacification and Edification of the Church of England:* the word ''priest'' was best discontinued and ''minister'' substituted; Bishops were of some usefulness but took to themselves too much glory and their powers were best reduced . . . The King's opening speech to the assembly of Lords and Bishops at Hampton Court on January 14th, 1603/4, follows Francis' recommendations practically point for point. So, Francis slipped into being his adviser, as he had been Elizabeth's.

Another paper for the King, touching the union of England and Scotland contains an aside: ''the Persian magic, which was the secret literature of their kings, was an observation of nature''. Spedding virtually confesses his ignorance of Persian magic when he says we need not trouble ourselves as to whence Bacon derived his idea of it. Bacon almost certainly refers to the teachings of Zoroaster, revered, with Orpheus and Hermes Trismegistis as one of the Magi, by Marsilio Ficino, who translated the *Corpus Hermeticum* and gave us our Plato. Bacon must have read Ficino.

In the Parliament, opened on March 19th, 1603/4, Bacon expressed a hope that, as Salt, Mercury and Sulphur are mixed but imperfectly by men, yet blend in plant or animal, so England and Scotland may be united in King James. Yet he hoped that using the single name of Britain for the whole island would not extinguish the names of England and Scotland.

That session the Commons made its first trial of strength against the King.

It was to the Earl of Devonshire, formerly Charles Blount, Lord Mountjoy, Essex' friend, that Francis wrote the long letter later printed as *Francis Bacon his Apologie in certain imputations concerning the late Earle of Essex.* (The word Apologie then meant Defence.) It begins:

It may please your good Lordship: I cannot be ignorant, and ought to be sensible, of the wrong which I sustain in common speech, as if I had been false or unfaithful to that noble but unfortunate Earl, the Earl of Essex . . . Whatsoever I did . . . was done in my duty and service to the Queen and the State . . . And if any man shall say that I did officiously intrude myself into that business, because I had no ordinary place; the like may be said . . . of all the business in effect . . . these many years, wherein I was continually used. For . . . The Queen . . . did not always tie her trust to place, but did sometime divide private favour from office.

Here we have the crux of the Queen's attitude to Bacon; she would not give him office, yet continually called upon his services as if he had it. By using him at all times of crisis, particularly such as concerned her own security, whilst always withholding any title to authority, she exposed him to envy and malignant gossip.

I was not only not opposite to my Lord of Essex, but . . . I did occupy the utmost of my wits, and adventure my fortune with the Queen to have reintegrated him, and so continued faithfully and industriously till his last fatal impatience (for so I will call it), after which there was not time to work for him; though the same my affection, when it could not work on the subject proper, went to the next . . .

The next can only be Southampton. There has always been mystery as to why Southampton was not executed. Mr. Robert Gittings says:[4] "He was lucky, for he had been in disgrace with the Queen for his marriage in 1598, cashiered by her from his post as General of the Horse in Ireland in 1599, and was by all accounts the ring-leader of the ill-guided conspiracy". Cecil would hardly have helped him, so deeply had he offended the Cecils. It seems obvious it was Bacon who persuaded the Queen to spare him.

1. British Museum, Additional MSS, 5503, f.19, b.
2. Lambeth MSS, 536, f.4.
3. British Museum, Additional MSS, 5503, f.25b.
4. *Shakespeare's Rival,* Robert Gittings (Heinemann, 1960), p.23.

CHAPTER 38

The Advancement of Learning

BACON'S first major work to be published was *The Advancement of Learning*, 1605. He explains that he is not concerned with mere scholasticism but with the importance of learning in the development of man as a whole. For if much learning can make men "perplexed and irresolute", it should teach them "how to carry things in suspense without prejudice till they resolve".[1]

He distinguishes three kinds of vain learning: fantastical, contentious and affected, and says, "the first distemper of learning is when men study words, not matter". The second is vain matter:[2]

This kind of degenerate learning did chiefly reign amongst the schoolmen; who having strong wits, and abundance of leisure, and small variety of reading . . . (chiefly Aristotle, their dictator) as their persons were shut up in the cells of monasteries and colleges; and knowing little history . . . did out of no great quantity of matter, and infinite agitation of wit, spin out unto us these laborious webs of learning which are extant in their books. For the wit and mind of man, if it work upon matter, which is the contemplation of the creatures of God, worketh according to the stuff, and is limited thereby; but if it work upon itself as the spider worketh his web, then it is endless, and brings forth indeed cobwebs of learning, admirable for their fineness of thread and work, but of no substance of profit.

He would have contemplation and action joined in "a conjunction like unto that of the two highest planets, Saturn the planet of rest and contemplation, and Jupiter the planet of civil society and action".[3]

He notes that according to the hierarchy of Dionysius,[4] after God, the first place is given to the Seraphim, or angels of love; the second to the Cherubim, or angels of light or knowledge; and "the following places to thrones, principalities, and the rest, which are all angels of power and ministry".

He recalls Moses was "*seen in all the learning of the Egyptians* . . . Plato brings in the Egyptian priest saying unto Solon: *You Grecians are ever children; you have no knowledge of antiquity nor antiquity of knowledge*".[5] As *Exodus* presents a solely negative picture of the Egyptians, it looks as though Bacon had been reading in addition to Plato, Neo-Platonic, Gnostic or Hermetic literature. We could not read the ancient Egyptian writings until Champillion published his decipherments of hieroglyphics from the Rosetta stone in 1824, but Renaissance man thought we had them in the body of Trismegistic texts, in Greek, but believed to have been translated from the Egyptian before the art of reading their hieroglyphics was lost. Ficino had given us in 1471 a Latin version of the *Corpus Hermeticum* and related texts. It was not until a few years after *The Advancement* was published that, in 1614, Casaubon drew attention to anachronisms implying an A.D. date for at least some parts of it. The spirit may nevertheless be rendered.

For biographers, it is good to know Bacon approved biographies, and wishes more were written.[6] He find the lives of individuals more interesting to read than compendious histories, wherein, to achieve compression, good stories are killed. Neither does he like ''ruminated history'', wherein one is treated to the author's constant reflections on the events narrated; he would rather be left to make his own.[7]

Poetry he esteems, because, while imposing a discipline with regard to measure, it offers licence in respect of matter. In Feigned History, whether in verse or prose (the historical poem, play or novel), the writer is not restricted to the chronicle of events, but free to show ''a more ample greatness, a more exact goodness, and a more absolute variety, than can be found in the nature of things . . . the acts or events of true history have not that magnitude which satisfieth the mind of man''.[8]

He divides poetry into Narrative, Representative and Parabolic: ''as hieroglyphics were before letters, so parables were before arguments . . . the secrets and mysteries of religion, policy, or philosophy are involved in fables or parables. Of this in divine poesy we see the use is authorised[9] . . . for the expressing of affections, passions, corruptions and customs, we are beholding to poets more than to the philosopher's works . . . but we stay too long in the theatre . . . ''[10]

So, he passes to Philosophy, Divine, Natural and Human. The divisions are not like lines that meet at an angle, but branches from one tree-trunk, or Philosophia Prima. ''Was not the Persian magic a reduction or correspondence of the principles and architectures of nature to the rules and policy of governments?''[11]

Is not the delight of the quavering upon a stop in music the same with the playing of light upon the water? . . . Are not the organs of the senses of one kind with the organs of reflection, the eye with a glass, the ear with a cave or strait determined and bounded? Neither are these only similitudes, as men of narrow observation may conceive them to be, but the same footsteps of nature, treading or printing upon several subjects or matters.[12]

The ''footprints of nature'' later formed a Rosicrucian image. A philosopher will be shown treading in them, in an illustration to Michael Maier's *Atalanta fugens,* Oppenheim, 1617.

The soul is not subject to those laws which Philosophy studies; knowledge of it can come only by the same inspiration as gave it being.[13]

He sent a copy of the book to Sir Thomas Bodley, the founder of the Bodleian, with a letter in which he said:[14]

I do confess since I was of any understanding, my mind hath in effect been absent from that I have done, and in absence are many errors which I do willingly acknowledge; and amongst the rest this great one that led to the rest: that knowing myself by my inward calling to be fitter to hold a book than play a part, I have led my life in civil causes; for which I was not very fit by nature, and more unfit by the preoccupation of my mind.

1. Spedding, III, p.271.
2. *Op.cit.*, p.285.
3. *Op.cit.*, p.294.
4. *Op.cit.*, p.296.
5. *Op.cit.*, p.297.
6. *Op.cit.*, p.334-37.
7. *Op.cit.*, p.339.
8. *Op.cit.*, p.343.
9. *Op.cit.*, p.344.
10. *Op.cit.*, p.346.
11. *Op.cit.*, p.348.
12. *Op.cit.*, p.349.
13. *Op.cit.*, p.379.
14. *Resuscitatio*, p.34.

CHAPTER 39

Gunpowder plot

THE King was to have opened Parliament on November 5th, 1605, but on October 26th Lord Monteagle received a letter warning him to keep away. An instant search discovered, in the cellar, a certain Guy Fawkes mounting guard over gunpowder and faggots.

This practically coincided with the publication of *The Advancement of Learning,* and Francis, sending Tobie Matthew a copy, says he encloses a brief relation of the recent attempted outrage, so far as known. It is a pity Matthew, who preserved for us Bacon's letters to him, suppressed this. Bacon, however, played no formal part in the trial of the conspirators.

Nevertheless, lines in *Macbeth,* II, iii, 9-12, "here's an equivocator that could swear in both scales against either scale; who committed treason enough for God's sake, yet could not equivocate to Heaven" glance at Father Garnet's use, whilst on trial, of the doctrine of equivocation.[1] Though Coke prosecuted, Bacon must have been in court, for he wrote to Cecil, now Earl of Salisbury, that he would attend him "after tomorrow's business" referring, as Spedding thinks, to the trial of Father Garnet, on March 28th, 1606.

King James was afraid of gunpowder because his father had been blown up by it. He also feared witches, as his special enemies. More than any other, *Macbeth* is the play written for King James.

It has, however, been suggested[2] that Catherine de Medici (whom Bacon could have met in France) was the model for Lady Macbeth. Her sleep-walking and attempts to wash blood from her hands has something in common with the inability of Charles IX to sleep after the massacre of the Hugenots, ordered by him under her influence, and his reported sweating of blood through his skin. There seems no reason for Macbeth's waiting for his wife to ring a bell to tell him when to kill his King, but in Paris on St. Bartholomew's Night posses of men in widely dispersed parts of the city waited for the great bell of St. Germain Auxerrois to toll, this being the tocsin at which they were to move, all at once, from their hiding-places, enter the marked houses and stab the inhabitants.

The 1606 Parliament saw Francis speak in a matter only to become significant later. There was in those days almost no salary paid to public men from public funds; no Civil List, no formal arrangement by which judges or other civil servants of the Crown could receive a living. What they all lived on was fees, that is, particular disbursements by private individuals, gratuities paid to the class which today is salaried. These were known as the ''perquisites'' of office. If one had to get a paper stamped, one gave something to the official who stamped it. After a law suit, it was usual for the victorious party to give something to the judge, and to the various clerks and persons about the court. In *The Merchant of Venice*, the judge and her clerk were being tiresome only in demanding of Bassanio and Gratiano the rings they were wearing, instead of leaving it to them and to Antonio to give a purse or valuable. There was a tendency for the amounts to become standardised, and in January 1605/6, a bill was brought by a disappointed jobber to reduce fees for copies in the Court of Record.[3] Bacon spoke against this, because it would be to ''take away other men's freeholds''. Some had served the Crown for very long before attaining to their present offices, and suddenly to deprive them of half their livelihoods would be to do them ''an infinite injustice''. Landlords were allowed to raise their rents, but the fees of office had continued at one rate. ''These offices are either the gift of the King or in the gift of great officers, who have their office from the King''. To reduce their fees would be to deny the King means to prefer servants, and the great offices of the state would be disgraced and impaired. Few could afford to assume them gratis. The bill was ''a slander upon all superior judges, as if they had tolerated extortions''. Lately, tables of appropriate fees had been hung up in courts, so that parties should know if they were giving suitable amounts.

1. *A Shakespeare Encyclopaedia*, 'Garnet' and *'Macbeth'* Campbell and Quinn (Methuen, 1966).
2. *Macbeth, King Lear* and *Contemporary History*, Lilian Winstanley (CUP, 1922), pp.117, 120-23.
3. *The Personal History of Lord Bacon*, William Hepworth Dixon (Murray, 1861), p.250.

CHAPTER 40

Marriage

ON May 10th, 1606, her fourteenth birthday, Francis married Alice Barnham. We have a description of the ceremony in a letter of May 11th from Dudley Carleton to John Chamberlain:

> Sir Francis Bacon was married yesterday to his young wench in Maribone Chapel. He was clad from top to toe in purple, and hath made himself and his wife such store of fine raiments of cloth of silver and gold that it draws deep into her portion. The dinner was kept at his father-in-law Sir John Packington's lodging over against the Savoy, where his chief guests were the three knights, Cope, Hicks and Beeston; and upon this conceit (as he said himself) that since he could not have my L. of Salisbury in person, which he wished, he would have him at least in his representative body.

The choice of purple was singular, because by a law passed in 1464, no commoner could wear purple. That was sufficiently recent for the association between purple and royalty still to be strong in people's minds, as indeed it is today. When his first biographer, Pierre Amboise, wrote in 1631 that he was "né parmi les pourpres",[1] he was intimating royal connections. It will be remembered that Leicester's friends, to show they favoured his marriage with the Queen, wore stripes of purple.

If Francis was Queen Elizabeth's bastard son, his marriage was important, as issue could create an alternative line of succession. It could be that this announcement of intent to marry a commoner, made in the letter to Cecil written so soon after the new King's accession, was in part intended to assure James he had no design upon the throne. His wearing now of purple would seem out of line, though he could have thought his loyalty was by this time so obvious that the little flourish would not provoke.

Yet Francis' choice of a bride remains mysterious. One feels she was not endowed with intellectual gifts or one would have heard of them. Perhaps one should not go beyond his own statement, that she was "an handsome maiden". Today we think of fourteen as far too young for marriage, yet it was not so then, although a difference in age of thirty-four years is strange.

Is there anything in Shakespeare written during the period 1603-04 showing us the courtship and marriage of a man of position and a girl hardly more than a child? There is *Othello*, written in 1604. This is interesting, because the Moor was Desdemona's father's friend, and it was listening to his talking of his life's experiences that her imagination was stirred, so that she became more than half the wooer. There is the hint he would not have thought his person appealing to her, dark—dare one say with ''tann'd antiquity''?[2] Othello refers to ''the young affects In me defunct'', not normally the qualification for a bridegroom. The plot concerning the wicked ensign who poisons the Moor's mind against his wife is, of course, from the novella of Cinthio, which it would seem the author of *Othello* must have read in the original Italian, since there is no English translation of that date known.

What is ironic is that the story of the tender courtship should have been set into one ending with the man's castigating himself for listening to another's accusation of adultery against his wife. Alice was not destined to prove faithful to Francis.

It may have been only towards the end he knew it for certain, but trouble began early. One of his best friends, Sir John Constable, had married Alice's younger sister, Dorothy, and their joint mother-in-law, herself at war within her own second marriage, was apparently meddling in both her daughters' when Francis wrote to her he could not suffer her to bring such dissensions between her daughters and their husbands as she had misery in her own case. Lady Packington must have thought he was on the point of ejecting Alice from his house, within months of the wedding, for he says that with regard to her kind offer to take her daughter back, cast off, it looked more likely he and Alice would have to take in her, cast off by her own second husband. Not yet apprehending the worst, he was, then, loyally trying to make the best of it.

King Lear was performed on December 26th, 1606. A series of eclipses in the autumn of 1605 had been followed by some strange events, such as the stupendous storm of March 30-31, 1606, and narrow the date of composition thought to underlie *King Lear,* I, ii, 112-19. One cannot say this dark tragedy sorts naturally with a bridal year, but if the idea of writing it was prompted by the publication of the anonymous *King Lear,* 1605, the more personal inspiration surely goes back to 1603, when the two married daughters of Sir Brian Annesley, Lady Wildgoose and Lady Sandys, sought to have their father declared insane with administration of his estate given to the husband of Lady Wildgoose. The youngest, Cordell, as yet unmarried, wrote to Cecil, pleading that her father, a Gentleman Pensioner of the Queen, deserved a better agnomination than at his last gasp to be registered as a lunatic. When eventually Annesley passed away, Lady Wildgoose petitioned to have his will set aside, but unsuccessfully. It left almost everything to Cordell. The overseer of the will was Sir William Hervey.

It looks then as if our dramatist had kept in touch with Hervey, despite his marriage to the Countess, and had heard the story from him. In II, iv, 46, when Lear hears how his messenger has been coldly turned away by Goneril and her husband, having got his money, the Fool comments,

"Winter's not gone yet, if the wild-geese fly that way". This sounds like a hit at Lady Wildgoose and her husband. But why does Lear go mad? The King Lyr, Ler or Leir of myth does not go mad, in any previous version of his story. He bears the usurpation by his daughters with patient sanity. Dr. Rowse makes the comment that the triangular relationship between Goneril, Albany and Edmund recalls that between Tamora, Saturninus and Aaron in *Titus Andronicus*. King Lear, amongst the mature plays of our author is the one which, in its stark cruelty, most nearly pairs with that early tale of horrors. Perhaps something had caused him to re-read "that blacke storie" as Hall called it. There, too, the central character, Titus, goes mad, in the end. Only, in *King Lear,* the madness is much more realistically depicted. O.J. Campbell says,[3] "Shakespeare's portrayal of each stage of Lear's tragic journey to insanity reveals his surprising knowledge of the onset of complete derangement." It is unlikely Cordell furnished the picture, as her case would have been that her father was of perfectly sound mind.

The total absence of allusion to Lady Bacon, even from documents concerning her estate at Gorhambury, during her last years, puzzles Spedding. He writes (Vol. XI, p.217):

The supposition which seems to me the most probable is that she lost the command of her faculties some years before her death, that the management of her affairs was taken out of her hands, and that somebody was employed to look after her. There are symptoms in her earlier correspondence of an excitement and irritability which might easily end in that way; and if it did, the silence would be accounted for. The only allusion to her later years which I have met with is in Bishop Goodman's 'Court of King James the First' and is in these words:- "But as for Bacon's mother, she was but little better than frantic in her age."

One remembers the terrible words she used, as long ago as 1589, to Captain Allen, of her very gentle and dutiful son, Anthony: "She let not to say you are a traitor to God and to your country; you have undone her; you seek her death; and when you have that you seek for, you shall have but a hundred pounds more than you have now . . . She says you are hated of all . . . and cursed of God in all your actions, since Mr. Lawson's being with you . . . She wished . . . you had been fairly buried, so you died in the Lord". Does one recognise Lear's comminatory style? Admittedly, Lady Bacon's was mainly a religious mania, and the above was because of reports Anthony had friends who were Catholic. But she had also an obsession that the family substance was being consumed by servants and hangers on, "sinful, proud villains, cormorant seducers and instruments of Satan". Could these have been the ancestors of Lear's "pelican daughters"? (11, iv, 77).

O.J. Campbell points out the way Lear uses the storm,[4] "The destructive power of the tempest is a manifestation of the forces of evil that have invaded Lear's mind . . . The storm is more than an adjunct to the old man's fury, it elevates his passion . . . He calls upon the elements of the storm – the rain, the thunder and the lightning . . . '' Back in 1595, Lady Bacon had written, of a wind that removed some tiles from the roof:

> One of the prophets, Nahum, I think, saith that the Lord hath His way with the whirlwind, the storm, and tempest, and clouds are the dust of his feet. The wind hath had great power . . .

As Spedding says, she probably grew worse with age. Ten years further on in time and frenzy, the even greater storm thought to have inspired *King Lear* will hardly have failed to set her off again. Francis, at Gorhambury, had to listen to her all the time. So, presumably, did Alice; which should be remembered in extenuation of her conduct.

And yet, behind a barren tragedy of such proportions, there should lurk surely something more than the ravings of an old lady, who, however much he might have to see of her, was not, it has been submitted, his real mother. I have wondered whether there is not in this picture of utter desolation something of Queen Elizabeth after the execution of Essex. It is a long shot, and the analogy cannot be pressed too closely, since, as the dramatist has reshuffled the pieces, it is not exact. Yet the play is about parents and children, strife between siblings and misjudgement by parents between their children. Each parent prefers the worse to the better. Queen Elizabeth preferred Essex to Bacon, and he may have seen himself in the role of Cordelia, uttering unpalatable truths where the other charmed.

It may seem strange to tax the greatest master of the English language with not being able to put his own case well. But if on the printed page the poet's words seem to the reader mellifluous, poets have, notoriously, been unsuccessful in the tender relations. Alfred de Vigny, has stated the dilemma in his poem *Moïse (Moses)*:

> Je comande à la nuit de déchirer ses voiles;
> Ma bouche par leur nom a compté les étoiles
> . . .
> Pour dormir sur un sein mon front est trop pesant
>
> I command the night to part its veils,
> My mouth has counted the stars by their names
> . . .
> To lie on a breast my head is too heavy

That is exactly it. The minor talent that composes a few pretty verses may serve as an adjunct to courtship or the pressing of a suit, but the head heavy with genius does not find the irresponsible words that gush forth to carry away. As Alexander Pope put it to his friend Spence,[5] Bacon, possessing intellectual capacities so far in excess of those of other men, could know no equal friendship, and therefore was condemned to a certain loneliness. Like de Vigny's Moïse, he would sometimes have liked to be rid of his capacities, to enjoy human relations unencumbered. Essex could promise the Queen the most total devotion, yet Francis, whose devotion was not the less sincere, could only tell the Queen she was demanding of the people too much in taxes, a plainness which caused her to cast him off as Lear did Cordelia.

1. Born amidst the purples.
2. *Sonnet* 62, 10.
3. *A Shakespeare Encyclopaedia,* Campbell & Quinn (Methuen, 1966).
4. *Loc cit.*
5. *Anecdotes.*

CHAPTER 41

Solicitor

MEANWHILE, a rumour concerning a possible promotion brought the Solicitorship into question again. Francis wrote to Salisbury:[1]

It is thought Mr. Attorney shall be Chief Justice of the Common Pleas. In case Mr. Solicitor rise, I would be glad now at last to be Solicitor.

Mr. Attorney (Coke) rose, but Mr. Solicitor (Doderidge) did not rise to take his place. A Sir Henry Hobart was put in as Attorney. To quote Spedding, "the sincerity of Salisbury's professed desire to raise Bacon falls under just suspicion". With the Cecils it was "like father, like son". Francis' reaction to this new passing over was almost violent. He wrote to the Lord Chancellor, Sir Thomas Egerton:[2]

It may please your good Lordship,
 . . . it were better for me that the King did blot me out of his book, or that I should turn my course to endeavour to serve him in some other kind, than for me to stand thus at a stop, and to have that little reputation which by my industry I gather to be scattered . . . by continual disgrace, every new man coming before me . . .

To Salisbury, he wrote very bitterly:[3]

I am not ignorant how mean a thing I stand for, in desiring to come into the Solicitor's place. For I know well, it is not the thing it hath been . . .

Further months passed. Summer turned to winter, winter to another summer. On June 25th, 1607, quietly, Francis became Solicitor.

That year, Tobie Matthew returned from his three year stay in Italy. It now came out he had been converted to Catholicism, which he had not mentioned in his letters, and which, since he was the son of Archbishop of York, shocked many. While his case was being considered, he was confined.

The Gunpowder Plot of 1605 had caused the passing of anti-Catholic laws, and these in their turn provoked anti-Protestant literature and a recrudescence of attacks on Queen Elizabeth. While she lived, it had been Bacon's role to reply to such. He did not fail her now that she was dead. Cynics have seen his praises of the living Queen as flattery; the charge can be dropped when one reads his *In Felicem Memoriam Elizabethae Reginae Angliae*. To write such an encomium in 1608 could advantage him not at all.

The title needs explanation. We shall later see from his essay ('Of

Fortune') that he considered it always wiser to speak of fortune than achievement. If a person was lucky, if his affairs seemed to arrange themselves with a certain felicity, it suggested the hand of Providence:

Nor ought the calamity of her mother to be admitted as an objection to the dignity of her birth: the rather because it is clear that Henry the Eighth had fallen in love with another woman before he fell in anger with Anne,[4] and because he has not escaped the censure of posterity as a man by nature extremely prone both to loves and suspicions, and violent in both even to the shedding of blood. And besides, the criminal charge in which she was involved was in itself, if we consider only the person to whom it related, improbable, and rested upon the slenderest conjectures; as was secretly whispered (as the manner is in such cases) even then, and Anne herself just before her death with a high spirit and in memorable words made protestation. For having procured a messenger whose fidelity and good will she thought she could trust, she sent to the King, in the very hour when she was preparing for the scaffold, a message to this effect: "That he kept constant to his course of heaping honours upon her; from a gentlewoman without title he had made her marchioness; he had then raised her to be the partner of his throne and bed; and now at last, because there remained no higher step of earthly honour, he had vouchsafed to crown her innocence with martyrdom." Which words the messenger durst not indeed carry to the King, who was then in the heat of a new love; but fame, the vindicator of truth, transmitted them to posterity.

One would dearly like to know through what agency this precious story, for which Bacon is our only source, descended. The person to whom Anne spoke these words probably desired Elizabeth should know them as soon as she was old enough to understand, but Elizabeth never published it. She could not declare her mother's innocence without implying her father's guilt, and many of her subjects liked to see him in her. That is doubtless why she never spoke of her mother. That she did hold her memory tenderly can be divined from the special kindness with which she treated all who had been her mother's faithful servants. She would hardly have told Francis, since she was not acknowledging him as her son, but she would have had few secrets from Leicester, and he may have thought Francis should know how his grandmother died.

There is a passage in *Felicem . . .* where the scholar in him seems to doze, when he writes of Queen Elizabeth, "Childless she was . . . as Alexander the Great, Julius Caesar . . ." Alexander did not live to see his child, but at the time of his sudden death Roxana was pregnant with the son she bore him posthumously. Julius Caesar had no legitimate child, but was the lover of Servilia, mother of Brutus, and it has been suggested that his abandonment of self defence against his assassins from the moment he saw the dagger in the hand of Brutus – "Et tu Brute? Then fall, Caesar"[5] – came from the shock of realisation he was dying at the hand of his son. Moreover, during his liaison with Cleopatra, she bore a son which she called after him, Caesar, plainly with his approval, since they were at the time living in Alexandria all three together, as domestically as any father, mother and child. At the time when Anthony was offering him the crown, she was in Rome with the little boy, and Weigall may well be right in his bold speculation it was Caesar's intention to let himself be crowned, legitimise their son and bring together the two halves of the civilised world in his person, making Caesarion heir not merely to the Egyptian throne but to the throne of Rome. If this is so, it is ironic Julius Caesar should have died at the hand of his elder son, and the drama takes on a possible element of fraternal jealousy. After his assassination, Anthony took Caesar's place at Cleopatra's side, but though he had two sons of his own by her, it was her son by Caesar upon whom he conferred the title King of Kings. Caesar's nephew, Octavian (Augustus), after his destruction of Anthony and Cleopatra, had the boy killed, on the simple excuse that it was dangerous for two Caesars to be in one world. It is difficult to imagine that Bacon, steeped as he was in Roman history, interested as he was in Caesar, knew none of this. For him to have said that Queen Elizabeth was childless like Julius Caesar, surely means she was without legitimate children, yet not without issue of interest and consequence.

Perhaps because it could raise awkward questions, Francis did not have *In Felicem Memoriam Elizabethae* printed while he lived, yet its composition was not casual, for in his will he left instructions for its publication.

Tobie Matthew's confinement can hardly have been to close prison, for on August 27th, Carleton wrote to Chamberlain:[7]

Tobie Matthew hath leave to go as often as he will with his keeper to Sir Francis Bacon, and is put in good hope of further liberty.

It must have been during this period that Francis lent Matthew some of his literary work, begging him to mark anything he thought infelicitous. In the letter inviting such criticism, he does not name the manuscripts, but they may have been first drafts of *In Felicem Memoriam Elizabethae* – ticklish to show to a Catholic – and his *Character of Julius Caesar*, for we later find him writing:[8]

I send you . . . a memorial of Queen Elizabeth . . . Of this, when you were here, I showed you some model; though at that time methought you were more willing to hear Julius Caesar than Queen Elizabeth commended.

The question is whether Bacon is here referring to the play or to the prose monograph. The play, *Julius Caesar,* having been performed in 1599, is probably the *Character* to which he had entertained Matthew. Yet the monograph makes explicit a feature of Caesar's character implicit in the play. In the *Character,* Bacon tells us that Caesar:

referred everything to himself, and was the true and perfect centre of all his actions . . . referred all things to himself.

In the play, Caesar says:

> Caesar is turned to hear
>
> *I, ii, 17*
>
> . . . for always I am Caesar
>
> *I, ii, 212*
>
> Caesar shall forth: the things that threatened me
> Ne'er looked but only on my back; when they shall see
> The face of Caesar, they are vanished.
>
> *II, ii, 10-12*

In these lines he does refer everything to himself.

Tobie Matthew now refused to take the Oath of loyalty required of Catholics, and so was confined to the Fleet. Bacon, plainly distressed, wrote to him picturing the late ''Powder Treason'' as an example of the horrors to which extremes could lead. Upon his intercession, Matthew was released, but upon condition of his leaving the country.

1. British Museum, Additional MSS. 5503, f.102.
2. British Museum, Additional MSS. 5503, f,37.
3. British Museum, Additional MSS. f.36.
4. Anne Boleyn.
5. *Julius Caesar,* II, i, 77.
6. *The Life and Times of Cleopatra,* Arthur Weigall (Butterworth, 1914). See also H. Volkmann's *Cleopatra,* translated by T.J. Cadoux, 1958, and article 'Cleopatra' by Dr. Cadoux in *The Oxford Classical Dictionary,* 1970.
7. Calendar of State Papers, Domestic, James.
8. Matthew, *Letters,* p.22.

CHAPTER 42

Death of Lady Bacon

THERE is a letter written by Francis:[1]

Sir Michael Hicks,

. . . I heartily wish I had your company here at my Mother's funeral which I purpose on Thursday next in the forenoon. I dare promise you a good sermon to be made by Mr. Fenton the preacher of Gray's Inn; for he never makes other. Feast I make none. But if I mought have your company for two or three days at my house I should pass over this mournful occasion with some comfort . . .

Your ever assured

Fr. Bacon

This Sunday the
27th of August, 1610

This is our source for the approximate date of Lady Bacon's death. She was buried in St. Michael's Church at Gorhambury.

---

1. British Museum, Lansdowne MSS. XCL, f.183.

CHAPTER 43

Jonson II

VOLPONE (1605) is a black comedy. Most of the characters are vile, yet there is nothing against the character of Sir Politique Would Be. His advice to Peregrine concerning the behaviour necessary to success in the world may be cynical, but he can – as played by Sir John Gielgud in 1977 – come over as a person of quiet dignity, slightly sad. He knows "the ebbes and flowes of state", is travelled and has had some experience of intelligence work, and he says:

> my fate hath beene
> To be, where I have beene consulted with,
> In this high kind, touching some great mens sonnes,
> Persons of blood and honour
>
> *II, i, 119–22*

He has made notes specially "for this meridian" and advises never to tell a truth, at any rate to strangers, and hardly even to express oneself in a fable, except with caution, yet to put into others' minds, at times, what they should say (III, i, 8, 13–17, 79–80). He has in his study no papers save "notes, Drawn out of play-bookes . . . And some essayes" (V, iiii, 40–43).

Montaigne (1533–1592) had written *essaies*, in France, but in England the term was new, so new that when, a few years later, Bacon presented a copy of his new and enlarged edition of his Essays, he apologises for it as a neologism. It is very difficult, therefore, not to think Sir Politique is meant for Bacon; yet in that case, why had his study no paper except drawn out of play-books?

The next play of Jonson was *Epicene or The Silent Women*. In this, there is a character called Sir John Daw. He must be a lawyer, for when asked whom he considers "the best authors" he replies, "*Syntagma Iuris civilis, Corpus Iuris civilis, Corpus Iuris Canonici . . .* " (II, iii, 81–2).

Another character comments below (95):

> I wonder hee is not called to the helme and made a councellor!

There then follows this dialogue, between Daw and Davphine, (107–20):

Davp. How can you justify your owne being of a *Poet*, that so slight all the old *Poets*.

Daw Why euery man that writes in verse is not a *Poet*; you have of the *Wits*, that write verses and are yet no *Poets*; they are *Poets* that liue by it, the poore fellowes that liue by it.

Davp. Why? would not you liue by your verses, Sir John?

Cle No, 'twere pittie he should. A knight liue by his verses? He did not make 'hem to that ende, I hope.

Davp. And yet the noble SIDNEY liues by his, and the noble family not asham'd.

Cle I, he profest himselfe; but Sir John Daw has more caution; hee'll not hinder his owne rising i' the state so much!

Here one has the nub of it. As in ancient Rome, the writing of verse was acceptable providing it was amateur. Sidney published his work, for sale, but he was not after a high office of state. Bacon was. He wanted to take the helm of the country, and would not hinder his chances.

CHAPTER 44

John Davies of Hereford

THE *Scourge of Folly,* by John Davies of Hereford, contains an epigramme:

> To the Royall Ingenious and All-learned Knight Sir Francis Bacon
> Thy *bounty* and the *Beauty* of thy Witt
> Compris'd in Lists of *Law* and the learned *Arts,*
> Each making thee for great *employment* fitt,
> Which now thou hast, (though short of thy deserts)
> Compels my pen to let forth shining *Inke*
> All to bedew the *Baies* that *deck* thy *Front*;
> And to thy health in Helicon to drinke
> As to her *Bellamour,* the *Muse* is wont;
> For thou dost her embossom; and, dost
> Her company for sport twixt graue affaires.
> So vtterest Law the liuelyer through thy *Muse*:
> And for that all thy *Notes* are sweetest *Aires*;
>   *My Muse thus notes thy worth in ev'ry Line.*
>   *With ynke which thus she sugars; so, to shine.*

Here we have in plain language a statement Bacon wrote poetry. Grosart glosses, "Miss Delia Bacon might have utilised this to her theory, as well as Bacon's enigmatical phrase to Sir John Davies of 'concealed poets'." He does not say he wrote Shakespeare, but the last line recalls "mellifluous and honey-tongued Shakespeare . . . sugared Sonnets among his private friends": Francis Meres, *Palladia Tamia,* 1598, and would have been likely to recall it to his readers.

There is also an epigram *To Our English Terence, Mr. Will Shakespeare.* This I would think is a genuine tribute to the actor, who, jointly with Burbage, is sympathetically saluted by Davies elsewhere, but the apostrophe as Terence doubtfully alludes to the writings. It is Terence himself who tells us in the Prologue to the *Adelphi* (160 B.C.), lines 15–21, that enemies say certain noblemen helped him to write his plays. This, he says, is really a compliment, for it means his plays are pleasing to those much admired citizens. Authorship is variously attributed to Scipio Africanus and C. Laelio and Terence never made serious efforts to refute it. John Davies of Hereford, if he thought Shakespeare was in the same case, may have thought it no detriment, but rather a grace to his personality, that one of higher position should condescend to use him as his mask.

CHAPTER 45

The Wisdom of the Ancients

DE *Sapientia Veterum* (1609), or in English *The Wisdom of the Ancients,* is Bacon's study of myth. Why did people, such as the Greeks, and other ancients, make up such extraordinary stories about gods and goddesses, heroes and monsters, making them do such fantastic things.

It was always a question with Bacon whether, "as hieroglyphics were before language",[1] fables came before the moralities read into them later; when he wrote *The Advancement of Learning* he inclined to think it so; now he returned to an earlier view, that they must have been devised to enshrine truths in parabolic form. Some of them were "so absurd and stupid upon the face of the narrative itself"[2] as to suggest there must be another meaning. As Plato told us the Greeks received their deeper knowledge from the Egyptians, these fables might carry over the profound teaching of the earlier sages.[3]

But the consideration which has most weight with me is this, that few of these fables were invented, as I take it, by those who recited and made them famous, – Homer, Hesiod, and the rest. For had they been certainly the production of that age and of those authors by whose report they have come down to us, I should not have thought of looking for anything great or lofty from such a source. But it will appear upon an attentive examination that they are delivered not as new inventions then first published, but as stories already received and believed. And since they are told in different ways by writers nearly contemporaneous, it is easy to see that what all the versions have in common came from ancient tradition, while the parts in which they vary are the additions introduced by the several writers for embellishment – a circumstance which gives them in my eyes a much higher value for so they must be regarded as neither being the inventions nor belonging to the age of the poets themselves, but as sacred relics and light airs breathing out of better times, that were caught from the traditions of more ancient nations and so received into the flutes and trumpets of the Greeks.

He goes on to the consideration of some of the mythological stories. The interpretations he offers are, he makes plain, not put forward as expositions of what the Greeks necessarily believed, but rather as his reflections upon the tales. For instance, when he reads the story of how Hippomenes won the race against Atalanta by throwing down golden apples, which she delayed to pick up, he thinks that as Atalanta (No. 25) was the one with the natural strength, the Hippomenes won against her by artfulness, so human Art will go faster than nature. The natural way for a fruit-tree to grow is from the kernel, but human art can obtain fruits much more quickly by grafting a slip of apple (or other) on to a mature trunk than by waiting for a pip to fall to the ground and germinate naturally.

Other of his interpretations are philosophical or scientific. For instance, No. 17 'Cupid or the Atom', reviews the role of the winged god in quite another light than that of amorous fancy. Of Cupid, he writes,[4]

This Love I understand to be the appetite or instinct of primal matter; or to speak more plainly, *the natural motion of the atom.*

He considers the attributes of Cupid. He is naked; it is compounds which are clothed. He is blind; he has very little providence:[5]

His last attribute is archery: meaning that this virtue is such as acts at a distance . . . Now whoever maintains the theory of the atom and the vacuum . . . necessarily implies the action of the virtue of the atom at distance for without this no motion could be originated, by reason of the vacuum interposed . . .

This slight volume 'The wisdom of the ancients' was destined to become one of the most popular in Bacon's name. It is saluted by Thomas Campion in his poem:

Ad Ampliss. totius Angliae Cancellarium,
Fra. Ba.
Debet multa tibi veneranda (Bacone) poesis
Ilo de docto perlepidoque libro,
Qui manet inscriptus Veterum Sapientia; . . .

Poetry owes you much, Bacon,
For the learned and most charming book
Inscribed The Wisdom of the Ancients.

The book of fables has great charm, yet it is not poetry but prose. Indeed, Rossi considers Spedding erred in classing it amongst the literary works; it is, he opines, one of the philosophical. So does not Campion's first line contain, however, a glance at something else? A second epigram by Campion, *Ad eundem* (to the same), contains the lines:

Quantus ades, seu te spinosa volumina iuris,
Seu schola, seu dulcis Musa (Bacone) vocat!

That is, "How great art thou present, whether the thorny volumes of the law, The school (of philosophy) or the sweet Muse, Bacon, calls thee". It is difficult to think what "the sweet Muse" could be, unless the Muse of poetry, alluded to in the first epigram of the pair. It would seem, then, that Campion knew of three separate bodies of Bacon's works; apparently of equal substance and importance: the legal, the philosophic and the poetic. Orthodoxy knows only of the legal and the philosophic.

1. *The Advancement of Learning,* Spedding, III, pp. 344-45.
2. *The Wisdom of the Ancients,* Spedding, VI, 697-98.
3ʹ. *Loc.sit.*
4. Spedding, VI, p.729.
5. Spedding VI, p.731.

CHAPTER 46

Age shall not wither her

IN 1607, the old Countess of Southampton died. Death often brings the review of a whole relationship; *Anthony and Cleopatra* is thought to have been written late in that year, or early in the following. The fusion of age with charm pervading the play is tell-tale. The historical Cleopatra was at the time of her meeting with Marc Antony twenty-eight, and North's Plutarch, supposed to be our author's main source, says that when she knew Caesar she was "'but a young thing, and knew not then what the worlde ment: but nowe she went to Antonius at the age when a womans bewtie is at the prime, and she also of best judgement." Here is the indication of maturity, but not such as of itself to justify the words our poet gives her on her own lips:

> serpent of old Nile
> . . . wrinkled deep in time
>
> *I, v, 25-29*

Surely, we are not with the historical figure but with that

> Carkase of a beauty spent and donne

so described when the author wrote *A Lover's Complaint,* the Dark Lady of the Sonnets in her magic and effulgent sunset.

Anthony and Cleopatra is the most richly poetical of all the plays, and rises to its peak in Enobarbus' description

> The barge she sat in, like a burnish'd throne

which, though indebted to North's Plutarch for the material details, the gold poop, the purple sails, the music, the cloth of gold, is particularised by this exclamation, not in the source:

> Age cannot wither her, nor custom stale . . .

She was, then, aged but with the ineffably puissant charm which, for the poet, perfumed her atmosphere for ever.

Deeply flawed she may have been, yet it is no mean glory in a woman to have inspired the greatest poetry the world has ever known.

In the chapter on *Promus,* phrases were noted which might have been fetched from that larder for this play. "Hail of pearl", f.101, seems to turn up in:

Ile set thee in a shower of Gold, and haile
Rich Pearles vpon thee.

notwithstanding that at their coronation eastern kings were powdered with gold-dust and seed-pearl. Seed-pearls are tiny things, whereas hailstones are big, and it is the image, perhaps drawn from the observation of the descent of actual hailstones, which gives a violence to Cleopatra's line.

One wonders what the first audiences made of "the wheeled seat of fortunate Caesar", IV, xiv, 75. He was not sitting on a wheel-chair. The image is not that of the spinning-wheel of fortune, turned by hand. Neither is the sense exactly that of the apparently proverbial saying, the world runs upon wheels, with an idea of giddiness or drunkenness (see the examples in the Variorum Shakespeare very appropriately annotated, *i.e.* "The third part of the world . . . is drunk . . . That it might go on wheels" earlier in the play.) It seems that "wheeled", here, carries the straightforward sense of "L'affaire va à quatre roues", the French proverb noted in the *Promus.* Here there is no hint of instability, but simply of progress. But "wheeled . . . fortunate" refers forward, also, to a very special view of Bacon's, which we shall find later expressed in his essay 'Of Fortune', wherein he tells how one who boasted his achievements saying, "In all this fortune had no part" never had fortune more, and another is commended for choosing the style "Felix" rather than "Magnus", for:

It is greatness in a man to be the care of the higher powers. So Caesar said to the pilot in the tempest, *Caesarem portas, et fortunam ejus* "You carry Caesar and his fortune".

That is why he speaks of the "felicity" rather than the greatness of Queen Elizabeth, whom he respected above all persons. "The wheeled seat of fortunate Caesar" carries three levels of Bacon's thought.

Of interest also is:

the air, which but for vacancy
Had gone to gaze on Cleopatra too,
And made a gap in nature
         II, ii, 221-23

Though this allusion is to Aristotle's *Physics,* at the disposition of all men, it is not all men who read Aristotle's *Physics,* and the scientific principle enunciated there is more likely to have interested Bacon than another.

Western Europe was entering its mini Ice Age. In the winter of 1607/8, the Thames froze. People could cross on foot from one bank to the other, and bonfires were lit on the ice. This is thought to underlie the line, "You are no surer, no, Than is the coal of fire upon the ice" in *Coriolanus,* I, i, 177, setting a date before which it cannot have been

written. Yet with it, we are back in the days of Essex. It may be said that
Essex, who courted popularity with the people, was the opposite of
Marcius, who was contemptuous of them and without ear for their
grievances, and that it was the revolts which started in Northamptonshire
in May, 1608, which prompted the writing of the play. But the
eponymous hero, grown too big for his boots, turning the gratitude of his
home state to fear of him, discontented and making his compact with the
Volsci, whom he had been sent to quell, and returning at their head to
threaten the walls of Rome, is very like Essex, overbearing and turning
the Queen's and his friends' love to apprehension, discontented, making
his private truce with the Irish, whom he had been sent to quell, and
returning to threaten the Queen.

Especially interesting is his development of the character of Volumnia.
In Plutarch, she does not appear until Rome is threatened when she
responds to Valeria's suggestion she and Virgilia should go out to meet
her son and persuade him to turn his wrath away from the city. Our
dramatist's representation of her in the earlier scene, in which she appears
as a most martial lady, the inspiration behind her son's deeds, is an
innovation. One cannot say she is Queen Elizabeth, for the Queen loved
peace, and always worried when Essex was on a military expedition,
whereas Volumnia would rather have her son dead than fail her high
expectation of him. Had he died:

> Then his good report should have been my son; I therein would have found
> issue. Hear me profess sincerely; had I a dozen sons, each in my love alike . . . I
> had rather had eleven die nobly for their country than one voluptuously surfeit
> out of action.
>
> *I, iii, 22–28*

One may feel the portrait is drawn larger than life; that no mother
would so inhumanly place principle before natural tenderness. Yet there
is a parallel to it. When Lady Bacon, fearing that Anthony's prolonged
stay in Montauban meant he was having to do too much with Catholics, it
will be recalled that his friend, Francis Allen wrote to him:[1]

> She is resolved to procure her Majesty's letter to force you to return; and when
> that should be, if her Majesty give you your right or desert, she should clap you
> up in prison . . . My Lady said she had rather you made the wars with the King of
> Navarre than to have stayed so long idle in Montauban, and with great
> earnestness, also tears in her eyes, she wished that . . . you had been fairly buried,
> provided you had died in the Lord.

The situation is different, yet there are sentiments common to these two
passages. Allowance made for translation into the terms of a pre-Christian
culture, the one could have been parent of the other.

But what is psychologically interesting in the play is the real dependence
of the towering, apparently heroic figure on his mother. His life turns

about her. She made him; and, when no other could, she undid him. The jibe, "boy of tears", V, vi, 101, which stings him to madness, points to his fundamental immaturity. Here, as well as in the sulks that provoked the disloyalty, is a very real parallel to Essex.

1. Lambeth MSS. 647, f.111.

CHAPTER 47

The Virginia Company

THE Charter of the Virginia Company of London of May 23rd, 1609, bears a complete list of the shareholders. These include investors from diverse walks of life, noblemen and commoners, sailors and landsmen, the Earl of Montgomery, the Earl of Pembroke, the Earl of Salisbury, the Earl of Southampton, Sir Francis Bacon Kt., Captain John Smith . . . The document does not specify the sums invested by each one, but granted to them, ''in form hereafter in these presents expressed, whether they go in their persons to be planters there in the said plantation or whether they go not but do adventure their moneys, goods and chattels . . . that they themselves should be one body or perpetual community . . . and . . . should be known, called and incorporated by the name of the Treasurer and Company of Adventurers and Planters of the City of London for the First Colony in Virginia'', the which company was granted a patent of rights.[1]

There had been an earlier charter but we do not know what names were connected with it. Bacon had had one known earlier ''adventure'' in the New World. In 1607 he had been one of the founders of the Newfoundland Company, a short lived and not very successful company for establishing a fishing colony in Newfoundland.[2]

Now, he was one of the founders of the Virginia Company.

1. *Records of the Virginia Company of London,* ed. G.M. Kingsbury (Washington D.C., 1915), vol. 4, p.363, and *The Three Charters of the Virginia Company of London,* ed. Samuel Bennis (1913).

2. *A Licence to Trade: the History of the English Chartered Companies,* Sir Percival Griffiths (1974), p.200.

CHAPTER 48

In setting forth

THERE is a sonnet known as the dated, No. 107:

> Not mine owne feares, nor the prophetick soule,
> Of the wide world, dreaming of things to come,
> Can yet the lease of my true loue controule,
> Supposde as forfeit to a confin'd doome.
> The mortall Moone hath her eclipse endur'de,
> And the sad Augurs mock their owne presage,
> Incertainties now crowne them-selues assur'de,
> And peace proclaimes Oliues of endlesse age.
> Now with the drops of this most balmie time,
> My loue lookes fresh, and death to me subscribes,
> Since spight of him Ile liue in this poore rime,
> While he insults ore dull and speachlesse tribes.
> And thou in this shalt finde thy monument,
> When tyrants crests and tombs of brasse are spent.

Unfortunately, there has been endless controversy as to the date indicated. Some writers have taken it as a reference to the climacteric or sixty-third year of Queen Elizabeth, passed through without mishap. This seems untenable. That year was not an especially peaceful one. Those who watch the waves know that every seventh is the biggest and starts a new cycle, and in this sense every multiple of seven in a person's life has been felt by many as climacteric; but no other instance has been produced of "endured" to mean survived. Though for many years I have watched out for it in the literature of the period, I have come on only one other instance of "to endure an eclipse", and that occurs in Bacon's *King Henry VIIth*, where he writes of the Queen Dowager, "This lady . . . hath endured a strange eclipse." He certainly did not mean she had survived a climacteric year; he meant she had passed into an obscurity from which she had not emerged, there being practically nothing recorded of her after a certain date.

A very strong clue as to the meaning of lines 7 to 9 is to be found in Bacon's *Apothegms,* where he tells that Queen Elizabeth, being importuned regarding the filling of certain offices, said,[1] "*I am sure my office will not be long void.* And yet at that time there was much speech of trouble and divisions about the crown, to be after her decease; but they all vanished; and King James came in, in a profound peace."

The meaning of these lines in the sonnet is, then, that Queen

Elizabeth has been eclipsed by death. The fears of civil strife concerning
the succession are seen to have been needless, since uncertainties have
been settled with the unopposed coronation of King James, who not only
came in peacefully, but concluded a Peace with Spain (1604), which,
being followed by a Peace between the United Provinces of the Protestant
Netherlands with Spain (1609) brings a profound universalisation of
peace.

In *Anthony and Cleopatra*, III, xiii, 153 when Anthony says "our
terrence moone is now eclipsed" he means Cleopatra. Moreover, in the
same play, IV, vi, 5, Caesar says "The time of vniuersal peace is near",
making a second parallel with the sonnet. But *Anthony and Cleopatra*, as
we have seen, was written late in the year the old Countess of Southampton died, so perhaps she is in the sonnet, too.

This brings us to the difficult question of "my love". For who, as late
as this, would Bacon have thought of as his love? Relations with
Southampton had suffered a very considerable chill since he had been
obliged to take the crown case against him as well as Essex, but though he
had prevailed with the Queen to spare him execution, on account of his
youth, he must have expected to see him confined within the Tower for a
long time, and the relief of seeing him released must have been
considerable. It may be that the term "my love" harks back to his
recollection of him as a boy, and that there is in it some spillage of the
emotion still felt towards his mother.

Note the sudden change from the 3rd to the 2nd person in the last line.
"Thou" is not the same person as "my love". Death subscribes to the
poet, because the poet's words outlive both the writer and the one of
whom he writes. The Countess, whom he addresses as "thou", is
physically in her tomb, but will find her truest monument not in the
tombstone but in his poetry.

What I suggest is that when he wrote this sonnet, Bacon had given his
permission to Hervey to have the *Sonnets* published.

Let us now look at the famous dedication:

TO. THE. ONLIE. BEGETTER. OF.
THESE. ENSVING. SONNETS.
MR. W.H. ALL. HAPPINESSE.
AND. THAT. ETERNITIE.
PROMISED.
BY.
OVR. EVER-LIVING. POET.
WISHETH.
THE. WELL-WISHING.
ADVENTURER. IN.
SETTING.
FORTH.
T.T.

The initials T.T., are generally thought to be those of Thomas Thorpe, the publisher. But how did Thorpe come to have the poems? They are addressed to more than one person, and we do not know whether the author kept copies. Even if he did, it would seem unlikely he gave them to Thorpe. It looks therefore, as though the poems, given out severally, had come into one hand, whose author composed the dedication attached to them when he passed them to Thorpe.

What I suggest is that, if the author is Bacon, Hervey approached him on the matter, some time after the old Countess' passing, and said something like "Now that she is dead, will you not allow those poems which you wrote, some to her, some to my step-son and some to me, to be published?" and that he received consent conditional on its being done in such a way the authorship could not be traced. The last thing Bacon would want, especially now that he was moving forward in his career, would be the laying bare of the most intimately tangled skeins of relationship. Neither would it be nice for Cordell, or for Alice.

The stops between the words leave the dedication without real punctuation. Mr. Cook, observing that in dedications of this shape, the usual order is: 1 the Dedicatee, 2 the Dedicator and 3 what is wished by the Dedicator to the Dedicatee, takes the sense to be: "To the sole author of the ensuing sonnets (for they are not an anthology of poems by different persons), Ship's Master William Hervey, in setting forth upon a new voyage, returns the good wishes wished to him by the poet, who has adventured money in the expedition".

The name of William Shakespeare does not, however, appear in the list of those who had adventured their fortunes in the Virginia Company (that is, the shareholders), published in its charter of 1609). Bacon's name appears, on the other hand, not only as one of those who had adventured money of his own, but as a member of the Council, or as we should say, now, the Board of Directors. William Strachey's book *The Historie of Travail into Virginia Britannia,* written 1612, is dedicated:

To the Right Honourable SIR FRANCIS BACON, Knight, Baron of Verulam, Lord High Chancellor of England, and of his Majesty's most honourable Privy Counsell.
Most wortheley honour'd Lord,
    Your Lordship ever approuving yourself a most noble fautor of the Virginian Plantation, being from the beginning (with other lordes and earles) of the principall counsell applyed to propogate and guide yt . . .

It sounds as though he regards Bacon as the chief inspirer.

---

1. *Apothegms* contained in the second edition of the *Resuscitatio,* ed. William Rawley (1661), No. 13, Spedding, VII, p.167.

CHAPTER 49

The mysteries

IT was as though with the publication of the *Sonnets* the past had been put behind him. After the great tragedies the romances, with a new cast of characters and a new idea running through them. The first of these is *Pericles,* printed 1609. It used to be thought that Shakespeare took over a play begun by an earlier author, but Professor P. Edwards has argued[1] that the whole is his sole work. Though superficially it may appear disjointed, in that Antiochus and his daughter, who dominate the first Act, disappear, the Flemish scholar Wilem Schricks has pointed out,[2] we come at the end to another father and daughter union, in different key. A dark father and daughter, whose relations were sin, have, since Pericles saw through them, been replaced in his life by a light father and daughter, symbolising virtue in their spiritual reunion. There is, then, perhaps intended an allegory of the human soul, the mystic theme of death and rebirth being reflected in the apparent drowning of Thaisa, to reappear in her daughter, Marina.

The two storms at sea, the one driving Pericles ashore at Tarsus, and the other in which Thaisa is thrown overboard, flanking as they do the marriage, may have been designed to recall the circumstances of King James' marriage to Queen Anne of Denmark. The ship that was to have brought her to Scotland for the marriage was beaten back to Norway, from where he had to fetch her, his own ship being then so battered by storms he was convinced it was the work of witches. Marina will represent their very young daughter, Elizabeth, who had been brought up by Lord and Lady Harrington, secluded in a country place near Coventry, until 1608, when the English Court saw for the first time the beautiful child of twelve, golden haired like her mother. She had been reared unspoiled, and it may have been the hope she would remain so, plunged amidst the sophistication and vices of the Court, which inspired the brothel scene. Her short flower-speech, IV, i, 15–17, will be found expanded in her development as Perdita.

She had two brothers, Henry and Charles. Prince Henry, the elder, was by Bacon's account a most personable young man, sedate and already kingly, yet ''easy to deal with.''[3] In May 1610, at the age of sixteen he was to be invested as Prince of Wales, and as the time approached poets burst into a florescence of tributes. Jonson wrote the speeches for an entertainment called *Prince Henrys Barriers,* based on an ancient British theme in which figured King Arthur and Merlin. Some months later, with Inigo Jones, he returned to its development in *The Masque of Oberon.*

The influence of Queen Anne is to be felt. Not possessed of the governing intellect of the sovereign Queen Elizabeth, art historians are yet grateful to her because in place of the neo-Mediaeval medallion-like portrait, in which no shadows were permitted on the sitter's face, she had herself painted · informally with her dogs jumping up around her. Neglected by James, who had eyes only for beautiful young men, and insulted by the reigning male favourite, Robert Carr, she gave herself to the delight of masques, which is why writers now turned to this genre. Samuel Daniel's contribution was *Thetys Festival,* in which Queen Anne appeared in the title role, Princess Elizabeth, aged fourteen, as The Thames, the Princes Henry and Charles as Meliade and Zephirus, while King James consented to appear as Ocean's King. Much is made in this of Milford Haven, as "That happy Port of Union", where King Henry VII had landed, who was to end the wars of the roses, and, from whom the Stuarts were descended.

Our author's contribution appears to have been *Cymbeline,* and Professor Glynne Wickham thinks he must have taken from Daniel the idea of making so much of Milford Haven.[4] Indeed, since the historical British king Cunobelinus reigned over a district north of the Thames, from a seat at Camuludinum, near the modern Colchester, it would have seemed more appropriate for persons travelling between it and Rome (of the time of Augustus) to do so via an Essex port, but that there was this special reason for bringing Milford Haven into everything.

Dr. Frances Yates suggests[5] the three children of Cymbeline; Imogen and the Princes in the cave are the three children of James, the Princess Elizabeth and the Princes Henry and Charles. She is probably right. But the cave is particularly curious, in that it seems to anticipate the *Fama Fraternitatis,* the cornerstone of Rosicrucianism, in its use of a cave as the place of finding something infinitely precious, long lost. It would seem that precious jewel, here, is the long lost unity of the island as a whole, the mythic Albion of pre-history, which became severed into England, Wales and Scotland, now brought together in the confluence of the English and Scottish crowns through the person of James, and investiture of the Prince. This, then, must be the meaning of the prophecy:

When from a stately cedar shall be lopped branches, which, being dead many years, shall after revive, be jointed to the old stock, and freshly grow; then shall . . . Britain to fortunate, and flourish in peace and plenty.

V, iv, 141–42

For Imogen, it may be objected she has a husband, which the Princess Elizabeth, only fourteen, had not yet; but Dr. Yates draws to our attention that his name, Posthumus Leonatus, seems to describe Brut, the legendry Trojan founder of Britain, who was a posthumous child and had the lion for his symbol and a wife called Innogen, which sounds very like Imogen. Our author would seem, therefore, to have fused the Princess Elizabeth with the legendary ancestress of the island, while also, perhaps, evoking in her the memory of Queen Elizabeth, as the Phoenix. Why else is it said of her, ''She is alone the Arabian bird'' I, vi, 17?

The Winter's Tale must have been written only shortly afterwards. Here, again, we have the follies of the elders resolved by the young. The past is recalled with Leontes' insane jealousy and unjust accusation of his Queen, Hermione. Her trial suggests that of Anne Boleyn, which Bacon considered to be unjust. Perhaps, then, Leontes is meant for Henry VIII. Yet the way in which he at the beginning presses Hermione to outdo him in exhortations to his friend, Polixenes, to tarry with them longer, reminds us of that passage in the old Countess of Southampton's letter to her father in which she explains it was only because of her husband's extraordinary liking for Dymock she tried to show herself friendly to him.

The superficial plot of the play is taken over from Greene's *Pandosto,* excepting that our author has switched around the kingdoms of the two kings. As this obliged him to credit Bohemia with a sea-coast, one wonders why he did it. Howard Bridgewater, a barrister, quotes Sir Edward Sullivan[6] for ''The mention of the oracle of Delphos suggests the Bohemia of a very much earlier date. Under the rule of Ottocar (1255–1278) . . . his dominions extended . . . from the Adriatic to the shores of the Baltic'', and glosses, ''Bohemia then comprised all the territory of the Austrian monarchy.''[7] Even the thirteenth century seems too late for a surviving cult of Apollo, yet the reference is not without its interest. Professor Ambros, in his article 'Bacon and Bohemia',[8] notices the arrival of certain Czechs in England in 1599, one of whom Zdeněk Brtnický, visited the Globe Theatre on July 3rd and August 2nd.

He notes also the visit to London of a Jan Diviš, who was of the family of:

Count Žerotín, who became closely related to Anthony Bacon. On his recommendation he was introduced to the Earl of Essex and other prominent members of the Queen's entourage. A certain Jacob Lesieur, a Frenchman by birth, was selected as personal guide to both these visitors.

Lesieur was both protegé and political agent to Essex and undertook several trips to the Bohemian lands between 1590 and 1614, and carried letters of importance backwards and forwards. He was very intimate with the later prominent leaders of the Czech Rising, and with many German Lutherans residing at Prague, as well. In 1613, Lesieur correctly informed James I that he expected a new wave of oppression of Protestants in Bohemia and Moravia.

Dr. Frances Yates is a Stratfordian, and is therefore unlikely to have seen this article, since it appeared in *Baconiana,* which is distributed only to members of the Francis Bacon Society. It is, therefore, of the more interest that a major theme of her books, *The Rosicrucian Enlightenment*

(Routledge, 1972) and *Shakespeare, The Last Plays* (Routledge, 1975) is that although the Rosicrucian manifestos were first published in Germany, the inspiration came from England, the liaison between England and certain groups in Bohemia and the Palatinate being mainly through the agency of travelling actors. She notes that during the years in which the Romances were presented, there was a certain inclination on the part of King James to have Prince Henry marry a Spanish Princess, which the Prince appeared to be resisting. Dr. Yates believes that in *The Winter's Tale,* Perdita stands for the Princess Elizabeth, the new Protestant hope, in whom, Phoenix-like, the old Queen was reborn.

Could this be the reason why the dramatist, in adapting Greene's tale, changed around the kingdoms of Sicily and Bohemia, so as to make the Prince whom Perdita marries heir to the throne of Bohemia?

Better to examine this thesis, let us look at some dates. The play was licensed by Sir George Hicks, who became Master of the Revels in August, 1610. It contains, in IV, iv, a passage about rustics who have danced as satyrs – the Servant calls them ''Saltiers'' – before the king, and it has been pointed out that this glances at the anti-masque of satyrs in Jonson's *Masque of Oberon,* in which, likewise, the satyrs' anti-masque follows the dance of the shepherds. *The Winter's Tale,* then, took shape some time between the performance of *The Masque of Oberon,* on January 1st, 1610/1, and May 5th, 1611, when Simon Forman saw a performance. It was performed at Court on November 9th, 1611. From the Venetian State Papers we gather that in November, 1610, Christian of Anhalt arrived in London to urge the King to join the Union of Protestant Princes and suggest a marriage between Princess Elizabeth and Frederick V, the Elector Palatine. Prince Henry was in favour. When the Venetian Ambassador called in August he found Maurice, Landgrave of Hesse with him, a testimony to his Protestant inclinations. There was nevertheless the fear among the English that King James intended to marry one of his children to a Hapsburg. However, early in 1612, the Duc de Bouillon, the uncle with whom the Elector had been brought up, arrived to negotiate terms, and in May – the month that Salisbury died – a marriage contract was signed. In October the Elector arrived and was shortly introduced to the Princess. The two sixteen-year-olds fell in love. (He is said to have been four days the elder, though there is some doubt whether Elizabeth was born on August 19th, 18th or even 15th, 1596).

The play, then, was written during the months of suspense. The Elector is Florizel. At any rate by the time of the wedding, the Spanish ambassador was startled to discover that people in England saw the princess as the future Queen of Bohemia, the Crown being here considered elective and likely to go to Frederick. The play, then, is saying let her marry the Elector and a great destiny may be theirs. Central Europe may be liberated from the Hapsburgs, and we may have our

English Princess beside her young bridegroom on the throne of Prague.
But what of the statue of Hermione? There was no statue in Greene's
novel. Professor Wickham notes that King James had commissioned two
painted statues, one of Queen Elizabeth – to whom Bacon had urged a
monument – and one of Mary Queen of Scots. The one of Elizabeth had
been finished in 1605, but that of Mary was delayed by the original
sculptor's death, after which the work was taken over by his son. We have
not the date of the unveiling, but it is thought to have been in 1611 or
1612. Professor Wickham therefore supposes that the statue of the dead
Queen Hermione, which proves to be the living woman, is introduced as a
tribute to James' ''piaculous action'' in resurrecting the memory of his
mother.

Dr. Yates, on the other hand, sees in the scene an allusion to the
Trismegistic literature, and in particular to the *Asclepius,* wherein it is
claimed that the ancient Egyptians had the art of drawing the souls of
their gods and goddesses into their statues, so that they were really alive,
capable of doing good or evil, wherefore music was played to please them.
Leontes, when Paulina shows him the statue, exclaims, ''There's magic
in thy majesty,'' and Paulina says, ''you'll think . . . I am assisted by
wicked powers''. Being authorised to proceed, she orders music to be
played, and the statue descends.

These two interpretations are not necessarily exclusive. Mary Queen of
Scots would have been a sore point for Bacon, since as a young man he
had been of the Parliament (his first) which condemned her. Nevertheless
the statue could have put him in mind of the magical ones in the
Asclepius. There was no English translation, but he would have read it in
the Latin of Ficino. He was interested in Ficino, in the Trismegistic
literature generally and in the legend of Asclepius, which he mentions
more than once.

But now another question rises. If the author had the mysteries in
mind, when he makes Perdita, with her flowers, speak of Proserpine, does
he intend her to represent Proserpine, or Persephone, because of her
relation to her mother? Sicily was sacred to Demeter and to Persephone.
Could that be another reason why the dramatist decided to change over
the kingdoms, making Bohemia that of the Prince's father, Sicily that of
Perdita's father and mother? Hermione is a title of both Demeter and
Persephone.[9] Demeter and Persephone are one and not one. As the old
corn she is cast on to the ground, is taken down to be the bride of the
underworld, and as Persephone she comes up as the new. This, though a
natural allegory, is believed to have been given, in the Eleusinian
mysteries, a spiritual meaning, the meaning at the heart of every true
religion, that one must die before one can be reborn. The fortunes and
goods of this world, though proper when they do not exceed their place,
have to be seen and felt as nothing before one can stand in one's spiritual

strength alone. In all works on esotericism, this is taken to have been the idea behind those rites in which the candidate for initiation had symbolically to die, before he could rise from the tomb, or the cave, purified and fortified. In Eleusis it has been suggested the mystery was staged, in some kind of a dramatic performance; indeed, it is probably from the sacred mysteries the profane theatre grew. One cannot push the thesis, because it is Leontes rather than Hermione who needs to be purged and to die to his former way of living; yet there is in all four of these last plays, *Pericles, Cymbeline, The Winter's Tale* and *The Tempest,* which we shall look at next, in one way or another the idea of a death of, or to, the old, with its miseries, after which a new and younger generation brings purity and regeneration. They are known as the Romances, but might better be called the Mysteries.

The Tempest must have been composed soon after, since it was performed at Court on November 1st, 1611, and was obviously inspired by the wreck of the *Sea Venture.* This ship had been one of nine which sailed from Plymouth on June 2nd, 1609, bound for Virginia. On the 24th they were struck by "a most dreadful Tempest", which drove the *Sea Venture* apart from the others. She carried the admiral, Sir George Somers, the governor designate, Sir Thomas Gates, Sir William Strachey (destined to succeed him) and the 1609 charter of the Virginia Company, signed by King James; and she was thought to have gone down with all aboard. In fact, she had been wrecked upon a shore between two rocks, but gently, so that although she was wedged between them and stuck in the ground, no one was harmed. The island, which was uninhabited, had a most balmy climate (it was Bermuda), and fruits, fowl and fish were all to be had for the taking, so that they spent pleasantly the months occupied in repairing the ship. They eventually arrived in Virginia in May of the following year, 1610, in much better condition than those they found there. The whole "plantation" seemed to have fallen apart since Captain John Smith, who had kept it together from the beginning, had returned to London, sick. Through whatever mismanagement, though the land was fertile, the colonists were in the last stages of starvation. Strachey was appointed secretary to the Council, and on July 7th, 1610, sent a letter home by Gates which begins "Madam", and contains the material used in *The Tempest.*

This is mysterious, because the letter was not published for fifteen years and contains an account of the lamentable situation found in Virginia which was certainly confidential. Professor Gayley worked out that the lady to whom it was addressed must be Elizabeth, the daughter of the Earl of Dunbar and wife of Lord Howard of Walden. She is called in the body of the letter "right Noble Ladie", signifying nobility below the rank of Countess, which would fit. She and her husband had their country seat in Saffron Walden, which was Strachey's home town, and he mentions that one of the mutineers (for they had a brief mutiny on Bermuda) was from near Saffron Walden, though he does not mention where any of the others came from. Her husband was heavily invested in the Virginia Company, and Professor Gayley supposes Strachey wrote it to her, that her husband might lay it before the Council in London.

Amongst the many similarities between the texts of the letter and play, perhaps the most striking is:

The heavens look'd so blacke upon us, that it was not possible the elevation of the Pole might be observed: not a Starre by night, not Sunne beame by day was to be seene. Onely upon the thursday night Sir George Somers being upon the warch had an apparition of a little round light, like a faint Starre, trembling, and streaming along with a sparkleing blaze, halfe the height upon the Maine Mast, and shooting sometimes from Shroud to Shroud, tempting to settle as it were upon any of the foure Shrouds; and for three or foure hours together, or rather more, halfe the night it kept with us, running sometimes along the Maine-yard to the very end and then returning.

Strachey

and Ariel's narration to Prospero:

I boarded the kings ship; now on the beak,
Now in the waist, the deck, in every cabin,
I flamed amazement. Sometimes I'd divide
And burn in many places. On the topmast,
The yard and bowsprit, would I flame distinctly,
Then meet and join

I, ii, 196-201

In parenthesis, it has been put to me by the head of a small Rosicrucian order, whom I cannot name as the conversation was informally *sub rosa,* that a member of the Christian faith, living before the devulgation of formerly esoteric works in the nineteenth century, would hardly have had the means to know that Ariel was one of the angels of the elements unless he had come to some knowledge of the Hebrew Cabala or Persian magic, as a Rosicrucian.[10] To pursue the question here would take us too far from Strachey.

It may be said that any returning member of the expedition might have described the phenomenon, St. Elmo's Fire, but when Strachey goes on to say:

Could it have served us now miraculously to have taken our height by, it might have strucken amazement, and a revenance . . .

one recognises the genesis of "flamed amazement" in Ariel's account of himself to Prospero. Then Strachey has:

fury added to fury . . . our clamours dround in the windes, and the windes in thunder. Prayers might well be heard in the hearts and lips, but drowned in the outcries of the Officers . . .

Shakespeare's Boatswain orders "Down with the topmast" and then hears "a cry within" and says, "A plague upon this howling! They are louder than the weather or our office." On the same page, Strachey speaks of "the glut of water"; Shakespeare has, "Though every drop of water . . . gape at the widest to glut him." This is the sole occurrence of the word "glut" in Shakespeare.

Miranda's "The sky it seems would pour down stinking pitch but that the sea, mounting to the welkins cheek Dashes the fire out . . . " I, ii, 3-5, seems close to Strachey's "swelling and roaring as it were by fits . . . did beat all light from heaven; which like a hell of darkness turned black upon us".

The springs, the berries and the sea-birds mentioned by Strachey all find their echoes in the play, but most extraordinary is:

Tortoise . . . such a kind of meat, as a man can call neither absolutely fish nor flesh, keeping most what in the water and feeding upon Sea-grasse like a Heifer . .

This becomes in the play Caliban, to whom Prospero says, "Come, thou tortoise", whom Trinculo dubs doubtfully, "man or fish" and for Stephano, is "moon-calfe" (the moon was ruler of the sea).

But overall, what comes over from Strachey is the sense of the miraculous, that they were all in the hand of Providence, which, though it contrived their wreck, provided also that not one of them should be harmed. In the play, they cannot get over the fact that their clothes are as fresh as when they set out.

The puzzle for Shakespeareans is, how did the actor from Stratford obtain access to Strachey's text? Professor Gayley wrote to A.W. Pollard of the British Museum to ask if there could have been a private printing, but received a negative answer. "It would have ruined Strachey's career to have published it at such a time; the wardens of the Stationers' Company would never have passed it . . . " The Company would not have wished to discourage further investment, which was most urgently needed, by publicising how the money already sunk in Virginia had been wasted.

In the *Introduction* to the play in the Arden edition, (F. Kermode, 1954), it is averred Shakespeare must have known some member of the Company who acquainted him with the details, and it is remarked that Shakespeare had acted in Jonson's *Sejanus,* and that when this was printed, in 1605, both Strachey and Sir Dudley Digges wrote laudatory verses for it. But that was before Strachey set to sea, and he did not return until after *The Tempest* was performed.

Moreover, the parts about the conditions found in Virginia being practically a state secret, it would have been a great breach of confidence on the part of any member of the Council to whom it had been circulated to lend it to the actor. But if the author of the play is Bacon, it would have come to his desk as a matter of course.

Sir A.W. Ward has suggested that Bacon wrote his essay "On Plantations" at this time.[11] If so, it ends on a gallant note: "It is the sinfullest thing in the world to forsake or destitute a plantation once in forwardness; for besides the dishonour, it is the guiltiness of blood of many commiserable persons."

In the play, however, nothing suggests Bermuda or an Atlantic island. The party wrecked were returning to Naples from Tunis, and much is made of its former state as ancient Carthage (actually, a few miles from it) and of Dido. This puts one in mind that Aeneas was driven by storm to land at Carthage, and that when he left it he came to Cumae, which is close to Naples, to consult the oracle and descend to Hades, before going further on his mission. The mariners were, then, retracing the journey of Aeneas. Was Capri the island on which they were wrecked? From it one can see both Naples and Cumae. Nobody in the play has to go down into the underworld, but the tasks set Ferdinand suggest an initiatory ordeal. Ariel's entry as a harpy in III, iii, is borrowed from the *Aeneid,* III, Ceres' salutation to Iris IV, i, 78–9, from the *Aeneid,* IV, showing how the Aeneid was running through the author's mind while he was writing *The Tempest.*

Prospero is a Mage, modelled as to his externals probably upon John Dee. There is in him a touch of Burghley, when, taking off his magic robe, he says "Lie there my art." This recalls Bacon's observation that Burghley, when he took off his robe of office and laid it over a chair, was wont to say, "Lie there, Lord Treasurer." The Oxfordians have drawn our attention to the somewhat obsessive attachment of Burghley to his daughter, and it may be this rears its head in several of the father-daughter relationships in the plays. Chiefly, however, one feels that Prospero is the author, and the magical world he has created that of the theatre. The received view that his renunciation of his magician's staff represents his intended farewell to it is almost certainly correct. Only, if the author is Bacon, the "Dukedom" he returns to take up will not be New Place at Stratford but the responsibilities of office, now coming so thick and fast as to leave him no further time for the shadow world he had made his own during the years that office was denied him.

But who is Miranda? It was suggested by Morton Luce (*Arden,* 1901) that she was Pocahontas, the daughter of the Red Indian chieftain, Powhatan, who rushed forward to save Captain John Smith, by laying her head on top of his on the block, as her father's executioners stood with their clubs poised to smash his brains out. Professor Bullough is against taking this too far, yet there is much concordance between the story told in *The Tempest* and by Smith. Pocahontas was very young at the time of the dramatic event of January 5th, 1607/8, in her father's wigwam at Werowocomoco, and Miranda seems to be hardly more than a child. She had never seen a white man before, and Miranda had never seen a man, other than her father, before. He was brought to the place as her father's captive, as Ferdinand was brought to the place as Prospero's captive. Powhatan, granted his daughter's plea for his life on condition of Smith's performing small menial tasks for them as Prospero set Ferdinand to carrying logs, which wore him out, so that Miranda tried to help him. Pocahontas probably knew better how to perform the tasks set by Powhatan than did Smith. After two days of this, Powhatan relented altogether, gave him an Indian name, Nantaquond, and said he would ever esteem him as his son. Ferdinand became Prospero's son-in-law. Powhatan released Smith and gave him a safe-conduct back to Jamestown; Prospero released his captives and their ship. Later, when Pocahontas would visit Jamestown, bringing food to the settlers, Powhatan would sometimes send to her a trusty servant Rawhunt ''exceeding in deformity of person, but of a subtle wit, and crafty understanding''. It looks as though Rawhunt was fused with the tortoise to make Prospero's and Miranda's servant, Caliban.

As to how the material could have been drawn upon, seeing that it has not been published, the answer comes easily if the author is Bacon. Smith was home, and what more natural than that Bacon should see him? The fact that the Pocahontas story does not feature in the earlier *True Declaration,* 1608, but, for the first time, in the fuller *General History,* 1624, has prompted some, who do not like Smith, to allege he invented it in 1624, it never having been heard of before. But now that we have seen it was used in *The Tempest,* 1611, the basis for that smear fails.

What is interesting is to see the way in which our author worked, taking three separate strands of material, the *Aeneid,* Strachey's unpublished letter about the wreck of the *Sea Venture* on the island of Bermuda in 1609 and Smith's unpublished account of how, in Virginia, two years earlier, his life had been saved by Pocahontas, and woven them together in ''something rich and strange''.

What has the classical *Aeneid* to do with Bermuda and Virginia? One must remember the nature of Aeneas' mission. After the destruction of Troy, he was instructed by the gods to sail west, and at a place to be later revealed to him, to make a settlement, in which civilisation should be reborn. He was driven by storm on to the coast of Carthage, where he was kindly received by Queen Dido, and could have spent his days in the debt of her hospitality, but that Mercury brought him a reproof from Jupiter Ammon; it was not for this his mother, the goddess Venus, twice saved him from destruction; he had to proceed on his mission, to sail onward until he came to the place where he must establish the lineage that would bring the whole world under the rule of law. So he had to leave Dido, and the ease she offered him (as Gates and his party had to leave the paradise of Bermuda), and set sail once more. At Cumae, he had to go down into Hades, pluck the Golden Bough, speak with the dead and receive certain prophecies of the Sybil. On surfacing, he had to push onwards into long toil and battle, before he could establish the stock that would found Rome, parent of the whole civilisation of western Europe, including Britain. Surely, this is what lies parallel in our author's mind to the westward voyages of his time, across the Atlantic. In the new world that was being discovered, less fettered by the mistakes of the past, the settlers had the chance to create a new and enlightened way of living, upon a land fair and fertile, and to establish, in justice and equity, a civilisation which might in the untold future rise to heights surpassing all that we knew.

The Tempest is about the founding of America.

One sees how these last plays have three levels of meaning. There is the simple romantic story, there is the political plane, apt for his day though probably escaping moderns; and there is the spiritual meaning, embracing the mysteries of death and rebirth, first tried out in *Pericles.* In *Cymbeline* there is the sleep mistaken for a death. In *The Winter's Tale* there is the death (apparent) of the mother, revived in the daughter, until finally, in *The Tempest,* there is the strange sleep of Miranda, after Prospero has told his story. I believe it a mistake to play this as though she were bored. He says the matter was "heavy" for her, and this may mean that a psychic shock has caused her to pass into a different level of consciousness, a momentary yet symbolic death, such as other characters in the play experience in different ways. The wrecked men "die" in the storm, to be reborn, to the level of their capacities, which vary, on the island, where they are tried and judged by Prospero. If we are on the right track, and the author really has gone to the Trisgemistic literature, does Prospero not here function as Osiris? The malicious brother by whom he was deposed set him and his child in a bark not, immediately, upon the open sea, but upon that long canal (which who would have known about who had not been there?) connecting Milan with the Adriatic. In this he resembles Osiris, who was cast by his evil brother, Set, into the Nile in a chest, magically to be revived by Isis, here replaced by Miranda. Is Caliban, then, Set, a reduplication of the wicked brother, in his monstrous form? Against this interpretation is that Caliban is (being half a Caribbean tortoise) associated with water, whereas Set was of a hot and dry nature, with red hair, like an ass, symbolising all that is contrary to spiritual evolution. Is there anything red about Caliban? He has freckles, and he curses Prospero with "The red plague . . . " Why the red one? This interpretation, though I submit it tentatively, would give a reason for Prospero's acknowledging "this thing of darkness" in some way his, presumably for ultimate redemption, a long way off. Wrecking the party that he might set them the ordeals he stands in the place of Osiris, with his crook and flail, before whom the Egyptian dead, as they rose from their bodies, had to appear for judgement.

But it is not merely the initiation of others which Prospero superintends. It is his own, too.

1. *Shakespeare Survey* 5, 1952, pp.25-49.

2. *Shakespeare Survey*, 29, 1976, 'Pericles . . . and some of the Play's Special Problems'.

3. *Memorial to Henry, Prince of Wales*, Spedding VI, p.327.

4. 'Shakespeare's Investiture Play', Glynne Wickham, *Times Literary Supplement*, December 10th, 1969.

5. *Shakespeare's Last Plays*, Frances Yates (Routledge, 1975).

6. 'Shakespeare and Waterways of North Italy', Edward Sullivan, *The Nineteenth Century*, 1908.

7. 'Shakespeare and Italy', Howard Bridgewater, *Baconiana*, October, 1938.

8. 'Bacon and Bohemia', M.V. Ambros, *Baconiana*, August, 1968.

9. *See Oxford Classical Dictionary* (1970), 'Hermione'.

10. Some confirmation may be found in the Cabalistic tables reproduced in *The Magus*, Francis Barrett, Introd. Timothy d'Arch Smith (New York, 1967), 'Talismanic Magic' p.112 and 'Ceremonial Magic', p.63.

11. 'Shakespeare and the Makers of Virginia', *Proceedings of the British Academy*, 1919.

CHAPTER 50

Attorney

THE year 1612 produced some curiosities. One was a posthumous edition of William Warner's *Albion's England*, embellished by the addition of two lines that did not appear in any of the nine editions printed in his lifetime:

> Hence Englands heires-apparent haue of Wales bin Princes till
> Our Queene deceast concealed her heire, I wot not for what skill.

Another was an emblem book called *Minerva Britanna* (sic) by Henry Peacham.

On the title-page between pillars, within a wreath of bays, a hand appears from behind a curtain and writes, upside down, the words MENTE VIDEBOR (By the mind I shall be seen). On p.34 we find Sir Francis Bacon, shown cutting a snake in two with a very long spear. The preceding page, 33, shows Lord Dingwall, but with an enormous spear-haft, grasped in a hand cut off at the wrist like that on the title-page by the curtain. The application to Dingwall is not obvious, and it has been suggested the drawings go with an idea found in *The Rape of Lucrece*, 1422–27:

> For much imaginarie worke was there,
> Conceipt deceitfull, so compact, so kinde.
> That for ACHILLES image stood his speare,
> Grip'd in an Armed hand; himselfe, behind,
> Was left vnseene saue to the eye of mind,
>   A hand, a foote, a face, a leg, a head
>   Stood for the whole to be imagined.

On p.35, that is "behind" Bacon is Prince Henry, with Prince of Wales feathers. These are proper to him, but it could have been artfully that, by the use of three successive pages, Bacon was placed between symbols relating to his alleged concealed authorship of the works of Shakespeare and his alleged real status as the deceased Queen's son.

The third curiosity is the portrait of Bacon used by Spedding as the frontispiece of his *Life and Works, I* (see our Plate 1). On p.xv he tells us it is from an old engraving by Francis Hall after Simon Pass, taken from a broken up copy of *Bazilogia*, (1612). What he does not tell us is what Bacon is wearing round his neck. It looks like a Masonic collar. What hangs from it is hidden by a small piece of paper which Bacon is holding up, apparently for no purpose but to prevent the pendant from being seen. There seems to be here a cryptic hinting at something, for if what hangs from the collar should not be seen, why wear the collar to draw attention to a mystery? The purpose might be to give the initiate a portrait of Bacon which they would appreciate, without baring the jewel to non-Masons. The breaking up of an emblem as indicated in the passage about Achilles' image accords with the Masonic ''lettering'' or breaking of a name, for secrecy, as ''Bo . . . as'' instead of ''Boas'' outright.

On the other hand, it is pointed out in an article in *Baconiana,* 1978, signed Joan Ham,[1] that although in all versions of this portrait forming title-pages to his books published during his life-time, the pendant is hidden, the posthumous 1640 edition of *The Advancement of Learning,* shows it as the medal of a Knight of the Garter. Bacon was not a Knight of the Garter. Her idea is that, as every Prince of Wales is invested with it automatically, the intention is to convey he was the true Prince of Wales. There could be this idea, or there could be a kind of double bluff, for the picture which shows him with the K.G. pendant from the collar also seats him in a chair, the visible side to the back of which is formed as a perfect Masonic ball on pillar.

If the Master Mason was a concealed Prince of Wales, his relations with the public one were friendly. In 1612 he sent the young Prince of Wales a copy of his new book, ''which I have ventured to call *Essays.* The word is late, but the thing is ancient.'' In their blend of psychological insight with shrewd wisdom, they are incomparable. Unhappily, on November 4th, 1612, the young Prince of Wales died, aged seventeen. It was Bacon who wrote his elegy, with evident regret and respect. There remained Prince Charles, but a great loss had been suffered. His sister's marriage was put back.

The new date, February 14th, 1612/13, occasioned John Donne's *Epithalamium,* in which St. Valentine is hailed as coupling ''two Phoenixes''. There is no record of contact between Bacon and Donne, yet both were close friends of Tobie Matthew. Plays presented before the couple included *The Winter's Tale, Much Ado About Nothing, The Merry Wives of Windsor, Othello, Julius Caesar* and *The Tempest.* Celebrations costing £53,000 (£26,500,000) practically bankrupted the royal exchequer. Gray's Inn and the Inner Temple contributed a masque, at a cost of £2,000 (£1,000,000), text by Francis Beaumont, dedicated to Francis Bacon, as the ''chief contriver'', who had spared no pains in ''setting forth, ordering and furnishing''. Entitled, *The Marriage of the River Thames to the Rhine,* it was on the evening of the 15th, brought up the river on a barge, but the King waved it away saying he could not keep awake to see it. Bacon pled with him not to ''bury them quick'' and they were given leave to come again another day.

On April 25th the newlyweds sailed from Margate, and progress down the Rhine culminated on June 7th with Elizabeth's first view of her future home, a fairy-tale castle, soft red upon its red sandstone cliff. John Donne followed later, to be Chaplain to the Ambassador. The word of God in Hebrew letters above the heads of the young couple in several designs suggests that Heidelberg held the matrix of what was to become the Rosicrucian movement.

In England, on August 7th, 1613, the Lord Chief Justice died. Bacon now wrote to the King suggesting Coke should be made Lord Chief Justice.[2] At the Common Pleas, Coke had constantly been challenging the Royal Prerogative. He could hardly refuse the move, since it was promotion, yet the higher position would give him less scope for vexing his sovereign. The present Attorney General, Sir Henry Hobart, could then be moved to the Common Pleas, an office better suited to his temperament and which he would be unlikely to abuse, and Bacon himself could be moved up to take the Attorney General's place, a promotion long overdue. It may seem strange Bacon should thus dispose of the places above his own, but the King made exactly the changes he suggested. Bacon became Attorney General in the autumn of 1613, Sir Henry Yelverton being put in to the place he had vacated, as Solicitor General.

The salary of the Attorney General, paid by the King, was £81.6s.8d, that is £40,667 in today's money, but the office was reckoned worth £600,000 (£300,000,000 in present day values), the extra being in fees or perquisites.

1. 'The First Sacrifice', Joan Ham (*Baconiana*, LXI, 178, 1978).
2. Lambeth, Gibson Papers, viii, f.257.

CHAPTER 51

The learned butcher's boy

ABOUT this time, Shakespeare withdrew to Stratford, where he had bought New Place, his purchase of the Gate House, Blackfriars, being solely as an investment. His purchase of the Stratford tithes brought him in an additional £60 (£30,000) a year. As early as January, 1597/8 one of his fellow townsmen, Abraham Sturley, had written to another, Richard Quiney:

Mr. Shaksper is willing to disburse some money upon some odd yard-land or other at Shottery or near about us; he thinketh it a very fit pattern to move him to deal in the matter of our tithes.

On October 25th of that year, Quiney wrote to Shakespeare:

Loving Countryman, I am bold to ask of you as of a friend, craving your help with xxx£ (£15,000 in today's money) upon Mr. Bushel's and my security or Mr. Myrten's with me . . . You shall friend me much in helping me out of all the debts I owe in London.

On November 4th, Sturley wrote to Quiney:

Yr letter of the 25 of October came to my hands the last of the same night per Greenway, which imported . . . that our countryman, Mr. Wm. Shak. would procure us money, which I will like of as I shall hear when, where or how, and I pray let not go that occasion if it may sort to any indifferent conditions.

Halliwell-Phillipps, presenting these documents, observes they afford fair grounds for the opinion Shakespeare lent money upon interest.[1]

One must be fair. In an age when there was no such thing as applying for a bank loan, because there were no banks, a private person who would make a business loan may have rendered service. It begins to look unpleasant, however, when these letters are read in conjunction with the case of another Warwickshire man, John Addenbrook, whom in 1608 Shakespeare had arrested and cast into prison for a debt of £6 (£3,000 in today's money). He was bailed out by the local blacksmith, Thomas Hornby, but jumped his bail, and Shakespeare sued Hornby for the debt and his costs.

One might be chary of borrowing money upon interest from one who, if one was unable to pay back, might have one put in prison. Somehow, it is not quite "Sweetest Shakespeare, Fancy's child" warbling his native woodnotes wild. He had the legal right, yet the proof that these episodes – which assort ill with "Neither a borrower nor a lender be" and "The quality of mercy is not strained'' - are unattractive, is that, short as is the authentic material concerning him, the popular biographies hardly hold them up for exhibition. They prefer to dwell on him as a ''sweet child of nature'', failing to perceive that the evidence of his supposed sensitivity to nature is derived only from the works accredited to him.

For contact with nature, one has only Aubrey's horrible story:

His father was a Butcher, and I have been told heretofore by some of the neighbours, that when he was a boy he exercised his father's Trade, but when he kill'd a Calfe he would doe it in a high style, and make a Speech. There was at this time another Butcher's son in this Towne that was held not at all inferior to him for a natural witt . . .

It has been pointed out that Shakespeare's father was a glover, that is, a man who would obtain from the butcher the hides of sheep and any of the smaller animals slaughtered (as opposed to cows', the hides of which would be purchased by the tanner), clean and prepare them as soft leather, which he would then sell to the makers of gloves, caps, purses and the like; that butchers and glovers belonged to different guilds and that a man could not belong to two guilds. Nevertheless, the story is an odd one to have been made up out of nothing. It could be that Shakespeare's father had a friend or relative in the slaughtering trade, from whom he would obtain hides at favourable prices.

Halliwell-Phillipps reminds us Malone discovered a notice of a Thomas Shakespeare, butcher, living at Warwick in 1610, and quotes from an original manuscript in his possession, an account of which can be found in Thorpe's Catalogue of MSS for 1836, p.395, a letter written by one I. Dowdall, on April 10th, 1693, to his cousin, describing a visit to Stratford-on-Avon:

The clarke that showed me this church is above 80 years old; he says that this Shakespeare was formerly in this towne bound apprentice to a butcher, but that he ran away from his master to London, and there was received into the playhouse as a servitore, and by this meanes had an opportunity to be what he afterwards became.

Halliwell-Phillipps sums up: ''however much it may shock our fancy'' the best evidence associates Shakespeare's early years with butchery.[2]

None of the anecdotes told of Shakespeare exhibit him as a profound man. He is given no wise sayings; not even represented with a book in his hand. The mythos is full of the ''jolly good fellow'' type of story, getting drunk under a mulberry tree, poaching and wenching, stealing another man's assignation with a woman. Nothing told of Shakespeare exhibits him as a lover of nature, or as sensitive or perceptive. The stories seem designed to reassure us that there was nothing too high, remote, or different from the ordinary man about him.

The will he made shortly before his death, in April, 1615, makes no mention of books, though it enters into details about furniture, plate and wearing apparel. This is singular, for there were no lending libraries in those days, and he would therefore have needed to own the many works ransacked for references and inspiration. Gone are the days when the great writer could be regarded as an ignoramus. To say he read Golding's Ovid and North's Plutarch will no longer explain all. *Shakespeare's Small Latine and Lesse Greeke,* W.T. Baldwin (Illinois, 1944) is an important work, wherein the possible sources of many classical allusions are investigated with care. In Vol. II, in the chapter on Ovid, p.426.f, following upon a dismissal of one of the instances brought up by Theobald, a Baconian, because it could be found quoted in the *Adagia* of Erasmus, a favourite Grammar School study, Professor Baldwin concedes, ''But enough instances hold to incriminate Shakspere of some knowledge of the *Heroides.* Besides the *Heroides,* it seems clearly proved that Shakspere used *Fasti* also, and with it at least one other author in the original Latin. For the *Rape of Lucrece* Shakspere used both the *Fasti* of Ovid, and the work of Livy, neither being yet in translation. Both *Fasti* and Livy were grammar school books.'' He next points to lines in the scene where Gaunt attempts to console his son for his banishment: ·

> All places that the eye of heaven visits
> Are to the wise man ports and happy havens

and points out that ''This is Ovid's

> Omne solum forti patria est, ut piscibus aequor,
> Vt uolucri uacuo quidquid in orbe patet.''

Shakespeare would have known A. Brooke's rendering of the passage, for he uses it in Friar Lawrence's advice to Romeo,

yet he uses the original Latin when he writes the banishment scene in *Richard II.* ''Omne solum'' on the background of the whole passage becomes ''All places'', and ''solum'' suggests ''sol'', the sun, which becomes ''the eye of heaven,'' which is also Ovidian, and ''visits'' all places. Then *forti* is literally translated ''to a wise man,'' and the verb *est* becomes ''are'' preceding, in accordance with English syntax. Finally *patria* is expanded into ''ports and happy havens.'' If anyone wants to know whether William Shakspere could read Latin, let him consider the process involved here.

He finds, p.430, evidence in *As You Like It* that Shakespeare knew ''the *Tristia* in the original''. On p.432 we read, ''Shakspere shows knowledge of the original of *Metamorphoses.*'' This is repeated. For *A Midsummer Night's Dream,* however, he must have used alongside Golding's translation an edition with the notes of Raphael Regius. On p.452 Professor Baldwin observes, ''even if at the end of his career Shakspere did use a translation as well as the original of the *Metamorphoses* . . . that fact does not prove he read Latin with difficulty.''

In the chapter on Virgil he shows us, p.465, how Perdita's speech about the flowers, *The Winter's Tale*, IV, 116-127, blends the lists and descriptions of them found in Ovid and Virgil (Ovid V, 392, 396, 399, and Virgil, *Eclogue* II, 45-50). He finds it doubtful whether Phaer's translation was used for the masque of Iris in *The Tempest*, where the author seems to have gone to the original of the *Aeneid*, IV, 700-702. With Ariel's clapping of his wings, ''Clearly, Shakspere's eyes were in this passage pretty closely fixed on Virgil's original.'' And again, p.484, ''Shakspere knew his Virgil well enough to draw upon widely separated parts of it for requisite materials, here a touch and there a suggestion.'' On p.496 he concludes: ''The knowledge displayed of the *Eclogues*, *Georgics* and *Aeneid* is such as Shakespeare should have acquired in grammar school. A great deal of it is not the kind of information which one could have picked up from reading a translation, even where a translation existed.''

Moving on to Horace, Professor Baldwin, on p.519, accepts Edmund Blunden's ''very brilliant'' demonstration that in *King Lear*, III, iv, where ''poor Tom'' is seen as a ''learned Theban'' and then as ''a good Athenian'', ''Lear is all the time contemplating the position through the first Epistle of the second book of Horace''. To Blunden's exposition, Professor Baldwin adds. ''Tom is not only 'this philosopher', but his loosely flowing blanket makes of him a Persian philosopher, one of the 'magi sapientes Persarum' alluded to by Horace.'' (One remembers Bacon's interest in ''Persian magic.'')

Two lines in the banishment scene of *Richard II* show close use of two in Ovid's *Fasti*, while in *The Winter's Tale* Perdita's speech about the flowers blends passages in Ovid and Virgil, and where translations available at the time have ''pale violets'' and ''white violets'', Shakespeare's ''violets dim'' follows neither of these, but yet translates Virgil's ''pallentes violas''.

Professor Baldwin finds, ''Shakespeare evidently knew in detail a fundamental point near the beginning of the *Ars Poetica . . .* and knew it as coming directly from Horace in the original''.

On the other hand, in *Othello*, III, iii, 158, he is translating a Latin sentence found in Camden's *Remaines Concerning Britain* 1605, p.107, adapted by Camden from Horace but not in Horace. (Shakespeare did not find that in a text set before him in Stratford Grammar School).

One sees, here, that our great genius had, at the highest level, a kind of magpie mind, picking upon bright things, wherever found, and weaving them into something of his own. Does this explain the name given by Jonson to Sir John Daw, sometimes called Jack Daw, in *The Silent Woman* (see above p.200)? The jackdaw, like the magpie, will fly into anyone's garden to pick up any bright object and carry it away to its nest. Rawley tells us Bacon ''would light his torch at every man's candle''.

Passing to Juvenal, Professor Baldwin accepts that the slander on old age in *Hamlet,* II, ii, 198–203, reproduces that in Juvenal's *Satire* X. He further notices that in *The Winter's Tale,* where Leontes, persuading himself his wife has been unfaithful, declares, "'tis far gone, When I shall gust it last", I, ii, 218–219, he reproduces from *Satire* X, Silus' idea that if he lies with Messalina, Claudius will hear of it in the end, though he will be the last whom it will reach. (Curious how our author is haunted by Claudius, his love life).

For Greek, Professor Baldwin tells us that this was taught in the highest forms, chiefly from the point of view of preparing scholars to read the New Testament in Greek. He points out that passages in *Love's Labour's Lost* and *The Merchant of Venice* show the author aware of the controversy concerning the proper translation of Greek ἀγάπη (Bacon was keenly concerned about this), and concludes, "It seems highly probable, therefore, if not absolutely proved, that Shakespeare had gone as far with Greek as the New Testament".

Professor Baldwin's thesis is that the education given by the Grammar Schools was of an exceedingly high order. He quotes Erasmus on how classics should be taught, and shows how his precepts were practised at Eton, Winchester, Westminster and Pauls. He notes that Sir Francis Bacon presented to the Grammar School of St. Albans a complete set of the works of Plato in the Latin of Serranus, and tells us that Saffron Walden Grammar School followed the Eton plan, with the omission of Greek. He has not been able to discover the curriculum of the Grammar School at Stratford-on-Avon, but presumes that as one of the townsmen, Richard Quiney, went to Cambridge, it must have prepared him to enter the University.

What may strike many people as unlikely is that a boy who had received such a very superior classical education would leave school to be apprenticed to a butcher. Indeed, Professor Baldwin feels that, for he will not believe either Aubrey or the old clerk, William Castle, who showed Dowdall round the church. He prefers the word of William Beeston, the actor, that Shakespeare had been a schoolmaster before he went on the stage. But why should Beeston, only seven at Shakespeare's death, and not a Stratford man, know better than the Stratford Townsman, Castle, christened July 17th, 1614, who took the visitors round the church?

Professor Baldwin's book has been opposed by J.A.K. Knight in his *Shakespeare and the Classics* (Allen & Unwin, 1952). Knight does not believe the education given in the Grammar Schools was anywhere near so high as Prof. Baldwin contends. He truly observes that today, when a boy is said to have "read the *Aeneid*", it means that, with the help of his teacher, he has struggled through one book of it. I must say, this had occurred to me. How many of us could easily have gone on from our set books to read further Latin works by ourselves? Thomson doubts whether it was much different then, even granting that, as fewer other subjects were studied, the emphasis on Latin was greater. He points out that Marlowe, who had been at Cambridge, translated Ovid's *Ars Amatoria,* but makes mistakes in the translation; and that the University Wits, though offering at first sight a show of being steeped in the classics, also make mistakes, even gross ones, such as bringing on to the stage together people who were not living at the same time. He warns us we should beware of supposing that a later author must have copied from a classical because of a similarity of ideas, since an idea could have occurred to him independently, without his knowing a classical writer had expressed it. Now, this is all very true, but the weakness of Knight's book is that he does not really meet Prof. Baldwin's examples head on. He does take him up on his observation that *Hamlet* V, i, 261-63.

> Lay her i' th'earth:
> And from her fair and unpolluted flesh
> May violets spring!

seems to come from Persius, 1,39-40.

> nunc non e tumulo fortuna atque favilla
> nascentur violae?
> (Now from your tomb and lucky ashes will not violets be borne?)

Knight sees no necessity for the Shakespeare to be derived from Persius: "For what would be more natural, especially for a brother, than the fancy that violets might spring from the grave of an unmarried girl?" In the London Library's copy, an unknown hand has pencilled a question mark in the margin.

Knight says it would be wrong to suppose *The Rape of Lucrece* LX must come from Ovid's *Metamorphoses* XV, 181-84, because, "Shakespeare has not gone behind Golding". The unknown penciller has, however, underlined the words "sequent" in the Shakespeare and "sequuntur" in the Ovid. Golding has "follow". The unknown penciller makes a valid point.

In *Titus Andronicus* Knight does find passages difficult to believe not based on the Latin of Seneca, also of Horace and Virgil. He finds something more astonishing. In I, i, 136-39 it is described how the Queen of Troy was armed for revenge "Upon the Thracian tyrant in his tent." Ovid says nothing about his tent. To know that it was in his tent the Thracian tyrant was blinded, it would have been necessary to read the *Hecuba* of Euripides, in Greek. Prof. Baldwin has assured us Greek was taught only in the highest forms of the Grammar Schools, and only for the reading of the New Testament, no classical Greek authors. Knight finds it so impossible the boy from Stratford read Euripides' *Hecuba* in Greek that he comes to the conclusion he did not write *Titus Andronicus.* Had he stopped there, I would agree with him. But Knight dissociates this one play from the rest, saying lovers of *A Midsummer Night's Dream* and *Romeo and Juliet* have always wanted to deny the horrific *Titus Andronicus*. Perhaps; but the works contain things many of us would be glad to do without, for different reasons. Some find the bawdy offensive (Bowdler offered an edition which removed it all). Women usually dislike *The Taming of the Shrew* (not only "Women's Libbers" of today: my mother and her mother before her hated it). But to make discards from the canon on the basis of our own sensitivities is dangerous. Dr. Rowse has pointed to a number of similarities between *Titus Andronicus* and *King Lear*, which seem to bind the two together. Knight does not suggest who amongst the known contemporary dramatists would have possessed the ability to read the *Hecuba* of Euripides in Greek needed to be the author of *Titus Andronicus*. Moreover, Knight gives positive opinion that before writing *Macbeth* Shakespeare must have read several of the tragedies of Seneca in Latin. Which of us knows a butcher's assistant who has read Seneca in Latin?

Knight is redoubtable as a classical scholar, but less reliable concerning Shakespeare. Thus he repeats Malone's ancient idea that the stage is referred to in Sonnet 110:

> Alas, 'tis true, I haue gone here and there,
> And made myselfe a motley to view,
> Gor'd mine own thoughts, sold cheap what is most deare,
> Made old offences of affections new.

The Variorum edition quotes several opinions that it has nothing whatever to do with the acting profession – with which I concur. I find it impossible to believe an actor would think of his appearances on the stage as "making a motley" of himself. It is not a career to which anybody is obliged, but one that offers excitement and glamour. Surely the lines:

> And worse essaies prou'd thee my best of loue
> . . .
> Mine appetite I neuer more will grin'de
> On newer proofe, to trie an older friend.

mean that he has been making a spectacle (a motley) of himself by running after other women. The Countess may have been trying, but he feels that to have paid court to others, to console himself, or to make her jealous, was a mistake.

But talk of the stage suggests another approach to the question. There is an anonymous academic play, *The Return from Pernassus*. (The spelling does not represent ignorance; *er* was then, more often than now, pronounced as a member of the *a* phoneme, as in clerk, sergeant, Derby etc.) It was performed at St. John's College, Cambridge, at Christmas

1601/2, printed 1606, and tells of the difficulties encountered by graduates in obtaining employment of a nature suited to their learning. At one moment they try their luck on the stage, and are interviewed by Burbage and Kemp, but do not care for the company. One of them says, in V, i:

> England affords these glorious vagabonds,
> Coursiers to ride on through the gazing streets,
> Sooping it in their glaring satten sutes,
> And pages to attend their maisterships:
> With mouthing words that better wits haue framed
> They purchase lands, and now esquires are made.

The reference seems to be to Shakespeare, his purchase of lands at Stratford and the grant of arms to his father so that he might style himself son of a gentleman. This is obviously resented. He may have acquired the title of gentleman but, in his glaring satin, he does not look like one. Is this the manner in which anyone would write of a man of the classical reading that has been shown? Note that there is the definite implication he did not write, but only mouthed, words given to him.

We should study beside this an anonymous pamphlet, *Ratseis Ghost* (undated, but entered in the Stationers Register May 31st, 1605). One Ratsey encounters at an inn a company of players, and reflects that while some are poor:

Others there are whom Fortune hath so wel favored that . . . are growne so wealthy that they have expected to be knighted . . .

He bids them perform something for him, and afterwards throws them gold, and says to the chief of them:

Get thee to London, for, if one man were dead, they will have much neede of such a one as thou art . . . I durst wager all the money in my purse on thy head to play Hamlet with him for a wager. There thou shalt learne . . . to feed upon all men, to let none feede upon thee; to make thy hand a stranger to thy pocket, thy hart slow to performe thy tongues promise; and when thou feelest thy purse well lined, buy thee some place or lordship in the country, that growing weary of playing, thy mony may there bring thee to dignitie and reputation; then thou needest care for no man, nor not for them that before made thee prowd with speaking their works upon the stage.

Halliwell-Phillipps takes the reference to be to Shakespeare, and the likeness of the characterisation to that in *Pernassus* is striking. But notice it is only through money he will purchase dignity. We are told nothing of his considerable dignity as a Latin scholar, and there is, more strongly than in *Pernassus,* the distinct implication he was not the author of the works he presented. Why should a man with such an extended classical education need others to make him proud by giving him their words to speak?

Apart from the absence of evidence he ever attended Stratford Grammar School, has anybody attempted to visualise what it would require in bookshelving to house not only all the classical texts, borrowings from which have been discerned, by Professor Baldwin, and also his Erasmus, but all the Italian comedies, in the original and in translation, traces of which have been found by Professor Bullough, all the historical works and chronicles drawn upon for the English history plays, as discerned by Professor Tilliard and Professor Bullough, not forgetting the skittish but voluminous and space-taking *Mirror for Magistrates* and his Malory, plus all the works of occasional reference, stretching in scope from the Essays of Montaigne to pamphlets on the Virginian venture, noted in the *Variorum* Shakespeare and by Professor Bullough, plus his earlier English authors, his Gower, his Chaucer, his Lyly and his Lodge, not to speak of his more or less contemporary authors, his Spenser and so on? List all these, and you have the inventory of a distinguished library. If it was disposed of before the will was made, one might have heard of the sale or gift.

With regard to the Italian works, traces of which have been found by Professor Bullough, though translations were sometimes used, or at any rate available, Professor Bullough thinks Shakespeare read in the original *Gl'Ingannati,* Nicolò Secchi, *Il Pecorone,* Giovanni Fiorentino, *Il Novellino* of Masuccio, and at least some of the *Hecatommithi* of Geraldi Cinthio and *Novelle* of Bandello. Now it may be said that to anybody who has learned Latin, Italian comes easily; yet not so easily as all that. I did several years of Latin at school, yet I certainly found it necessary to work through an Italian grammar before I could attempt to read Dante. With these sallies into the literature of mediaeval Italy we are beyond the curriculum of the Grammar School, howsoever classical.

How could a man of such extended reading be contumeliously described as "mouthing words that better wits haue framed"? The jibe would, however, sort with the butcher's apprentice, turned actor, whose new gentility was resented. Is it not obvious we have in this figure, and in the scholar discerned through professorial scrutiny of the works, two different men?

Somebody is sure to ask whether the works do not show traces of Warwickshire speech. The word "rother" in *Timon of Athens,* IV, iii, 12, has been linked with the Rother Market at Stratford; but "rother" was the old word for cattle, in general usage. The homespun word "muck" has been cited as though it could only be used by a countryman; but Bacon does use "muck", meaning, obviously, manure. As soon as one turns to an academic study, *Shakespeare's Pronunciation,* Helge Kökeritz (Yale, 1953), one sees how thin is the evidence. For the pronunciation of the West Midlands, Professor Kökeritz has only one exhibit to show. It comes in *The Merry Wives of Windsor,* I, iv, 22,

where in the Folio there is reference to a ''wee-face''. In the Quarto, the
same character has a ''whay coloured beard''. Professor Kökeritz
therefore takes it that ''wee-face'' means ''whey-face'', which would
show Gloucestershire dialect, because ''whey'' is pronounced ''wee'' in
Gloucestershire. But this is a frail argument. The concept of ''whey''
may have got displaced from the beard to the face as the Professor thinks,
or the bard may simply mean ''small-face''. We cannot be sure.

A short *o* before nasals as in ''mon'' for ''man'', Professor Kökeritz
tells us, is very typically Warwickshire, and does occur in Shakespeare;
but it can be found also in other poets, notably in London born Spenser.
Shakespeare's rhyme ''shorter''/''departure'' accords with Warwickshire but the same sound changes have been traced through place-names
in Middlesex, Essex and also Surrey. Shakespeare's rhymes, ''young''/
''belong'' ''tongues''/''tongs'', ''wrong''/''rung'', are in line with
present day Warwickshire, but we cannot dismiss the possibility
that the same levelling of Middle English ĭn/ŏn, ŭng/ŏng occurred also
in the London area. In short, there is nothing that can be pinned down as
exclusively Warwickshire.

On the other hand, there is evidence in the plays of a tendency to
pronounce the short *a* as the fronter and closer more *e*-like sound that it
was becoming in London and the home counties, rather than as the backer
and more open one which remained in the provinces. Where this occurs
in *King Henry IV*, it could be argued the dramatist was deliberately trying
to represent a typical London pronunciation, but that would not explain
why he should lend it to Ophelia: see *Hamlet*, IV, v, 26, ''sendall' for
''sandal''.

Professor Kökeritz writes, p.163, ''As an actor Shakespeare may have
found it expedient to exchange his native Warwickshire *a* for the more
fashionable London *ae?*'' From the Stratfordian position, that is the best
that can be said; but if the Warwickshire origin of the author is in
question, this Londonism must count against it.

But what about Jonson's Ode *To the Author, Mr. William Shakespeare?*
Why write a tremendous hymn of praise, unless sincerely? Yet how could
he possibly write:

> And though thou hadst small Latine and lesse Greeke,
> From thence to honour thee, I would not seek . . .

the works being so full of compacted classical allusions? Moderns may
miss these where they are concealed. Many who have not read Ovid or
Virgil take Perdita's speech about the flowers as evidence of direct
observation in the fields and hedgerows around Stratford. Jonson, whose
works contain many concealed classical borrowings was surely equipped
to discern the like in those of his great contemporary. The sense is usually
taken to mean, ''Although thou hadst small Latin etc''; but then, should

not sequence of tense call for ''I do not seek''? Is not the intended sense, ''Even if you had had small Latin, etc . . . I would not seek . . . ''?

Is there not something a little strange about the hesitation shown at the beginning lest praise from Jonson might damage the reputation of the one he idolises:

> as some infamous Baud, or Whore,
> Should praise a Matron. What could harm her more?

How could the praise of Jonson, an actor playwright of respectability harm another actor playwright? It might conceivably harm someone of more exalted social standing or more serious vocation. In the *Discoveries,* against *Scientiae liberales,* Jonson writes rather oddly, ''The power of liberall studies lyes more hid, then that it can be wrought out by profane wits . . . Science is not every mans *Mistress.* It is as great a spite to be praised in the wrong place, and by a wrong person, as can be done to a noble nature.'' Whose was the noble nature he was the wrong person to praise?

He calls him ''Sweet Swan of Avon!'' yet he says:

> he seems to shake a Lance,
> As brandish't at the eyes of Ignorance.

The natural object of plays is to entertain. Perhaps the entertainment may be used as the vehicle of some moral instruction, as by displaying the ill results of envy, greed, jealousy, but that is hardly to tilt at Ignorance. To combat Ignorance was specifically the object of Bacon's philosophic or scientific works.

He says:

> Leaue thee alone, for the comparison
> Of all, that insolent *Greece,* or haughtie *Rome*
> Sent forth . . .

We shall see him later apply the same compliment to Bacon. If these observations seem strained, one should look at the book of *Epigrammes* Jonson published in the following year, including:

> On Poet-Ape
> Poore Poet-Ape, that would be thought our chiefe,
> Whose workes are eene the fripperie of wit,
> From brocage is become so bold a thief . . .
>   now growne
> To a little wealth and credit in the *scene* . . .
> Foole, as if halfe eyes will not know a fleece
> From locks of wool, or shreds from the whole piece?

There has been understandable academic controversy as to whether this is or is not meant for Shakespeare. The reference to ''brocage''

240   *Francis Bacon*

suggests the money-lending in Stratford, "scene" recalls Greene's jibe at "the only Shake-scene in a countrey" and "wool" could glance at his father's subsidiary dealings in that commodity. On the other hand, even if the epigram had been written at an earlier date than the memorial ode, and repented, why publish it in the collection published the following year? It seems scarcely credible the two poems were written to the same man. If they were not, is it the epigram or the ode which has to be referred to another?

1. *The Life of William Shakespeare*, Halliwell-Phillipps (1848), p.177.
2. *The Life of William Shakespeare*, Halliwell-Phillipps (1848), pp.87-88.

CHAPTER 52

The veiled and feathered sunburst

IN 1616, Francis leased Canonbury Manor, usually known from its most conspicuous feature as Canonbury Tower. Then in the country, now engulfed in slummy north-east London, it is even today a mysterious place. At first sight there seems to be no way in. A rounded, high, old wall wraps itself round much of it. In what should be the front, there is no door, and a small, side one, in the tower itself, is not conspicuous. It stands within a complex of buildings that belonged to the Knights of St. John of Jerusalem, but if they built it, it is not known at what date. At a later date, likewise unknown, it became the Priory of St. Bartholomew, and in Canonbury Place as a whole can still be discerned the lay-out and vestiges of the Priory. For the construction of the Manor, within the Priory, we do have a date, 1362. The brick tower is said by Stowe to have been added between 1509 and 1532, by Prior Bolton of Smithfield. Underground passages are said to run from its base to St. Bartholomew's at Smithfield and to certain other foundations. With the dissolution of the Monasteries by Henry VIII, it became Crown property. Henry VIII granted it first to Thomas Cromwell, then to Leicester's father, on whose execution it reverted to the Crown. Queen Elizabeth granted it to Lord Wentworth, who sold it to Sir John ("Rich") Spencer. On his death, in 1610, it passed to his only child, Elizabeth, and to her husband, William, 2nd Lord Compton, later 1st Earl of Northampton. It was from this couple Bacon leased it. What was its interest for him?

Within the Tower, the handsomest of the rooms to which one climbs is that now known as the Compton Oak Room. One turns at a sharp angle from the staircase to enter by a small door at the side of one wall. There is, then, a fireplace on the right. Pillars are carved on the walls in bas-relief, as in an ancient temple. One cannot say that they exactly reproduce any of the classical Greek orders, but some of the major pillars, the widest amongst those of full height, have Corinthian capitals, with volutes and acanthus, while the shafts, ornamented with a fine design in which figure pomegranates, rest upon tall bases. Of these Corinthian pillars there are two on the west, one on the east side of the south and two on the east walls. On the north wall, flanking the fireplace, are two which, by their absence of bases or of ornamentation on the shafts, suggest the austerity of Doric. In the middle of the east wall, flanked by the two Corinthians, is a single pillar of which the shaft, though ornamented, is slenderer than that of the Corinthians, its lighter grace evoking the Ionic. Since together

they seem to make a temple, the presence of the three orders may be
intended to represent the three aspects of the Deity. Since most temples
face towards the east, the single Ionic probably stands for the First, the
Deity as Ruler. It will be noticed there are eight major pillars altogether.

But what of the smaller carvings? Above the door, in the east of the
north wall, is that roseate form, suggestive of a cross, seen in the arch of
church windows, but here enclosed within a crescent, which, if we are in
the domain of mystic symbolism, stands for the human soul, as a cup or
chalice, open to the descent of the divine spirit, here represented by the
rosy cross. But there are flanking forms, at first strange. I puzzled over
them for long, until it came to me that what were hooked upon the
straight shafts, continuing the horizontal arms of the cross, were two
flattened crescents, horned at one end, barbed at the other, which could
only represent anchors. Perhaps we should think of St. Paul's Epistle to
the Hebrews, VI, 19, ''Which hope we have as an anchor of the soul . . . ''
(The image is used in *The Faerie Queene,* I, 10, 22.)

Beneath this lovely and composite design, there is something on the
keystone. From a knob at the top, there descend two legs, like those of a
compass, open to sixty degrees, except for enlarged ''knee-joints'' at
which it is intersected by a similar, though not identical, figure, inverted.
The knob at the bottom rears arms, but they have ''wrists'' that turn in
at the top. They are not a second pair of compasses, but a pair of tongs.
The House of Solomon included in its furnishings a pair of gold tongs,
near the gold candlesticks, *I Kings,* VII, 49. The two figures, with their
opposed apexes, are reminiscent of the interlaced triangles of the
Theosophical Society, symbolising the union of the human with the
divine spirit, of the Jewish Star of David, or of the Freemasons' square and
compasses.'

In the centre of the north wall is the great fireplace, presumably once
ablaze with logs. The mantelpiece displays a floral design. Acorns and
oak-leaves, wide open roses and rose-leaves, wide open honeysuckle
flowers and honeysuckle leaves all spring from a single graceful stem,
from the sides towards the centre. The oak must stand for Strength, the
rose for Beauty or Love, the honeysuckle perhaps for Wisdom, hidden as
the nectar down at the bottom of the long tubes behind the flowers, here
concealed by their opened faces. So, here again one has the three aspects
of the Deity.

In the centre of the mantelpiece is a figure surely intended to represent
the Deity: a point off which radiate forms I cannot identify, encompassed
within a circle, within a square. The radiating forms could possibly be
seen as a conventionalised lion's face, his mane combed upwards to make
a corona. But the point within a circle is the astrological symbol for the
sun, and symbol of the Deity.

Above the mantelpiece are two human figures representing Faith and

Hope. If Charity is elsewhere, perhaps it is in the Cup over the door, with the cross and anchors.

As one looks around the room, one sees several introductions of a cord motif. In the four corners of the room there are minor pillars, paired, so that there are eight minor as eight major. On the bases of each of the minor pillars are tassels. In certain chivalric and mystic orders, a cord is placed around the waist of the initiate at his initiation, and he is told it links him with all of the others, past, present and future. Here, however, the positioning of the tassels at the four corners suggests the fastening of cords that perhaps run all round the walls. The cords perhaps enclose the rectangle to protect the sacred rites performed within it from alien influences. The making fast of the four corners by tassels suggests cardinality or hinging. An astrologer might think of the four cardinal signs, but in Christian symbolism the four hinges would more likely stand for the four Cardinal Virtues, Prudence, Temperance, Fortitude and Justice, which, with the three Theological Virtues, Faith, Hope and Charity, make up the septenary of evolved man.

The cornice above the two Doric pillars is formed by two faces, one a lion's – a real lion's this time, with the proper ears – and one a human's, very soft, both surrounded by drooping frondlike leaves. If one is familiar with the Tree of Life in the Kabbala, the mystic tradition within Judaism, the two heads might seem fit to epitomise the two columns of Justice and Mercy. Christians of Bacon's time would not normally know the Kabbala, though the paired principles of Justice and Mercy were represented in the division of the law-courts into those of Justice and Equity. There should, however, be some Christian Biblical pair of opposites the heads are carved to represent, something meaning the Grace and the Power of the Lord: the Power and the Glory, if they are not the same? Whilst I was contemplating these paired heads a waking vision came to me. As if from the wood, a bird in the shape of a peacock stepped towards me. Its feathers were not, however, peacock's feathers, but aquamarine sequins, reflecting the light from every angle. It was entirely composed of these sequins, except for the legs, feet, bill and quills, which were all of a white metal, lighter than silver. A bird that never was, and never could have been, it stepped towards me with astonishing vigour, raising its feet very high, its neck arching, head darting, crowned baubles waving, tail trailing, all a shimmer. It was totally unexpected, its brilliance strange against the old wood, and when it had vanished I was not further informed, but had a further symbol to interpret. It had perhaps been the ''sole Arabian bird'', the Phoenix, incorruptible, ever reborn from its ashes, a resurrection symbol. Did it explain the paired heads? In Solomon's temple were carved lions, together with cherubim and palm-trees, *I Kings*, VII, 36. There must be further layers of meaning here.

In a thin band of decoration just beneath the ceiling on the east wall is discernible what might be a conventional phoenix, rising body in the middle with wings spread out on either side.

On the base of the Ionic pillar is the face of a lion with a ring in its mouth. Could it stand for all those lions whose mouths were shut by the hand of an angel, so that they should not harm Daniel (*Daniel, VI,* 22); a symbol of God's protection and redemption of his chosen, the lion of Judah?

On the bases of the two Corinthian pillars in the west wall, and the southern of the Corinthians in the east wall, is an extraordinary face, rounded, plump and full. Over the forehead there are lines, but they are not the right shape for wrinkles. They appear also round the tip of the nose, and, notably, around the chin. They are the folds of a veil. Descending folds from it swathe the neck. Mrs. Brameld[1] believes it is Truth piercing the veil. It could be. Yet why should Truth have such a round face? Sages and ascetics are depicted with lean faces. This is so full as to suggest the solar orb. Is it a sunburst? From the head springs a corona of rays. Yet rays taper to the tips, whereas these broaden out, slightly scolloped and curling. Is it a headdress of plumes? Is it a sunburst both feathered and veiled?

On the bases of the Corinthians on the south wall and the north of the east wall, is a version in which the veil is replaced by a beard. In *The Wisdom of the Ancients, VI,* "Pan; or Nature", it is observed with reference to Pan's beard that sometimes the sun, when the upper part is clouded, its rays breaking out below "has the appearance of a face with a beard"; and a little further on it is said that Pan's emblems are of two kinds, "one of harmony, the other of empire". This provides another analogue for the paired faces of woman and lion.

On the cornices above the Corinthians are faces which, except for being surrounded by fig-leaves and figs instead of by cords, are identical with those in the bases, the two bearded sunbursts, if that is what they are, above the two bearded sunbursts, the three veiled sunbursts above the three veiled sunbursts. This suggests the principle of reflection: in Kabbalistic language, "Kether is in Malkuth, Malkuth is in Kether", in the Lord's prayer, "on earth as it is in Heaven", in Masonry the Blazing Star reflected in the star beneath. A sunburst with face inscribed is a Masonic symbol for the Deity. Is one in a Masonic Lodge?

In Whitney's *Choice of Emblems,* published right back in 1586, when Bacon was only twenty-five, there appeared, on p.53, a curious design, featuring two very Masonic looking pillars standing upon a row of arches in a wilderness. In the foreground is a sow and a young man who is directing her attention to them. Around the pillars is draped a ribbon bearing the words PLUS OLTRE and over the sow's back is written ULTERIUS. The pig could be taken as a rebus for Bacon, but it is also possible to find the letters F.BACON tucked away in the design. It looks, then, as if people associated Masonry with him from early in his life. Nevertheless, the carvings in Canonbury Tower were executed in 1599–1600, while it belonged to Sir John Spencer, to whom it will be remembered that Bacon had written in 1593, on Anthony's behalf, signing himself "Your very loving friend". What sort of a person was Spencer? His wealth was self-made, in trade with Spain, Turkey, Venice and Tripoly. He was a member of the Clothworkers Company and he was Alderman, then Sheriff, then Lord Mayor of London. He was one of the richest men in Europe, a Protestant, and apparently a Mason. For since he had a room in his house converted into a Lodge wherein the brethren might meet, presumably he was given some dignity within it. As owner of the property, he would be the natural guardian of the portals. If any who were not Masons called, unaware that something was going on that they might be interrupting, it would be he who would have to go out to speak to them, prevent their entry into that room and tactfully see them off the premises. Perhaps he was the original Senior Warden.

There is a legend that Francis Bacon was the founder of Freemasonry and Rosicrucianism. It must be said the literature on these movements is most diverse in the choice of origins offered. Suggested founders of Freemasonry are King Solomon, Pharoah Totmes III, Pompilius Numa, King Athelstan and Sir Francis Bacon, whilst the origins of Rosicrucianism have been seen amongst the Ancient Egyptians, in the Eleusinian mysteries, in the rites of the Druids, in the monks of St. Columba and in the Trismegistic movements of Renaissance Europe. Are Rosicrucianism and Freemasonry the same, or linked at their origins? This has been indignantly denied by some masons, and yet they share symbols and the 18th degree, in Freemasonry, is the Rose-Croix.

The most prosaic account of Masonry, preferred by Gould and Knoop, is that it originated in the craft guilds of the Middle Ages, its only mysteries being those of the building trade. But even if the workmen took to moralising upon their tools, and invited friends who were not in the building trade to come and do it with them, it seems a vast leap from this to the elaborate rites in gorgeous vestments known to the eighteenth century. It is admitted, even by the most sober of Masonic historians, that there is a gap. The period of the transition is not recorded nor the manner of it explained. There is, therefore, room for some particular individual to have stepped in and taken a hand.

The cornerstone of Rosicrucianism is a curious little pamphlet, the *Fama Fraternitatis,* usually known for short as the *Fama,* published anonymously, in German, in 1614, in Kassel. It starts off with an apparently historical story of a German, Christian Rosenkreutz, of the fourteenth century, who went to Damascus, and there met with sages who revealed to him the secrets of nature. On his return to Europe he drew around him brethren, who were bound by special oaths, to heal the sick, gratis. Together they founded a college, in which all the arts and sciences were studied in greater depth than in the general world. They did not live monk-like, within the college, or wear distinguishing dress, but were to meet at regular intervals. Because of their understanding of the laws underlying natural phenomena, their lives came to be unusually long. The difficulty with the *Fama* is to be sure at what point history leaves off and fantasy takes over. In the place of the signature, at the end, are the words, *Sub Umbra Alarum Tuarum Iehova,* Beneath the shade of thy wings, Jehova. Sacred secrets are communicated *sub rosa,* beneath the rose, as symbol of holiness and silence.

Dr. Yates believes Christian Rosenkreutz to have been an invention of the author of the *Fama.* Yet Damascus, in the fourteenth century, would not have been an unlikely place in which to pick up ideas of the nature described. It was in the Lebanon that the teachings of the eleventh century mage, sage and scientist, Sheikh-el-Djebel,[2] 'The Old Man of the Mountains'', fused with those of the Druses, and remains of this culture seem to have lingered on at least until the time of the crusade led by Louis IX.[3]

The *Fama* was succeeded in the following year by the *Confessio,* again published in Kassel, 1615, this time in Latin; but both in the *Fama* and the *Confessio* it is stated that there was simultaneous publication in five languages. It is not known whether this was true.

A third Rosicrucian publication, *Die Chymische Hochzeit Christian Rosenkreutz,* written in German and published in Strassburg, 1616, is probably by Johann Valentin Andreae, who later claimed authorship of it. He does not claim, however, to be the author of the first two. Dr. Yates discerns in *Die Chymische Hochzeit* numerous references to the court at Heidelberg. Certainly some of the designs she exhibits depict the young couple, the Elector and his bride, beneath Jehova's wings.

John Dee's symbol, the *Monas hieroglyphica,* appears in *Die Chymische Hochzeit.* However with his conjurations of angels Dee seems disconcertingly credulous, and uncritical of the purported communications, whereas the Rosicrucians, with their emphasis of following in Nature's footsteps, seem more inclined to investigation along the channels of rational science. They have been too much mocked for their terms ''invisible brethren'' and ''invisible college.'' They seem to mean little different from what Christians do by the Community of Saints, except that their canon is wider, admitting the sages of antiquity. It has, alternatively, been suggested the invisible college is what was later to become the Royal Society, since, until eventually granted a charter by Charles II, it existed only in the conceptions of those who desired its creation. The *Fama* and the *Confessio,* in Thomas Vaughan's translation, formed part of the Library of Sir Isaac Newton.

In our day, we tend to think of rational and hermetic science as opposed, but Dr. Paolo Rossi, in his history of the evolution of attitudes, *Francis Bacon: From Magic to Science,* shows how the one had its roots in the other. Bacon was the turning-point, but he did not throw out all that had gone before. On the contrary, he saw in the myths and fables of the ancients the traces of a deep teaching enshrined in these popular forms. He would, then, have no reason to see harm in the promulgation of a latterday fable, as the apparently absurd vehicle of matter that was really serious. In the place of the signature, at the end, are the words *Sub Umbra Alarum Tuarum Iehova* (Beneath the shadow of thy wings, Jehova). Sacred secrets are communicated *sub rosa*; beneath the rose as symbol of silence and of holiness.

Dr. Yates, finding no trace of any distinctively Rosicrucian rite, hazards the guess that Masonry was the rite of the Rosicrucians. She could even be right.

The earliest reference to Masonry is said to be that in a poem about the neighbourhood of Perth published in Edinburgh, in 1638:

> For what we do pressage is not in grosse,
> For we be brethren of the Rosie Crosse;
> We have the Mason word and second sight,
> Things for to come we can foretell aright . . .

The next is an entry in the diary of Elias Ashmole, under October 16, 1646, ''I was made a Free Mason at Warrington in Lancashire . . . ''

These references are, however, preceded by the lines in *Anthony and Cleopatra,* II, iii, 6–7:

> I have not kept my square, but that to come
> Shall all be done by the rule.

As these lines can only refer to the Masonic square and rule, the inference is that a Masonic lodge existed at least as early as the play was written, c.1607, that is seven years before the publication of the *Fama.* Moreover, at least some members of the expected audience must have belonged to it, as well as the poet, otherwise the allusion would have been understood by no one.

C.W. Leadbeater, in *The Hidden Life in Freemasonry* (Adyar, 1928), says of Bacon, p.15, ''In Co-Masonry we refer to him as the Head of all True Freemasons''. Supposing this should be so, what should Bacon, as we know him from the works that stand in his name, want with anything so mysterious? As Margery Purver has made plain in her excellent work, *The Royal Society, Concept and Creation* (Routledge, 1967), Bacon, though the Royal Society was founded to undertake the work he had indicated, was not himself a scientist. He never attempted, himself, to make all the detailed enquiries into the realms of astronomy, physics, chemistry, climatology and the like which he saw as needed. His business, as a philosopher, was to discern the lines along which enquiry should be made, so laying the bases on which the men with particular knowledge should work. In an age scarcely emancipated from Mediaevalism, any attempt at study along these lines was likely to be assimilated to magic and witchcraft. One has only to read Robert Greene's treatment of his namesake, Roger Bacon, *Friar Bacon and Friar Bungay,* to realise the ridicule which a pronounced undertaking to seek to learn the secrets of nature must court, not to speak of the charge of anti-Christianity.

Even Bacon, taking note that the angels of knowledge were placed lower than the angels of love, showed himself aware that scientific enquiry could lead to strange ills if not subjected to the higher law of charity. He did not wish to father wickedness. If his researchers were not to abuse the powers they might acquire, they must submit themselves to moral discipline. Here would be the utility of some kind of rite, which would take in not only the scientists but all who entered into the spirit of the great work, and give a sense of corporate identity to those living in the world without distinguishing habit, bridge any possible religious differences by uniting them in a ceremonial which avoided the familiar points of controversy, and by its poetry lift their thoughts and feelings to the highest level. Gesture and posture affect mind. This is known to yogis and eurhythmic dancers. Colour and symbol affect mind. This is known to artists. Words may divide, where division is not intended. They lend themselves to dissensions. But a beautiful rose, fresh with the dew, the sun on the golden stamens within the rosy heart, seems to say something about love and goodness, faith and forgiveness, grace in living and sweet-smelling life; and the cross something about austerity and sacrifice. The two impaled, the one upon the other, make a spiritual impact, susceptible to multi-directional interpretation, which would be only weakened by verbalisation. A man coming forward with one shoe off and one shoe on may seem eloquent of the human condition, a candle's flickering flame the neophyte's aspiration, while a blazing star above, reflected in a pool, or from a lower point in the lodge, dramatises the reflection of the divine spirit in the human being. Much ink has been expended in commentaries on the rite, but perhaps the intention was simply that it should be lived, as the musician lives the music he is playing, playing it, not analysing it. If two shake hands in a particular way, it is to experience brotherhood, and the same idea may underline the holding of the dinners which are a feature of Masonry.

If one wants a link with the operative side one might consider Bacon's friendship with Jonson. He was not a stone-mason, but, step-son of a master brick-layer, he had practised brick-laying. Both crafts use a level and plumb-rule. The idea of re-building Solomon's temple is biblical, but Bacon was also inspired by the mystery religions.

Acacia is special to Masons, and it seems not to have been understood why. After the candidate for the Master's degree has undergone his symbolic death, burial and resurrection from the tomb, he is told a story about how King Solomon's architect, Hiram Abiff, was murdered and the Masons went looking for his body. By accident, one of them found it, shallowly buried, and stuck a sprig of acacia at the head. When a Mason dies, the members of his Lodge do not attend his funeral, but sometime afterwards may visit his grave and lay on it a sprig of acacia. I have also noted that in the *Papyrus of Ani*[4] the Cat of the Sun stands, to behead the Snake of darkness, before a tree which Wallis Budge identifies as an acacia: "Behind the Cat is the famous Acacia Tree which flourished in very early times in Anu, i.e. On, or Heliopolis."[5] The allusion is apparently to the ritual slaying of the foes of Ra which took place there. The fields of Anu are those to which the souls of the blessed go after death, as those of the Greeks to Elysium, which seems to give the acacia connection with death and rebirth into these fields. As, however, Budge elsewhere translates, "I am the Cat which fought near the Persea Tree in Anu on the night when the foes of Neb-er-tcher were destroyed",[6] I thought I should check the species of the tree with both the Keeper of Egyptian antiquities at the British Museum and the Librarian of the Royal Botanic Gardens at Kew. The former T.G.H. James thought that the shape of the tree was too conventionalised to permit botanic identification. From Kew, however, Rosemary Angel wrote that the Persea or Laurel family was native to America and could not possibly have been known to the ancient Egyptians, whereas the Acacia, a member of the Pea family, grew in Egypt. The connection with the Masonic Third Degree seemed to gather strength from Ani's post-mortem salutation to Osiris, as Judge of the Dead, "Homage to Thee, O Lord of the Acacia Tree".[7]

Further, the prayer made by the deceased in respect of his corpse, "That my intestines shall not perish . . . My head shall not be separated from my neck. My tongue shall not be removed" recalls, by inversion, the penalties the Masonic candidate calls down upon his head should he break his Oath. If the origin is in ancient tradition, that could explain its grisly character.

It is not being suggested that these texts, which, though believed to have been written about B.C. 1250, were not available to scholars until the nineteenth century, could have been perused by Sir Francis Bacon; but unless these connections are coincidental and meaningless, he might have come across some true reminiscence of them in the "Egyptian", i.e. Trismegistic literature, in which he was certainly plunged.

I came back to that strange sunburst face. The sunburst with face inscribed is a Masonic symbol, known by Masons as the Sun in Splendour. Only it does not usually have a chin, a chin whose purpose is to make evident the folds of a veil.

In *The Rape of Lucrece,* one reads:

Revealing day through euery crannie spies,
And seems to point her out where she sits weeping,
To whoom she sobbing speakes, o eye of eyes,
Why pry'st though through my window? leaue thy peeping.

1086-89

There is here an obvious link with ''Reuealing day through every cranny
peeps'' (Northumberland Manuscript). Could it be possible that the
sunburst face which comes through the veil in that room is Revealing Day
peeping through the veil of clouds, the sun piercing the clouds of
ignorance?

The symbol was in use before it was carved in this room, for it appears
in the centre of the headpiece of the first editions of both *Venus and
Adonis* and *The Rape of Lucrece,* less round, and peeping over, instead of
through, a veil, but the symbolism is recognisably the same, and it is
surrounded by the same corona of what seem to be feathers arranged like
rays. It is not one of the set headpieces of Richard Field, the printer, so
may have belonged to the author. It appears on one other book, the 1612
edition of the Authorised Version of the Holy Bible. I enquired of
Lambeth Palace why this should share a headpiece with *Venus and
Adonis* and *The Rape of Lucrece,* but the answer was they did not know,
and I had the impression it had not been drawn to their attention before.
They recommended me to ask at Bible House. I did, but they did not
know there, either. It is not being suggested Bacon wrote the Bible, but
he was certainly interested in the translation, as we know from a letter he
wrote the King, and if the headpiece belonged to him he might have lent it
for what he considered a worthy purpose.

A version of the face appears also on the first edition of the *Sonnets,*
without veil, and chubbier, but with the reminiscent corona of plumes,
now recognisably those of the ostrich, suggestive of Prince of Wales
Feathers.

We have, therefore, in this veiled and feathered sunburst-face, a symbol
linking Bacon, through his tenancy of the room, with both Masonry and
Shakespeare. I take it that ''Rich'' Spencer, being a high-up Mason, had
made the room available to Bacon, upon an informal basis, so that he
might conduct the rites in it, rites in which Spencer presumably played a
part. This would explain why, after Spencer had died, Bacon found it
necessary to obtain from his daughter and her husband William, 2nd Lord
Compton, later the Earl of Northampton, a formal tenancy, so as to be
able to continue holding the Masonic meetings there where so much
loving care had been expended upon the carved symbolism.

---

1. Secretary of the Francis Bacon Society. The Tower still belongs to the Marquess of
Northampton, and is let, together with the adjoining theatre, to the Tavistock company, with a
provision one room should be made available to the Francis Bacon Society for use as its headquarters.

2. See my books *The Magical Dilemma of Victor Neuburg* (W.H. Allen, 1965), the chapter entitled 'Templars and the Tradition of Sheikh-el-Djebel', and *Shelley* (Cape, 1968), the chapter entitled 'The Assassins and the Discovery of Ariel'; also references to Rosicrucianism *passim* in both books.

3. See *Le Vieux du Montagne*, Lisle de Sales (Paris, 1799), four volumes.

4. British Museum, 10470, on public exhibition; also facsimile edition by Trustees, 1894, sheet No. 10, vignette top left.

5. *The Book of the Dead: Papyrus of Ani*, ed. Wallis Budge (Medici, 1913), I, p.264.

6. Budge, *op. cit.*, II, p.390 (from Papyrus of Nebseni, sheet 14, British Museum, 9900).

7. *Papyrus of Ani*, sheet 19, the Litany (columns headed in red), col. 5, reading from right; (translation in Budge, op, cit., II, p.492).

CHAPTER 53

The Overbury murder

WE now come to one of the strangest murder mysteries of all time. On September 15th, 1613, a young man of twenty-two, Sir Thomas Overbury, died while a prisoner in the Tower. Nobody thought anything of it, at the time; the death was certified by the doctor, de Mayerne, as consumption.

Three months later, on December 26th, 1613, there took place an expensively celebrated marriage. The bridegroom was a young Scot, born Robert Carr, the King's favourite, created by him Earl of Somerset; and the bride a young woman, born Frances Howard, who had been married to the new young Earl of Essex, son of the one who had been beheaded. She had obtained an annulment of her marriage to him on the ground that it had not been consummated, and now came to the altar with her hair down, as was done by virgins. As in Queen Elizabeth's day, the giving of presents was still an indispensible social obligation, and everybody who had any pretentions to position felt obliged to give the very utmost he could afford. Bacon, though he seems not much to have cared for Somerset, gave *The Masque of Flowers*, from Gray's Inn. Yelverton, the new Solicitor General, offered to share the cost with him but he preferred to bear the whole. Somerset had been a friend of Overbury, but it was two years before anybody connected the marriage with the murder.

How it came out is not clear. A boy named Reeve, who had been a servant to the apothecary of de Mayerne, is said to have made a death-bed confession which was reported to Winwood, Secretary of State; but it is also said that a chance remark by the Earl of Pembroke, that he would prefer not to make the acquaintance of Sir Gervase Helwys, Governor of the Tower, until the latter had been cleared of suspicion connecting him with the death of Overbury, that caused enquiry.

High names quickly becoming involved, Coke was put in charge of the investigation and made over 300 interrogations for the preparation of what he called his ''great oyer of poisoning''. Helwys said the first he had known of it was when the underkeeper, Weston, had indicated a tart brought for Overbury by the Countess of Essex, as she was then, asking if he should give it to him now. He thought the meaning was the tart was poisoned, and had it put aside; it turned black, as did other tarts sent from the Countess, which likewise he put aside. He pled not guilty, but on the scaffold confessed he had not done all he might have to prevent the murder of Sir Thomas Overbury. The Countess being affianced to the

Earl of Somerset, he had feared to offend great persons, and even the King, by obstructing them.

Weston pled guilty to having given the prisoner meats, tarts and jellies which came from the Countess, knowing them to have been poisoned; and, these working but slowly, to have administered the clyster (enema) that killed him.

Also caught in the net was Anne Turner, dressmaker to the Countess. She confessed the Countess had sent her to a magician, Simon Forman, to obtain two potions, one to avert her husband's lusts from her and the other to draw to her the love of Robert Carr, now Earl of Somerset. The potions seemed to work, for Essex did desist from pressing his conjugal rights and agreed to an annulment of the marriage, and Carr became her lover and was willing to marry her but for the opposition of his friend, Sir Thomas Overbury. Forman having died, the Countess now sent her dressmaker to one Franklin, who supplied poisons. On the scaffold, Anne Turner asked permission to say a prayer for ''that poor lady''.

Franklin, too, was executed, in November, 1615.

By this time the Somersets had been arrested. Even previous to his implication, the Earl's relations with the King had become impaired. Royal favourites are a special breed. Having risen by their charms, they tend to a vanity and arrogance that ends by destroying the royal favour that made them. The King wrote a letter to Somerset in which he accused him of trying to rule him, and not by affection but by ''awe''. He was now delighted by the young Villiers. Some writers have doubted whether James, who was a devout reader of the Bible, would have committed sexual acts forbidden in it, but the Queen, Anne, resented Somerset and complained that he and Overbury mocked her, and one has only to read the King's letters to Villiers to see they are homo-erotic. There was a violent scene between Somerset and Villiers before the King, and the King told Somerset he was still welcome to his presence but must accept the rise of Villiers. Somerset was with the King when Coke's messenger arrived with the warrant for his arrest; the King is said to have given him a parting kiss, but did nothing to save him.

The ''great oyer'' was now taken out of Coke's hands and given into those of Francis Bacon. As Coke had been very diligent, there has been some speculation as to why the case was taken away from him, but it may have been precisely because the matter was coming rather near the King that the King preferred it should be handled by Bacon, on whose judgement and discretion he had come to rely.

We now find a number of letters from Francis both to the King and to Villiers about the impending trial. Francis must have taken to the young Villiers, for whereas he had always written to the King direct, now frequently he wrote through Villiers or to both. On February 21st, 1615/6, he expressed to Villiers the wish the King might make him a

Privy Councillor, so that it might not be said he dealt in matters above his station. For the Attorney's office, he had applied to the King direct.

It was in those days usual for the Sovereign to have conference with the judges before any case involving the crown, but what strikes one, as one reads Francis' letters to the King and Villiers is that they are not discussing whether Somerset is guilty. That, they take for granted. What concerns them is how he can be induced to make a confession so that he may be pardoned. Neither does this care proceed from love of him. Francis says the slowness and coldness of the poisoning makes the crime one which repels all sympathy. The Countess will plead guilty and ask for mercy; but if the Earl persists in his present intent of pleading not guilty, there are no grounds upon which he can be given clemency, the implication being if he sees himself about to die he may, becoming "desperate",[1] speak things touching the King. That is the danger, which has to be circumvented.

It is all the odder because Francis refers to a letter brought to Somerset by one Ashton,[2] containing a phrase implying it was Somerset who had induced the death of Prince Henry, and that the murder of Prince Charles, as next in line to the throne, was intended. It now begins to look to him as though Somerset and Overbury were in the service of Spain. Somerset was in the habit of betraying all the King's letters to Overbury and they corresponded with one another in a "jargon" in which the King, the Queen and all members of the royal family were referred to by code-names, and all their doings noted.

If Somerset had really poisoned the Prince of Wales (who was rumoured earlier to have been in love with the Countess), it was a much more important matter of state than the wretched Overbury – whom Francis dismisses as a young man of little virtue and much vain glory, "naught and corrupt", that however being no matter now that he had been so foully murdered. One might have expected a search for further evidence, to support a charge of having murdered not only Overbury but the late young Prince of Wales, but that seems to be almost beside the point. The only practical point is how to manage things so that Somerset shall not become so desperate as to speak.

We are in the face of blackmail.

Francis says bluntly that he cannot present the case without making plain the responsibility of the sovereign; for the safety of a prisoner in the Tower is the responsibility of the sovereign. He is really saying the King will have to accept part of the odium, otherwise it will look too obviously as though he is being spared.

On May 24th, 1616, the Countess of Somerset, dressed in black, as a penitent, appeared briefly in court and pleaded guilty, begging pardon.

At 10.00 the next morning began the dreaded trial of Somerset. Bacon, presenting the case for the crown, said that in the beginning Somerset and

Overbury had been the greatest friends, but ''the best things are in their corruption worst, and the sweetest wine makes the sharpest vinegar; so fell it out with them, that this excess (as I may term it) of friendship ended in a mortal hatred''.

Somerset became the lover of the Countess while she was still married to the Earl of Essex, and proposed after the annulment of that marriage to marry her. This was violently opposed by Overbury, who ''was loth to have any partners in the favour of my Lord of Somerset.'' Overbury threatened that if the marriage went forward he would disclose the indiscretion of Somerset in making him privy to papers of the King.

Somerset and the Countess therefore conspired to be rid of Overbury, by murder. They decided to poison him, and in order to get him into a situation in which he would have to eat food prepared by themselves, determined on his incarceration in the Tower. To bring this about, Somerset first contrived that Overbury should be offered a post abroad in his Majesty's service and then advised Overbury, privately, against accepting it. This would technically constitute treason and render him liable to imprisonment in the Tower, but Somerset represented to him that it would be to his interest as he would very quickly get him out of it. The unsuspecting Overbury walked into the trap, not dreaming ''that death should be his bail''. Once in the Tower, he was systematically poisoned, by tarts and other sweetmeats sent as gifts. His friends were turned away, and a servant who wished to share his cell that he might tend him was told by Somerset it was needless as his release was imminent.

Somerset admitted having intrigued to get Overbury into the Tower in the manner Bacon had described, but said it had never been his intention to have him poisoned whilst there, but only to have him kept there until after his marriage, so that he should not make trouble. He had not known his wife had been sending him poisoned foods. He himself had sent tarts, but the tarts he had sent were wholesome.

He was found guilty. He began to speak but was told the time for giving evidence was over and that he might speak now only to say whether there was any reason why sentence should not be passed upon him. He then said he claimed his privilege, as a nobleman, of being beheaded. Commoners were hanged.

He and the Countess were conveyed back to the Tower. Time passed and neither was executed. After some years, both were released and allowed to live obscurely.

In a book, *The Great Oyer of Poisoning,* published in 1846, Andrew Amos expressed the view that Overbury, Somerset and the King were all homosexuals, which was what Overbury threatened to disclose, to prevent the wedding, and which it was feared Somerset would disclose, at his trial. This may very well be true. However, Amos goes on to impugn the evidence on which Somerset was convicted and to assert the real murderer was the King, who, wishing to be rid of not only Overbury but also Somerset, had his physician, de Mayerne, who was also physician to the Tower, administer the fatal clyster, and then had Somerset framed for it.

This seems far-fetched. It is true that Franklin, though he knew Weston, said "The man was not known that gave him the clyster, and that it was that did the deed." But Weston admitted giving it. It is true de Mayerne was not called to give evidence, which seems to Amos suspicious, yet there could be a more innocent reason for it. Though James had confidence in him it has been suggested he was not a very good doctor, and if it was brought out that he could not tell the difference between a death from consumption and one really occasioned by prolonged intake of white arsenic, roseaker and mercury sublimate, he might lose much of his fashionable practice. Yet it is improbable any physician of the period could have distinguished.[3]

1. British Museum, Additional MSS. f.82.
2. *Loc.cit.*
3. On this point I consulted Dr. Margaret Little, who sent me a photocopy of *A Mechanical Account of Poisons,* by Richard Mead, M.D. (1702), a classic work but exhibiting knowledge inadequate to make diagnosis in such a case.

CHAPTER 54

Bacon to Villiers

FIVE days after the trial, on May 30th, 1616, Bacon wrote to Villiers,[1] asking him to remind the King some further advancement was due. "If you would put your strength to this business, I know that it is done". Villiers must have replied saying the King offered him the choice of becoming either a Privy Councillor or Lord Chancellor. Both were offices in which Francis had earlier expressed interest; but it was at a time when the present Lord Chancellor, Egerton, later Lord Ellesmere, had been so ill it seemed likely he would retire, that Francis had written to the King saying he would like to take over in that eventuality. Now, Egerton had recovered. Francis had at once rejoiced in the recovery of a good man and told Villiers he would like to be made a Privy Councillor. He may, therefore, have been surprised now to hear he could have either post, with a little delay in the case of the Chancellorship, but he did not wish Egerton to feel he was being hurried out, as he might if a successor were appointed. Francis therefore replied to Villiers[2] saying the King had given him a noble choice, but that as he hoped the Lord Chancellor would live long, and expected to do the same himself, he would prefer for the present to be made a Privy Councillor, and to let the Chancellorship wait upon "the accident of time". He owed Egerton more than anybody "after the King and yourself", and would not like him burdened by the appointment, while he was still in office, of a successor.

One may think it shows sensitivity and delicacy on Francis' part to forego the making certain of his eventual appointment, so that an elderly man should not feel they were waiting for him to go.

The temptation must have been enormous, because the office was worth a great deal in fees, unofficial fees or gifts.

The King must have asked Bacon to prepare the patent for the creation of Sir George Villiers, for in a letter to the King of July 28th, 1616, Francis says that he encloses this,[3] and a day or two later he wrote to Villiers saying he was sending his bill for Viscount. He said the King had wished him to keep his proper name, "Therefore I have made it Viscount Villiers."[4]

A week later, on August 12th, he sent him the patent, and with it advice to think goodness better than greatness and to be careful the men he advanced were good ones. "For in the time of the Cecils, the father and the son, able men were by design, and of purpose suppressed . . . rather make able and honest men yours, than advance those that are otherwise because they are yours . . . ' " ⁵

The creation was at Woodstock, Oxfordshire, on August 27th, 1616.
Apparently the newly created nobleman had taken Francis' stern little
morality in good part and even asked his counsel, for Francis, emboldened
to oblige, now sent him a letter remarkable for the frankness with which it
treats the position of royal favourite:[6]

> You are now the King's favourite . . . then give me leave to tell you . . . the
> duty that lies upon you towards the King . . . If the King hath made choice of you
> out of his affection, or out of his opinion of your worth, to communicate his
> bosom thoughts with you . . . you are bound in gratitude to return so much as
> possibly you can to advance your Master's service and honour. But were it . . . to
> interpose you between himself and the envy of his people . . . then you are bound
> for your own sake to watch over your actions.
>
> Remember then what your true condition is. The King himself is above the
> reach of his people but cannot be above their censure; and you are his shadow, if
> either he commit an error and is loath to avow it, but excuses it upon his
> Ministers, of which you are the first in the eye; or you commit the fault, or have
> willingly permitted it, and must suffer for it, so perhaps you may be offered as a
> sacrifice to appease the multitude.

One sees how far this is from a conventional letter of congratulation.
He even warns the young man to be on his guard against finding himself
the King's scapegoat, should one be needed.

1. Lambeth, Gibson Papers, Vol. viii, f.33.
2. Lambeth, Gibson Papers, Vol. viii, f.34.
3. Lambeth Fortesque papers.
4. Lambeth MSS, Gibson Papers, Vol. viii, f.40, copy by Meautys.
5. Lambeth, Gibson Papers, Vol. viii, f.41, copy by Meautys.
6. Lansdowne MSS.

CHAPTER 55

The suspension of Coke

DURING this while, tension between the King and Coke had been mounting. Though hardly by temperament democratic, Coke had since he had been moved to the Common Pleas identified with Common causes. Between the Common Law Courts, that is the King's Bench and Common Pleas, and the Courts thought of as being on the King's side, particularly the Chancery, there existed an opposition of character analogous to that between the House of Commons and House of Lords. It needs to be understood that during the whole of the reign of James, the Commons were working up to that trial of strength with the King which in the succeeding reign, of Charles I, became the Civil War. Already they were tough and aggressive in a way that would have been inconceivable in the time of Elizabeth, so that Coke was riding on a rising tide. Coke was making sallies at the King's prerogative, and was using an instrument known as the Praemunire to prevent persons discontent with the judgements they had received at the King's Bench or Common Pleas from appealing to the Chancery. The King, reacting, went to the Star Chamber and read out a declaration that just as there was the King's Bench for criminal causes, so there was the Chancery, ''the disposer of the King's conscience . . . mixing justice with mercy.''[1]

Bacon, as Attorney-General, was by function defender of the King, and looked up precedents for him; he found that from the time of Henry VII judgements at the King's Bench and Common Pleas had been subject to appeals to the Chancery. This was set out in a decree by the King on July 18th, 1616,[2] and must have relieved the Lord Chancellor. It was a defeat for Coke.

It should be noticed that despite the personal rivalry between Coke and Bacon which parallelled the rivalry between the kinds of courts they represented, Bacon had never acted against Coke save as his office compelled. He had taken occasion to pay tribute to Coke's handling of the earlier stages of the enquiry into Overbury's murder. But the question now was what was going to be done about Coke. The King wanted to be rid of him; but Bacon joined with the Lord Chancellor in sending the King a letter over both their signatures saying a man of Coke's eminence could not be dismissed without being given public opportunity to defend himself.[3] Villiers replied on the King's behalf, to Bacon only; dressed in polite language, his letter meant the King would prefer to be rid of Coke without granting him a hearing.[4] Faced with this, the Lord Chancellor

(Egerton) and Bacon were courageous enough to send a second joint letter to the King, submitting that if Coke was to be charged he must, in justice, be heard.[5] The King's reaction to this was, on November 10th, simply to inform his Privy Council that Coke was to be removed from office.

Then things took a very surprising turn. Coke, who had an unmarried daughter, Frances, heir through her mother to Hatton House, Corfe Castle and a vast fortune suggested to Villiers the advantage of an alliance. For Villiers had an unmarried brother.

1. Lambeth MSS, 174, f.119.
2. Lambeth, Gibson Papers, vol. viii, f.51.
3. Lambeth, Gibson Papers, vol. viii, f.50.
4. Lambeth, Gibson Papers, vol. viii, f.51.
5. Lambeth, Gibson Papers, vol. viii, f.52.

CHAPTER 56

Lord Chancellor

LORD Ellesmere's last years as Lord Chancellor had been discomforted by aspirants to his office. Where Bacon had declined to be nominated to the succession while Ellesmere lived, Sir John Bennett had offered the young Villiers, now Earl of Buckingham, £30,000 (that is £15,000,000 in today's money) to recommend him to the King for it.[1] Buckingham was in many ways so corrupt, it should be remembered to his credit that in this at least he appears to have dealt straightly, refusing this, and similar inducements from others, to recommend to an office already promised by the King to Bacon, free.

Ellesmere reckoned his office as worth between £10,000 and £15,000 a year;[2] (in today's values, between £5,000,000 and £7,500,000 a year). That means, in fees and perquisites. Every law-suit began with the issue of a writ, which had to be stamped by the Great Seal, and every imposition would command the payment of a fee. Then, after the conclusion of a case heard before him, the winning party would probably present a gift bearing some relation to the extent by which he had benefited from the judgement.

Bacon gave £8,000[3] (£40,000,000), not to Buckingham but to Lord Ellesmere, for his retirement. There was no automatic entitlement to a pension, so it was really for the successor to help make a retirement possible. Lord Ellesmere resigned the Great Seal on March 6th, 1616. (Later, the King sent him word by Bacon, that he intended conferring on him a pension of £3,000 (£1,500,000) a year for life, but he was on his death-bed and only survived the news half an hour.)

On March 7th, 1616 the King conferred on Sir Francis Bacon the title of Lord Keeper of the Great Seal of England. He now stood where his father, or putative father, had stood, and York House, where he had "first breathed" was after brief formalities leased to him by the Archbishop. Francis Bacon now held the highest secular office in the land. In stately procession he would walk directly after the Archbishop of Canterbury, the Great Seal carried before him. It would also be carried before him whenever he entered or left court. He was known as Lord Bacon. This was not, as people today sometimes imagine, an ignorant usage. It was correct according to the courteous usage of the time. From the moment Coke became Lord Chief Justice, Bacon never failed to address or refer to him as "My Lord Coke". For the higher office, Lord Bacon was the accepted style.

Bacon's procession to Westminster Hall on May 7th was splendid. He was dressed in purple satin, as on his wedding day, and as he rode along the Fleet Conduit and Strand, he was escorted by the nobility and other gallants to the number of 200 horse, besides the Judges and the Fellows of the Inns of Court.[4] The King was in Scotland, but the Queen and Prince of Wales sent all their followers to swell the train, and the ordinary citizens of London tacked on to the procession massively.

From the marble chair within the Hall, his speech, however, was workmanlike. There was to be a speeding up of legal procedures; he told the assembly, because of the arrears, the afternoons would be worked as well as the mornings and two weeks taken from the vacation and added to the term.[5]

An odd memorandum in his hand says,[6] "Yesterday, which was my weary day, I bid all the Judges to dinner (which was not used to be)."

On the day following his installation, Francis wrote to Buckingham, now in Scotland with the King,[6] "Yesterday I took my place in Chancery . . . There was much ado, and a great deal of world. But this matter of pomp, which is heaven to some men, is hell to me . . . "

In the middle of July, Tobie Matthew returned to England, and stayed with Francis at Gorhambury. There was speculation that, since his conversion to Catholicism, he had been allowed to return to England only on condition the Lord Chancellor assumed responsibility for his good behaviour.

The sky was blue. A thunderstorm broke without warning.

Coke, when last we heard of him, had been dismissed from office but, nothing abashed, had offered his daughter in marriage to Buckingham's brother. Coke's own marriage had proved unhappy in the extreme. Lady Hatton – she was not unique amongst noble women in retaining her title after remarriage – made an immediate objection, declaring their daughter was affianced already. During the summer, Coke and Lady Hatton were having "great wars at the Council table" over money and property. Now, while Coke sent the Secretary of State to Scotland to talk with Buckingham about the match, the mother removed and hid the girl. Lady Compton, Buckingham's mother,[7] came to York House to ask the Lord Keeper for a warrant empowering Coke to regain possession of his daughter. Bacon refused the warrant.

However, he wrote to Buckingham, advising him against the marriage of his brother to Coke's daughter. "The mother's consent is not had, nor the young gentlewoman's."[8] Though Lady Hatton had a great fortune, if the daughter were married without her consent, it was doubtful whether anything was to be expected from her. For Buckingham's brother to marry Coke's daughter would be to marry into a house disgraced by the King; it would be to marry into a house troubled by the quarrels of man and wife, and it would cause Buckingham the loss of all such of his friends as were adverse to Coke (himself excluded)...

On the afternoon of the same day that he sent this letter, Lady Hatton, accompanied by Lord Hallam, came to York House and asked to see the Lord Chancellor. They were told he was unwell, and lying down. Indeed, Francis had not been well. Lady Hatton asked to be allowed to sit in the room next to his so as to be the first to speak with him when he stirred forth. A chair was brought for her, but she presently rose from it and knocked on Bacon's door. Francis, startled by the knocking, called out to his serving-man, and as they opened the door to attend him she went in with them, to tell him, where he lay, that her husband had stolen her daughter away from her. Apologising for her boldness in intruding, she said she was ''like a cow that had lost her calf''. Coke, she said, had obtained a warrant from Winwood, Secretary of State, empowering him to take their daughter into his own custody; she wanted a counter-warrant, to regain her. Francis must have asked her to make her application through the official channels, for on the following day, July 13th, 1617, it was received at the Council table. Her husband had, she said, come with ten or more men, and using a piece of timber smashed down the door of the house in which she was keeping their daughter and dragged her to his coach. She petitioned for immediate recovery of her daughter so that she might receive medical treatment for the shock caused by her abduction. A letter was sent by the Board to Coke requiring him to deliver his daughter to the Clerk of the Council, to be kept at the latter's house until the hearing of the case.

Coke delivered up his daughter to the Clerk of the Council, but on the following day appeared before it to charge his wife with having intended to take her to France in order to break off the match he intended. He was asked for proof of his wife's intention of taking the girl to France, and failing to produce it, was told he would have to face a charge in respect of the damage he had done to the house of Sir Edward Withipol, from which he had taken her. Husband and wife were asked to agree upon a neutral person in whose house their daughter could reside, and both were enjoined to forbear violence touching her.

Though these measures were enacted by the Council as a body, it is to be presumed they represented Francis' judgement, and he must have been considerably startled when, a couple of days later Coke was able to appear before the Council again, showing a letter from the King approving all that he had done with regard to his daughter, and by implication disapproving the warrant by which he had been compelled to surrender her. It could not be the business of His Majesty's Privy Council to act contrary to the King's wishes, and the Council was made to look foolish, as not in fact privy to the royal purposes. It was unmannerly in the King not to have sent his communication to the Council but to Coke, one of the interested parties, finding in his favour without the aid of the Council judging the matter. In the circumstances, the Council, nonplussed, directed that the daughter should live at Hatton House, with both her parents together, and left the issue of the matter "wholly to his Majesty's pleasure" when he should return from Scotland.

Bacon wrote to the King saying his great obligations made it suiting he should be "freer than other men in giving your Majesty faithful counsel . . . " He would therefore speak "in plainness". The Justices of the peace were on the whole more obsequious and all mutinous spirits disposed "to draw in their horns" since the King's action in dismissing Coke; if he were now to be restored, by an alliance with Buckingham's family, this pacification would be lost. His Majesty would never be able to go to Parliament with the Council united, if again "that man come in". Nevertheless, if it was the King's will this match should go on, he wished his Majesty would give him his commands, so that he might conform himself thereto and speak with the mother, for though he did not promise to be able to change women's minds, "I can prevail more with the mother than any other man". If the command came from his Majesty he must obey it; nevertheless, if only the Earl of Buckingham addressed him he would go against him, and that for his own sake, as what he had a mind to was not in his interest. "I would rather go against his mind than against his good."[9]

On the same day, July 25, 1617, he wrote to Buckingham, saying he had received no reply to his earlier letter concerning his brother's marriage. "As I then showed my dislike of the matter, so the carriage of it here in the manner I dislike as much."[10]

In retrospect, the two letters written this day, to the King and to Buckingham, can be seen as Bacon's greatest mistake. For worldly tactics, he had indeed been too plain.

Four days later, having still heard nothing from Buckingham, he wrote to him again, not mentioning controversial matters but simply hoping the country air did his health good and that when he returned to England he might have greater leisure for correspondence. He ended, "God bless and prosper you". The shock must have been great when he received a little note in the most coldly formal terms, saying, "In this business of my brother's that you overtrouble yourself with, I understand from London by some of my friends that you have carried yourself with much scorn and neglect towards myself and friends . . . "[11]

What had happened? In the past the younger man had accepted advice, but it looks as though he had been carried away by the idea of alliance with Coke's money.

The King must have written in similar vein, for we have Francis' reply.[12] thanking him for his letter though it distressed him more than anything in his life. He confessed his attitude to Buckingham was "a little parent-like" and said he did not doubt his discretion, though he feared "the height of his fortune might make him too secure''. He would now do what he could to forward the match.

To Buckingham he wrote, revealingly, ''I did ever fear that this alliance would go near to loose me your Lordship that I hold so dear.'' He had heard Buckingham's mother and brother had spoken of him with bitterness, but would try to bear it. Yet he hoped Buckingham did not wish him ''vassal to their passions, especially so long as they are governed by Sir Edward Coke and Secretary Winwood; the latter of which I take to be the worst . . . ''[13]

From Buckingham he had a chilling, one-sentence reply, from the King a very long fulmination concerning ''the theftous stealing away of the daughter from her own father''.[14] The King had taken in ill part Bacon's remarks about Buckingham. ''You say that you were afraid that the height of his fortune might make him too secure. Now we know not how to interpret this in plain English otherwise than that the height of his fortune might make him misknow himself . . . '', in other words that it might make him conceited. He taxed Bacon with fault in refusing Buckingham's mother the warrant for Coke, and his reported ''slight carriage to Buckingham's mother . . . '' So, Lady Compton had complained she had been slightingly received when at York House. In truth, Bacon had probably felt it was none of her business to come about a warrant enabling a man to whom she was in no way related to deprive his wife of their daughter. His sympathies had certainly been with Lady Hatton.

Yelverton, Solicitor General, now wrote to Bacon warning him of what he doubtless guessed, that Coke was using every means in his power to ''have at'' him, and that by ''the weightiest instrument, the Earl of Buckingham, who as I see sets him as close to him as his shirt, the Earl speaking in Sir Edward's phrase and as it were menacing in his spirit . . . '' Buckingham was speaking ill of Bacon in every way. Yelverton warned Francis that ''it is common in every man's mouth . . . your greatness shall be abated''.[15]

Bacon must have felt he had risen to the highest office only to lose real power; which lay only in Buckingham, as the King's favourite.

However, soon after the return of the King and his retinue, he had to see Buckingham about a small practical matter, and at once relations were considerably restored, as appears from a letter Buckingham wrote him afterwards. He says that, seeing him again, he no longer feels the unkindness he had conceived towards him while away, but sparks of old affection. The King had been saying he would put some mark of public disgrace on him, but he had dissuaded him from this. Despite a postscript asking him to keep this letter to himself, and hinting at something sinister that was going on behind the scenes, Bacon's relief must have been enormous.

Seven days later Coke's daughter was married to Buckingham's brother; Coke was received back on the Privy Council and tried to have his wife charged before the Star Council with having abducted their daughter. It now appeared that she could not be compelled to settle her fortune on the reluctant bride, and that all the coveted wealth was vested in her so that apart from the £30,000 (£15,000,000) Coke had already paid down as her dowry there was nothing. Buckingham and the King were therefore disappointed, and the girl, doubtless because she had hated the forced marriage, eloped with somebody else.

If Bacon felt like saying "I told you so," he had to keep it to himself. On January 7th, 1617/8, Buckingham refused to be made an Admiral, giving as his very good reason that he knew nothing about naval matters, and was therefore made a Marquis. At a dinner the following Sunday to celebrate his Marquisate, Francis Bacon was made Lord Chancellor.

1. *Personal History of Lord Bacon,* William Hepworth Dixon (John Murray, 1861), p.233.
2. *The Story of Lord Bacon's Life,* William Hepworth Dixon (John Murray, 1862), p.367.
3. *Personal History of Lord Bacon,* William Hepworth Dixon (John Murray, 1861), p.236.
4. Chamberlain; State Papers Domestic, James I, Vol. xcii, No. 18.
5. State Papers Domestic, James I, Vol. xcii, No. 13.
6. Lambeth, Gibson Papers, Vol. viii, f.63.
7. Not to be confused with her sister-in-law, from whom Bacon rented Canonbury Tower.
8. Stephens First Collection, p.207.
9. Lambeth, Gibson Papers, vol. viii, f.71.
10. Stephens' first collection, p.213.
11. British Museum, Birch MSS. f.4260.
12. Lambeth, Gibson Papers, vol. viii, f.69(a).
13. Lambeth, Gibson Papers, vol. viii, f.70.
14. Lambeth, Gibson Papers, vol. viii, f.69(b).
15. Lambeth, Gibson Papers, vol. viii, f.74.

CHAPTER 57

Baron Verulam

ON May 12th, 1618, Francis was created Baron Verulam of Verulam. He signed his letters now Fr. Verulam, Canc. Rising in state, he improved his dwellings. At Gorhambury he added a portico and a gallery over it, with windows on which were painted birds, animals and plants. In the grounds, he set tulips and paeonies beneath the trees, amidst wild flowers. Like the French impressionist painter, Monet, three hundred years later, he made no flower-beds, but stowed his cultivated flowers cunningly, as peeping from under a stone, to give the illusion of their having been sewn by nature's hand. *Ars est celare artem.*

At York House he had an aviary built, and pipes laid to the Thames to bring water within-doors. This must have meant installing a pump to raise the level of the water, probably worked by a waterwheel, based on the tides, such as was in use at London Bridge. We do not hear much of the march of the water-closet across England, yet since it had been invented by Sir John Harrington and Queen Elizabeth had had the first installed in her Palace at Richmond, to possess one must have been the ambition of all who could rise to the expense. Also, Bacon certainly bathed; for he writes of the virtue of red rose petals thrown in the bathwater.

Sir Nicholas Bacon had had water inducted through Gorhambury Manor, but one year the level in the reservoir at Gorhambury sank, and this gave Francis the impetus to have a second house built, within the grounds, nearer the ponds: Verulam House. It cost him £9,000 (£4,500,000 in today's money) to have built, to his own design, the chimneys gathered together in the middle and seats ringed round them, with a carved wooden staircase and the doors painted with classical figures. His servants wore livery with his crest, a boar, and all wore boots in Spanish leather, for he disliked the smell of calf.

The ponds he had lined with pitch and set with coloured pebbles to make designs that could be seen through the clear water; and on the island in the middle of one he built a banqueting house, floored with black and white marble. Aubrey writes, that when His Lordship was at Gorhambury, "St. Albans seemed as though the Court were there, so nobly did he live."

Captain John Smith of Virginia now wrote to Bacon to ask for backing for an attempt to found a colony in New England. "With a stock of 500£ [£2,500,000] I durst venture to effect it, though more than

100000 [£50,000,000] hath been spent in Virginia and the Barmudas to small purpose''.[1] Bacon's reply seems not to have been preserved.

In central Europe there were developments of the utmost consequence. Earlier in the year (March 10th, 1618/9), the Holy Roman Emperor had died. One should understand Europe was divided into two camps. One was formed by the alliance between the two Hapsburg houses, of Spain and the Holy Roman (ie German) Empire and the Papacy. In the Protestant world, this was regarded with odium, as representing the ultimate in reactionary tyranny, the Inquisition. In the Protestant camp were Calvinists, Lutherans, all free churches, mystics, hermeticists, Rosicrucians and scientists; all, in short, who wanted freedom to think in their own way. The Imperial crown was supposed to be elective, as were those of Holy Roman member states such as Bohemia and the Palatinate, but had tended to descend through the Hapsburg family as though it went by the blood. The passing of the Emperor Matthias gave the Protestants a great hope they could get the Hapsburg dynasty out. The architect of the rebellion, Christian of Anhalt, was a friend of Count Rožmberk, of Bohemia, patron of esoteric studies. Bohemia had for a long time been a centre of such. John Dee had visited it, to try to interest the Emperor Rudolph II; and it is curious that Rudolph, although a Hapsburg, had been so drawn to the occult that he moved the Imperial capital from Vienna to Prague; and it was because this city had enjoyed his protection that when he was succeeded by his brother, Matthias, the Protestants in it felt the reaction badly. Prague yearned towards Heidelberg, as a Rosicrucian centre, protected by the Elector Palatine. The latter now sent a messenger with a letter to Bacon, which has been lost, but apparently suggested his uncle, the Duc de Bouillon, leader of the French Protestants, might be made Emperor, and we have Bacon's reply, in French assuring him he would do his best in the advice he gave the King. However, the Catholic states were sufficient to secure the election of Ferdinand, the cousin of Matthias, who had been imposed by the latter on the Czechs as King of Bohemia. Within two days of the election of Ferdinand as Emperor, the Czechs deposed him as King of Bohemia. That was on August 16th, 1619. They then offered the Crown of Bohemia to Frederick V, the Elector Palatine.

Should be accept it? Much was at stake, for the Elector Palatine and the King of Bohemia had one vote each in the election of the Emperor, and if Frederick had both, the Protestants had the necessary majority to get the Hapsburgs out of central Europe. It may even have been the idea of Christian of Anhalt that Frederick, though still only twenty-three, might one day become not merely King of Bohemia but (combining the titles, like the lately deposed Ferdinand II) Emperor as well. The death of Prince Henry had left him the white hope of the Protestants.

Elizabeth wrote immediately to the Duke of Buckingham, asking him to ask her father's advice whether her husband should accept the Bohemian Crown and whether he would help them. It shows how remote was James that even his daughter should have had to write to him not direct but through this favourite. The Baron of Drona would furnish him with all particulars. A postscript adds:[2]

I am entreated by the Prince of Anhalt, for fear he should be censured in counseling the Prince to the wars, to entreat you not to believe of him anything hardy, but to be assured he will counsel nothing but what shall be for the Prince's good.

We know (from a letter of Buckingham) that Bacon went to Windsor to confer with the King about what had happened, but not what was said. His links were entirely with Elizabeth and Frederick, and he probably regarded this invitation as a great opportunity. From the Hague, Sir Dudley Carleton wrote to Naunton, "if the Bohemians be oppressed, the consequences of their loss will fall upon their neighbours, whose defence is like to coat as much in blood with much less fruit than this acquisition". This was probably Bacon's view, too.

King James summoned the Council, but only to acquaint it with his own determination:[3]

. . . he would not engage himself unto the quarrel afore he were satisfied of the justice of the States of Bohemia's proceeding in the renouncing of Ferdinand, whom they had formerly chosen for their King. Besides that he said the business did not require such a haste of his resolution . . . Upon which speech of his Majesty's all the Board remained mute, there being but very few among them that had other affections than to favour the lively embracing of the cause . . .

In Heidelberg, Frederick's mother, daughter of William the Silent, pleaded with him not to accept, as it would be too dangerous. Elizabeth is said to have favoured acceptance. Nevertheless, it was without hearing from Bacon, Frederick wrote that he would accept the Crown. It was a letter from the Archbishop of Canterbury which, in after years, Elizabeth was to show, as the instrument which had affected them to make their fatal decision.

They set out from Heidelberg on October 7th, taking with them their small son, Elizabeth's pet monkey and much of their library. Giving audience to deputations on the way, they crossed the border on the 23rd. As they neared Prague, about 400 peasants approached in procession, armed with scythes, hatchets and other implements, which they clashed together to make a welcoming noise, and so escorted them to the Hradčany, neither of them knowing a word of Czech. Elizabeth wrote the next day to inform Buckingham. Frederick was crowned in St. Vitus Cathedral on November 4th, and Elizabeth three days later.

In England, Londoners who had lit bonfires and were ringing joy-bells were ordered to desist. King James, in a panic, had written to the King of

Spain to ask his opinion whether his son-in-law's acceptance of the
Bohemian Crown was legal, knowing that as the Spanish royal family
were not Spaniards but Hapsburgs the answer would be negative. In
Prague innocents produced an emblematic picture of Frederick and
Elizabeth in their coronation robes, with orb and sceptre, the name of God
in Hebrew letters above their heads (proclaiming the design Rosicrucian)
and four lions supporting them, the Palatine lion, the double-tailed lion of
Bohemia, the British lion, with sword in paw and the Netherlands lion,
and one of the verses beneath assuring that their new Queen's father
would not desert them. In England, James was, in Dr. Yates' words,
"disowning all responsibility for his son-in-law's Bohemian enterprise to
every court in Europe",[4] or as C.V. Wedgwood puts it, "denying to
every court in Europe that he had countenanced or even known of the
project."[5]

We have no comment from Bacon, probably because his views were
opposite to the King's; he could hardly say his Majesty's attitude was
deplorable, neither would he be its mouthpiece. But the Earl of Pembroke,
freer because merely a peer, showed, in a letter to Frederick's
representative, that he was really ashamed of his King's behaviour, for
which he virtually apologised.

In Bohemia, Frederick and Elizabeth received assurance of support
from Bethlem Gabor, Prince of Transylvania, King of Hungary.

But the forces of Ferdinand II were massing.

There was another ill matter. Sir Walter Raleigh had been in the Tower
since his supposed complicity in a plot to put Lady Arabella Stuart on the
throne instead of James. Prince Henry had said of this long confinement
that only his father would keep such a fine bird in a cage. Raleigh had at
last thought to propose that if liberated he could lead an expedition to a
gold mine, near the Orinoco River. James, his finances in a bad way, put
him in charge of shipping. The Spanish Ambassador expressed anxiety
lest Spanish towns be attacked. Raleigh found no gold and a Spanish town
was attacked by his son. On his return, the Spanish Ambassador
demanded his execution. It was at this point Bacon was called in. He set
up a commission consisting of himself and five others, one of whom was
Coke. Their finding, sent to the King over the signatures of Bacon and
Coke, was that as Raleigh had been legally dead since sentenced to death
so many years ago, the case could not be tried in a court of law, since a
court of law could not try a dead man. While there was nothing legally to
prevent his execution upon the old judgement, they did not advise it.
They advised he should be given a hearing in York House, to which the
public should be admitted.

James preferred the cowardly advice of Buckingham, to have him
executed without hearing, secretly. At the scaffold, all hearts were with
him.

The King's finances grew worse. Francis sent him a detailed statement of his accounts, "like a perspective glass, to draw your estate nearer to your view". (Galileo's telescope, invented nine years earlier, must already have become a household word.)

There is a letter from Bacon to Buckingham,[6] dated December 12th, 1619, saying he has been going into the proposition made to him by the King with regard to the grant of a monopoly patent for Inns and Hostelries to Sir Giles Mompesson. The proposition was that Mompesson should receive a fifth, and the King and Buckingham the rest. Bacon was never keen on monopoly patents, which he regarded as "the canker of trading", but found that Queen Mary had granted one such. "The King's estate, if I should die and it were opened, would be found on my heart as Queen Mary said of Calais."[7]

1. Public Record Office (Kew), CO 1/1, f.42.
2. Bodleian, Tanner MSS, 74.209.
3. British Museum, Additional MSS, 4176, f.262.
4. *The Rosicrucian Enlightenment*, Frances Yates (Routledge, 1972), p.21.
5. *The Thirty Years' War*, A.C.V. Wedgewood, p.108.
6. Lambeth, Gibson Papers, vol. viii, f.119.
7. Bodleian, Tanner MSS, f.67.

CHAPTER 58

The *Novum Organum*

THE *Novum Organum*, described by Bacon as "a new logic, teaching to invent and judge by deduction", may be considered as the cornerstone of modern scientific method. In order to appreciate it, one should first realise how abysmal was the state of knowledge of the time, and how inhibiting the ways of thought. It was supposed that man had progressively degenerated from a golden age in which there was more profound knowledge. Therefore, learning took the form of trying better to understand what the ancients had really said, in the hope to recover some part of their wisdom. The Aristotelian logic was an excellent tool for testing the validity of a chain of reasoning, but could not lead to the discovery of new information, the scholiasts of the Middle Ages and early Renaissance spun theories out of theories, never making contact with reality, and the laboratories of the alchemists were given over to the pursuit of a trivial and venal purpose.

Bacon's revolutionary enterprise was to postulate that we could enquire into nature for ourselves.

Near the beginning he lists four Idols, by which he means types of false notion which obstruct clarity of thought. Idols of the Tribe are those which suppose the common sense of the community necessarily to correspond to what is absolutely true, for it may but reflect the false perceptions of individuals. Idols of the Cave are similar, but relate to the individual, who has a "cave or den of his own", within which he hatches out ideas, often from reading books, not realising the extent to which they are coloured by a particular predisposition. Idols of the Market Place are those that arise from "the ill and unfit choice of words" in the everyday associations and discourse of men. "For men believe that their reason governs words; but it is also true that words react on the understanding."[1] We have, therefore, to be sure that one word means one thing, both to speaker and hearer, or confusion follows.

Lastly, there are Idols which have immigrated into men's minds from the various dogmas of philosophies, and also from wrong laws of demonstration. These I call Idols of the Theatre; because in my judgement all the received systems are but so many stage-plays, representing worlds of their own creation after an unreal and scenic fashion.[2]

He observes that:[3]

The sciences which we possess come for the most part from the Greeks . . . Now the wisdom of the Greeks was professorial and much given to disputation; a kind of wisdom most adverse to the inquisition of truth . . . Nor should we omit that judgement, or rather divination, which was given concerning the Greeks by the Aegyptian priest that they were always boys, without antiquity of knowledge or knowledge of antiquity.

It is useless merely to read up what others have said, and then to try to form an opinion on that. What is needed is fresh observation of the universe.[4]

Those who have handled sciences have been either men of experiment or men of dogmas. The men of experiment are like the ant; they only collect and use: the reasoners resemble spiders, who make cobwebs out of their own substance. But the bee takes a middle course; it gathers its material from the flowers of the garden and of the field, but transforms and digests it by a power of its own.

What is needed is the ''firmness of mind and purpose resolutely to ''sweep away all theories and common notions, and to apply the understanding thus made fair and even, to a fresh examination of particulars''; then:[5]

not to extract works from works or experiments from experiments (as an empiric) but from works and experiments to extract causes and axioms.

He goes on:[6]

It may be thought also a strange and a harsh thing that we should at once and with one blow set aside all sciences and all authors; and that too without calling in any of the ancients to our aid and support, but relying on our own strength. . . . But for my part, relying on the evidence and truth of things, I reject all forms of fiction and imposture; nor do I think that it matters any more to the business in hand, whether the discoveries that shall now be made were long ago known to the ancients, and have their settings and their risings according to the vicissitude of things and course of ages, than it matters to mankind whether the new world be that island of Atlantis, with which the ancients were acquainted, or now discovered for the first time.

A new philosopher, J. Krishnamurti, has said that the difficult thing is to ask the right question; when the right question is asked, the answer comes. The alchemists, when they enquired of themselves how to turn base metals into gold were asking a poor question, which if answered would merely enrich themselves, or debase the currency, whilst the end, taken in isolation, would hardly add to our understanding. Francis, asking, here in the *Novum Organum,* what is the nature of heat, and how is it that friction or the movement of one thing against another causes it, and what is the nature of light? is laying the foundations of physics. A single passage shows both how deficient was the knowledge of his time and how far forward he is reaching through it. He observes that most things that give out light give heat as well, for instance the sun, or flame; but yet the moon gives out light but not heat; and so do fish-scales at night, and glow-worms, by which one cannot warm oneself. (He does not know that the moon's light is merely reflected and the fish-scales and glow-worm's tails phosphorescent.) Some believe the sun and flame are different in nature, but he believes they are the same; for butterflies stupid from cold, if brought indoors and set near a fire, will revive in the grateful warmth as if in the sun (it must have been his custom to take pity on them). Suddenly, he is light-years ahead:[7]

Even in sight, whereof the action is most rapid, it appears that there are required certain moments of time for its accomplishment; as is shown by those things which by reason of the velocity of their motion cannot be seen – as when a ball is discharged from a musket. For the ball flies past in less time than the image conveyed to the sight requires to produce an impression.

This fact, with others like it, has at times suggested to me a strange doubt; viz. whether the face of a clear and starlight sky be seen at the instant at which it really exists, and not a little later . . .

Does one experience a *frisson?* We know now that we are seeing the stars not as they are but as they were, millions upon millions of years ago. His analogy with the musket-ball may be a little faulty, since there, it is the mechanism of the eye which fails to perceive its passage; small matter when, with this question, he is at the beginning of modern stellar astronomy, as, with the question about the generation of heat from the passage of one thing against another, he is at the beginning of thermodynamics.

Coming to biology, he has some nice touches, as:[8]

. . . the root of the nerves and faculties in animals is the head, while the seminal parts are the lowest – the extremities of the legs and arms not reckoned. In a plant on the other hand, the root (which answers to the head) is regularly placed in the lowest part, and the seeds in the highest.

There is something for the Rosicrucian type of mind here; for in esoteric teaching the capacity of a creature to stand upright and to raise its head, so that it obviously dominates and governs what is beneath, is an index of its place in the scale of evolution.

Of the germination of seeds:[9]

. . . we must . . . observe (as we may easily do, by taking out day after day the seeds that have lain in the ground two days, three days, four days and so on, and carefully examining them) how and when the seed begins to puff and swell, and to be as it were filled with spirit; secondly how it begins to burst the skin and put forth fibres, at the same time raising itself slightly upwards, unless the ground be very stiff . . . In the same way we should examine the hatching of eggs, in which we might easily observe the whole process of vivification and organisation . . .

The experiment, he observes, could not be made with mammals, as to cut the foetus from the womb would be "too inhuman". In the case of mammals, one must be content to be dependant on the accident of an abortion, producing the incompletely formed young prematurely, or the death of a pregnant animal by misadventure, when one could open it up as it was dead already. (There is not, here, the soul of a vivisector.)

There is a great deal about horticulture, in which is shown his love of gardening and knowledge of plants. In this unlikely place one finds the suggestion that as a tree grows better from a graft than from its own seed, so an onion seed, grafted into an onion, should mature ahead of one set in the soil.

But perhaps his most charming aside concerns the extraction of infusions, and particularly of the scent of violets:[10]

. . . in an infusion of rhubarb the purgative virtue is extracted first, the astringent afterwards. And something of the kind I have found on steeping violets in vinegar, where the sweet and delicate scent of the flower is extracted first, and then the more earthy part of the flower, which mars the scent. Therefore, if violets be steeped in vinegar for a whole day, the scent is extracted much more feebly; but if you keep them in for a quarter of an hour only and then take them out, and (since the scented spirit in violets is small) put in fresh violets every quarter of an hour as many as six times, the infusion is at last so enriched that although there have not been violets in the vinegar, however renewed, for more than an hour and a half altogether, there nevertheless remains in it a most grateful odour, as strong as the violet itself, for an entire year.

He must have been using an odourless vinegar, probably made from wine.

1. Spedding, Vol. IV, p.61.
2. *Op.cit.*, p.55.
3. *Op.cit.*, pp.72–3.
4. *Op.cit.*, pp.92–3.
5. *Op.cit.*, p.104.
6. *Op.cit.*, pp.108–9.
7. *Op.cit.*, p.211.
8. *Op.cit.*, p.166.
9. *Op.cit.*, pp.201–02.
10. *Op.cit.*, p.213.

CHAPTER 59

Herbert's Tribute

THE publication of the *Novum Organum* occasioned the best known of several tributes from the pen of a younger man, George Herbert, aged twenty-seven, Public Orator at Cambridge, perhaps already beginning to write those religious poems which became known to his private friends long before they were eventually published in the volume, *The Temple,* which has earned him the title of "an all-but canonised Anglican saint."[1] This tribute, *In honorem illustrissimi domini Francisci de Verulamii . . .* is composed in Latin in lines of twelve-syllable iambics, which I shall endeavour to render into English iambic pentameter:

> Who is this, then? No quotidian face
> Is walking. Know you not? Then harken.
> Leader in ideas, Truth's High-Priest,
> Lord of inductive method, Verulam,
> Master of what's real, not artful theory,
> Pine of profundities, elegancies,
> Scrutator of the natural world; Philosophy's
> Foundry; of experience Trustee,
> Of speculation; Equity's standard-bearer;
> Liberator of Science, till now in pupilage;
> Dispenser of light; Disperser of idols and clouds;
> Colleague of the Sun; Certainty's corner-stone;
> Sophistry's scourge; Literary Brutus,
> Despoiling Authority's tyranny; Admirable
> Arbiter of reason and of sense;
> Polisher of minds; Atlas of Physics,
> To whom yields the Alcides, the Herculean
> Sage of Stagira born, Aristotle;
> Dove of Noah, finding in old arts no perch,
> Homing in his strength to the Ark, his mother;
> Gimlet of subtlety, Grandson of Time;
> By his mother, Truth; Hive of Honey;
> Unique priest of the World and of Souls;
> Axe of error; innate grain
> Of mustard; self-growing, pungent to others.

Although this may be hyperbole, written in his public capacity at Cambridge, there seem to be in it points of possible private reference. "Literary Brutus" is peculiar. There were several Bruti, none of them writers. Herbert probably means not Caesar's assassin but that first, semi-legendary Brutus who, in as much as he slew the tyrannic Tarquin king, founded the Roman republic. Bacon's inductive method seems to be seen as slaying the tyrannic authority of the school-men, but would not "Philosophic" rather than "Literary" have been more apt, if that had been the only reference? If Herbert knew his Livy—and Livy's history of early Rome is our primary source of information concerning this ancient Brutus—then he might have had in mind that in Livy I, one reads, "Brutus deliberately assumed a mask to hide his true character." This could be an allusion to Bacon's use of Shakespeare as a mask for his more literary compositions.

Again, "Colleague of the Sun" might seem exaggerated and empty apostrophe, but assumes pertinent meaning if Herbert had been received in Canonbury Tower and knew the symbolism of the veiled sunburst face. In that case, as King Henry V ascended the throne, a glorious sun to disperse the clouds which had been permitted to "smothere up"[2] the beginning of his day, so the sun of Bacon's inductive method dispels the fictitious conceits and superstitions which had clouded the beginnings of the day of philosophy.

1. Article on George Herbert by John Heath-Stubbs in *The Concise Encyclopaedia of English and American Poets and Poetry*, ed. Stephen Spender and Donald Hall (Hutchinson, 1963).

2. *I King Henry IV*, I. ii, 221.

CHAPTER 60

Lord St. Alban

IT was feigned by Gondomar that the movement of troops from the Spanish Netherlands was intended only for the invasion of Bohemia, where King James acknowledged his son-in-law's cause unjust. When, on the way, they deviated into the Palatinate, it was too late to do anything about it, and on September 5th, 1620, Heidelberg was occupied. Even to James, this was a provocation. Till now, he had permitted Frederick only to recruit in England at his own expense, for the defence of the Palatinate (not of Bohemia). Now, he was willing an army should be sent from England, to recover the Palatinate, if the cost was not prohibitive. As it would take time to call a Parliament to discuss and vote funds, Bacon drew up a *Circular Letter from the Council to the Nobles,* inviting them to contribute treasure for the provision of forces to recover the Palatinate heritage of his Majesty's grandchildren. The Archbishop of Canterbury's name appeared beneath, then his own and some others. The date was October 25th 1620. Prince Charles contributed £10,000, Bacon and some others £1,000 each (£500,000 each in today's money). Two English ambassadors, Sir Edward Conway and Sir Richard Weston, now arrived in Prague, but explained to Elizabeth, who received them in her husband's temporary absence, that on instructions from her father, they might only address her as the Princess Palatine, not as Queen of Bohemia. A letter she received from Sir Henry Wotton made the same point. It is not unlikely this abandonment depressed the Bohemians. In November, they were routed, by a Bavarian army, on the White Mountain. Frederick and Elizabeth with their family had only just time to escape, from a city which became the scene of massacre.

There was now a question of where they could go. German states were nervous of harbouring them, in case it caused them, too, to be attacked. King James was not willing to have them in England. It was Holland who gave them sanctuary.

Again, we have no record of Bacon's reactions, but his feelings would have been opposite to those of the King.

At home, his old friend Yelverton had been suspended, for inserting in the charter of the City of London clauses infringing the King's prerogative. Many thought his real offence was to have opposed the monopoly patent for gold and silver thread, which was a source of income to Buckingham's brother. Coke demanded a vicious fine of £6,000. Francis could not deny there had been an offence, but brought the fine down to £4,000. It will be seen from these figures that nobody expected Yelverton to be living on his salary as Attorney General, £81 odd. It was understood that it was out of the unofficial perquisites or perks of office that such a fine could be paid. When the Attorney General's place had become vacant, on Bacon's elevation, Sir James Ley was said to have offered Buckingham £10,000 to recommend him for it.[1] Why offer £10,000 for £81 per annum, unless the unofficial fees made the post worth far more than the salary? In this instance, either the bribe to Buckingham had been insufficient, or the King could hardly fail to accept Bacon's recommendation as to who should fill the place from which he had moved upwards. But note that it was because he had crossed swords with Buckingham that Yelverton was brought down.

Francis was becoming more than ever concerned over monopoly patents, and was courageous enough to write to Buckingham, on November 29th, 1620, advising him that in the coming Parliamentary session three patents in which he, Buckingham, had interest, would be brought into question. One was that for Inns and Hostelries, which had been granted Mompesson for the King's benefit. Francis told Buckingham roundly they should be terminated. The increasing number of these monopoly patents, reserving to a particular person the exclusive right to trade in certain things, was provoking public resentment. But Yelverton had opposed a patent in which Buckingham had an interest, and afterwards found himself disgraced from his post as Attorney-General, and Bacon, when he wrote to Buckingham urging him to "put off the envy of these things" (patents) must have known he risked a like fate.

Buckingham referred Bacon's letter to the King, who referred it to the Privy Council. Bacon urged that the three patents be terminated before the opening of the new Parliament. The King, who was the principal beneficiary of the Mompesson Patent, was opposed to this, and other members of the Council suggested the patents could be given up as a graceful gesture in response to the Commons' concern, when expressed. Delay won the day, as Bacon was out-voted.

On January 7th, 1620/1, the King announced Francis was to be made a Viscount. His sixtieth birthday, a few days later, was the occasion of a banquet at York House, at which Ben Jonson read a poem he had composed in his honour:

> Haile, happie *Genius* of this antient pile!
> How comes it all things so about thee smile?
> The fire, the wine, the men! and in the midst,
> Thou stand'st as if some Mysterie thou did'st.

The "antient pile" is York House, but Masons have felt that the fire refers to that on the altar of the Lodge, or to the firing-glasses, the wine to the cup of charity, and the Mystery performing stance of Bacon (at the dining-table surely seated), to his officiation as Grand Master. If so, Jonson was one of the initiates of the temple of Canonbury Tower.

On January 30th the new Parliament was opened. Bacon had persuaded the King to call it. James hated Parliaments, even though they were his only means of obtaining a subsidy; that was perhaps why he preferred to increase patents. Francis, taking seat upon the crimson Woolsack for the first time, the Great Seal in its embroidered purse beside him, must have felt the King and Buckingham would have to face a buffeting from the lower chamber; probably he thought his tact would be needed to steer them through. The King made his opening speech, and Bacon, speaking next, paid him a graceful tribute, quoting Solomon: ''The words of the wise are as nails and pins driven in and fastened . . .''

On February 3rd, 1620/1, Francis said good-bye to the name of Bacon when he was created Viscount St. Alban. Lord Carew carried before him the robe in which he was to be invested, Lord Wentworth the coronet.

After the ceremony, he wrote to the King, thanking him for having raised him so high.

1. *The Personal History of Lord Bacon*, William Hepworth Dixon (Murray, 1861), p.257.

CHAPTER 61

Scandal threatens the King

ON February 6th, 1620/1, the Gold and Silver Thread patent was brought up in the Commons. This was an old patent, but the beneficiaries now were the King and Sir Christopher Villiers, another of Buckingham's brothers, the holder being Sir Giles Mompesson. This being the same person as held the Patent for Inns and Hostelries, for which the beneficiaries were the King and Sir Edward Villiers, question of one led to question of the other. In connection with the first, Sir Edward Sackville had said that those who had advised his Majesty it was good should bear "the blame and share of it", and in connection with the second Coke at first said it was "good in law but ill in execution". The research committee was noted it had been referred to the then King's Attorney-General (Bacon), the Lord Treasurer and others . . . The next day Coke said it was an exorbitant grievance both in itself and in the execution. The same afternoon the Patent for Ale-houses was brought up, and the attack turned upon the execution of it, by a Sir Francis Michell. On February 20th Coke said Michell was unworthy to be a Justice of the Peace and should be removed from his place and walked through the streets to imprisonment in the Tower. Michell was called to the Bar to hear his sentence on his knee and refused permission to speak after sentence.

This alarmed Mompesson, who tried to forestall a similar fate by sending the House a voluntary confession that he had erred in the manner of his execution of his patent. So far from saving him, this provided ground for the issue of a warrant for his arrest. He jumped through a window and took ship, and it was suspected Buckingham had paid for his not being hindered in his flight.

The manner in which Mompesson had erred, it now came out, was in refusing licences to respectable inn-keepers unless they could afford to pay him enormous bribes, but granting them to those who ran their inns as brothels. As the King was the principal beneficiary, this meant that his Majesty was living largely off the proceeds of prostitution. The vision James' subjects must have had of a paederast King and his boy-friend living off the exploitation of women makes comprehensible the growing association of the idea of reform with Puritanism. The Civil War might have been brought forward from the reign of Charles I into that of James I, had not the momentum of the rising tide been at that moment broken, or rather turned, by a diversion in the direction of Bacon, whom it was to engulf.

CHAPTER 62

The Sacrifice

ON March 14th, 1620/1, a certain Christopher Awbry presented to the House of Commons a petition alleging that some two and a half years ago, having a suit in Chancery, he had given the Lord Chancellor £100; the Lord Chancellor had taken the money but given judgement against him. On the same day, a similar complaint was made by a certain Edward Egerton (not to be confused with the previous Chancellor), that some three years previously, while he had a suit in Chancery, he had given the Lord Chancellor £400 in gold and a basin and ewer worth £50; the Lord Chancellor had accepted the gifts but given judgement against him. That these two strange charges, both made by men proclaiming their own intention to corrupt, on occasions between two and three years back, should have been made on the same day, suggests they had been put up to it. Neither had anything to gain, unless he were being paid to proclaim his own corruption in order to inculpate Bacon.

It will be noticed that Bacon was not, and never has been, accused of giving a corrupt judgement. The notion of him as a corrupt judge is therefore false. The complaint was on the contrary, in each case, that he had failed to deliver the corrupt judgement for which the bribe had been given.

Bacon wrote that evening to Buckingham, "I know I have clean hands and a clean heart . . . "[1]

From March 15th to 17th, the Commons heard the witnesses and debated what was to be done. Bacon was not without defenders. John Finch, the Member for Oxfordshire said he hoped "so great a man would not fall by the testimony of one who had most reason to excuse himself for . . . the delivery of a bribe." The man who had received the money on Bacon's behalf could, he suggested, have kept it for himself, and in any case, he averred, no judge could be expected to remember the names of all those who had suits to be heard before him. Gifts could therefore be received without consciousness they came at an improper time, while a suit was pending, and receipt of gifts during improper time could not constitute corruption unless there was a compact that they were to procure the verdict.

It needs to be grasped how general in those days was the custom of giving presents. Christmas cards had not been invented, but at New Year everybody gave presents to everybody, costly ones; it was expected, and upon birthdays and numerous other occasions affording pretext for celebration. A gift at the conclusion of a law-suit was usual; only if it was received *pendente lite,* while the case was on, or pending, was there impropriety of time.

Edward Alford, a respected barrister, rose to say he had seen the ledger of a great Baron in Henry VIII's time wherein a payment to the Lord Chancellor at the conclusion of a case was set down as a normal expense.

The point has, however, been made that Chancery was hated by common lawyers because it took business from the King's Bench and Common Pleas[2] and Coke used the occasion to mount his guns, as of old, against the Chancery. It was he who first used the word ''bribe'' in connection with untimely fees allegedly paid to Bacon.

The case was referred to the Lords.

Francis, as Leader of the Lords, sent them a letter saying he would not attend as he was suffering from heart and back-ache, but that if they would settle some convenient time he would look into the matter and tell them what he could remember about these fees. Obviously, he would not store all fees in his head and would have to ask questions of those who received them for him or consult any records that were kept.

Buckingham (now Lord Admiral) brought the letter to the House of Lords, and the Earl of Southampton moved that a verbal reply be sent that the Lords would proceed with the hearing of witnesses; and during the ensuing days a procession of persons, climbing on this strange band-wagon, presented themselves to say they had given the Lord Chancellor such and such gifts.

Francis remained at York House, and on March 25th wrote to the King, ''I have been no haughty or intolerable or hateful man . . . I have inherited no hatred from my father . . . Whence should this be?'' When the book of hearts should be opened, he hoped he might not be found to have a corrupt heart, ''however I may be frail and partake of the abuse of the times.''

The next day the King went to the Lords and announced his decision to ''strike dead'' the Patents for Inns and Hostleries, Ale-houses and Gold and Silver Thread. He omitted to mention that Bacon had, the previous November, urged him to do this, and that he, the King, had put it off to the last possible moment, when the bursting scandal forced it on him.

Francis had sufficiently recovered to withdraw to Gorhambury, and made his will: ''My body to be buried obscurely. My name to the next ages and to foreign nations . . . '' He gave all his books to Sir John Constable, and all his unpublished manuscripts, suggesting he publish such as seemed to him fit but particularly enjoining him to publish his tribute to Queen Elizabeth *In felicem memoriam Elizabethae, Reginae Angliae (In felicitous memory of Elizabeth Queen of England).*

At this time he also composed *A Psalm or Prayer,* in which he said, ''. . . I have hated all cruelty and hardness of heart: I have (though in a

despised weed) procured the good of all men. If any have been mine
enemies, I thought not of them . . . I confess before thee I am a debtor to
thee for the gracious talent of gifts and graces, which I have neither put
into a napkin, nor put . . . where it might have made the best profit; but
misspent it in things for which I was least fit; so as I may truly say, my
soul hath been a stranger in the course of my pilgrimage.''[3]

On his return to London a few days before Parliament was to reopen,
Francis had an appointment with the King, on April 16th, 1621. We
have his notes of what he intended to say. He distinguished three kinds of
payments to judges:

1. The first, of bargain or contract for reward to pervert justice, *pendente lite.*
2. The second, where the Judge conceives the cause to be at an end by the
   information of the party, or otherwise, and useth not such diligence as he
   ought to enquire of it.
3. And the third, where the cause is really ended, and it is *sine fraude* without
   relation to any precedent promise.

Of the first, he was as ''innocent as any born on St. Innocent's day.'' It
was the second he was looking into, to see whether there were any
moneys he had received supposing causes ended that were not ended. At
his coming in as Lord Chancellor he had received an enormous number of
presents, and perhaps he had not made enquiry as he should have done
whether any were from givers who had suits in Chancery; and likewise
subsequently at New Years, when the number that arrived was great.

One may suggest that it might seem almost pedantic to return
acquaintances' presents saying, ''You mustn't give me a present this
year; you have a suit coming up in Chancery.'' With the smaller
population, one was inevitably hearing the cases of persons known to one
socially, and from whom New Year's presents would normally be
received. Also, a case could seem to be over, yet break out again, so that
an ''after'' could become a ''before'', innocently.

Francis went to the King, then, to defend himself and tell him how he
would defend in the Lords. When he came out from that audience,
everything was changed; the King had faced him with a request or
command that must have been to him an overwhelming shock.

Thomas Bushell, one of Francis' secretaries, after Francis, the King and
Buckingham were all dead, put on record for posterity what happened:

. . . there arose complaints against his Lordship and the then Favourite at Court,
that for some days the King was put to this quere, whether he should permit the
Favourite of his affection or the oracle of his Council to sink in his service.

Whereupon his Lordship was sent for by the King, who, after some discourse,
gave him this positive advice, to submit himself to the House of Peers, and that
upon his princely word he would then restore him again . . .

Now, although my Lord saw his approaching ruin, and told his Majesty there was little hope of mercy in a multitude, when his enemies were given fire, if he did not plead for himself, yet such was his obedience to him that he resolved his Majesty's will should be his only law, and so took leave of him with these words:

Those that strike at your Chancellor – it is much to be feared – will strike at your crown; and wished that as he was then the first so he might be the last of sacrifices.

Francis had warned Buckingham, on his coming in as Favourite, that to be near a monarch was not without perils; for should the people be angered, the monarch might, to save himself, use one near to him to put the blame on. He had meant this as a warning to the beautiful boy; yet in a way, it cannot have been beyond his conception that it should be not the Favourite but himself who would be chosen for the sad role.

1. Lambeth, Gibson Papers, vol. viii, f.220.
2. *Francis Bacon,* Catherine Drinker Bowen (Hamish Hamilton, 1963), p.148-151.
3. British Museum, Birch MSS, f.110.
4. Lambeth, Gibson Papers, vol. viii, f.146.
5. Spedding, XIV, p.149.

CHAPTER 63

The submission

BACON wrote his submissive letter to the House of Lords, desiring his Majesty would take the Great Seal into his own hands, and trusting he would be spared entering upon further particulars.

On April 24th, 1621, the Prince of Wales read this out in the House. Afterwards there was a long silence. Then Lord Pembroke, as the Lord Chamberlain, said the question was whether the letter was sufficient. The Prince and Buckingham said they thought it would be considered so; but Suffolk, against whom Francis had given judgement in 1619, said it would not be sufficient, for it confessed nothing in particular and therefore gave no grounds upon which a sentence could be passed. The Prince and Buckingham said to lose the Seal was surely sufficient, without passing of a sentence, but the Earl of Southampton, who probably had never forgotten standing beside Essex in Court while Francis acted for the crown, said he was charged by the Commons with corruption and no confession of corruption was in his submission; there must be a confession of particulars.

There was further discussion, as to whether the charges could be sent to Bacon in writing for him to answer in writing, or whether he be required to come to the House. Buckingham and Pembroke urged he should not be required to come. In the end, a list of twenty-eight charges was sent to him. He was not supplied with the names of those who witnessed against him.

Francis replied, "I do plainly and ingenuously confess that I am guilty of corruption . . . The particulars I confess and declare to be as follows . . ."

Paragraphs 1 and 2 dealt with the Egertons, Sir Rowland and Edward. There had been more than one suit between them. Shortly after his coming to the Seal, there was amongst the many presents a purse from Edward Egerton containing £400. From the words of him who brought it, he thought it was presented in respect of a suit past, not thinking there was another to come. In the one which afterwards came, he gave judgement against Edward Egerton, and Sir Rowland afterwards gave him £500.

In 3, the present came a fortnight after the case was ended.

In 4, between the Lady Wharton and coheirs of Sir Francis Willoughby, he found the £310 from the Lady Wharton to have come in *pendente lite*; and yet he recalled some shuffling of the date of entries between Mr. Shute and the Registrar, which he distasted.

In 5, the present was a year after.

In 6, the purse containing £100 was received at New Year, and since it came amongst the New Year's gifts he neglected to enquire whether the giver had a suit filed, as in fact he had. This one, therefore, he now realised came in *pendente lite.*

In 7 and 8, the present was after.

In 9, when he was brought to see the present, a cabinet said to be worth £800, he thought it of too great value and asked him who brought it to take it back. This he would not. During the ensuing months he several times asked Sir John Kennedy, from whom it came, to have it taken away, which he did not, and so it remained, still awaiting collection.

In 10, the party against whom he gave judgement had lent him money from before the hearing, and he had asked the King's permission to have the amount restored to him out of the fine.

In 11, 12, 13 and 14, the present was after.

In 15, he granted to William Compton delay in the settlement of a debt of £1,002, and during the time granted him in which to pay, a suit broke out between Compton and another . . .

In 16, he could recall £100 from Awbry but not the circumstances.

17 and 18 were after.

In 19, at his coming to the Seal, he received £200 from Sir George Reynell towards the furnishing of York House; he thought this was for diverse former favours and in fact believed it was before any suit had begun. Yet the ring from him, received at New Year, was *pendente lite,* and he thought now that it was of too great value for a New Year's gift.

In 20, he borrowed from one Peacock, but it was before any suit.

In 21, the cause between Smethwick and Wick, the servant who received the fine brought with it £200 received earlier, which when he understood the nature of the extra he had him return.

22 and 23 were after.

24, 25 and 26 did not concern judicial business but a matter concerning three business companies which he settled unofficially, in a manner such as all were pleased; and if it were considered a fault in him to have accepted the moneys they paid him for his pains, he knew not how it could have been concealed since the sums must of necessity have appeared in the account books of the three companies.

27 again was a non judicial matter in which, by request, he had treated between vintners (to save their having to have a suit at law) and took from them £1000 for settling the matter.

28, he had given way to great exactions by his servants.

One sees that in the whole there is not one single confession to a charge of bribery. There were three cases in which, through confusion or oversight, something had come in *pendente lite.* As John Finch had said in the House of Commons, an untimely receipt, *pendente lite,* could not in itself be deemed corrupt without proof of corrupt intent. His whole position was one he would have been prepared to defend, and had he not, used the form of words "I confess' it is doubtful whether he could have been convicted.

The King sent the Lord Treasurer, the Lord Steward, the Lord Chamberlain and the Earl of Arundel to recover from Francis the Great Seal. They found him very sick.

There ensued, in the Lords, a discussion of the sentence, whether a fine, imprisonment and disqualification from office should suffice or he should also lose his titles. Southampton, unforgiving, voted for his degradation. This was not carried, Cambridge speaking against it and followed in that by the Prince; Buckingham being against a sentence.

In the end, he was sentenced to a fine of £40,000, imprisonment in the Tower during the King's pleasure, disqualification from any office of State, from sitting in Parliament or coming within the verge of the Court. There was only one dissenting vote, that of Buckingham.

That Buckingham dissented from the sentence should be remembered as perhaps the one brave thing he ever did. Yet his role remains odd. His power was immense; how had it dwindled to almost nothing at this moment?

Bacon was left at York House, and it was Southampton who pointed out, venomously, that he had not yet been taken to the Tower, and urged his transference be no longer delayed. Buckingham said it had been delayed because of his sickness.

The exact date of his transference there is not known. From the Tower he wrote on May 31st, 1621, to Buckingham: "Good my Lord, Procure the warrant for my discharge this day . . . " He has been the "perfect servant . . . the justest Chancellor that hath been in the five changes since Sir Nicholas Bacon's time."[1]

This letter surely tells the whole tale. He had proved himself the perfect servant to the King by pleading guilty when he was not guilty, and expected the release he had been promised. The pretence of corruption was for public show only; he had made of his own reputation an oblation to save the King's.

His release was procured, almost at once, and Francis accepted an invitation from Sir John Vaughan to stay for a while at his home in Fulham.

On June 5th saw a motion in the House of Commons which was virtually a vote of confidence in the King. Francis wrote to Buckingham. "I hope his Majesty may reap honour out of my adversity . . . His Majesty knows best his own ways, and for me to despair of him were a sin . . . "[2]

The King, as though not understanding what he had done to Bacon, wrote asking his advice how he should reform his courts of justice, a role Francis pointed out to him in his reply was not now fitting.[3]

In fact, the King had eliminated from his service and thrown to the wolves the one person who, had he held in his hands the helm, could have prevented the Civil War which broke out in the succeeding reign. The history, not only of England but of the world would have been different.

1. Lambeth, Gibson Papers, vol. viii, f.147.
2. Lambeth, Gibson Papers, vol. viii, f.219.
3. Lambeth, Gibson Papers, vol. viii, f.251.

CHAPTER 64

The empty dishes

AUBREY begins his life of Bacon, "In his Lordship's prosperity, Sir Fulke Greville, Lord Brooke, was his great friend and acquaintance; but when he was in disgrace and want, he was so unworthy as to forbid his Butler to let him have any more small Beer . . . "

Timon of Athens perplexes Shakespeare scholars. It was not acted in Shakespeare's time. Does this mean he was dissatisfied with it? There are passages of prose, not only in the mouths of menial characters. Does this show Shakespeare's practice was to write in prose first and to versify later, in this case failing to complete the versification? If he tired of it, why? Does the evident disgust with sex and harping upon venereal desease relate to a bad experience of the author's? What is the date? No topical allusions have been found to the events of any year within Shakespeare's lifetime. What are the sources?

The author has taken the names of some of the minor characters from Plutarch, presumably North's. But Plutarch does not tell us why Timon lived apart from his fellows, hating mankind. For the information that once he had been rich, and that friends to whom he had been over-generous deserted him in his adversity, the source is the Greek of Lucian of Samosata. This had been translated into Latin, Italian and French, but not into English. Professor Bullough, who appears to have studied it in all four versions, indicates to us one verbal reminiscence which must be either of the Greek or of the Latin. There was also, found among the Dyce MSS, now in the Victoria and Albert Museum, 52, an anonymous academic play, in English, based upon Lucian's theme and containing a banqueting scene in which Timon served his worthless acquaintance painted stones. This surely must be the ancestor of that in Shakespeare, where he serves them hot water, and there seems to be a reminiscence of the academic play where one of the disappointed guests, referring to the hot water, says, "One day he gives us diamonds, next day stones." The academic play, since it borrows from three of Jonson's, Every Man Out of His Humour, Cynthia's Revels and The Poetaster, must have been written subsequent to them, but it was never published, and, though it was presumably acted in a college of a university, or in a school, was not acted in the Inns of Court or on the public stage. Professor Bullough cannot think how Shakespeare could have come to his apparent knowledge of it, though he supposes it possible both had borrowed from an antecedent source, of which we do not know. Finally, Professor

Bullough endorses Professor Farnham's suggestion that the contrast between the characters of Timon and Apemantus is built on a passage in Montaigne's essay 'Of Democritus and Heraclitus' in which are contrasted Timon and Diogenes the Cynic. This would explain all the allusions to dogs in connection with Apemantus.

One can say, then, that we know what our author had on his desk while he worked, Plutarch's *Lives,* Lucian, either in the Greek or in the Latin translation made by Erasmus, probably the latter, and Montaigne's essays.

If, as I contend, the author is Bacon, and he wrote it now, he had also, to move him, terrible anger and disgust. Greville's case may have been glaring, but he is unlikely to have been the only one from whom slights were experienced. Professor Bullough avers that, neither a tragedy nor a romance, *Timon* is, alone of Shakespeare's works, a morality. Bacon may well have written it as such. In that case, the thought in it is, "When I was high, I was needlessly lavish; now I am fallen, my case is Timon's." His suppositive mother had thought him extravagant and uncritical where the handling of his finances was concerned, and it has been suggested it was not really necessary for him, at his installation as Chancellor, to dine at his own expense all the judges in the kingdom. Sir Fulke will have been among the feasted. And how many of the two hundred horse and footfollowers who brought up his train received, on their arrival at Westminster, not perhaps the judges' dinner but something to eat and drink?

For the prose patches, I would think it unlikely the plays were written first in prose and then versified. To the poet, form and content come so much together, that would hardly be practicable. But Wordsworth said poetry was "Emotion recollected in tranquillity", and it is the experience of most practising poets that work written too close to an acute emotional experience tends to lack poetry. It may be that bitter thoughts were at this moment coming too fast for poetic clothing.

But Timon is contrasted with Alcibiades, and this is the hinge of the matter. Timon was not banished; he outspent his means and left the city to live on roots. It is Alcibiades who has been banished. The reason for the historical Alcibiades being banished was, Plutarch tells us, that he had "offended against the goddesses, Ceres and Proserpina, counterfeiting in mockery their holy mysteries, and shewing them to his familiar friends in his house, himself apparelled and arrayed in a long vestement or cope, like unto the vestement the priest weareth . . . " Why has this been changed in the play to pleading before the Senate for the life of a friend who had killed another in self-defence? Even if such a plea had been refused, it seems most unlikely the pleader would have been punished. Let us look into the arguments. Alcibiades says his friend "in hot blood Hath stepp'd into the law", but was apart from this a man of virtue, who responded to a challenge manly. The first Senator tells him he is making an ugly deed look fair, "To revenge is no valour, but to bear." Alcibiades then asks pardon if he speaks like a captain.

> Why do fond men expose themselves to battle
> And not endure all threats? . . .
>   If there be
> Such valour in the bearing, what make we
> Abroad? why then, women are more valiant
> That stay at home, if bearing carry it;
> And the ass more captain than the lion, the felon
> Loaden with irons wiser than the judge,
> If wisdom be in suffering.   *III, v, 42–51*

This comes very close to Bacon's feeling about the Bohemian's overthrow of their tyrant King, to offer the Crown to Frederick. (This feeling we shall later learn from a private letter of Bacon to Prince Charles.) It was a taking of the law into their own hands, which, as a lawyer, he would have to see as being validated by their own constitution as an elective monarchy, yet if the legal position was difficult to understand, he did not wish them to suffer, and help to Frederick and Elizabeth must be brought by whatever means possible. Francis thought the Hapsburg tyranny odious, and his sympathies were wholly with the Bohemians in their desire to be free of it and to have Frederick and Elizabeth to govern them instead. It would be so infinitely to the betterment of the enlightened world to have Florizel and Perdita in Prague that we should be justified in supporting them, though the rising had been in hot blood. That this point of view and feeling was totally opposite to that of King James, despite that it was his daughter and son-in-law who were involved, may explain why we have no public pronouncement of Bacon's. James' view was evidently that the Bohemians' proper role was simply to bear their afflictions, not to liberate themselves; so King and Chancellor would have been at loggerheads. Is it possible Bacon thought this was why his fall had been engineered?

If this is the proper interpretation, he was Alcibiades as well as Timon; and whilst Timon can only hurl curses at those who have let him down, and indeed upon all mankind, Alcibiades learns to discriminate, and forebears destruction of the city as a whole.

Bacon could not give the play to be acted, now Shakespeare was dead.

Happily, there were some who, unlike Fulke Greville, were not changed towards him by his fall. Ben Jonson was later to write:[1]

My conceit of his Person was never increased towards him, by his place or honours. But I have, and doe reverence him for the greatnesse, that was onely proper to himselfe, in that hee seem'd to mee ever, by his worke, one of the greatest men, and most worthy of admiration, that had beene in many Ages. In his adversitie I ever prayed, that God would give him strength: for *Greatnesse* hee could not want. Neither could I condole in a word, or syllable for him, as knowing no Accident could doe harme to vertue; but rather helpe to make it manifest.

1. *Discoveries,* 1641; *Ben Jonson,* ed. Hereford and Simpson (Oxford, 1947), VIII, 592.

CHAPTER 65

Henry VII

FRANCIS now began a biography of King Henry VII. Unfortunately, most of the papers he needed were in Sir Thomas Cotton's library, which was within the forbidden "verge of the court". Cotton looked up and copied out passages for him, but that was not the same as seeing the sources for himself. At Gorhambury, he worked from Cotton's extracts and from Holinshed, Polydore and Fabyan.

For his most interesting material, however, he had no known source. He says that Henry VII owed his stability rather to his wife, as daughter of Edward IV, than to his own descent from the house of York, and, resenting this, always diminished her. He could never bear to hear her cheered by the people. Though cold to his Queen, he had, however, no mistresses, known of, nor yet male favourites either.

He was frugal, so the resources of the Crown built up.

He was "never found to be enterprising or adventurous"[1] but chose safe courses, avoiding calamity. His greatest strength was that he "was not afraid of an able man, as Lewis the eleventh was",[2] but set the ablest in positions of responsibility. "Neither did he care how cunning they were that he did employ; for he thought himself to have the master-reach. And as he chose well, so he held them up well. For it is a strange thing, that though he were a dark prince, and infinitely suspicious, and his times full of secret conspiracies and troubles, yet in twenty-four years reign he never put down or discomposed counsellor or near servant, save only Stanley",[3] who had been false to him.

For a country to be strong, "it requireth men bred not in a servile or indigent fashion, but in some free and plentiful manner. Therefore, if a state run most to noblemen and gentlemen . . . you may have a good cavalry, but never good stable hands of foot . . . And this is to be seen in France and Italy . . . where . . . all is noblesse or peasantry . . . and no middle people."[4] Henry VII encouraged a middle class.

His laws were "deep and not vulgar",[5] not made upon the spur of particular occasion but with providence for the future. He was not loved, but he was respected.

The book was dedicated to Prince Charles.

1. Spedding, VI, p.235.
2. Op.cit., p.242.
3. Op.cit., pp.242-43.
4. Op.cit., p.95.
5. Op.cit., p.92.

CHAPTER 66

The rape of York House

To Prince Charles, Francis wrote thanking him for his goodness at the time of his troubles, and to William Herbert, Earl of Pembroke, Lord Chamberlain, for his handling of his part of the matter. To Gondomar the Spanish Ambassador he had already written, from Fulham, thanking him for a surprisingly nice letter on the occasion of his fall.

The one who was letting him down was Buckingham. He sent Bacon the King's warrant for his pardon, signed on October 12th, 1621, but it was odd the new Lord Keeper, Bishop Williams, officiously delayed putting his seal on it until Parliament should have met again, and it began to be noised abroad that Buckingham desired the delay which would end the restraint upon Bacon's entering London as he had conceived an envy of York House. Moreover, he held aloof.

Francis was anxious, as we know from a memorandum of what he should say to him if granted the interview for which he asked:[1]

Your Lordship knoweth as well as I what promises you made me, and iterated them both by message and from your mouth, consisting of three things, the pardon of the whole sentence, some help for my debts, and an annual [pension] which your Lordship ever set as £2,000 obtained and £3,000 in hope. Of these . . . there is effected only of the remission of the fine and the pardon now stayed . . .

That such an enormous pension, £1,000,000, certainly, and £1,200,000 hopefully, in present day value, should have been promised him is surely suggestive of inducement to plead guilty, not being so.

The interview was not granted. Francis wrote to Buckingham he did not refuse to sell him York House, but it was dear to him; he would give him Gorhambury.

Still Buckingham held off, and the pardon left unsealed so that Francis could not re-enter York House.

Lord Montgomery and Sir Edward Sackville procured an interview with Buckingham for Bacon's wife, who of course was not forbidden London. The result must have been unsatisfactory, for Sir Thomas Meautis, Bacon's secretary, writes to him that Sackville thinks Lady St. Alban should now appeal to the Prince of Wales.

At this juncture the Duke of Lennox wrote to Bacon offering to buy York House from him, tendering in addition to money a smaller house in London, suitable for the residence of Lady St. Alban when in town.[2]

Francis' reaction was violent. ''York-house is the house where my father died and where I first breathed, and there will I yield my last breath.''[3] He had not refused it to Buckingham, yet his letter had been so like a refusal that he could in no case receive any other offers.

This, when it reached Buckingham's ears, restored his humour, and Sackville, profiting of it went to see him again. After the interview he wrote to Francis,[4] ''If York-house were gone, the town were yours, and all your straitest shackles clean off . . . Seem not to dive into the secret of it, though you are purblind if you see not through it.'' Buckingham did not wish to appear as having forced him out of it and his request was therefore that Francis should offer it to Cranfield, from whom he would afterwards buy it. There was a sinister hint that if Francis did not do this, he could have more troubles than had come his way already.

Then Francis knew he would never be allowed to re-enter York-House. So he offered it to Cranfield, as bid; his pardon was sealed and the sentence of banishment lifted. He took a house for a while at Chiswick, then moved to Bedford House on the Strand, within sad sight of York house. That, today, is no more; and many have felt it ironic that nearby streets commemorate the name of the usurper, Villiers Street and Buckingham Street.

It was not that, at the time he forced Francis out of it Buckingham was deficient in residential accommodation. He had already Wallingford House on Whitehall, and a fabulous country seat, Newhall, near Chelmsford, which he had purchased in 1622 from Lord Suffolk for £20,000, that is in present day values, £10,000,000, and which he was engaged in rendering grander, at heaven knows what fantastic expense, by the inset of marble paving and importation of marble blocks and pillars which had to be brought specially from the Aegean, paintings from Italy and Holland and, presumably for the curtaining or upholstery of furniture, Persian cloth of gold.

1. Lambeth, Gibson Papers, vol. viii, f.244.
2. Lambeth, Gibson Papers, vol. viii, f.158.
3. Lambeth, Gibson Papers, vol. viii, f.159.
4. Lambeth, Gibson Papers, vol. viii, f.177.

CHAPTER 67

Bacon and the Queen of Bohemia

BACON sent a copy of his *Henry VII* to the exiled Queen of Bohemia, with a letter saying:[1]

It may please your Majesty,

I find in books (and books I dare alledge to your Majesty in regard of your singular ability to read and judge of them even above your sex) that it is accounted a great bliss for a man to have Leisure with Honour. That was never my fortune; nor is. For time was, I had Honour without Leisure; and now I have Leisure without Honour . . . But my desire is now to have Leisure without Loitering . . . but to yield some fruit of my private life. Having therefore written the resign of your Majesty's famous ancester. King Henry VII . . . I could not forget my duty so far to your excellent Majesty (to whom, for that I know and have heard, I have been at all times so much bounden as you are ever present with me both in affection and admiration) as not to make unto you in all humbleness a present thereof, as now being not able to give you tribute of any service . . . I most humbly pray your Majesty graciously to accept of my good will, and so with all reverance kiss your hands, praying to God above, by his divine and most benign providence to conduct your affairs to happy issue, and resting.

Your Majesty's most humble
and most devoted servant
Fr. St. Alban

In ordinary circumstances, this might pass for a conventional letter. It is when one reads it in the context of King James' instructions to his subjects to address her still only as Electress, not as Queen, that the repeated style ''your Majesty'' takes on the significance of a declaration. Spedding says we cannot know what view Bacon took with regard to the legality or otherwise of Frederick's acceptance of the Bohemian crown. In this letter, it is revealed in every line.

She replied to him:[2]

My Lord,

I thank you very much for your letter and your book, which is the best I ever read of the kind; and though my wit does not deserve the honour which you give me, yet with the little wit I have I consider that worthy Prince fortunate in having so faithful a biographer as you are, and I am very sorry that I cannot show otherwise than by my letters my gratitude for this and other benefits for which I am beholden to you: and though your fortunes are changed (for which I grieve)

believe that I shall not change to be what I am,
                                Your very affectionate friend,
                                              Elizabeth
The Hague, the 11th of June, 1622

1. Lambeth, Gibson Papers, vol. viii, f.166.
2. Spedding, XIV, 366.

CHAPTER 68

De Augmentis Scientiarum

FRANCIS was now translating *The Advancement of Learning* into "the universal language", Latin. In this task he received some help from George Herbert. Could he but have known it, many continentals today find it easier to read in English, so he need not have undertaken this labour for their sakes. Nevertheless, as he translated, he expanded, and at some points revised opinion.

In the *Promus,* he had jotted an Italian proverb, "L'Astrologia e vera ma l'astrologuo non si trova." (Astrology is a true science but a [true] astrologer cannot be found.) In the *Advancement* he dismissed astrology. In *De Augmentis,* he comes back to the sense of the proverb. As practised, it is so full of superstition, it is hard to find anything reliable in it. He does not believe in "planetary hours", despite that to this ancient scheme we owe the order of the days of the week. Neither does he see the reason for dividing the zodiac into its twelve signs. If the Sun, Moon and planets in their movement affect us, it would seem to him they should do so most strongly when nearest to the Midheaven, their rays beating then straightest down, also in proportion to their elevation in the ecliptic, and in their passage over the place of stars, as well as in their conjunctions with one another.[1] But the matter should be researched retrospectively, as by casting horoscopes for the inceptions of past wars and noticing whether Mars was always prominent, or if not, whether there was some other constant factor.

The study should not be allowed to undermine the sense of moral responsibility for our actions.

Coming to instruments, he asks for one to collect the sounds for the deaf. Also, as spectacles make small things large enough to assist those with poor vision (an invention of his spiritual forbear, Roger Bacon, 1214-92), why should not a glass be made so strong as to bring into visibility things invisible to the best normal sight? Beneath such a glass, a smear of urine might show us things undreamed of, which would help in diagnosis of disease. (Physicians already inspected urine, in a glass instrument known as a urinal, but with their unaided eyes.)

Following passages on Hieroglyphics and Writing, he inserts a section on Cyphers, demonstrating one which involves use of two founts of type, at first glance identical, though minutely differentiated, for the concealment of a hidden message within an open text.

But thus to pick out passages is to miss the intention of a great work.

As Margery Purvor has pointed out,[2] he was a philosopher, the parent of scientists but not a scientist. That is, he was not the man who would choose one small area of study and devote his life to the pursuit of special particulars. He was the one who saw which questions needed to be researched, which is a higher thing than to do the detailed work. That is why he wanted a college. Neither Queen Elizabeth nor King James were interested. Charles I was too troubled, and it was necessary to wait for Charles II to give the Royal Society its charter. That is why the frontispiece of Sprat's *History of the Royal Society* shows Charles II in the middle, an angel floating down from Heaven to place a wreath on his head, the first President and Francis Bacon one on either side of him. Bacon was laying ''great bases for eternity.''[3]

1. Serious astrologers do give value to all the points he mentions, but also to the point at which the ecliptic intersects the eastern horizon, known as the Ascendant.
2. *The Royal Society, Concept and Creation,* Margery Purvor (Routledge, 1956), pp.52-3.
3. Sonnet No. 125.

CHAPTER 69

The New Atlantis

THE *New Atlantis* is a fable, Bacon's only experiment with the form. It begins, "We sailed from Peru," and relates the adventures of a party driven by winds until they lose their bearings, eventually coming ashore in a land that has never been known. As they step down from the ship, the porters who come to take their luggage refuse tips, smilingly explaining that they are paid already.

In this land, it is discovered, children revere their parents, but the parents leave them free to marry for love, and the spouses, having chosen one another, are faithful. There is no desire for "meretricious embracements".

The government is by philosopher-scientists. They had to take an oath of secrecy. This was so that the results of experiments should not be divulged excepting after full consultation between all, as to "which of the inventions and experiences which we have discovered shall be published, and which not". This is probably because he forsaw that inquisition into nature could lead to the acquisition of powers dangerous to man: we have seen nuclear fission lead to the atomic bomb. Such knowledge should not be divulged to people not morally prepared to use it only for good. Rosicrucians, who tend to take *The New Atlantis* for a Rosicrucian book, see here a parallel with the Masonic oath.

They had perspective-houses, sound-houses and perfume-houses, wherein the properties of light, sound and smell were experimented (Bacon believed odours, like foods, to affect the health). There were engine-houses, wherein were produced by experimentation carriages that would fly in the air and ships that went under the sea.

There were extensive orchards and botanical gardens, in which experiments with grafting were made and new varieties induced. There was also a zoological garden, containing every kind of beast, bird, reptile and insect. These would serve not merely the curious interest, to look upon, but for making trials and dissections, so learning much that could apply to the body of man. This comes as a shock to those of us whose regard for animals is tender, but as he told us in the *Novum Organum* it would not be possible to cut a dog open unless it had died from misadventure, it would seem certain that by dissections he means of dead animals. It is also probable that when he speaks of making trials of this or that upon them, he makes a distinction between the higher animals, such as are companions to man, and show distinct personality, intelligence, affections and feeling, and the many less evolved creatures in which these qualities are not greatly evident. (It does not appear that Bacon ever performed an experiment upon an animal.)

Rawley tells us he had intended to go on to describe the laws, but gave it up because he wanted to write his *Natural History.* Rawley was well placed to know Bacon's attitude to his books, because an anecdote relayed by Archbishop Tenison reveals he was the scribe who took at least one of them down.[1]

Whilst I am speaking of this work of his Lordship of *Natural History,* there comes to my mind a very remarkable relation reported to me by . . . the Reverend Dr. Rawley. One day his Lordship was dictating to that Doctor some of the experiments in his *Sylva.* The same day he had sent a friend to Court to receive for him a final answer touching the effect of a grant which had been made to him by King James. He had hitherto only hope of it and hope deferred; and he was desirous to know the event of the matter and to be freed, one way or other, from the suspense of his thoughts. His friend returning told him plainly that he must thenceforth despair of that grant, how much soever his fortunes needed it. *Be it so,* said his Lordship; and then he dismissed his friend very cheerfully, with thankful acknowledgements of his service. His friend being gone, he came straightway to Dr. Rawley, and said unto him, *Well, Sir, yon busines won't go on: let us go on with this, for this is in our power.* And then he dictated to him afresh for some hours, without the least hesitancy of speech or discernible interruption of thought.

So Bacon was an author who dictated. In a letter to Tobie Mathews, of June 26th, 1623, he mentions that his *Advancement of Learning, Henry VII* and *Essays* are being translated into Latin ''by the help of some good pens which forsake me not.''[2] Now this could mean that friends did the translating for him, yet more likely I think it means they took down in Latin from his dictation. George Herbert, we are told, was one of those who helped with turning the *Advancement* into Latin. He was a good writer in Latin, but Bacon needed no help with Latin; I fancy it means he was one of the good pens who, like Dr. Rawley, took down from dictation. Right back in his Twickenham days we found him inviting a friend to come for a while to Twickenham Lodge where there were some pens idle. This suggests a continuous custom. Since the work was presumably unpaid, and the interest of it the only reward, Bacon would try to reserve the dictation of each book to a scribe who would find some pleasure in the matter. And that is where I think Shakespeare came in, as his dramatic secretary, though in his case there was probably some agreement as to the division or allocation of the proceeds.

1. Spedding, XIV, p.525.
2. Lambeth, Gibson Papers, vol. viii, p.232.

CHAPTER 70

The quest for longevity

BACON left other work unfinished, now, to push on to his *Historia Naturalis*. The first book of this is an enquiry into winds, their nature and origin. He had meant to follow with a study of the density and rarity of matter, but skipped it to proceed to a subject interesting him more vitally.

This was the *Historia Vitae et Mortis (History of Life and Death)*, which might be called the search for longevity, being an enquiry into the ageing process with the end of defeating it. He says most people seem to think that those aspiring to eternity ought not to interest themselves in prolonging earthly life; yet many of the Fathers, especially the holy hermits, lived to great age, so he cannot think there should be anything anti-Christian in seeking long life. The ages ascribed to the Patriarchs suggest this blessing to be natural. If it is wrong living that has shortened our span, we should try to discover our errors.

He starts by seeking analogies in the plant and animal kingdoms. Lettuce, borage, cereals and many others die each year, but hyssop, thyme, savory, basil, marjoram and wormwood live longer. Rosemary will live for sixty years, a vine bear at so many. Ivy will live for a hundred, an oak for eight hundred years. Hardness and density seem to go with longer life. The trees that come into leaf the latest in the year, such as the oak, live the longest.

Animals that have a long period of gestation live longer than those with short. Those that bring forth numerous young at a time, and several times a year, such as rabbits and hare, are short lived; those producing fewer at a time and less often live for longer. Thus, the longest lived is the elephant, which is said to be the slowest in reproduction. It is also the largest, but he thinks rarity of progeny to be a better guide than size. The horse lives not so long as should be expected, barely reaching forty; but we know not the ages of horses we have not bred to our use. The donkey, though smaller, lives to the same age, but the mule, that is a hybrid between them, incapable of begetting or conceiving, outlives either. The dog lives not long for the size and power of the larger breeds, but produces many litters and is a notably hot animal. The age of the cat he gives as only six to ten years. Presumably, this was true of the cats of his day, which were not well cared for, but the pets of our own time live to fourteen or nineteen, exceptionally even to thirty years. Caring owners advise, however, that even when the queen is not spayed, the number of litters she is allowed to bear in a year should be limited, since it is the frequent kittening allowed by nature that wears her out. There is, therefore, here an interference with nature's law that goes toward the making of Bacon's point.

Birds, he notes, for their size, are longer lived than mammals. This may be because feathers protect better than fur, but he rather thinks it is because they have in them more of the nature of the female.

For he begins to distinguish two natures at work in all things: one hot, fiery, lascivious, male and short lived; the other cool, moist, chaste, female and long lived. The former are, while they live, more robust, with greater show of strength; the latter paler, with less show of strength though living longer. The question is, of which kind one would rather be? Hot foods and lusts will make one of the first kind; a cooler way of living, of the second. Perhaps one should take something of both, so as not to be too short lived, yet not too cold. Herbs of the two kinds recommended by him are: *Hot,* saffron, folium Indum, lignum aloes, citron rind, balm. basil, cloves, gilliflowers (carnations or pinks), mons, rosemary, mint, betony, carduus benedictus and – these to be taken only with caution – garlic, watercress, germander, angelica, vervain, valerian, myrrh, spikenard, elder-flowers and chervil; *Cold,* roses, burnet, sandal-wood, camphire, juice of sweet lemons, oranges and apples, and all plants that are under nitre, borage, bugloss, langue de boeuf, strawberries, raspberries, cucumber, vine-buds, violets and all things which have a smell like that of good and pure earth lately turned and dug. Floral odours he deems curative, particularly the scents of violets, roses, wallflowers. carnations and pinks, bean-blossoms, lime flowers, clary, lavender and strawberry plants; but they should be inhaled from the growing plants; when they have been cut their virtue is much less. One should walk or sit among the breaths of such plants.

Odours work most upon the spirits. To treat the heart by vapours he would throw equal parts of vinegar, rose-water and wine upon a hot iron plate, in the morning or at noon; but any heroic desire strengthens the heart.

Procurers of sleep are violets, lettuce (especially boiled), syrop of dry roses, saffron, balm and apples.

Commonly, people feast and make love when in cheerful spirits but neglect pleasures when depressed. This is a mistake; it is when depressed that the spirits need changing and cheering by hot foods.

Age is associated with dryness and shrivelling; one should therefore aim at preserving oils and moistures. Oils of almond and olive conduce marvellously towards longevity and preservation from shrivelling, and should be used for cleaning the skin. Oiling protects it from cold in winter and from sun in summer; only it tends to keep in perspiration so care must be taken the bowels work sufficiently. Woollen garments, having in them something of the sheep's oil, do not draw moisture from the skin as does linen, which absorbs it. One can slightly oil the skin before taking one's bath, which is better not too hot; a little whey or roses may be thrown in one's bath-water.

He wonders the practice of making hot drinks, common amongst the Romans and Greeks, has fallen into disuse. What one wants first thing in the morning, to break one's fast, is not cold fruit juice, beer, whey or barley-water, on one's empty stomach, to chill it, but some hot drink. (Bacon lived before coffee or tea.)

Except in sleep, it is not good for the body to remain long in one posture. If writing or reading, one should make a point of getting up and moving about from time to time. Nevertheless, he doubts if violent exertions improve health. Games or sports involving running, at the utmost of one's strength, over-tire; but bowls, archery, dancing or riding are beneficial, moving the body harmoniously without causing exhaustion.

For those with strong stomachs, a glass of cold water taken last thing before going to bed procures sound sleep.

He fears some of his recommendations may seem a little commonplace but it would hardly be believed with how much care they have been studied.

CHAPTER 71

Sylva Sylvarum

SYLVA *Sylvanum* is a book of jottings. Rawley tells us Bacon would not organise them, saying the present form would better encourage others to add their own.

With every herb, there is an optimum time for infusion. Infuse in one water for half an hour; take out and infuse in a second for like time, and in a third for like time. Then smell and taste the three waters. Usually it will be found the first smells the sweetest, the second tastes the best, and the third is the worst.

Milk is a remedy for consumption but not all can stomach it. If while milking the cow you put in the pail two bags, one containing powder of mint, the other of red roses, the nauseous effect will be taken off. But the pail should be in a larger one of warm water so that the milk is drunk before cooling.

Aristotle believed trees lived longer than animals because their parts which became young and new each year – leaves – drew up the sap, which, passing through the older parts, revivified them. We have no leaves to put forth, yet we do have some parts which retain capacity for renewal: skin, hair, nails. They should be encouraged. Daily friction is a means to this, with the hands, or with a cloth wetted with almond oil or bay-salts.

In medicines and in foods, one should not continue with one for long, though it be good. Things have their strongest effect at first, afterwards losing their power. Change to another, and come back to the first again after one has been off it long enough for it to seem new.

There seems to be a sympathy between certain parts of the body: the feet, being warmed, will cure a head cold, while juices of gilliflower (carnation), rose campion or garlic applied to the wrists and palms have cured long-standing agues of the heart. In fever it is good to hold in the palms alabaster eggs or crystal balls.

There are two great families of things: oil and water. To turn one into the other would be a greater marvel than base metals into gold.

Water is best that runs over pebbles, next best over chalk; worst over mud. He refers to the conservatories of rainwater at Venice as though he had seen them.

Grains of wheat steeped before planting in man's urine, horse's dung, powdered chalk, soot, ashes, bay salts, came up in that order; next, those he had left untreated and last those soaked in warm water; but those soaked in malmsey and spirit of wine came not up at all.

Bringing them indoors, he has had violets, strawberries and peas all the winter. The November rose has a specially sweet scent. Plants which draw different things from the soil help one another, particularly sweet and bitter. Roses smell sweeter if garlic is planted with them; wormwood or rue makes lettuce, cauliflower and artichoke taste sweeter, if grown near to them.

A cucumber has crept towards a pot of water. He has trained cucumbers to grow into strange shapes . . .

CHAPTER 72

"Had I but served my God . . ."

ON January 10th, 1622/3, a report was sent to King James that Bacon had applied to see papers relating to the time of Henry VIII. The question is whether he wanted access with regard to his prose history of that reign, of which he only wrote two pages, or the play *Henry VIII*. Baconians generally feel that in the fall of Wolsey, Bacon was describing his own, but there are difficulties.

First as to date: on July 2nd, 1613, Sir Henry Wotton wrote to Sir Edmund Bacon describing a performance of "a new play called *All is True*" at which, when the cannons were fired, on Henry's entry to Wolsey's house, the Globe caught fire and burnt down. It is generally thought the reference is to "chambers discharged", *Henry VIII*, I, iv, 49. The late Dr. Gerstenberg, on the other hand, wrote to me that none of the other history plays by our author have titles like *All is true*. All have simply the King's name. Samuel Rowley's play about Henry VIII was entitled *When You See Me You Know Me*, and Thomas Heywood's about Elizabeth *If you know not me you know nobody*. He thought the Globe must have burned down at a performance of a lost play by Heywood. However, Sir Thomas Puckering, writing the day after the fire, says it happened, "while Bourbage and his companie were acting at the Globe the play of Hen:8."

Some have contended different hands were at work in the play. Spedding and Hickson made metrical tests, as a result of which they assigned to Shakespeare I, i, and ii; II, iii and iv, III, ii from the beginning of line 203; and V, i. The rest they gave to Fletcher. These tests have been criticised, notably by Peter Alexander, and by F.J. Furnivall, who said, "Counting words can never be a better judge than real criticism." Professor Partridge agreed that metrical tests within isolated lines were inapplicable, yet felt that the style of the alleged Fletcher parts was more modern. He therefore made his own tests, which he presents in his book *Orthography in Shakespeare and Elizabethan Drama* (Arnold, 1964). Counts had shown that "has", "does", " 'em" and "ye" or "y" to be used more frequently by Fletcher than by Shakespeare, who used relatively more of "hath", "doth", "them" and "you", the Fletcher forms representing the modern trend of the period. He, therefore, counted up the number of instances of each of these forms in each scene of the play and tabulated his results, which do correspond to those of the metrical tests. The only reason for calling the modern forms "Fletcher" is that he was a younger dramatist writing in the more modern style. I have, however, noticed that there is a great deal of " 'em" in *Timon of Athens,* which may mark a transition in Bacon's style. Since he had thought to bid farewell to the theatre with *The Tempest,* Bacon had risen to the highest office in the land, and now was dashed to nothing. Shakespeare was dead, so unless he had a new scribe he would have to write with his own hand. It is a fact that when an artist or writer leaves off for a very long period, his style, when he begins again, is often different, more in keeping with the later times.

In any case, critical opinion is now moving back towards acceptance of the whole play as Shakespeare's. R.A. Foakes, in his Introduction to it in the New Arden, 1958, stresses its tonal oneness with the Romances, its similarities with *Cymbeline,* and its counterpointing of *King John,* the earliest of the great series. He sees in the pageantry of Anne Boleyn's coronation a reflection of that at the Princess Elizabeth's wedding, and supposes it was this that sent the author's mind back to the wedding of Henry VIII and Anne.

Dr. Yates, endorsing this view, points out that the cedar-image and prophecy, in *Henry VIII* as in *Cymbeline,* refers to King James, and supposes *Henry VIII* to have been written in the brief period between the Princess Elizabeth's wedding and the Bohemian tragedy.

Indeed, it is difficult to conceive Bacon would pen a tribute to him after he let his daughter down. It is possible that he wrote the play, in 1613, in one mood, and later took it up again, when bitter experience had caused him to have more feeling for Cardinal Wolsey in his fall.

Edward Castle, a barrister, is interested in the pageantry, too, but from a different point of view.[1] He notices that the stage directions concerning the two processions, into the ecclesiastical courtroom at Blackfriars, II, iv, and for Anne's coronation, IV, i, appear very full, yet are not impeccable. An attempt has been made to give to all the dignitaries their correct insignia. The Archbishop of Canterbury enters, followed by Bishops, then Cardinals Wolsey and Campeggio; yet only two silver crosses are borne by the attendants. From Cavendish, the dramatist's apparent source, we know that Wolsey had two silver crosses, one as Archbishop, the other as Papal Legate; if the two borne are both for him, Campeggio who was also a Papal Legate, and the Archbishop of Canterbury are both denied. On the other hand, things are borne which have no place to be there. The purse containing the Great Seal and the Cardinal's hat are for Wolsey, but what is the silver mace doing? Bacon, when he sat in Chancery, was preceded, as he entered and left, by gentlemen, the one bearing the purse with the Great Seal, upon a cushion, the other bearing his mace. Wolsey doubled his ecclesiastical offices with the Chancellorship, so that purse and mace would have preceded him when he appeared in his office as Lord Chancellor; but would he have brought these things into an ecclesiastical

court, where he sat as Cardinal and Legate but not as Chancellor? The
purse is mentioned before the hat; and in the coronation procession, the
hat has been forgotten. Wolsey's power was mainly as Papal Legate, but
the dramatist is conscious of him chiefly as Lord Chancellor.

Castle supports Lord Campbell's opinion that to Shakespeare's law
there can be "neither writ nor demeurer", but does not think it could
have been picked up by perhaps working for a time in a lawyer's office, or
even that the mind at work is that of a country judge. Details point to the
Chancery. In the coronation procession, we read, "Mayor of London
bearing his mace," which seems hard on him. Surely he would have had
his mace-bearer to carry it before him. Mayors, like ecclesiastics, are not
observed closely. But nothing is missed relating to the "Lord Chancellor,
with purse and mace before him."

It was, however, Dr. Gerstenberg who drew to my attention that to the
historical Wolsey, in his fall, came only two people to take the Seal away
from him; in the play, as to Bacon, four.

I checked this, with A.F. Pollard's *Wolsey,* (1929), pp.254-55,
278-29, and with Holinshed, who would have been the dramatist's
source. It was two persons only, the Dukes of Norfolk and Suffolk, who
came to require the Seal of Wolsey. So why, in the play, where
Holinshed's text is otherwise followed very closely, do we read, "Enter to
Wolsey the Dukes of Norfolk and Suffolk, the Earl of Surrey, and the Lord
Chamberlain"? Why should Shakespeare have invented the extras?
There entered to Bacon, to take the Seal from him, four, The Lord
Treasurer (Suffolk), the Lord Steward, the Lord Chamberlain and the Earl
of Arundel (Spedding, XIV, p.262). It is also interesting that in the play,
whereas Norfolk, Suffolk and Surrey all use contumelious language to
Wolsey, the Lord Chamberlain does not so, but breaks the flow of their
invective, saying, "Press not a falling man too far . . . My heart weeps to
see him so little of his great self." (III, ii, 333-36). Note that the scene is
one of those containing the modern forms. Since the Lord Chamberlain
did not come at all to Wolsey, but only his two bitterest enemies,
Norfolk and Suffolk, this would seem to be an inexplicable invention of
the dramatist. But the Lord Chamberlain of Bacon's time was the Earl of
Pembroke, who was one of the best friends of his latter years. He would,
therefore, have hated being one of the four sent to take the Seal from him,
and if the other three had been contumelious in their bearing towards
Bacon, it is likely he would have dissociated himself from the insults
offered, as he is shown doing in the play.

Wolsey's policy had been quite different from Bacon's. But they had
both, while in office, been magnificent, and Bacon, after his fall, would
have felt the similarity in their cases. In the play, Wolsey says:

Had I but served my God with half the zeal

I served my King, he would not in mine age
Have left me naked to mine enemies.

III, ii, 455-57

On September 5th, 1621, Bacon had written to the King concerning the want into which his fall had plunged him. To the body of the drafted letter, he added a postscript:[2]

Cardinal Wolsey said, that if he had pleased God as he pleased the King, he had not been ruined.

The postscript was omitted from the fair copy sent, but remains to show us the trend of his thoughts.

1. *Shakespeare, Bacon, Jonson and Greene,* Edward Castle, (Sampson Low, 1897).
2. Lambeth, Gibson Papers, viii, p.242.

CHAPTER 73

Considerations touching
a war with Spain

AT the turn of the year 1622/3, Francis gave up Bedford House, and
from now onwards stayed, when in London, at Gray's Inn.

King James was convinced the only way to recover the Palatinate was
to engage Prince Charles to the Spanish Infanta and ask the return of his
other child's (and his spouse's) country as part of the marriage
settlement. Moreover, the King of Spain played him along. This makes it
very peculiar that Prince Charles and Buckingham now left for Spain in
feeble disguise, with false beards, apparently without King James'
knowledge. As he was the person who most desired the match, one
wonders whether the appearance of their having stolen away was to divert
from James the wrath of the English, to whom the idea would be most
unwelcome. In Spain, the Prince was received cordially, but it was made
plain the Infanta's hand was his only on condition of his becoming a
Catholic. There was an alarming episode in which Prince Charles, in a
rowing boat, the sea turning choppy, was nearly drowned, and
the excursion ended bitterly.

The relief in England was enormous, and the return of the travellers
greeted with bonfires and rejoicings. Ostensibly, the celebrations were for
Prince Charles' physical safety, actually, for his coming back with all
thoughts of the Spanish match abandoned.

Bacon had been silent whilst the Spanish negotiations were in progress,
but now he sent Prince Charles a paper, *Considerations touching a war
with Spain:*[1]

Your Highness hath an imperial name . . . A War with Spain (if the King shall
enter into it) is a mighty work; it requireth strong materials and active motions.

The aim should be the recovery of the Palatinate. As to Bohemia, he
did not claim perfectly to understand its customs and constitution. Yet he
would say in passage, that in an elective monarchy, the monarch could
not be so free and absolute as in an hereditary.

So that if the part of the people or estate be somewhat in the election, you cannot
make them nulls and ciphers . . . And if it be said this is a dangerous opinion for
the Pope, Emperor and all Elective Kings, it is true it is a dangerous opinion, and
ought to be a dangerous opinion, to all such personal Popes, Emperors or Elective
Kings as shall transcend their limits and become tyrannical.

In other words, he feels that the people of Bohemia had some right to depose Ferdinand II and offer the Crown to Frederick and Elizabeth. But while that was a matter debated, there could be no doubt that the Spanish incursion into the Palatinate was wrongful; "the Palatinate is in their talons".

He goes on to practical considerations. Spain appears a formidable power, yet he thinks her strength not in truth so great. "Spain is no overmatch for England."

He sent a copy of this paper to the Queen of Bohemia.

To go to such lengths, he must have felt very deeply. It was probably this which had caused King James to fear him as Chancellor.

No English intervention was made on the continent. What had come of the brave Bohemian venture was the beginning of the Thirty Years War, by which central Europe was devastated. Perhaps, had we gone in we should have had a central Europe closely affiliated to ourselves. But our present Royal family descends from Elizabeth, the Queen of Bohemia; who was Imogen and Perdita.

1. British Museum, Harleian MSS, 37, f.2(A).

CHAPTER 74

The painting and the bust

SOME time between Shakespeare's death and now, the memorial bust by Gheerat Jansen was errected in Holy Trinity Church, Stratford-on-Avon. Many people feel it to be of the same man as the Chandos painting in the National Portrait Gallery labelled 'William Shakespeare'. Experts, Dr. Roy Strong and Mr. David Piper, confirm it to be of his period, without finding proof of identification. The gold earring suggests an actor in one of his parts. In 1719 George Vertue recorded he had been told by the antiquary, Francis Keck, who gave as his source the actor, Thomas Betterton, that it had been painted by the actor, John Taylor, and given by him to the actor Sir William Davenant. Betterton had acquired it after Davenant's death, Keck after Betterton's. As there was no actor John Taylor known of, it is always supposed the reference was to Joseph Taylor, though not a painter, the actor brought in from a different company to replace Burbage on his sudden death. Yet this provenance is curious. Portraits, because not usually made unless commissioned, tend to become property of the sitter, and so to descend through his family, whereas this has descended through the theatre. There is no mention of it in Shakespeare's will, and it is strangely like the self-portrait by Burbage, the actor, who also painted, which hangs in the Dulwich Art Gallery. Forehead and hair, eye-colour and face, small white collar on black suit and the angle at which the head is turned to the viewer are all the same. It is as though the Chandos were a professional artist's painting made from the actor's amateur self-portrait. The illness of Burbage was so sudden he had no time to make a written will, but only a nuncuperative, a statement by mouth before witnesses, that he left to his wife all sources of income that would survive him. A portrait could have been forgotten. Actors tend to keep in their dressing-rooms things they like to look at, old playbills, pictures of themselves in former roles. Taylor would have moved into the dressing-room which had been occupied by Burbage, and the things in it, unless somebody came for them, would come to be thought of as his; the portrait, if it was there that it was kept, along with the ''props'', the make-up and the nick-nacks.

In the Stratford bust the features are too small and too close together for the face, but the high domed skull and hair-shape appear to have been suggested by the Chandos, and the same little white collar is worn. He holds a pen, with which he appears to be writing, not upon the sheet of paper beneath the left hand, but upon the cushion, which serves him in the place of a desk or table.

It was first noticed by Charlotte Stopes that the reproduction of it in Dugdale's *Antiquities of Warwickshire*, 1656, is dissimilar in giving the figure a lean and scraggy type of face, and instead of the flat and neat cushion, ''a large cushion, suspiciously resembling a woolsack''.[1]

And Charlotte Stopes believed Shakespeare wrote Shakespeare! But it is true that in the Dugdale one sees clearly a large, softly bulging sack, open at both ends, the four corners tied with cords. Wool, and no other commodity, is regularly kept in sacks such as this. Was Dugdale, by making it more obvious, seeking to draw attention to the nature of the cushion used by the sculpted figure to write upon? Baconians have contended that the present bust was substituted for an original one, which resembled that shown by Dugdale, taken down in the eighteenth century for repairs. This view is based largely on reference by the Rev. Joseph Greene to ''the original'' monument. Scrutiny of Greene's correspondence,[2] however, convinces me that he is comparing the new monument to Shakespeare within Westminster Abbey with the original one in Holy Trinity, where he was Rector, and for which he had a patriotic preference. Dugdale may have been having his own little joke, but the Woolsack in the House of Lords is neater and flatter than the vulgar ones used in the trade, a smoothly stuffed rectangle, without bulges, secured at the four corners not with cords but with elegant tassels, such as tie that smooth cushion in Holy Trinity Church.

If what we see there today is the original, then our greatest poet has sat from the beginning writing his immortal works upon what looks suspiciously like the Lord Chancellor's seat in the House of Lords.

---

1. 'The Story of the Stratford Bust', Charlotte Stopes, *The Monthly Magazine*, 1904.
2. *The Correspondence of the Rev. Joseph Greene of Stratford-on-Avon, 1712-80* (H.M. Stationery Office).

CHAPTER 75

The Folio

THE first Folio edition of Shakespeare's plays appeared in 1623. On the title-page is an engraving of Shakespeare, by Martin Droeshout, from an unknown original. The huge domed forehead looks almost hydrocephalous, there is no proper modelling of the face, the head does not grow naturally from a neck, but is stuck upon a huge, plate-like wire collar, with no opening, so that the wearer could never get out of it, beneath which are shoulders far too small. These are strangely clad, for the figure is wearing two left sleeves one of them sewn to the doublet back to front. The chin-line is so hard as to suggest the edge of a mask. The whole impression created is of a primitive; yet art was not primitive in 1623.

Sir Edwin Durning-Lawrence thought Droeshout must have been instructed to represent an impossible figure that could not be mistaken for anything but a mock-up. Stratfordians suppose Droeshout to have been an inexperienced artist, unable to do better. Yet, if he could do no better, why did those who produced the volume not obtain somebody who could? A considerable price was charged for it, £1; that is £500 in today's money, per copy. Publishers producing such a *de luxe* volume would surely not hesitate to pay the fee of a competent artist.

Whereas *Venus and Adonis* and *The Rape of Lucrece* had been dedicated to the Earl of Southampton, the Folio is dedicated to the brothers, William Herbert, 3rd Earl of Pembroke, and Philip Herbert, Earl of Montgomery. Bacon's relations with Southampton had ceased to be friendly, but Pembroke must have done something at the moment of his fall to lessen the blow, for Bacon wrote to thank him for it. Moreover, Pembroke had been trying to obtain support for Frederick and Elizabeth, and was of Bacon's view concerning Bohemia and the Palatinate. Of his brother, Bacon was in the following January to write, "There is not an honester man than Montgomery",[1] and again, "Montgomery is an honest man and a good observer."[2] They were relatives of George Herbert.

This is the more interesting in that Greg remarks that if Pollard should be right in supposing the first edition of the Folio to have been of only 500 copies, or even if the editors of the Oxford facsimile edition should be correct in giving the number as 600, with the price of £1 (£500), it would hardly have been an attractive commercial proposition, unless the publishers received some support "from the Earls of Pembroke and Montgomery, and our debt to those two noble brothers may be greater than we have hitherto suspected.''³

Commander Pares thinks it may have been intended as a present to Bacon, to make up for what had happened.⁴

One immense question looms up. If it happened in this way, did he know about it whilst it was going through the press? One major problem of Shakespeare scholarship would be solved, that which concerns the plays, *Hamlet, Othello, 2 King Henry IV* and *Troilus and Cressida*, the texts of which have mysteriously altered and expanded since their appearance in Quarto. The usual explanation offered is that the printers must somehow have obtained alternative texts, full texts of which the Quartos represented versions with stage cuts. There are difficulties to this theory. One is that a producer cutting to reduce the time a play will take to act tries to take out only the dullest passages, whereas, as Commander Pares has shown in the case of *Othello,*⁵ some of the lines imagined to have been cut are most dramatically effective. If, however, the author was in the know concerning the production, there is a simpler solution: he took the opportunity to work over and expand some of the plays. But there are what appear to be errors in pagination or printers' mistakes. There are three possibilities:

He did not see the proofs

He was a poor proof-reader

They are not mistakes

Baconians generally favour the last solution.

I know no way in which the question could be treated, except by dealing separately with each and every one. I will therefore limit myself to the indication of a few places where there is strong Baconian contention the text is correct as it stands.

Mr. Ewen Macduff objects to the customary emendation of ''latten'' to ''Latin'' in *The Merry Wives of Windsor*, IV, i, 50. ''Latten is a word!'' The line is ''Hang hog is latten for Bacon.'' (Folio). The pretext for changing ''latten'' into ''Latin'' is that Mistress Quickly's cue is ''Hung, hang, hog'', Evans' attempt at ''Hic, hac, hoc.'' Latten is an alloy of copper, zinc, lead and tin. This, to Mr. Macduff, suggests a mix up not of molten metals but of Bacon. He sees an analogy with the *Apothegms* in which Sir Nicholas Bacon is cited as telling a felon who claims kindred with him because his name is Hog, ''Hog is not Bacon until it is well hanged''.⁴ The *Apothegms* were a collection of witty sayings, by many persons, ancient and modern, made by Bacon but some were not published until after his death, by William Rawley. This particular one comes from the third edition, which Spedding considers to have been augmented by spurious ones, though Mr. Macduff considers this one genuine. In as much as the possibility is there, it would perhaps be preferable for editors of the play not to presume to know better than the author what he meant.

However, quite the most famous textual emendation ever made is that to *King Henry V,* II, iii, 17–18. Mistress Quickly tells us how Falstaff died: "his nose was as sharp as a Pen on a Table of greene fields." The eighteenth century editor, Theobald Lewis, decided this did not make sense and emended to "his nose as sharp as a pen 'a babbled of greene fields." This was such a touchingly idyllic conversion as to seem inspired, though some pointed out that "a Table" for "a babbled" would be an aural mistake, not such as would arise from the compositor's misreading of the author's handwriting. Moreover, nothing in the character of Falstaff, as it has been built up, suggests that he would, in his last moments, babble of green fields.

Mr. Roderick Eagle contends the words are correct as printed in the folio.[7] He points out that the symptoms of approaching death, as described by Mistress Quickley, so closely tally with those listed by Hippocrates as to suggest the author's familiarity with that ancient writer. He knows of no English translation in Shakespeare's time, though there were Latin versions. In most, the Greek word Χλωρός was rendered "pallidus", yet the later physicians, Galen and Cardan, explained that it meant light green. He quotes Galen:

> The ancients assumed that Χλωρός means merely pale; it is rather the colour of cabbage or lettuce.

and the sixteenth century Italian Cardan:

> The difficulty is what does Χλωρός mean? . . . Who does not know that in Greece the face of a dying man is of a green colour?

Mr. Eagle reminds us Sappho wrote:

> My face is paler than the grass,
> To die would seem no more.
> *(Thomas Davidson's translation)*

Mr. Eagle then quotes *The Rape of Lucrece,* line 72, and *Sonnet* 2, for the use of "field" to mean face. Had Mr. Eagle's mind been bawdy, he could also have found "field" used for other parts of the body, in the sense of field for conquest, with overtones that marry with the bawdy use of "nose" and "pen" for penis.[8]

We now have an image of extraordinary power; the old lecher dies, his nose, the flesh shrunk from it, sharpened to a plain penis-symbol, jutting over, not the warm fields of a woman's declivities, but the flattened fields of his own cheeks, turned the green of death.

Is anybody going to say this came by a printer's error?

1. Lambeth, Gibson Papers, vol. viii, f.179.
2. Lambeth, Gibson Papers, vol. viii, f.192.

3. 'The First Folio and its Publishers', W.W. Greg; in *Studies in the First Folio* (O.U.P. for the Shakespeare Association, 1923), p.156.

4. Pares to myself, oral.

5. 'Othello', Martin Pares (*Baconiana*, December, 1973).

6. Spedding, VII, p.185.

7. 'The Death of Falstaff', Roderick Eagle (*Baconiana*) 1972, December.

8. *Shakespeare's Bawdy*, Eric Partridge (Routledge, 1947), pp. 159 and 163.

CHAPTER 76

Cryptomenytices

IN Germany, but with the text in Latin, there now appeared a book, *Cryptomenytices et Cryptographiae Libri IX. In quibus & planissima Stenographiae a Johanne Trithemio* . . . Gustavi Selini (Lunaeburg, 1624). With such a title it is hardly surprising its elaborately pictorial title-page (Plate 17) should itself have been scanned for possible cryptographic significance.

Above and beneath, to right and to left of the entablature are pictures. Those which flank it are the easiest to understand, and are plainly paired.

In the one on the left, we see a man wearing a tall hat giving a book, or rectangular sheet of paper with writing, where one would expect to see the title of a book, to a man who is wearing actor's buskins, and who holds in his other hand a long spear and a hat, from the band of which projects a sprig of leaves, the shape of bays. He carries on his back a satchel. It would not be usual for a man wearing or carrying a civilian hat (which presumably he has doffed to the tall hatted man, who is more nobly dressed) while carrying a spear, so perhaps there is cryptic significance. Let us look further. Behind these two foreground figures, there is, on the road to a town nestling under a mountain, what appears to be the actor again, for he has the same buskins, and the same hat, though now on his head, and he is still carrying the spear, in one hand, whilst with the other he leans on a stick. Again, it is difficult to envisage the circumstance in which a man would go out with a spear in one hand and a walking-stick in the other, since he could not be at once so strong as to be able to throw a spear and so feeble as to need a stick. We do not, now, see the book: on the other hand, the satchel, which before had hung on his back as if empty, is now bulging. He must have put the book in the satchel, or rather, a great many books. It looks as though he went to the tall-hatted gentleman to get his satchel filled. Within the town to which he goes, there rises one dominating building, with high walls, rounded. Is it a round fortress? Within and above the outer walls is a small, raised rectangular part. No, it is not a fortress, it is a theatre, a round one, and this highest part is that which houses the wires and other mechanisms for the floating of fairies and deities, raising and lowering of curtain or backcloth or other contrivances necessary for stage effects. Behind the town with the theatre is a mountain, sloping from the left to the right, then dipping slightly, as if to a pass, though the entablature prevents our seeing the other side. In the sky is a large bird, holding in its beak another book or paper with writing. The bird is set amidst lightning flashes. Towards this flies a missile, with arrowhead and feathers.

On the left of the entablature we see the same man, on horseback this time, still in his actor's buskins fitted now with a very large spur and wearing the same hat, with the leaves. He is not an experienced rider, for he lets the reins hang so loose that should the horse bolt he would be unable quickly to regain control. His satchel is now strapped behind him on the horse's back, and in his hand he holds a horn, which he is blowing. He is nearer than before to the town, where the theatre is prominent. We see the mountain again, this time sloping from the right towards a peak, from which there is a slight descent leftwards towards a central pass. For it is obviously the same mountain, which appears in the two pictures flanking the entablature. It is a two-peaked mountain, with the entablature between the peaks.

Let us look again at the gentleman in the left-hand picture. He wears Bacon's tall hat, with the curving brim that distinguishes it from the Puritan tall hat, with the hatband shown in the Simon Pass and the brim turned up in the way that Spedding takes to identify any descendant of the Pass.[1] The design on his sleeves, though sketchily indicated, looks much like that shown in the Van Somer, but there is something odd about what purports to be his cloak. From his neck, it falls down his back, opening out to become a three-dimensional bag, closed at the base, so that it could never be drawn round him, but is bulked out to show that it has concealed contents. He carries something secret in the folds of his cloak. Perhaps it is from his cloaked bag that he gives to Shakespeare the book which the latter puts into his satchel.

Durning-Lawrence, though he did not notice the cloak-bag, took the designs to represent Bacon giving the plays to Shakespeare and the latter riding away with them. The spear and spur he took as alternative rebuses for the second syllable of the actor's name, which some scholars believe to have been pronounced short. The horn would be to create publicity for the plays, which he was taking to the town. Unaccountably, Durning-Lawrence missed what I believe to be the only picture of the Globe Theatre. The Globe was not set amongst mountains, but then the twin-peaked mountain behind it is obviously Mount Parnassus, which had twin peaks. The big bird, Sir Edwin suggests, is Jove's eagle; the missile will have to wait for explanation.

In the picture below the entablature are again two men. One is seated at a desk, on which he is writing. As he is indoors, he is not wearing a hat. But though he is now clothed in a long and comfortable looking gown, the sleeves which appear through its shorter ones bear the same pattern as in the first picture, of him in his tall hat. The other man, who stands behind him, looks oddly unreal. If he is meant to represent the spearbearer of the first picture, he is no longer in his coarse cloth, but in what looks like silk, or perhaps, since it shows up the pattern so sharply as to suggest that it is very shiny, satin. His head is not properly located on his shoulders. It is set so far to one side that the distance from the other is impossibly long. Indeed, as in the Droeshout, it does not grow from the shoulders on a neck, but sits impossibly on its wired collar. This is the more remarkable in that all the other figures are perfectly well drawn, showing the artist's ability correctly to depict the human figure when he wished. I cannot identify the cord-like object held in his left hand, one end of which goes half round his own waist while the other seems to be attached to the belt of the seated author; but in his right hand he holds above the author's head, like a crown, a cap of maintenance, symbol of dignity. Behind him there is a huge curtain, which is unrelated to the windows and seems to descend from the centre of the ceiling, looped up at the side. It looks like one of the pair of curtains draping the proscenium arch of a theatre, being partially drawn back. To the right is a notable arch. This may be decoration, or, in connection with the curious crown, intended to suggest the Royal Arch degree in Masonry.

Durning-Lawrence refers the reader to *The Return from Pernassus* (see above p.236); the passage about the actors:

> England affords these glorious vagabonds,
> That carried erst their fardels on their backs,
> Coursers to ride on through the gazing streets,
> Sooping it in their glaring satten sutes,
> And Pages to attend their maisterships:
> With mouthing words that better wits have framed,
> They purchase lands, and now Esquires are made.

He thinks it is Shakespeare, who is shown in the picture on the left of the entablature with a fardel on his back, in the picture on the right on his courser, and here in the bottom picture ''sooping it in satten''.

Durning-Lawrence further directs the reader's attention to William Camden's *Remaines Concerning Britaine,* 1605, where, in the chapter on surnames, one will read:

Break-speare, Shake-speare, Shot-bolt, Wagstaff, Bagot in the old Norman; the same with Scipio, that is a stay, or walking staff with the Latines, which became a surname, for that Cornelius served as a stay to his blind father.

Durning-Lawrence thinks that on this basis Wagstaff and Shot-bolt are being used in *Cryptomenytices* as synonyms for Shakespeare (he might have added that Nicholas Brakespeare was, until Bacon's time, the only famous man of St. Albans). That, Sir Edwin Durning-Lawrence thinks is the reason why in the left-hand design Shakespeare walks with a staff in the hand not holding a spear. A further point he might have made is that Scipio was the distinguished Roman suspected of writing Terence's plays for him. But in any case, Scipio means staff, so that Wagstaff and Scipio seem to bridge the gap between Shake-speare and Shot-bolt. As one cannot see whether it is from a bow or a crossbow the feathered missile in the left-hand picture has been shot, one cannot say whether it is an arrow or a shot-bolt.

If this is the key, then the eagle presenting the book to the shot-bolt, as synonym for Shakespeare, simply reduplicates the representation of Bacon giving the book to the buskined actor.

Did Camden construct the passage with forethought as to the cryptic meaning that could be derived from it? The ornament beneath the chapter-heading is upside down, an apparent printer's mistake which Durning-Lawrence believes often used to signify something cryptographic to follow. Spedding refers us to a copy in Camden's *Annales* in the Cottonian library which bears on blank pages notes in the hand of Bacon. Spedding says:

I suppose that Camden had lent the MS to Bacon to read and criticise; that Bacon had returned it with these passages suggested for insertion; and that they had been inserted accordingly, either by Camden himself or by someone to whom the MS was entrusted.

Spedding, VI, p.352.

Above the entablature, is the only picture contained not in a rectangle but in an oval. The three grotesque faces supporting it are probably, as Durning-Lawrence says, the conventional masks of Tragedy, Comedy and Farce. But what is depicted within? There are men in a rowing-boat on a choppy sea, making for a shore on which there is a town sporting beacon-baskets. I am not happy about Durning-Lawrence's interpretation of this:

It represents *The Tempest* of Shakespeare and tells you that the play is filled with Bacon lights. (In the sixteenth century Beacon was pronounced Bacon. 'Bacon was the Beacon of the state').

Laymen seldom realise how complex is the history of sound-changes. The sound heard in ''beacon'' would then have been more open, but so would that in Bacon. In phonetician's language, the sound heard in ''beacon'' today is a close front vowel (English vowel no. 1); in those days it would have been a half-close front vowel, nearer to Cardinal vowel No. 2. The sound in Bacon today is a diphthong, but would then have been a half-open front vowel, near Cardinal vowel 3. The sounds would, then as now, have been in different phonemes, with about the same interval between them.

Imperfect puns have always been with us, but to me the scene evokes not *The Tempest* but the return of Prince Charles after his narrow escape from drowning in the rowing-boat in the water off Spain (one of the figures in the boat is not rowing but a passenger) and the bonfires that were lit in London to welcome him. It is not an uninhabited island to which the little boat is putting in, for it is a town which is putting out the beacon-baskets, a town in which one sees again the Globe Theatre, and behind it, as before, Mount Parnassus. One sees both of its peaks.

The book, then, is surely the work of an Englishman, very glad, as were the people of London, to have Prince Charles safe˙back home, having escaped engagement to marry the Spanish Infanta. I think it is his cryptographic dedication of the book to Prince Charles.

1. Spedding, I, p.xviii.

CHAPTER 77

The starting of a witch

THERE is a pastoral fragment, entitled *The Sad Shepherd,* commonly printed as part of Jonson's works because found amongst his papers after his death. Yet it is totally unlike anything to which he put his name while he was alive. First there is a question as to date. The Prologue begins:

> He that hath feasted you these forty yeares,
> And fitted Fables, for your finer eares,
> Although at first, he scarce could hit the bore;
> Yet you, with patience harkning more and more,
> At length have growne up to him . . .

Here is the indication that it was a mature work, also the suggestion the reader needed to have matured, along with the author in order to be ready for it. From the internal evidence I can suggest a date. It is set in Sherwood and an attempt is made to imitate the dialect of the district, the characters often using for the present participle "and" instead of "-ing", as "barkeand" and barking. In Jonson's masque *The Fortunate Isles,* 1625, designed for the Court on Twelfth Night but finished by December 1624, Jophiel inappropriately drops into this on just one occasion, as "tinkling rime! and flowand verse!" As there is no reason why Jupiter's Intelligencer should speak with the dialect of Nottinghamshire, I think it must have been in 1624 that Jonson was deep in *The Sad Shepherd.* But I do not think he wrote it.

That it has Shakespearean connections has been noted with respect to *Othello.*[1] The belt described by the witch Maudlin to help her daughter recognise her, as she will be:

> In mony shapes tu day; where you spie
> This browdred belt, with Characters, 'tis I.
> A Gypsan Ladie, and a right Beldame,
> Wrought it by Moone-shine for mee, and Star-light,
> Upo' your Granams grave, that verie night
> We earth'd her, in the shades; when our Dame *Hecat,*
> Made it her gaing-night, over the Kirk-yard,
> With all the barkeande parish tykes set at her,
> While I sate whirland of my brasen spindle:
> At every twisted thrid my rock let flie
> Unto the sew'ster . . . which ran each spell
> She stitched in the worke . . .

II, iii, 37–49

has some community with the handkerchief given by Othello to Desdemona, which had been given to him by an Egyptian enchantress, as having been stitched by a Sybil, who had worked her prophetic fury into it.

I shall seek to show that the fragment exhibits far closer links with *The Tempest*, also to some extent with *Two Gentlemen of Verona.*

It opens with Robin Hood's decision that he and his men should give a banquet in the forest to all the shepherds and shepherdesses. One swain, Aeglamour, is however, too sad to accept, weeping for his lost love, whom he believes drowned in the Trent, declaring that when her body is washed up, he will still embrace it, to show that not even death can lessen his devotion. In *Two Gentlemen of Verona,* that other play concerned with the Robin Hood legend, Aeglamour swore eternal chastity on his dead love's grave. Why are these two themes for the second time connected? The *alfresco* banquet to which Robin and his guests were about to sit down is, however, stolen from them by the witch, Maudlin, disguised as Maid Marian. This is a reversal of the situation in *The Tempest,* where the banquet the ship-wrecked men were about to consume is snatched and made to vanish by Ariel, disguised as a harpy. We next learn that Earine was not, as Aeglamour thinks, drowned, it was the witch Maudlin who had "shut the maiden up in a tree, as her sonnes prize, if he could winne her; or his prey, if he would force her." This recalls the witch Sycorax, who had shut Ariel up in a tree, and her son Caliban's attempt on Miranda.

There is another curious resemblance. In *The Tempest*, Caliban is afflicted with:

> cramps,
> Side-stitches that shall pen thy breath up
>
> *I, ii, 325-26*

Prospero is unable to improve Caliban, for:

> . . . as with age his body uglier grows,
> So the mind cankers.
>
> *IV, i, 191-92*

and shortly after that he says:

> Go, charge my goblins that they grind their joints
> With dry convulsions; shorten up their sinews
> With aged cramps.
>
> *IV, i, 259-61*

The notion witches' spells may cause all manner of evils is as ancient as it is primitive, but note that the afflictions here brought together are all symptomatic of old age.

Now listen to the witch Maudlin cursing the cook:

The Swilland Dropsie enter in
The lazie Cuke, and swell his skin;
And the old Mort-mal on his shin
Now prick, and itch, withouten him.
. . .
The Paene wee call S.Antons fire,
The Gout, or what we can desire,
To crampe a Cuke . . .

II, vi, 61-68

Friar Tuck perceives the effect of the spell:

Poore Tom, the Cooke, is taken! All his joynts
Do crack, as if his Limbes were tied with points:
His whole frame slackens; and a kind of rack
Runs downe along the Spondylls of his back;
A Gowt, or Crampe, now seizeth up his head,
Then falls into his feet; his knees are lead;
And he can stirre his either hand, no more
Than a dead stumpe . . .

II, vii, 1-9

Every one of the complaints is a symptom of old age. One of the shepherds says, "Shee must by some device restrained bee." Robin and his men then go off upon "Witch-hunting, Or starting of a Hag." As one bores one's way into this fragment, one may come to wonder if it is not the witch as a malevolent old woman but old age, personified in the witch, the hunters are trying to run to earth:

Within a gloomie dimble, shee doth dwell,
Downe in a pitt, ore-growne with brakes and briars,
Close by the ruines of a shaken Abbey
Torne, with an Earth-quake, down unto the ground,
'Mongst graves and grotts, neare an old Channell house
. . .
                                    in the foggs
And rotten Mistes, upon the fens and boggs . . .

II, viii, 15-25

This knobbly piece of Gothic is, in the very texture of the verse, as well as in the mood, far more "Shakespearean" than Jonsonian, and may explain the "unwholesome fen" Caliban thought of as the habitat of his mother, though so unlikely either on Bermuda or a Mediterranean island. But I think what the hunters are after is the cause of old age and death.
    In the Prologue, it is said:

Old Trent . . .
. . . shall grow young againe

29-30

If one leaves out the intervening words, one has simply the statement, "Old shall grow young again", and this, I believe, is the real theme of the play, not enciphered but enfolded within the cover-story.

The name Earine is the Greek word for Spring with "'ine'" added—perhaps by way of Martial's epigram (IX, xi, 1-2) on a slave, Earinos, whose name meant Spring—and Aeglamour repeatedly relates Earine to the season and its flowers. She is, then, as surely as Perdita, Proserpina. We are still in the atmosphere of the Mother and Daughter mysteries, Demeter and Persephone for the Greeks, Ceres and Proserpina for the Romans. Since we have Proserpina, is Ceres somewhere about?

The fragment refers (II, ii, 20) to "An aged Oake, the King of all the field". In Sherwood, this can only be that massive oak, venerated for its antiquity and because it is said that Robin Hood hid in it, and that it formed a rallying point for his men. This oak, as I realised while walking in its neighbourhood, stands near to a grotto or "gloomie dimble" and cave in the escarpment of a stream. This, if the author walked there, with his mind running, as so often, on the *Aeneid,* would have been enough to put him in mind of that other oak, near to both the Sybil's cave and the gateway to Avernus, from which Aeneas had to pluck the Golden Bough before Proserpina would permit him to descend into Pluto's kingdom and to return alive. It would not come off unless he were really one whom the Fates called; the Golden Bough, having been plucked would immediately regrow, so as to be ready for the next candidate, resembling the phoenix, ever reborn, as it burned away.

In the Prologue to the fragment, play is made with the name of Hood as a head-covering. In the circumstances, this recalls Pluto's helmet of invisibility.

If Bacon saw this place in his uncharted youth, and felt that the natural configuration of the landscape suggested that other, it could have given him the idea of creating on English soil a mystery-rite comparable to that of the ancients.

Between the oak and the cave is a pillar, with a ball on top. It has weathered so that, as I first saw it, in May 1971, the globe looked dark against the sky, the column white against the dark trees. I made a pen and ink sketch on the spot and took five photographs, from which I made a painting showing a view no longer obtainable, the trees having grown up much more closely round it. It seems to have been set up in the wilderness, at random; yet, though no road connects them, if one lays a ruler across the map from the oak to the pillar, it goes practically through the spot; and it looks to me like a Masonic pillar.

The escarpment with the cave belonged then to Sir George Savile, perhaps related to the Sir Henry Savile esteemed by Bacon as a scholar; the land on which the pillar stands belonged, in 1589, to a Mr. William Lodge, Alderman of the City of London. It is not known to have been used except as a game reserve. Mr. Carter the head game-keeper, told me he had heard said the coaches used to pull up at it, but they would only have done so because it was a landmark already existing. Mr. Paul Sykes, Principal Librarian to the City of Nottingham, could find nothing about it and could only imagine it to have been set up as a decorative milestone. Yet it does not bear a milestone's information.

The column is fluted, but near the top is smoothed to the likeness of a label going part of the way round a bottle. It is rectangular, longest in its horizontal dimension, but surmounted by the vestiges of a crest, arc or small triangle. The whole could be a Masonic apron with flap, above the border. It is quite high up. Even standing upon the plinth, and stretching up, my finger-tips reached only to a foot or more below the lower border of the apron. The apron is divided vertically and horizontally. Half way up, upon each side, one sees from underneath a dark shadow. On the left, this is the underside of what has been a small ledge or projection, on the right a hole, into which a similar one must have been fitted. The right and the left sides reproduce each other, in a manner suggesting the parallel columns of the Kabalistic Tree of Life. They are, perhaps, justice and mercy, or in Bacon's words on Pan's emblems, empire and harmony. In the upper hemispheres are crosses. They could be Christian crosses, or as the long descending arm tapers to a point, swords, hilt up, point down. So placed a sword is sometimes called, in esoteric tradition, a sword of justice, or down-pouring of the divine spirit. In the lower hemisphere are what look to me like bees, with their wings open at an angle of about 60 degrees. They could equally be moths, which likewise fold their wings so, but I fancy the designer would rather have chosen bees as the recipients of the divine inspiration. With their heads pointing upwards, they form the lower triangle of the well-known Masonic device, and perhaps the down-pointing swords form the upper. The two columns are divided by an arch, coming to a point in the middle, beneath the flap. Can it be because it is here that the left and right columns meet that the arch is the highest degree in Masonry?

But what of the globe? Solomon's temple had two portal pillars, Jachin and Boas (I, *Kings,* VII, 21 and II *Chronicles,* III, 17), related to establishment and strength. The Bible does not say they carried globes, so why do the Masonic ones? Perhaps in Bacon's mind they fused with the "pillars of his sacred will" (CIVth Psalm) which supported "the fixed earth". But why are there two? Perhaps one is celestial.

I noticed on the map that near to the pillar was Ceres Lodge, and wrote to the Managing Director of the estate asking why it was so named. Mr. McFerran replied:

. . . all the Lodges round the Park were called after Greek Gods, thus we have Cameleon Lodge, Proteus Lodge and Ceres Lodge. We have no precise

information about when these were either built or named, but they are not shown
on the map dated 1730.

Nevertheless, it seemed to me strange so to have called shooting or
hunting lodges unless in perpetuation of names already existing.

In Bacon's *Wisdom of the Ancients,* XXIX, 'Proserpina or Spirit', one
reads, "By Proserpina the ancients signified that etherial spirit which,
having been separated by violence from the upper globe, is enclosed and
imprisoned beneath the earth (which earth is represented by Pluto) . . .
The air meanwhile, and the power of the celestial region (which is
represented by Ceres) strives with infinite assiduity to win forth and
recover this imprisoned spirit again''. The upper globe then corresponds
to Ceres.

Bacon related the return from the realm of death that was permitted if
one plucked the golden bough to the conquest of the ageing process. "I
am satisfied that the ancients regarded the conservation, and to a certain
extent the restoration, of natural bodies as a thing not desperate, but
rather abstruse and out of the way''. As the golden bough was plainly a
graft upon the holm-oak, he thought this would come about by art and not
by unaided nature.

Cameleon is not a deity, but the chameleon (then sometimes spelled
without the *h*) is a reptile, lizard-like, with unusually long, prehensile tail,
which changes colour with its surroundings. The name transliterates the
Greek for "ground-lion", but it is an exceptionally torpid creature,
which goes for a very long time without eating, and was then believed to
live on air. Hamlet relates it to futurity, when he says that he fares "of the
chameleon's dish: I eat the air, promise crammed''. (*Hamlet,* III, ii, 98).
There is no chameleon in *The Wisdom of the Ancients.* The nearest I find
is in XXVI, 'Prometheus or the State of Man', where Bacon notes that so
ungrateful were men for the gift Prometheus had brought them that they
betrayed him to Jupiter, from whom he had stolen it, but that Jupiter and
the gods "not only indulged mankind with the use of fire, but presented
them likewise with a new gift, of all others most agreeable and desirable—
perpetual youth. Overjoyed with this, the foolish people put the gift of the
gods on the back of an ass. The ass on his way home, being troubled with
extreme thirst, came to a fountain; but a serpent, that was set to guard it,
would not let him drink unless he gave in payment whatever that was he
carried on his back. The poor ass accepted the condition; and so for a
mouthful of water the power of renewing youth was transferred from men
to serpents . . . Now for the gift . . . the unfading flower of youth; it seems
to show that methods and medicines for the retardation of age and the
prolongation of life were by the ancients not despaired of, but reckoned
rather among those things which men once had and by sloth and
negligence let slip . . . in that having received this gift of the gods, they

committed the carriage of it to a lazy and slow-paced ass . . . a thing stupid and . . . tortoise-like . . . As for the transfer of the gift to serpents, it seems to be an addition merely for ornament; unless it were inserted in shame of mankind . . . '' Zoological classifications were less exact then, and the term ''serpent'', from Latin *serpere*, to creep, may have been extensible to the chameleon, as a creature more sluggish than either ass or tortoise, but, as the toad that carries the jewel of wisdom in its head, the leaden casket containing the supreme prize of futurity.

Now we can understand Desdemona's fault. Having received a holy gift, ''dyed in mummy'', a gum to preserve the body for ever, which ''To lose or give't away, were such perdition As nothing else could match'' (*Othello,* III, iv, 67-8), ''she let it drop by negligence'' (*Othello,* III, iii, 311), it was carried by a silly ass to the serpent Iago and she was punished by death.

The mention of the tortoise makes one think of that other ''tortoise'', Caliban, and his counterpart in the fragment, the witch's son, Lorel. Lorel identifies himself by his bristling chin with Pan (II, ii, 8). Now we can understand why Caliban offers the natural treasures of the islands, nuts, a jay's nest with eggs, while Lorel, wooing, presses upon Earine milk and curds, cheeses, swarms of bees, ''An hundred Udders for the payle I have''. Even the ''aged Oake'' is in his gift (II, ii, 15-20). In *The Wisdom of the Ancients,* VI, 'Pan, or Nature', Bacon avers that the parents of Pan (Greek for ''All'') are the ''Divine Word'' and ''confused matter''.

Two references to the chameleon are in *Two Gentlemen of Verona,* wherein Proteus is a character. In that early comedy he cuts a sorry figure, but in mythology Proteus was a god. Shepherd to Poseidon's herd of seals, he would emerge from the sea each day at noon, count them and then sleep. He could prophesy, but would only do so if one could seize and bind him. That was not easy to do, as he would continually change shape, but if one could hold on and secure him he would revert to his own, and then he would tell the future truly. In *The Wisdom of the Ancients,* XIII, 'Proteus, or Matter', Bacon says ''The sense of this fable is related, it would seem, to the secrets of nature and the conditions of matter''. He takes the counting of the seals and then sleeping as nature's creating the species and then, apparently, sleeping, as though the work were done. It is human beings who carry it further. It is not possible to annihilate matter, for in whatever manner one may attack it, it does but assume another form. Yet, ''if a man knew the conditions, affections and processes of matter, he would certainly comprehend the sum and general issue . . . of all things past, present and to come''.

This, then, is the opposite pole to Ceres, spirit never subject to matter. In mythology the two do not enter into the same stories. As corn and seal-herd they are not related. It is solely in Bacon's special interpretation they are meaningfully juxtaposed. We now have the two Masonic globes or north and south poles of head and fundament.

In the fragment, Proteus seems to be represented by the witch, Maudlin, forever changing her shape, so that only by the "browdred belt" can she be known. Momentarily she deceives even Robin into mistaking her for his true love, Maid Marian, who seems to be Ceres. So disguised, she cheats him of the venison on which he had invited all the shepherds and shepherdesses to feast. Marian had, at his request, brought down and presented the stag. As Robin Hood was the famous archer, it is significant he had to ask this of her. The guests represent, probably, the generality of mankind. It is a banquet intended for them by the heavenly spirit that was stolen. In *The Wisdom of the Ancients,* V, 'Styx', Bacon writes that the penalty for breaking an oath on "the fatal river across which no man can return" was exclusion "from the banquet of the gods". The banquet of the gods consisted of ambrosia and nectar, which, if partaken of by mortals, would confer on them immortality. So it was the gift of immortality they let slip. One of the shepherds advises Robin only "to await the issue" (I, vii, 37). He retorts, "The dead or lazie wait for 't; I will find it". (I, vii, 39). Here it is very plainly no ordinary dinner which is in question. The generality of mankind accept the gift of immortality as lost; he will find it again.

Almost at the end, in III, ii, he catches the witch by the belt, when, like Proteus, she reverts to her own shape. The future may, then, soon be revealed.

Near the end of the fragment, Aeglamour tells us that Earine is destined to become an eighth sphere.

Throughout the play, there have been passages in which, if one has counted, there have been found eight things of a kind. Whether or not this is connected with its always being in the eighth Canto of a Book of *The Faerie Queene* that King Arthur appears, to effect the miraculous deliverance of one of his knights from some peril, in *The Sad Shepherd,* when Earine was thought drowned, eight rivers shrank themselves dry with weeping, eight gifts were offered by Lorel, the witch's son, when laying siege to Earine, locked in her tree, poor Tom is seized by eight kinds of affliction or in eight parts, a shepherdess cites eight birds and animals to symbolise young and innocent love, and now in the conclusion, Aeglamour tells us that there are to be, from now on, eight spheres, Sun, Moon, Mercury, Venus, Mars, Jupiter, Saturn and Earine. Earine is to have the special property of tuning all the rest, so that on this earth the result of her apotheosis will be felt as the harmonising of all discords.

> O what an age will here be of new concords!
> Delightful harmonie! to rock old Sages,

Twice infants, in the Cradle . . .

III, ii, 33-36

This passage and indeed the whole play may become more meaningful if one is acquainted with the Trismegistic literature, and in particular with the *Corpus Hermeticum, I, Poemandres the Shepherd of Men;* (24) ''Man-Shepherd said; . . . The body's senses . . . resurrect as energies . . . (25) And thus it is Man doth speed . . . upwards through Harmony . . . And . . . cometh to that Nature which belongeth to the Eighth [Sphere].''[2] Old shall become young again.

Is this not Bacon hinting, as he dared not even in the *New Atlantis,* that he is on the point of finding what he was looking for when he wrote the *Historia Vitae et Mortis,* the very principle of the ageing process, and hence the possibility of arresting it?

In that work he had referred to ''a young Frenchman of great wit'' whom, in his continental travels as a youth, he had met at Poitiers. This French wit was unkind about old men, alleging:[3]

the defects of their minds had some parallel and correspondence with those of the body. To dryness of the skin he opposed impudence; to hardness of the bowels, hardness of the heart; to blear eyes, envy, and the evil eye; to sunken eyes and bowing of the body to the ground, atheism (for they no longer, he says, look up to heaven); to the trembling of the limbs, vacillation of purpose and inconstancy; to the bending and clutching of the fingers, rapacity and avarice, to the tottering of the knees, timidity; to wrinkles, cunning and crooked ways

If Bacon stored this in his memory through a lifetime, to reproduce it in a serious work of his advancing years, it was because, although outrageously onesided and therefore to be repudiated, there was sufficient truth in it to throw his spirit into rebellion. He did not wish to succumb to exemplification of this picture, or that others should do so. In the *Sonnets,* the begetting of progeny is urged as the means of replacing time's ravishments, but there must be a better way than that. In the *Vitae et Mortis* he had affirmed his faith that care continually to bend and stretch the parts should prevent the stiffening of the joints, oils and frictions keep at bay the drying and wrinkling of the skin, but perhaps there was something else to be found. What seems to be promised in *The Sad Shepherd* is the reversal (to some extent achieved by yogis) of the ageing process.

Shakespeare was dead, and no further plays could be fathered upon him. *The Sad Shepherd* was too late for inclusion in the *Folio.* I think Bacon asked Jonson to take it down for him.

1. See Elze in *Shakespeare Jahrbuch,* xi, 299, and editorial notes to related passages in the *Variorum Shakespeare* and in Hereford and Simpson's *Ben Jonson.*

2. *Thrice-Greatest Hermes,* trans. and ed. G.R.S. Mead (Watkins, 1949), II, pp. 15-16. See also note, 'The Eighth Sphere', p.42.

3. Spedding, V, 319.

CHAPTER 78

Charles I

SHORTLY before Christmas, 1624, King James, ailing and failing, wrote Buckingham the letter that makes clear the relationship:

My only sweet and dear child,
. . . I cannot content myself without sending you this billet, praying God that I may have a joyful and comfortable meeting with you, and that we may make at this Christmas a new marriage, ever to be kept hereafter; for, so God love me, as I desire only to live in this world for your sake, and that I had rather live banished in any part of the earth with you, than live a sorrowful widow-life without you. And so God bless you, my sweet child and wife, and grant that ye may ever be a comfort to your dear dad and husband,

James R

He passed away at Theobalds on March 27th, 1625.

Charles I had, like his father, an outbreak of plague to coincide with his coronation. A purer man than his father, he followed the same fatal policies, because he knew no other. Afraid of his Parliament – not without reason – he tended to put off calling it, so depriving himself of the subsidies only it could vote him, and obliging himself, for income, to create more of the hated monopoly patents. He had fallen totally under the influence of Buckingham, and his French bride, Henrietta Maria, was of a temperament ill-suited to help him understand his people.

Never was there a young King in sadder need of the counsel Bacon would have given him. But Bacon, at Gorhambury, was laid up with a ''grave sickness''.

CHAPTER 79

The Psalms

In 1625, Bacon published the only collection of works in verse that stands in his name, his translation of several of the psalms. There is a dedication: "To his very good friend Mr. George Herbert. The pains that it pleased you to take about some of my writings I cannot forget; which did put me in mind to dedicate to you this poor exercise of my sickness . . . Your affectionate friend, Fr. St. Alban." Over the translation of the first psalm one reads the name of God in the four Hebrew letters.

Since Psalm No. I was also, later, translated by Milton, occasion is afforded to compare Bacon's verse-style with that of one generally acclaimed our greatest poet after Shakespeare. It must be remembered translation is a difficult genre, especially of sacred scripture, where religious respect would be likely to inhibit any too free handling of the material. One should not, therefore, expect to find either poet at his most creative.

Bacon's rendering is:

>Who never gave to wicked reed
>   A yielding and attentive ear;
>Who never sinner's paths did tread,
>   Nor sat him down in scorner's chair;
>But maketh it his whole delight
>   On law of God to meditate,
>And therein spendeth day and night:
>   That man is in a happy state.
>
>He shall be like the fruitful tree,
>   Planted along a running spring,
>Which, in due season, constantly
>   A goodly yield of fruit doth bring:
>Whose leaves continue always green,
>   And are no prey to winter's pow'r:
>So shall that man not once be seen
>   Surprised with an evil hour.
>
>With wicked men it is not so,
>   Their lot is of another kind:
>All as the chaff, which to and fro
>   Is toss'd at mercy of the wind.
>And when he shall in judgement plead,
>   A casting sentence bide he must:

So shall he not lift up his head
In the assembly of the just.

For why? the Lord hath special eye
To be the godly's stay at call:
And hath given over, righteously,
The wicked man to take his fall.

Milton's is:

Bless'd is the man who hath not walk'd astray
In counsel of the wicked, and i' the way
Of sinners hath not stood, and in the seat
Of scorners hath not sat. But in the great
Jehova's law is ever his delight,
And in his law he studies, day and night.
He shall be as a tree which planted grows
By watery streams, and in his season knows
To yield his fruit, and his leaf shall not fail,
And what he takes in hand shall prosper all.
Not so the wicked, but as chaff which fann'd
The wind drives, so the wicked shall not stand
Its judgement, or abide their trial then,
Nor sinners in the assembly of just men.
For the Lord knows the upright way of the just,
And the way of bad men to ruin must.

Both have made rhymed versions, Milton in five feet, Bacon in four.
There is enjambement in the Milton, as suits the pentametre, whereas
Bacon, mindful that the psalms were meant to be sung, has kept the style
of a song, and therefore the sense stops with the ends of the lines, as in the
songs in the plays.

Each has a tautology in the same place, Bacon "running springs",
Milton "watery streams"; however, the Authorised Version has "rivers
of water". Milton has "planted grows", which is very awkward. Bacon
has avoided this. The most singular infelicity of the Milton is "chaff
which fann'd the wind drives". As one first reads it, chaff seems to be
fanning the wind. One has to go back over it, puzzled, to work out that
the chaff, having been fanned, is driven by the wind. Professor Berry has
defended Milton's omission of a comma in "Haste thee nymph"
(Allegro), as showing how the phrase was meant to be read aloud,
trippingly, without pause;[1] but even were "fann'd" to be marked off with
commas, the syntax is still strained, un-English. It is an example of Dr.
Leavis' criticism that Milton's Latin constructions involve a "rejection of
English idiom . . . So complete . . . is Milton's departure from the English
order, construction and accentuation that he often produces passages
which have to be read through several times to see how they go."[2] Bacon,
for all his Latinity, writes an English much closer to the vernacular; he

has even the old word ''reed'', in the meaning of counsel, probably derived from reading Chaucer.

But to get the full power, sweep and majesty of Bacon's religious verse one should read his translation not of the Ist but of the CIVth Psalm:

Father and King of Pow'rs, both high and low,
Whose sounding fame all creatures serve to blow;
My soul shall with the rest strike up thy praise,
And carol of thy works and wondrous ways.
But who can blaze thy beauties, Lord, aright?
They turn the brittle beams of mortal sight.
Upon thy head thou wear'st a glorious crown,
All set with virtues, polish'd with renown:
Thence round about a silver veil doth fall
Of crystal light, mother of colours all.
The compass heaven, smooth without grain or fold,
All set with spangs of glitt'ring stars untold,
And strip'd with golden beams of power unpent,
is raised up for a removing tent.
Vaulted and arched are his chamber beams
Upon the seas, the waters, and the streams:
The clouds as chariots swift do scour the sky;
The stormy winds upon their wings do fly.
His angels spirits are, that wait his will,
As flames of fire his anger they fulfil.
In the beginning, with a mighty hand,
He made the earth by counterpoise to stand;
Never to move, but to be fixed still;
Yet hath no pillars but his sacred will.[3]
. . .

In parenthesis, does not the tenth line show that Bacon knew it was the pure or white light which gave birth to the colours? This was not scientifically demonstrated until by Newton in 1666.

1. *Poetry and the Physical Voice,* Francis Berry (Routledge, 1962, p.94.)

2 *Revaluations,* F.R. Leavis (Chatto, 1936, p.53.)

3. Sir Sidney Lee, who was a Stratfordian, but neither a poet nor a poetry critic, asserted that Bacon's ''effort to write verse'' (that is in the translations) sufficiently proved him incapable of having written the poetry assigned to Shakespeare. Whilst I, as, in a modest way, a poet, made quite a different estimation, I might, as a Baconian be taxed with bias, in a sense opposite to Lee's. What was therefore needed was a critic who would judge Bacon's verse without knowing whose it was; a witness unawares. I sent two samples, including the above, to Mr. Martin Booth, poet, winner of a number of poetry prizes, poetry critic for the *Times Literary Supplement, Times Educational Supplement, Poetry Review* etc. and publisher of modern poetry from his Sceptre Press. Except that I told him the enclosed verse translations were not by myself, I gave him no clue as to the authorship, but asked him whether he would take them for the work of a scholar who had written practically no verse excepting for the enclosed, or a part of the work of a major poet. Mr. Booth replied:

''The mastery of subtle techniques, usually lacking in the 'initiate' (ie amateur) poet, are present here. Structure tight and controlled, neat, subtle and forceful, using the poetic imagination to express the original, also the use of imagery. If it was a modern, I'd say the person had written little because of the cliché imagery . . . But if the person is pre-Eliot, then – yes. They must either have written other verse and destroyed it, or read very widely . . . Too good for a non-poet. A poetically knowledgeable person . . . The work of a poet who has written . . . Has impulsive sense of the intention of the original writer . . . No awful jarring smashes at the literary face that occur in premature writing . . . tightly controlled: metre firm, seldom fails if at all; Rhyme good if a little old-fashioned, and rhythm very good . . . So, who is it?''

CHAPTER 80

The Essays

IN 1625 Bacon published his final edition of the Essays. They had been growing up gradually all through his life, but since the 1612 edition had been augmented by twenty new ones and much expansion of those existing.

Of all the works standing in his name, this is certainly the most popular, endlessly reprinted to this day. In it, we seem to come nearest to Bacon in the affairs of every day. Although some of them may be intended as advice to persons in high positions, the hints in them can be applied at any level. For instance, No. 11, 'Of Great Place' may have been thought of as useful for senior Ministers of the Crown, but could as well serve for the Chairman or Secretary of a business or of any small cultural society. On coming in:

Use the memory of thy predecessor fairly and tenderly; for if thou dost not, it is a debt will be sure paid when thou art gone.

In policy, try to steer a course which is regular, so that those in inferior place may know what to expect. Nevertheless, it may sometimes be necessary to change policy. In such case:

Therefore always when thou changest thine opinion or course, profess it plainly, and declare it, together with the reasons that move thee to change; and do not think to steal it.

Otherwise, integrity is doubted.

One should respect the rights of the offices inferior to one's own, and not impinge on them, and think it one's honour to direct in chief, and not be busy in everything. If any come to offer help or advice or to bring information, such should not be treated as meddlers but accepted in good part. Yet one should not be too facile, and one should remember that any show of favouritism, except upon ground of obvious merit, leads to suspicion of undue influence or corruption. On the other hand, in dealing with those beneath one must never be rough; ''reproof from authority ought to be grave, and not taunting.'' When one is not acting in one's official capacity, one should not bear oneself with airs that seem to seek too much to remind people of one's office, but rather let it be said, ''When he sits in place he is another man.''

No. 9, 'Of Envy' has some shrewd observations that will be recognised by people in the professions. Those who rise suffer most envy from those who were once close to and level with them:

Lastly, near kinsfolk and fellows in office, and those that have been bred together, are more apt to envy their equals when they are raised. For it doth upbraid unto them their own fortunes, and pointeth at them.
This is because; when the distance is altered; ''it is like a deceit of the eye, that when others come on they think themselves go back.''

It is always a matter of comparison, which is why kings are not envied, excepting by other kings; and envy is a tare ever destroying the wheat, of all affections the vilest.

It can be largely mitigated by giving full respect to those beneath, and is most excited by public display. Moreover, in moments of glory or triumph, the inward spirits of the person seem to externalise, and so meet the blow.

In No. 21, 'Of Delays', he warns that ''If a man watch too long it is odds he will fall asleep.'' It is interesting that he goes on:

For the helmet of Pluto, which maketh the politic man go invisible, is secrecy in the council and celerity in the execution. For when things are once come to the execution, there is no secrecy comparable to celerity.

''The helmet of Pluto'' takes us back not only to the *Promus* but to Hall's satires.

In No. 36, 'Of Ambition', he says that he who endeavours to achieve eminence amongst able men sets himself a great task, but one that is good for the public interest:

But he that plots to be the only figure amongst ciphers is the decay of a whole age.

In 49, 'Of Suitors', he gives a warning for consideration by all who in any cause find themselves asked to supply a reference or give a letter of introduction:

Nothing is thought so easy a request to a great person, as his letter; and yet if it be not in a good cause, it is so much out of his reputation.

In No. 40, 'Of Fortune', he examines what we now call luck. It is perhaps, like the Milky Way, comprised of numbers of stars too small to be seen separately, yet making together a visible band of light. Yet the Italians say of a lucky person that he has ''Poco di matto'' (a little madness), and indeed it is often those who have in them something of the fool who seem favoured. Perhaps this is because they do not presume too much on their virtues or merits. It is always very unwise to attribute any stroke of fortune to one's own deserts. The Athenian, Timotheus, who made a long speech about the successes of his government saying of each, ''and in this Fortune had no part'' never prospered in anything afterwards. Fortune had turned her face away. If one wants to enjoy the favours of Luck, one must give her credit.

The wise, not presuming on their works ascribe any rise to Providence or Fortune. Moreover, this does them no harm in others' eyes:

It is greatness in a man to be the care of higher powers.

It is better to let oneself be known for one's Felicity than Greatness.

In No. 33, 'Of Plantations' (Colonies), we find close practical thought. In the beginning, it is better not to take out wheat, oats or barley; they demand too laborious preparation of the soil, cultivation and harvesting before they yield the grain from which can be made bread. The space in the ships would be better filled with beans and peas, which are easy to put in the ground, come up quickly and yield immediate food. Have we here his reflections on the mystery of the colony that was found in Virginia starving, in a fertile land?

There is nothing about the theatre, but an essay 'Of Masques and Triumphs' (No. 37) which shows a ''stage'' knowledge of the effects of lighting. ''The colours that show best by candle-light are white, carnation and a kind of sea-water green; and oes or spangs, as they are of no great cost, so they are of most glory. As for rich embroidery, it is lost and not discerned.'' This is even more true of the modern footlights; any actress knows it is better to have cheap sequins or huge spangles or artificial jewels than small real ones or embroideries, which are not discerned.

In No. 23, 'Of Wisdom for a Man's Self', he says, ''be so true to thyself, as thou be not false to others'', which has affinity of thought with:

> To thine own self be true
> And it must follow, as the night the day,
> Thou canst not then be false to any man.
> *Hamlet, I, iii, 78-80*

He is not a lover of that classic art which seeks to make every feature regular. ''There is no excellent beauty that hath not some strangeness in the proportion.'': 'Of Beauty' (No. 43).

There are the biographical insights. In No. 7, 'Of Parents and Children' he tells us, ''the noblest works and foundations have proceeded from childless men; which have thought to impress the images of their minds, where those of their bodies have failed.'' Bacon was childless.

In the following one 'Of Marriage and Single Life', he observes that men without responsibility for wife and children are the most apt for great enterprises, whether of virtue or mischief, and that unmarried men make the best friends, masters and servants, but not always the best subjects or citizens, for they can the most easily run away. He thinks, also, that unmarried men may be the more hard-hearted, because their tenderness is not so often called upon. ''Chaste women are often proud and froward, as presuming upon the merit of their chastity''. Does this describe Isabella in *Measure for Measure?*

Some consider cold his essay, No. 10, 'Of Love':

The stage is more beholding to Love, than the life of man. For as to the stage, love is ever a matter of comedies, and now and then of tragedies; but in life it doth much mischief . . .

But this was his own experience. To create a Juliet was one thing, but he had not found one, only hurt through love. "The speaking in a perpetual hyperbole is comely in nothing but in love." Touchstone mocks it in *As You Like It*. He thinks the wise manage not to be transported by the madness of love, for "It is impossible to love and to be wise."

This recalls:

> But you are wise,
> Or else you love not, for to be wise and love
> Exceeds mans might.   *Troilus and Cressida*, III, ii, 162-5.

In *The Advancement of Learning*, Bacon had expressed the same thought: "It is not granted to man to love and to be wise."[1]

He has better to say of friendship (No. 27) 'Of Friendship':

For friendship maketh indeed a fair day in the affections, from storm and tempests; but it maketh daylight in the understanding, out of darkness and confusion of thoughts.

This imagery shows affinity with that of two of the *Sonnets*:

> Shall I compare thee to a Summers day?
> Thou art more louely and more temperate:
> Rough windes do shake the darling buds of Maie
>
> *Sonnet 18*

and

> Why didst thou promise such a beautious day,
> And make me travaile forth without my cloake,
> To let base cloudes o'ertake me in my way . . .
>
> *Sonnet 34*

A great town is a great solitude, "because in a great town friends are scattered". He anticipates modern psychology, when he says, "We know diseases of stoppings and suffocations are the most dangerous in the body; and it is not much otherwise in the mind." Medicines will open the body, but only a friend can open the heart, "a true friend; to whom you may impart griefs, joys, fears, hopes, suspicions, counsels" and whatever lies on it.

There are the amusing ones. "Riches are for spending" is his beginning to No. 28, 'Of Expense'. This precept had certainly guided him. But he adds a true observation. What is dangerous is not the single extravagance, which a man is aware of, and indulges consciously, but the small expenses, that will recur, that seem as nothing yet aggregate to a considerable charge. "A man ought warily to begin charges which once begun will continue''.

"Houses are built to live in, and not to look on'', is the beginning of No. 45, 'Of Building'. The Vatican and the Escurial look very fine from the outside, yet have not "a fair room in them''. This sounds as though he had included in his travels both Rome and Madrid. He probably means that they are warrens of small rooms. He would have comfort and convenience first in the design, not sacrificed to regularity of facade.

But he begins No. 46, 'Of Gardens', "God Almighty first planted a Garden. And indeed it is the purest of human pleasures''.

His suggested lay-out implies far vaster acreage than most of his readers of today are likely to possess, but in principle, he would have part lawn, part cultivated flower and herb gardens, and part left wild, yet with the wild flowers cunningly placed, as something fragile peeping up from under a stone. One should study the nature of one's soil, not fight against it, and put in those plants that will thrive in that soil which one has. In so far as possible, group within one place those that will flower in the same season, so that at any particular moment there is one corner of the garden that will be all open blossoms, unmixed with dead ones or dormant plants. For the wild part, he will have violets, primroses, strawberries, sweet briars and honeysuckle; for the cultivated, he gives long lists appropriate to each month, including evergreens for winter.

And because the breath of flowers is far sweeter in the air (where it comes and goes like the warbling of music) than in the hand, therefore nothing is more fit for delight, than to know what be the flowers and plants that do best perfume the air . . . That which above all others yields the sweetest smell in the air, is the violet.

1. Spedding, III, p.328.

CHAPTER 81

The chill in the snow

AT the end of December, 1625, Francis made his last will, "'For my burial, I desire it may be in St. Michael's Church, near St. Albans . . . for my name and memory, I leave it to men's charitable speeches, and to foreign nations, and the next ages . . . '' Constable, as in the former will, was his literary executor and received as his legacy all Bacon's books. Many things were to go to his wife, but beneath the main body of the will, there is a codicil, dated December 19th, 1625:

> Whatsoever I have given, granted, confirmed or appointed to my wife, in the former part of this my will, I do now, for just and grave causes, utterly revoke and make void, and leave her to her right only.

What had happened? Within four months she was married to her gentleman-usher, Sir John Underhill; perhaps Francis had found them together. There is, however, a point to be noticed in Aubrey's *Brief Lives*. He says:

> His Dowager married her Gentleman usher Sir Thomas (I think) Underhill, whom she made deafe and blinde with too much of Venus.

Aubrey means she infected him with syphilis, a point which seems to have escaped Bacon's biographers. It is, however, inherited syphilis which tends to cause deafness and blindness, rather than syphilis contacted. If Underhill went deaf and blind soon after his marriage to the Viscountess St. Alban, it would be unlikely to be because she had infected him. On the other hand, it is a most extraordinary allegation for Aubrey to make; and if his medical knowledge, or that of his informant, was insufficient to appreciate this point, that such a thing should be believed points to a reputation for insatiability. For, since Bacon showed no signs of the disease, it must have been believed she had been unfaithful to him with lovers preceding Underhill. If Bacon had any suspicion his wife was infected, it could explain the sickened allusions to syphilis in *Timon*, where he seems to think of women as good for nothing but to spread it: an inexplicable intrusion into the plot, usually taken by Shakespeareans to mean the actor from Stratford had suffered a touch of ''the clap''.

If Bacon had had his suspicions earlier, there must yet have been something which he discovered right at the end which caused him to revoke his bequests to her. He speaks of ''just and grave causes'', in the plural. That could mean either adultery with more than one man, or adultery and something else, perhaps financial sharpness. When after his passing Sir Thomas Meautis and Sir Thomas Rich, as executors, were to bring a bill in Chancery against herself and Underhill for ''Fraudulent conveyances and deeds of gift'' in respect of jewels, plate, pictures, hangings, which should have been sold for the payment of Francis' creditors, she defended, saying that some of these she had bought with her own money, and that it was because she had refused to join with her husband in selling lands that he had left her society. So there had been disputes and estrangement long before the last discovery which caused him to add to his will that codicil depriving her of all but her legal right in his estate.

There was no comfort for Francis in his home, and not much in the way the affairs of the nation were shaping. The Parliament which met in February, 1625/6 was that which impeached Buckingham. Francis was not present. He had received his writ to attend, as usual, but his health did not permit him to use it. His appeal to Sir Humphrey May to try to obtain for him a pardon of the whole sentence appears to have brought no fruit, probably because King Charles was too much taken up with Buckingham's and his own troubles with Parliament.

At the end of March, Francis, returning from London to Gorhambury, took cold, and instead of continuing to Gorhambury, stopped at a house belonging to Lord Arundel, where the steward prepared a bed for him. This we know from a letter written by Francis to Arundel, hoping he would forgive the steward.

Rawley tells us he died in the early morning of April 9th, 1626, of a fever and defluction of rheum so plentiful he suffocated.

Did Rawley see this or take it from the steward? The question is asked because it has not been possible to ascertain the place of Bacon's burial. It used to be thought it was under the statue erected to him by Meautis in St. Michael's, Gorhambury, but recent excavations revealed there was no coffin. The inscription reads not ''hic jacet'' but ''sic sedebat'' and the present Verulam family are adamant he was never interred there. The relevant page from the burial register is missing and it has not been possible to discover any reference to his funeral.

There is a legend that at Highgate he simply gave the world the slip and sailed via Holland for America. The end, like the beginning, is mystery.

CHAPTER 82

Manes Verulamiani

IN 1626, an anthology of poems to his memory was printed under the long title of *Memoriae Honoratissimi Domini Francisci Baconis de Verulamiano Vice-Comitis Sancti Albani Sacrum* generally known as *Manes Verulamiani.*

Not all the elegies are signed. Of those whose names or initials appear, most seem to be Cambridge or legal men. They are: W. (William) Rawley, S.T.D. (Bacon's Chaplain); S. Collins, R.C.P.; George Herbert; R.P.; William Boswell; T. Vincent, Trinity College; I. Vincent, Trinity College; R.C.T.C.; T.P.; Williams; H.T., Fellow of Trinity College; Thomas Rhodes, King's College; Robert Ashley, of the Middle Temple; E.F., King's College; William Loe, Trinity College; James Dupont, Trinity College; C.D., King's College; Henry Ferne, Fellow of Trinity College; G. Nash, Pembroke Hall; James; R.I., Henry Ockley, Trinity College; William Atkins, His Lordship's Domestic Attendant; Thomas Randolph, Trinity College.

Names that surprise by their omission are Tobie Matthew and Ben Jonson, but Rawley, as editor, says, "very many poems, and the best, too, I withold from publication." Was this because they were too revealing?

Even in the poems published, there is a repeated association of Bacon with Apollo and the Muses, suggestive of poetry rather than prose. All the tributes are in Latin. Perhaps the most beautiful is that from George Herbert:

> Dvm longilentiq; gemis sub pondere morbi
> Aetq; haeret dubio tabida vitae pede;
> Quid voluit prudens Fatum, jam sentio tandem:
> Constat, Aprile uno te potuisse mori:
> Vt Flos hinc lacrymis, illinc Philomela querelis
> Deducant linguae funera sola tuae.

I render into the best English verse I can:

> Long a heavy illness made you groan,
> With weakening foothold upon life you clung;
> What Fate intended now is plain. Alone
> In April could you die, that sole
> The weeping flower and plaintive nightingale
> Might celebrate the funeral of your tongue.

These are the obsequies of a poet for a poet.

Two Dutch title pages

IN 1642 there appeared from Lugduni Batavorum, Holland, an edition of Bacon's *Henry VII,* with a curious title page (see Plate 18). Fortune stands upon a globe, holding a bridle without a bit and a salt (symbol of wisdom). To her left, a venerable gentleman with roses on his shoes stretches forward his arms, one in the light and one in deep shadow, to hold her there, while behind him peeps over a man in a helmet, who likewise stretches forward to touch the figure of Fortune. On the right of the picture we see the same two men. The one in the helmet is now the nearer, and we see that he wears actor's buskins and, on one foot only, a prominent spur (as in *Cryptomenytices*). His sword is awkwardly slung across his buttocks and his lace collar looks unmilitary. He bends forward, to touch with his left hand the Globe upon which Fortune stands, while with his right he shares with the reverend gentleman the hold of a very long spear. This spear intersects Fortune's wheel, dividing it into two hemispheres. The spokes of the wheel in the upper terminate in three crowns, a spade and Bacon's tall hat, those of the lower in a jester's coxcomb, a bowl, a scourge and a mirror, symbolising perhaps comedy, tragedy, satire and Hamlet's advice to the players. Bacon's higher or public life seems to be divided from that he shares with the actor. What is shown plainly is a partnership, since the hold on the spear is joint. The helmet could be ''Plutoes helmet'' (*Promus*) transferred to Shakespeare, in his Falstaff aspect, who seems to be playing Sancho Panza to Bacon's Don Quixote.

Three years later, in 1645, from the same was published an edition of his *De Augmentis.* On the title page (Plate 19), Bacon is seated at his desk. He is wearing his tall hat again, and his long gown. His foot intersects the entablature, showing the page was cut as a whole. On the desk is a large open book, and the light falls on this, and on his right hand, placed on it. His left arm and hand are in deep shadow. With this shadowed left hand he holds up a little figure in goatskins, who holds a small book, fastened close, as if offering it to a temple on a rocky crag. There are lightning flashes in the sky, so perhaps we have to do with Mt. Parnassus again. The mannikin does not, this time, have actor's buskins, so the small book may not necessarily represent the plays. It may be the secret as opposed to the open book of Bacon's life, or secret knowledge of the laws of nature, not confided to *De Augmentis.* Yet the word tragedy has been thought to derive from τραγῳδοί goat-singers, so that his goat-skin could stand for tragedy, while in the fold of Bacon's gown, just above where it falls over his foot, is picked out in dots a face, in what might appear to be the sunburst we met first in the temple-room of Canonbury Tower, save that one of the rays flops over so as to form a jester's coxcomb. Tragedy and comedy seem, therefore, to be counterpointed within a complex symbolism.

None of these symbols are mentioned in McKerrow or Praz, probably because they are particular to these two volumes, and R.V. Gibson's *Bibliography* of Bacon's works offers no comment on them.

Van der Werff's portrait of Elizabeth

THE illustrations in the *Histoire d'Angleterre, d'Ecosse et d'Irlande*, Isaac de Larrey (Rotterdam, 1707), were first drawn to Baconian attention by Dr. Gerstenberg. The author's preface explains the artist had begged to be allowed to contribute to the volume drawings in which he endeavoured symbolically to encapsulate what appeared to him essential in the characters' lives. Thus Cranmer and others burned have stakes, flames and martyrs' palms. Those beheaded have an axe woven into the design, together with some detail suiting the case: Charles I has an axe and an overturned crown, Anne Boleyn an axe hidden in voluptuous draperies. Henry VIII is in a mirror held in the hand of a naked woman; Buckingham is given peacock's feathers and a dagger. He was vain as a peacock and died with a dagger in his back. In none of these is the symbolism so obscure as to defy interpretation. So why is Queen Elizabeth given three children? (Plate 8).

At first one sees only two, both in the full light. The higher placed wears a cloak buckled on one shoulder, like a Roman Imperator, and holds a martyr's palm. The only martyred military commander of Elizabeth's reign was Essex. The child in the centre has his arm around an instrument, which is partly a musical one, of the viol family, and partly a quarter rudder, with helm. One remembers Pierre Amboise wrote that Bacon saw himself destined to hold in his hands "le timon du royaume", the helm of the kingdom. Perhaps this is it. De Larrey's text is in French, so he can have read Amboise. The helm grows from where the peg would, from the neck of the rudder-viol, which passes into shadow behind the child's dark side, suggesting a secret musicianship. It is difficult to convey in a picture that a man is writing poetry, for if one puts a pen in his hand what he is writing with it might be prose. Poetry, however, is often thought of as a kind of music. The hand positioned, as if to play on the strings holds, however, not a bow but sprigs of corn. As I asked myself the meaning of these, I had, whilst seated at my typewriter, a waking vision: a girl, with slender, pale face and wreath of poppies in a cloud of hair, so dark it faded as a dark nimbus into the night, seeming in some way mystical. As it vanished, I asked myself its meaning, and its relation to the sprigs. Poppies grow in corn, yet connect with death, whether by blood and Flanders fields or opium sleep. A mythological figure combining the

ideas of harvest with being the bride of death? As the Demeter-
Persephone legend came into my mind (from which evolved, also, my
interpretation of *The Winter's Tale*) I thought that what Van der Werff
must have tried to convey with his sprigs was resuscitation or
immortality. But I see from Oliver's *Dictionary of Symbolic Masonry*
(Spencer, 1853) that corn is a Masonic symbol of resurrection. Van der
Werff may have thought his picture would speak to Masons.

But who is the third child, who stands in the shadow, by an altar on
which there burns a flame, above which he holds what looks like an
inverted saucepan or enormous candle-snuffer? Professor Henrion thinks
he must be a child born prior to Bacon and Essex, who in his begetting
extinguished the vestal flame of Elizabeth's virginity. He does not suggest
who this earlier child might have been.

My mind goes back to the earlier scandal affecting Elizabeth. After the
death of Henry VIII she was placed in the care of Catherine Parr, who
then married Sir Thomas Seymour, younger brother of Edward Seymour,
Duke of Somerset, the Lord Protector. Despite the vigilance of her
governess, Catherine Ashley, Elizabeth was subjected to indecent
familiarities by her step-mother's new husband. He slashed her gown in a
romp, took to visiting her in her room in the mornings before she was up,
tickled and slapped her buttocks as she lay in bed, and pocketed the
bedroom key. What passed as horse-play assumed another character when
her step-mother came upon them alone together, in each other's arms.
Elizabeth, then fourteen and a half (it was May, 1548) was sent away
immediately, to a house in the country, at Cheshunt, where, falling sick
during the summer, she was hardly seen for the rest of the year. She knew
she was suspected of being pregnant by Seymour, for at the end of
January, of the following year, she wrote to the Lord Protector, asking
permission to come to court and show herself as she was. Is it possible she
had already been delivered?

In 1587 there presented himself in Spain a man calling himself Arthur
Dudley, who claimed to be the son of Elizabeth and Leicester. He made a
statement for the English Catholic Sir Francis Englefield, today in the
Simanca. It has always struck me as odd in the first sentence he refers to
Catherine Ashley, which sends the mind back to a period ten years
previous to Elizabeth's intimacy with Leicester. Nowhere in his long
statement does he give the date of his birth, which one would have
thought material to the attempted establishment of his claim. He may not
have known it exactly, but surely he could have given the year in which,
as he says, Catherine Ashley gave him as a baby to a servant of hers,
Robert Southern, to be brought up as the child of Southern and his wife.
Later he learned it was John Ashley, husband of Catherine Ashley, who
paid for his education, and much later extracted the information he was
the Queen's son. Why did he say his father was Leicester? Perhaps he was

confused, or thought Leicester's the weightier name to play with. At the end of his statement there is an enigmatic sentence which may be the give away: "As for the Earl of Huntingdon and Beauchamp, son of the Earl of Hertford, both of them are descended from Adam, and perhaps there is someone who is their elder brother." Lord Beauchamp was Edward Seymour, son of the Earl of Hertford, son not of Thomas Seymour, Elizabeth's friend, but of his elder brother, the Lord Protector. It looks as if Arthur was trying to have it all ways. Yet, where Francis and Essex had been grafted upon high placed families, he had been put out to servants; he had some reason to feel aggrieved.

Elizabeth's name is broken by the feet of the child holding the viol-helm, so that one reads ELIZABE TH. There would, therefore, be room for one or two hidden letters. I tried to think of such as would, added to her name, form an anagram for a significant word, or which joined to an abbreviation of it could form the anagram of a soubriquet, but nothing came to me.

As I went over the picture, inch by inch, closely, suddenly something appeared which no one seemed to have noticed. It was a sphynx, in the deepest of the deep shadow. Something told me it was not a good sphynx. Why, otherwise, draw it so carefully and yet hide it as though it were a dark secret? It was not the Egyptian sphynx, with man's head and lion's body, but the Greek one, with woman's head and wings: the Theban sphinx, that posed the riddle to Oedipus.

Who was Van der Werff? He knew it all.

The establishment of Essex' birth data from a manuscript horoscope in the British Museum

I was at first puzzled to find the date of Essex' birth differently given in different works of reference. The *Dictionary of National Biography* gave it in early editions as November 10th, 1567, but in 1908 silently changed it to November 19th, 1566. Why had the year been changed and also the day? G.B. Harrison, in the 'Notes' appended to his biography, *Robert Devereux, Earl of Essex* (Cassell, 1937) explained the reason. The 1567 date had been taken from a book about coats of arms by Thomas Miles, *Catalogue of Honour*. Writers of the period sometimes reported a person of ''30 year'', regardless whether he had completed thirty or was in his thirtieth, and the *Dictionary of National Biography* had changed the date by one year less nine days after the discovery of a manuscript horoscope in the British Museum, Sloane MSS. 1697f, 54b. Harrison wished to check but had not the knowledge of astrology; he, therefore, had the manuscript examined for him by one D.C. Collins. He does not tell us the qualification of Collins to examine an astrological map, and in my judgement he was incompetent and completely misled Harrison.

The report Collins made for Harrison started off by saying the horoscope could not have been calculated for November 19th, for on the 19th (Julian) the Sun would have been in Sagittarius, whereas the horoscope showed it in Scorpio. So far so good, and had he stopped there, he would have rendered valuable service. Unfortunately, he attempted to go further into it, and became confused. He made out a table showing the zodiacal signs in which the Ascendant, Descendant and 8th cusp would be posited on the two dates. In doing this he showed his own ignorance that because these factors depend on the diurnal rotation of the earth they will, like the hands of a clock, make a complete circuit of all the positions on every day. To make an analogy, 9.0 p.m. will occur not only upon November 10th but upon November 19th and upon every day of every year, and no differentiation can be made upon this basis. The zodiacal degrees in which the Ascendant, Descendant or any one of the twelve cusps find themselves is capable of differentiating dates only if linked to an exactly stated time, because all come round approximately four minutes later each day. Perhaps Collins merely forgot to explain, but worse follows.

He goes on to say that on the basis of the horoscope no discrimination can be made between one year and another:

The positions of the stars noted in the horoscope are no indication of the year, because between 1566 and 1567 the changes were so slight as to be barely noticeable. Indeed, Hartgyll's table [in the *General Calendar of Astronomicall Tables* George Hartgyll, 1592] was intended to serve for forty years.

It is here that complete miscomprehension shows itself. It is very rare for astrologers to insert in the chart any of the stars proper. They insert against the Ascendant, Descendant and other cusps, the zodiacal degrees, calculated from the moving Vernal equinoctial point, which are intersected by the said cusps at a given Sidereal Time. Within the houses so marked off, they insert the zodiacal degrees (still in the equinoctial zodiac) of the Sun, Moon and planets. As these all move at different speeds, they never come back, all at the same time, to the same positions *in zodiaco* and in relation to one another, as they have previously occupied. Thus, it is impossible to confuse a horoscope cast for one year with one cast for another, even should the day of the year be the same.

G.B. Harrison, not understanding that his informant must be wrong, was so discouraged by the ''information'' that he discarded the horoscope as incapable of affording information, even as to the year of birth, and preferred the 1567 date from the book on heraldry, not as being necessarily correct but as being at least clear and unambiguous, whereas, as it appeared to him from Collins' account, the horoscope contained some internal inconsistency.

That it is quite otherwise, I shall endeavour to explain. Even without seeing the Hartgyll, I felt sure as I read the passage quoted, that it must have been misunderstood, and that what Hartgyll had claimed for his tables was that the Sidereal Times would hold good for forty years. Sidereal Time is the interval, in sidereal hours, minutes and seconds, since the preceding meridian passage, at a given place, not of a star but of the True Equinox or First Point of Aries.[1]

When I went to the British Museum, inspection of the Hartgyll confirmed this surmise. What he claims for the table which occupies pp.15-52 of his book is that it is calculated for 1612 but will serve ''without sensible error'' for 30 (not 40) years before and as many after, ie from 1582 to 1652. This was a modest claim considering that for 1612 the Sidereal Times, starting from the Noon on the day of the Vernal Equinox were, by the Hartgyll:

H	m	s
0	0	0
0	3	40
0	7	21

and for 1979, by the current Raphael:

23	53	38
23	57	35
0	01	32
0	05	28

0 exactly is the same as 24 exactly. The regression of the equinoctial point for 367 years is shown as so slight that to use one for the other would, for the majority of purposes for which an astrologer would require it, serve "without sensible error". I thought 1612 had been chosen by Hartgyll (writing in 1592) because in that year Noon on the day of the Vernal Equinox would be 0h 0m 0s, neatly.

The zodiacal positions of the planets, day by day, during any particular year does not appear in Hartgyll's table, or anywhere in his book. There is a column against that in which the Sidereal Times appear day by day in which are entered planetary symbols, and these may be what Collins perhaps thought referred to planets, apparently standing fixed in their positions for many years. But if he had looked to the head of the column, he would have seen the word 'Nature'. Now Hartgyll does not explain, but any astrologer would know, that the word 'Nature' in such a context refers to the 'Natures' of the stars, described in terms of the supposed likeness of their influence to that of planets, as set out by the 1st century Alexandrine Astrologer, Claudius Ptolemy, in his *Almagest*. What Hartgyll is setting out is the 'Nature' according to Ptolemy of the star nearest the Meridian at Noon on each day of the year, starting from the Vernal Equinox. Indeed, he has set small numbers against each one, and if one refers to an earlier table in his book, pp. 1–13, one finds that against the numbers are set the names of stars. Thus, it can be seen that the symbol for Saturn is written in the 'Nature' column against 0 0 0 because, on the day of the Vernal Equinox, the star nearest to the Midheaven at Noon is that which the Arabs called Difda and modern astronomers *Beta Ceti,* to which Ptolemy ascribed the 'Nature' of Saturn. One can check the whole of 'Nature' column for the 365 days of the year against Ptolemy, and the entries will be found to tally.

The positions of the planets are not indicated by Hartgyll because there would be no space for them within this kind of table, and because he supposed the kind of person who would be using his book would be provided with a set of ephemerides giving the position of the Sun, Moon and planets for each day of each year. Only in such annual ephemerides can be found the data distinguishing one year from another, and, within each year, one day from every other day. Before he can begin to cast a horoscope, an astrologer needs to take from a table such as Hartgyll's, or the modern Raphael, the Sidereal Time for the Noon on the required date, which, plus or minus the hours and minutes the subject's birth was anterior or posterior to that Noon, will, in conjunction with a set of tables setting out the zodiacal degrees corresponding to every four minutes of Sidereal Time at a given degree of Latitude (that is another set of tables) enable him to calculate the Medium Coeli or Midheaven and the Ascendant (point at which the ecliptic intersects the eastern horizon) at the time and place of his subject's birth. There is more to it than Collins realised. To find the Sidereal Time is needful, in order to find these cusps, but bears to what follows only such relation as does finding the ignition key to the car to the journey intended. Once he has the cusps, he has to look in the annual ephemeris for the zodiacal positions of the Sun, Moon and planets at the Noons preceding and following his subject's birth, and then either by Diurnal Proportional Logarithms or, as these had not at this early date been discovered, by a series of proportional sums, work out the zodiacal positions at the time of the birth.

I went to the Manuscript department and applied for Sloane 1697f, and found indeed on f.54b a horoscopic chart, in the centre of which was written:

1566

die	ho	m	November
9	21	45	p.m.

Robertus Comet Essex

In other words, Robert Earl of Essex was born 21 hours and 45 minutes after the Noon of November 9th, 1566, which is 9.45 a.m. of November 10th. This has the interesting result of restoring to Essex his traditional birthday, November 10th, although in the year previous to that given by the writer of the book on heraldry.

In the case of an a.m. birth, astrologers often prefer to add the time of birth to the Sidereal Time of the Noon of the previous day, rather than subtract it from the Noon of the day itself. "Always add, never subtract," is even a precept with some.

Hartgyll does not name his months and days, but if one turns to his page for the entry of the Sun into the sign of Scorpio and counts down, one will find against what must be November 9th and 10th Julian:

h	m	s
16	38	49
15	42	57

Now, whether one adds the birth-time to the first or subtracts it from the second, one will arrive at a Sidereal Time for Essex' birth corresponding to a Midheaven of Libra 22°, at Greenwich which is extremely close to the Midheaven of the chart, which is carefully written in as Libra 21°40'. This minute displacement shows that the astrologer has made allowance for about 20 seconds of Longitude west of Greenwich, though there was no observatory at Greenwich when he lived. That he has not used merely the nearest round degree shows that he has taken immense pains with this chart to get it accurate to within fractions.

But how had first the *Dictionary of Natural Biography*'s informant, then Collins, made of the 9 a 19? Beneath the 9 is a mark which they must have taken for a mishapen and displaced figure 1. It is not, it is the symbol for Saturn, and denotes that November 9th was a Saturday, which (I have checked with the *Calendar of State Papers*)) was the case in 1566.

. The zodiacal positions shown within the chart are: Sun Scorpio 27°12', Moon Scorpio 11°04', Mercury Scorpio 11°18' Venus Scorpio 0°03', Mars Scorpio 29°46', Jupiter Libra 27°50', Saturn Virgo 13°09'. Not having the ephemeris from which the ancient astrologer worked, I completely recalculated them from the modern *Planetary Lunar and Solar Positions 601 B.C. to A.D. 1649,* Bryant Tuckerman (Philadelphia, 1962). Here are tabled the positions of Saturn, Jupiter and Mars for every 10th day, and Venus, Mercury and the Moon for every fifth day. They are expressed in the Julian calendar, in Right Ascension, and are given for 7.00 p.m. Local Mean Time, Babylon. This being perhaps a homage to the ancient Chaldean masters of the art, who reckoned the rising of the stars and planets from the moment the small points of light became visible in the darkening sky, it is necessary first to convert Babylon to Greenwich, and then, by a longish series of proportional sums, to find the positions of the Sun, Moon and planets not at 7.00 on the nearest given dates on either side of the date sought, but on the date sought, November 10, 1566, and then not at 7.00 p.m. but at the more usual Noon, and finally at the time required on that date, 9.45 a.m. Very roughly, as I have worked it, the positions come out as Sun Scorpio 27, Moon Scorpio 6, Mercury Scorpio 7, Venus Scorpio 0, Mars Scorpio 27, Jupiter Libra 27 and Saturn Virgo 12. Considering the number of manipulations involved, and that the Tuckerman tables, being calculated by computer, can take no account of acceleration or deceleration (in the case of the Moon considerable), this is a remarkably close result, placing the date of Essex' birth beyond dispute and fully justifying the ancient astrologer. I should like to salute him, the unknown confrere who did this work three centuries before me. There is no clue to his identity. His hand is not that of the fanciful John Dee or the careless Simon Forman. He was a master. I shall call him Magister.

But a horoscope does not exist in vacuo. It is cast for some particular Longitude and Latitude. With regard to the former, in Elizabethan times, there was some problem. We reckon it from Greenwich, but the Observatory had not then been built. Sailors reckoned it from Cap Verde or the Azores, landsmen from the capital cities of their own countries, somewhat crudely. Also, since four minutes of clock time correspond to the passage of a zodiacal degree at the Midheaven, if confronted with an unlikely looking longitude, before concluding that the subject must have been born on a raft adrift on the sea, it is prudent to consider whether the astrologer, faced with a birth-time looking suspiciously as though it had been rounded up to the nearest hour, may not have, in order to obtain a map better corresponding to the subject's appearance or circumstances, made a discreet addition or subtraction of 4, 8, 12, 16 or more minutes to or from the round time given, which would have the same effect upon the map as a Longitudinal displacement. For instance, in the horoscope of Essex' infant son, though the Longitude looks adjusted, the Latitude is that of the family's home in Herefordshire, and I think that is the place for which the nativity is cast, since, unlike his father, he was christened in the local church, as recorded in the register. However, having made these reservations about Longitude, I do not think we need be too difficult about accepting Magister's subtraction of 0° 20' West Longitude for the birth of Essex, since this would be too fine to effect his appearance or destiny.

About Latitude, happily, it is possible to be precise. This is because, unlike Longitude, it is related neither to the clock nor to any starting-point agreed by convention. Latitude is something real. A given Midheaven can only occur in combination with a given Ascendant at a certain parallel of Latitude. If one looks, for instance, at a horoscope for King Philip of Spain, which though in another hand is bound into the same MS, one sees as Ascendant of Libra 26° 44' with a Midheaven of Leo 0° 39'. A glance through Raphael's *Tables for Northern Latitudes* shows this combination could not be found anywhere in the British Isles, and that one would have to go a long way south to obtain it.

The chart for Essex shows an Ascendant of Sagittarius 19° 00' with a Midheaven of Libra 21° 40'. This could not have occurred so far north as the family's home in Herefordshire. Neither would one find it even in London. To obtain it, one has to go south from London, though not a great distance. Using Raphael's *Tables of Houses for the British Isles,* I noted that the combination sought would fall somewhere between the parallels given for London, 51° 32', and Taunton, 51° 01'. At Taunton, a Midheaven of Libra 21° corresponds to an Ascendant of Sagittarius 18° 47', a Midheaven of Libra 22° to an Ascendant of Sagittarius 19° 33'. The difference is 60 between the Midheavens, 46 between the Ascendants. At London a Midheaven of Libra 21° corresponds to an Ascendant of Sagittarius 18° 14', a Midheaven of Libra 22° to an Ascendant of Sagittarius 19° 00'; the differences are the same, 60 and 46. What we want is a Latitude at which a Midheaven of Libra 21° 40' will correspond to an Ascendant of Sagittarius 19° 00'.

As a first step, let us establish what would correspond to a Midheaven of Libra 21° 40' at either parallel. I approach the question like this: 40 is ⅔ of 60, and the same proportion of 46 is just over 30. Adding 30 to the lower figure for the Ascendants at either Latitude gives us Sagittarius 19° 17' at Taunton, Sagittarius 18° 44' at London, when Libra 21° 40' is on the Midheaven.

Now, the difference between 18°44′ and 19°17′ is 33, and ⅔ of 33 is 22. Adding this to the lower figure gives us Sagittarius 19°06′, which is near enough. It is already obvious we are going to be somewhere in Surrey. The distance between 51°01′ and 51°32′ is 31. ⅔ of this is just over 20. Adding this to the lower figure gives us 51°21′. This is our parallel, for which the horoscope is calculated.

At this stage, I open out an Ordnance Survey map for Greater London and take a ruler. The parallel for 51°21′ runs just south of Ewell. The meridian of 0°20′ west runs through the east of Claygate. The co-ordinates meet, then, at a point very slightly south-east of Claygate, where the map shows nothing. But this is just three and a half miles (a horoscopically insignificant distance) east of Nonsuch Park, through which the parallel of 51°21′ actually passes.

---

1. Entry under 'Sidereal Time' in the 'Notes on Astronomical Terms' in *Norton's Star Atlas and Telescopic Handbook,* Arthur P. Norton, B.A. and J. Gall Inglis, F.R.A.S. (Gall and Inglis, Edinburgh and London, first published in 1910 and regularly updated ever since).

Pope's tribute

THE year 1741 saw the unveiling of the statue to Shakespeare in Westminster Abbey. This presents certain oddities which have caused some to regard it as a cryptographic piece. Are the heads of Queen Elizabeth and two earlier sovereigns of England which adorn the plinth intended to suggest some association with the monarchy? Are the crossed legs, clad in stockings embroidered with cruciform roses, intended to form a rebus, ROSY CROSS? We must be careful not to be led into idle fancies, especially as cross-legged statues go back into classical times. But the long narrow face bears less resemblance to the Droeshout, the Chandos portrait or the Stratford bust than to portraits of Bacon, so far as his hat will let us see him. Baconians have looked closely at the text on the scroll. It appears to be a quotation from *The Tempest*, IV, ii, 151-56 but as such is incorrect.

The Folio text of the passage used is:

> And like the baselesse fabricke of this vision
> The Clowd-capt Towres, the gorgeous Pallaces,
> The solemne Temples, the great Globe it selfe
> Yea, all which it inherit, shall dissolue,
> And like this insubstantiall Pagent faded
> Leaue not a racke behinde

What is carved in the marble is:

> The Cloud cupt Tow'rs,
> The Gorgeous Palaces
> The Solemn Temples,
> The Great Globe itself
> Yea all which it Inherit,
>   Shall Dissolue;
> And like the baseless Fnbrick of a Vision
> Leave not a wreck behind.

This statue was erected on the initiative of four people, the 3rd Earl Burlington, Alexander Pope, Dr. Richard Mead and Dr. Thomas Martin, at their own expense, save for some minor contributions from well-wishers.[1] Burlington was the neighbour and patron of Pope, and would perhaps have supported any cultural project about which the poet was enthusiastic. Martin was a fellow of the Society of Antiquaries. Mead was a Fellow and former Vice-President of the Royal Society; he was a physician, the author of a celebrated work on poisons,[2] and discoverer of the mite which caused the itch. He also had scattered amateur interests, in antiques, in Roger Bacon and in Shakespeare. Pope was the foremost poet of the day, and one of its foremost Shakespeare scholars, the editor of an edition of Shakespeare's works printed in 1725. It is obvious that, in such a company, Pope would be thought of by the others as the literary one, on whom responsibility for the selection and accuracy of the quotation would naturally fall. In his edition of the Works, he had made emendations where he fancied desirable but no such apparently impertinent re-casting of a whole passage, as appears on the marble.

Baconians have wondered if the distortion was made to bear a cipher. I have generally avoided involvement with cipher, for it is a specialised domain and one, moreover, in which it is easy to lose reality in illusion. The most serious attempts to find cipher have, however, a common feature which is simple, that the letters of the alphabet should be numbered straight through from A to Z, 1 to 24 (J and V being treated as forms of I and U, respectively, as in Latin). By this count, the letters BACON add to 33, which is the highest degree in Masonry, and those interested in the possibility of cipher look at the 33rd page, line, word or letter of a text. Alfred Dodd made an experiment based upon the number of letters in the inscription, but this appeared to me to leave unexplained the change of ''racke'' (a vestigial trace of cloud) to 'wreck'', since the number of letters is the same.

Where Dodd had counted letters, Mr. T.D. Bokenham peered into them.[3] He noticed that the word too easily read ''Fabrick'' was ''Fnbrick'' (this I have checked against the marble). As the intrusive *n* stood between an *F* and a *b*, Bacon's initials, and was the 33rd letter from the *S* of ''Shall Dissolve'', inset as if to suggest a starting-point, and *N* was the 13th letter of the alphabet, he decided to count in 13s. From the *b* of ''Fnbrick'', this brought him to the *n* of ''Vision'', the *c* of ''wreck'' and (passing from the end to the beginning of the inscription) the *o* of ''Cloud'', the *h* of ''the'' and the second *a* of ''Palaces''. He now had NNCOHA. Starting from the *F* of ''Fnbrick'', brought him to the *i* of ''Vision'', the *r* of ''wreck'', and *C* of ''Cloud'', the *s* of ''Tow'rs'' and the first *a* of ''Palaces''. With the FNB, he now had altogether COSHAAFNSBINRC. Discarding the H on the authority of Camden,[4] he was left with an anagram for FRANCIS BACON.

For all my suspicion of cipher, this does seem to be neat. Especially satisfactory is that it accounts meaningfully for ''wreck'', for what the anagram needs from the word is the *R*. It was necessary for the cipherer to move the *R* of ''racke'' from its position as the first (which would have been only 12 from the *I* of Vision) to that of the second letter of the word, where it is found in ''wreck'', a word that by good fortune carries something the same meaning. If Pope was doing this deliberately, then he was being marvellously adroit.

It is, therefore, interesting to turn to the Fourth book of his *Dunciad,* wherein one finds a comment on the statue and an apparent mockery of the "most critical Curators" for their exhibition of "the first specimen of an edition of an author in Marble, where (as may be seen on comparing the Tomb with the Book) in the space of five lines two Words and a whole Verse are changed". But those responsible were himself and his three colleagues, so that if they are Dunces, he is the chief of them, unable to get it right. But note that he refers not to "mistakes" but to "changes", so perhaps he intended them. The life of Pope exhibits pranks. If he had made in marble his supreme practical joke, he may have been surprised the alterations had caused no earlier outcry and decided to signpost them for posterity.

Mr. Bokenham supposes Pope may have been informed by Mead of a Baconian tradition within the Royal Society, but wonders why he should have reburied it, in marble, instead of writing something about it openly. All reason for secrecy had surely ended with Bacon's death.

Here my experience suggests an explanation. Persons who have received information under seal of secrecy can be very reluctant to break it, even when the apparent need for it has gone. They feel there may be some remaining reason for it of which they do not know, and that it is not for them to vulgarise what others have kept close. Somebody who has, from the outside, picked up what seem to him to be indications of a secret tradition is free to pubish his speculations, but Pope, if indeed he had received certain information *sub rosa,* may have felt it impossible to break the trust by publicising except in the cryptic manner hallowed by the tradition.

If Pope did believe that Bacon was not only the father of physcial science (of more interest to Mead than to himself) but of the works of Shakespeare he had so reverently edited, it would explain why, despite his role in obtaining the erection of the statue to the dramatist in the Abbey, he should, in the conversations with Spence, towards the end of his life, have talked to him not of Shakespeare but of Bacon, saying, "Lord Bacon was the greatest genius that England (or perhaps any other country) has ever produced".[5]

1. *The Gentleman's Magazine,* February, 1741, p.105.
2. Referred to above, p.322n.
3. 'The Shakespeare Monument in Westminster Abbey' in 'Those Shakespeare Manuscripts', T.D. Bokenham (*Baconiana;* 1975).
4. *Remaines Concerning Britain,* William Camden (1605), the chapter 'Anagrams': "The precise . . . are only bold with an H, either in omitting or retaining it . . ."
5. *Anecdotes,* Joseph Spence (ed. Singer, 1820).

The Gorhambury Quartos

EARLY in the present century, the Manor in which Bacon had lived was felt uncomfortable and a new residence was built within the grounds at Gorhambury. Everything in the old house was transferred to the new, and as the library was carried over, it was noticed that the books included seven Shakespeare Quartos:

Romeo and Juliet	1599
Richard III	1602
Hamlet	1605
King Lear	1608
Titus Andronicus	1611
I King Henry IV	1613
Richard II	1615

one copy of each, bound into two volumes with other writings of similar dates.

It is not known how they came to be there. The present family of Verulams think they must have formed part of Bacon's library, simply because they cannot think of anybody else who lived in that house who would have been likely to bring in Shakespeare Quartos. The binding could have been done by a more recent occupant, who thought good to secure together things of similar character.

The likelihood of Shakespeare Quartos being acquired casually recedes with distance from the time in which they were produced. They have now been transferred, for safe-keeping, to the Bodleian. There are so few of them altogether, it is rather odd that seven should have as their provenance that house.[1]

---

1. As the dates of the *Hamlet* Quarto are generally given as 1602, "the bad Quarto", and 1604, "the good Quarto", the 1605 puzzled me and I wrote about it to the Bodleian; the Keeper of Printed Books, Dr. R.T. Roberts, replied to me, "There are seven known copies of the second or 'good' quarto of *Hamlet*. Of these, three bear the date 1604 and four the date 1605. The Verulam copy is one of the latter. The texts are otherwise identical and the reason for the change of date is not known. There is, I suppose, a possibility that the title-pages were printed about the turn of the year".

Bibliography

MANUSCRIPTS

Alnwick Castle *The Northumberland Manuscript*
Rousham *The Countess of Southampton's Letters*
Lambeth Palace Library *Tenison Manuscripts; Fortescue Papers*
British Museum *The Promus; Passports to Navarre of Anthony Bacon and train; Lansdowne Manuscripts; Harleian Manuscripts; Additional Manuscripts; Birch Manuscripts*
Public Record Office *The Duke of Norfolk's Confession; Mother Dowe's Confession; State Papers*
University of London Library *Corton Cowell's two addresses to the Ipswich Philosopical Society, MS 294*
Somerset House *Sir Nicholas Bacon's Will*
City of Westminster Civic Library (Archives) *Francis Bacon's Baptismal Registration*
Hatfield House *Cecil Papers*

BOOKS

(the place of publication is London except where otherwise stated)
The Works, the Letters and the Life of Francis Bacon, James Spedding (Longmans, 1858-74), fourteen volumes
A Conference of Pleasure, ed. Spedding (Longman, 1870)
Promus of Formularies (British Museum, 1898)
Sir Francis Bacon's Letters, ed. Scrinia Ceciliana (1663)
A Collection of Letters made by Sir Tobie Matthew Kt., with dedicatory letter by Dr. Donne (1660)
Collotype Facsimile & Type Transcript of an Elizabethan Manuscript Preserved at Alnwick Castle, Northumberland, Transcribed and Edited with Notes and Introduction by Frank J. Burgoyne, Librarian of the Lambeth Public Libraries (Longmans, Green, 1904)
Of the Advancement of Learning, interpreted by Gilbert Wats (1640)
A Translation of Certain Psalms (1625)

BACON STUDIES (orthodox)

Amboise, Pierre, *Histoire Naturelle de François Bacon, Baron de Verulam, Vicomte de Saint Alban et Chancelier d'Angleterre* (Antoine de Somaville et André Sombron, Paris, 1631)

Bevan, Brian, *The Real Francis Bacon, a biography* (Centaur, 1960)
Bowen, Catherine Drinker, *Francis Bacon, the Temper of a Man* (Hamish Hamilton, 1963)
Campbell, Lord John, *The Life of Francis Bacon* (Murray, 1853)
Crowther, J.G., *Francis Bacon, the First Statesman of Science* (Cresset, 1960)
Dixon, William Hepworth, *The Personal History of Francis Bacon* (Murray, 1861)
Dixon, William Hepworth, *The Story of Lord Bacon's Life* (Murray, 1862)
du Maurier, Daphne, *Golden Lads, a study of Anthony Bacon, Francis and their Friends* (Gollancz, 1975)
du Maurier, Daphne, *The Winding Stair, Francis Bacon, His Rise and Fall* (Gollancz, 1976)
Farrington, Benjamin, *Francis Bacon, Philosopher of Industrial Science* (Collier, New York, 1961)
Gibson, R.V., *Francis Bacon, a Bibliography of his Work and of Baconiana to the Year 1750* (OUP, 1960)
Macauley, Thomas Babington, *Lord Bacon* (Longman, 1852)
Mallet, David, *The Life of Francis Bacon, Lord Chancellor of England, 1740*
Rawley, William, D.D., *Resuscitation; or bringing into public light several pieces of the works, civil, historical, philosophical and theological, hitherto sleeping, of the Right Honourable Francis Bacon, Baron of Verulam, Viscount St. Alban, according to the best corrected copies,* prefaced by a *Life of the Honourable Author* (1657)
Rossi, Paolo, *Francis Bacon, from Magic to Science* (Routledge, 1968)
Tenison, Thomas, Archbishop of Canterbury, *Baconiana* (1679)
Vickers, Brian, ed., *Essential Articles for the Study of Francis Bacon* (Ardon, Connecticut, USA, 1968)
Wats, Gilbert, *Of The Advancement of Learning, interpreted* (1640)

BACONIAN THEORY

Bacon, Delia, The *Philosophy of Shakespeare's Plays Unfolded* (1857)
Baker, H. Kendra, *Bacon's Vindication* (Bacon Society, undated)
Baker, H. Kendra, *Pope and Bacon: the meaning of the "Meanest"* [arguing meanest meant most modest] (Bacon Society, undated)
Baker, H. Kendra, *Who Wrote Love's Labour's Lost?* (Bacon Society, undated)
Baker, H. Kendra, Barrister-at-Law, *The Persecution of Francis Bacon* (Bacon Society, 1978)
Begley, Rev. Walter, of St. John's College, Cambridge, *Is it Shakespeare?* (John Murray 1903)
Bokenham, T.D., *The "Original" Shakespeare Monument at Stratford-on-Avon,* (Francis Bacon Society, 1968)
Bridgewater, Howard, [Barrister-at-law] *"Shakespeare" and Italy* (Bacon Society, 1938)
Bridgewater, Howard, [Barrister-at-law], *Evidence Connecting Francis Bacon with Shakespeare* (George Longworth, 1949)

Brown, Basil, *Law Sports at Gray's Inn* [arguing Shakespeare wrote the plays but with help and protection from Bacon] (New York, 1931)

Bunten, Alice Chambers, *Twickenham Park and Old Richmond Park and Francis Bacon, Lord Verulam's connection with them* (Robert Banks, 1912)

Bunten, Alice Chambers, *A Life of Alice Barnham, 1582-1650* (Page & Thomas, 1919)

Castle, Edward James, One of Her Majesty's Counsel, *Shakespeare, Bacon, Jonson and Greene* [arguing a collaboration between Bacon and Shakespeare] (Sampson Low, 1897)

Churchill, R.C., *Shakespeare and his Betters, a history and a criticism of the attempts which have been made to prove that Shakespeare's works were written by others* [Stratfordian] *(Reinhardt, 1958)*

Crouch Batchelor, H., *Francis Bacon Wrote Shakespeare, the arguments pro and con frankly dealt with* (Robert Banks, 1912)

Deventer von Konow, Amelia, *Francis Bacon, Last of the Tudors* (New York, 1924)

Dodd, Alfred, *Shakespeare, Creator of Freemasonry* (Rider, 1937)

Dodd, Alfred, *The Secret History of Francis Bacon* (Rider, 1941)

Dodd, Alfred, *The Personal Poems of Lord Bacon* (Daily Post Printers, Liverpool, 1944)

Dodd, Alfred, *The Martyrdom of Francis Bacon* (Rider, 1946)

Dodd, Alfred, *Francis Bacon's Personal Life Story* (Rider, 1949)

Douse, Thomas le Marchant, *Examination of a Manuscript* [Stratfordian] (1904)

Durning-Lawrence, Sir Edwin, *Bacon is Shakespeare* (Smith Elder, 1915)

Eagle, Roderick L., *Shakespeare Forgers and Forgeries* (Bacon Society, undated)

Eagle, Roderick L., *The Death of Falstaff* (Baconiana, 1972)

Eagle, Roderick L., see also under Hapgood

Gerstenberg, Joachim, *Bacon, Shakespeare and the Great Unknown* (Bacon Society, 1967)

Gerstenberg, Joachim, *Strange Signatures* (Bacon Society, 1967)

Gerstenberg, Joachim, *Coincidences,* (Kalamakion, Corinth, Greece, 1969)

Gibson, E.N. *The Shakespeare Claimants* [Stratfordian] (New York, 1962)

Goldsworthy, William Lansdowne, *Shakespeare's Heraldic Emblems* (Witherby, 1928)

Goldsworthy, William Lansdowne, *Ben Jonson and the First Folio* (Cecil Palmer, 1931)

Greenwood, Sir George Granville, of the Middle Temple, Barrister-at-Law, *Shakespeare's Law* (Cecil Palmer, 1920)

Greenwood, Sir George Granville, *Ben Jonson and Shakespeare* (Cecil Palmer, 1921)

Greenwood, Sir George Granville, *The Shakespeare Signatures, a reply to* (Cecil Palmer, 1924)

Greenwood, Sir George Granville, *The Stratford Bust and the Droeshout Engraving* (Cecil Palmer, 1924)

Greenwood, Sir George Granville, *Shakespeare's Handwriting and the Northumberland Manuscript* (Cecil Palmer, 1925)

Greenwood, Sir George Granville, see also under Smithson

Gundry, W.G.C., of the Middle Temple, Barrister-at-Law, *Francis Bacon, a Map of Days, A Guide to his Homes and Haunts* (Bacon Society, 1946)

Gundry, W.G.C., of the Middle Temple, Barrister-at-Law, ed. *Manes Verulamiani*, the 1626 edition in photo-facsimile, with translation from the Latin, introduction, notes and appendices (Privately Printed at the Chiswick Press, 1950, distributed by The Bacon Society)

Hapgood, F.E.C. and Eagle, R.L., *The Stratford Birthplace* (Bacon Society, 1947)

Johnson, Edward D., *A Short History of the Stratford Monument* (Bacon Society, 1963)

Melsome, W.S., *The Bacon-Shakespeare Controversy* (1947)

Pares, Martin, *A Pioneer, in Memory of Delia Bacon, February 2nd, 1811, to September 2nd, 1859* (Bacon Society, 1958)

Pares, Martin, *Knights of the Helmet* (Bacon Society, 1964)

Pares, Martin, *Who was Shakespeare?* (Aylesford Review, Summer-Autumn, 1964)

Pares, Martin, *The Tempest and the Mysteries* (Privately printed, 1969)

Pares, Martin, *Francis Bacon and the Utopias* (Privately printed, undated)

Pott, E.W. (Mrs. Henry), *The Promus of Formularies (being private notes circa 1594 hitherto unpublished) by Francis Bacon, illustrated and elucidated by passages from Shakespeare* (Longman's Green, 1883)

Pott, E.W. (Mrs. Henry), *Did Bacon Write Shakespeare?* (1884)

Pott, E.W. (Mrs Henry), *Francis Bacon and his Secret Society* (Robert Banks, 1911)

Smith, William Henry, *Was Lord Bacon the Author of Shakespeare's Plays* (Skeffington 1856)

Smithson, E.W., and Greenwood, Sir George Granville, *Baconian Essays* (Cecil Palmer, 1922)

Theobald, R.M., *Shakespeare Dethroned, a collection of letters contributed to "The Daily Telegraph" with the Preliminary Editorial Papers* (Sampson Low, 1888)

Woodward, Parker, *The Early Life of Lord Bacon* (1902)

SHAKESPEARE STUDIES

Akrigg, G.P.V., *Shakespeare and the Earl of Southampton* (Hamish Hamilton, 1968)

Arnold, Paul, *Esotericisme de Shakespeare* (Paris, 1955)

Baldwin, T.W., *William Shakespeare's Small Latine and Lesse Greeke* (Illinois, 1944) two volumes

Bartlett, John, *A Complete Concordance . . .* (Macmillan, 1966)

Berry, Francis, *The Shakespeare Inset* (Routledge, 1965)

Bradbrook, Muriel, *The School of Night* (CUP, 1936)

Brown, Ivor, *The Women in Shakespeare's Life* (Bodley Head, 1968)

Bullough, Geoffrey, *Narrative and Dramatic Sources of Shakespeare* (Routledge, 1964-75) seven volumes

Burgess, Anthony, *Shakespeare* (Cape, 1970)

Campbell, Lord John, *Shakespeare's Legal Acquirements Considered* (1859)

Chambers, Sir E.K., *William Shakespeare, a Study of Facts and Problems* (OUP, 1939) two volumes

Cook, Canon A.M., *The Lincolnshire Background of Shakespeare's Tragedy of Richard II* (Lincoln Civic Trust, 1964)

Cook, Ivor, *William Hervey and Shakespeare's Sonnets (Shakespeare Survey,* No 21, 1968)

Cook, Ivor, *Titchfield - Shakespearean Treasure-house (Hampshire,* Vol. 11, 8, 1971)

Cook, Ivor, *Shakespeare's Sonnets and Mr. W.H. (The Times,* 1969)

Dowden, Edward, *Shakespeare, A Critical Study of his Mind and Art* (1875)

Gittings, Robert, *Shakespeare's Rival* (Heinemann, 1960)

Gollancz, Sir Israel, *The Sources of Hamlet, with an essay on the legend* (OUP, 1926)

Gray, Arthur, *A Chapter in the Early Life of Shakespeare* (CUP, 1926)

Greg, Walter William, *Sir Thomas More,* ed. (Malone Society, 1911)

Halliwell-Phillipps, James Orchard, *The Life of William Shakespeare* (1848)

Hinman, Charlton, *The Printing and Proof-Reading of the First Folio of Shakespeare's Plays* (OUP, 1963), two volumes

Hotson, Leslie, *Shakespeare Versus Shallow* (Nonesuch, 1931)

Hotson, Leslie, *I, William Shakespeare do appoint Thomas Bushell* (Cape, 1937)

Hotson, Leslie, *Mr. W.H.* (Hart-Davis, 1964)

Hotson, Leslie, *Shakespeare, by Hilliard* (Chatto, 1977)

Jones, Daniel, *Shakespeare in the Original Pronunciation,* in *English Pronunciation through the Centuries* (Linguaphone, undated)

Jones, Ernest, *Hamlet and Oedipus* (Gollancz, 1949)

Kerr, Jessica, and Dowden, Anne Ophelia, *Shakespeare's Flowers* (Methuen, 1972)

Kott, Jan, *Shakespeare our Contemporary* (Methuen, 1965)

Lee, Sir Sidney, *A Life of William Shakespeare* (Smith Elder, 1899)

Lee, Sir Sidney, *The Herbert-Fitton Theory* (1907)

Malone, Edmund, *An Attempt to Determine the Order in which the Plays of Shakespeare were Written* (1778)

Marrian, F.J.K., *Shakespeare and Gray's Inn* (Villiers, 1967)

Partridge, A.C., *Orthography in Shakespeare and Elizabethan Drama* (Arnold, 1964)

Partridge, Eric, *Shakespeare's Bawdy* (Routledge, 1947)

Pollard, A.E., *Shakespeare's Hand in the Play of Sir Thomas More* (1962)

Prince, F.T., *Shakespeare: The Poems* (Longman, 1963)

Rowse, A.L., *William Shakespeare, A Biography* (Macmillan, 1963)

Rowse, A.L., *Shakespeare's Sonnets, ed. with an Introduction and Notes* (Macmillan, 1964)

Rowse, A.L., *Shakespeare's Southampton, Patron of Virginia* (Macmillan, 1965)

Rowse, A.L., *Shakespeare, the Man* (Macmillan, 1973)

Schoenbaum, S., *Shakespeare's Lives* (OUP, 1970)

Schoenbaum, S., *Shakespeare, a Documentary Life* (OUP, 1975)

Schricks, Wilem, *Pericles in a Book-list of 1619 from the English Jesuit Mission and some of the Play's Special Problems* (Shakespeare Survey, 29, 1976)

Speaight, Robert, *Shakespeare, the Man and his Achievement* (Dent, 1977)

Spurgeon, Caroline, *Shakespeare's Imagery* (OUP, 1935)
Stopes, Charlotte Carmichael, *The Bacon-Shakespeare Question* (1888)
Stopes, Charlotte Carmichael, *The Story of the Stratford Bust* (Murray, 1904)
Stopes, Charlotte Carmichael, *Shakespeare's Southampton, Patron of Virginia* (CUP, 1922)
Tannenbaum, Samuel, *Problems in Shakespeare's Penmanship* (Century, New York, 1927)
Tannenbaum, Samuel, *Shakespeare and Sir Thomas More* (Werner Laurie, 1929)
Thomson, J.A.K., *Shakespeare and the Classics* (Allen & Unwin, 1951)
Thomson, Patricia, *The Date Clue in Shakespeare's Sonnet 98* (Neophilologus, Groningen, 1966)
Tilliard, R.M.V., *Shakespeare's History Plays* (Chatto, 1944)
Tilliard, R.M.V., *The Elizabethan World Picture* (Chatto, 1945)
Tilliard, R.M.V., *Shakespeare's Problem Plays* (Chatto, 1964)
Tilliard, R.M.V., *Shakespeare's Early Comedies* (Chatto, 1966)
Tyler, R., *The Herbert-Fitton Theory of Shakespeare's Sonnets* (1898)
Wickham, Glynn, *Shakespeare's Investiture Play* (*Times Literary Supplement*, December 10th, 1969)
Wilson, John Dover, *The Copy for Hamlet, and the Hamlet Transcript of 1588* (1918)
Wilson, John Dover, *Bibliographic Links* (1923)
Wilson, John Dover, *The Essential Shakespeare* (1932)
Winny, James, *The Player King, A Theme of Shakespeare's Histories* (Chatto, 1968)
Winstanley, Lilian, *Hamlet, Macbeth and King Lear and Contemporary History* (CUP, 1922)
Yates, Frances, *A Study of Love's Labour's Lost* (CUP, 1936)
Yates, Frances, *Shakespeare's Last Plays* (Routledge, 1975)
Zeefeld, W.C., *The Influence of Hall on Shakespeare's Historical Plays* (1937)
Shakespeare Ready Reference
A Shakespeare Encyclopaedia ed. Oscar James Campbell and Edward G. Quinn (Methuen, 1966)
A Shakespeare Companion, F.E. Halliday (Duckworth, 1952)

GERMANE CONTEMPORARY WORKS

Daniel, Samuel, *Delia* (1592) and other poems
Davies, Sir John, *The Complete Works*, ed. Grosart, A.B. (1876)
Davies, John, of Hereford, *The Complete Works*, ed. Grosart, A.B. (1878) two volumes
Drayton, Michael, *Idea's Mirror* (1594) and other poems
Florio, John, *First Fruites* (1578), *Second Fruites* (1591), *A World of Words* (1598); *Giovanni Florio*, Longworth Chambrun (Favot, Paris, 1931)
Greene, Robert, *Friar Bacon and Friar Bungay* (1591), *A Groat's Worth of Wit* (1592)

Hall, Joseph, Bishop of Exeter and Norwich, *The Collected Poems*, ed. Davenport, A. (Liverpool Univ., 1949)

Harvey, Gabriel, *Three Proper, and Wittie, Familiar Letters* (1580), *Four Letters and Certain Sonnets* (1592)

Hayward, John, *The Life and Raign of King Henrie IIII* (1599)

Heywood, Thomas, *If you know not me you know nobody* (1606)

Jonson, Ben, *Ben Jonson* Collected Works ed. Herford, C.H. and Simpson, Percy (OUP, 1925) eleven volumes; Gilchrist, D.G., *An Examination of the Charges maintained by Messrs. Malone, Chalmers and others of Ben Jonson's Enmity towards Shakespeare* (1806); Mort, J., *Ben Jonson and Shakespeare's Sonnets, a commentary of Jonson's Lines Prefaced to First Folio* (1914); Rendall, Gerald R., *Ben Jonson and the First Folio of Shakespeare's Plays* (1937); Knoll, Robert R., *Ben Jonson's Plays* (Nebraska, 1964); Thayer, C.G., *Ben Jonson: Studies in the Plays* (Oklahoma, 1963)

Marston, John, *The Works*, ed. Bullen, A.E. (John C. Nimmo, 1887) three volumes; Caputi, Anthony, *John Marston, Satirist* (Cornell, 1961)

Nashe, Thomas, *The Works of*, ed. McKerrow, R.B. (OUP, 1966) three volumes

Sidney, Sir Philip, *Astrophel and Stella* (1591), *The Prose Works* ed. Feuillerat, Albert (CUP, 1963) three volumes

Spenser, Edmund, *Poetical Works*, ed. Smith. J.C. and de Selincourt E., (CUP, 1912, ed. 1970); *The Sources of Spenser's 'Mother Hubberd's Tale'*, Edwin A. Greenlaw (Modern Philology, January 1905); *The Influence of Machiavelli on Spenser*, Edwin A. Greenlaw (Modern Philology, October, 1909); *Spenser and the Earl of Leicester*, Edwin A. Greenlaw (Modern Languages Association of America, Vol. 25, 1910); *The Shepherd's Calendar*, Edwin A. Greenlaw (Modern Languages Association of America, September, 1911); *Spenser and British Imperialism*, Edwin A. Greenlaw (Modern Philology, January, 1912)

Wyatt, Sir Thomas, *Collected Poems*, ed. Kenneth Muir (Routledge, 1949); Thomson, Patricia *Sir Thomas Wyatt and his Background* (Routledge, 1964)

Anon, *The Three Parnassus Plays (1598-1601)*, ed. J.B. Leishman (Nicholson & Watson, 1949)

Anon, *Histriomastix*, attrib. Marston, (1599)

Anon, *Satiriomastix*, attrib. Dekker and Marston, (1601)

PHILOLOGY AND PHONETICS

Wright, Joseph, *Grammar of the Gothic Language* (OUP, 1910)

Wright, Joseph, *Old English Grammar* (OUP, 1925)

Wright, Joseph and Elizabeth Mary, *An Elementary Middle English Grammar* (OUP, 1928)

Sweet, Henry, *A Student's Dictionary of Anglo-Saxon* (OUP, 1896, rev. 1928)

Sweet, Henry, *An Anglo-Saxon Reader . . . with Grammar . . .* (OUP, 1876, rev. 1943)

Jones, Daniel, *An Outline of English Phonetics* (Heffer, Cambridge, 1947)

Jones, Daniel, *The Pronunciation of English* (CUP, 1950)

Jones, Daniel, *The Phoneme* (Heffer, Cambridge, 1950)

Jones, Daniel, *Shakespeare in the Original Pronunciation* (in *English Pronunciation Through the Centuries*, Linguaphone, undated)
Gimson, A.C. *Introduction to the Pronunciation of English* (Arnold, 1970)
Kökeritz, Helge, *Shakespeare's Pronunciation* (Yale, U.P., 1953)
Dobson, E.J., *English Pronunciation 1500-1700* (OUP, 1957) two volumes

PORTRAITS

Strong, Roy, *Portraits of Queen Elizabeth* (OUP, 1963)
Strong, Roy, *Tudor and Jacobean Portraits* (H.M. Stationery Office, 1969)
Strong, Roy, *The English Icon* (Mellon, 1969)
Strong, Roy, *The Elizabethan Image* (The Tate Gallery, 1969)
Gibson, Robin, and Roberts, Keith, *British Portrait Painters* (Phaidon, 1971)
Spielman, M.H., *The Title-Page of the First Folio . . . A Comparative Study of the Droeshout Portrait and the Stratford Monument* (OUP, 1923)
Stopes, Charlotte, *The Story of the Stratford Bust* (*Monthly Magazine*, 1904)
Piper, David, *O Sweet Mr. Shakespeare I'll have his picture* (National Portrait Gallery, 1964)

CRYPTIC PICTURES [BOOKS CONTAINING]

Peacham, Henry, *Minerva Britanna* [sic] (1612)
Selini, Gustavus, *Cryptomenytices* (Lunaeburg, 1624)
Bacon, Francis, Lugduni Batavorum, *Historia Regni Henrici Septimi* (Rotterdam, 1642)
Bacon, Francis, Lugduni Batavorum, *De Augmentis Scientiarum* (Rotterdam, 1645)
de Larrey, Isaac, *Histoire d'Angleterre, d'Ecosse et d'Irlande* (Rotterdam, 1707)

DEVICES Etc.

R.B. McKerrow, *Printers' and Publishers' Devices in England and Scotland, 1485-1640* (Bibliographical Society, 1913)
Praz, Mario, *Studies in Seventeenth Century Imagery* (Warburg Institute, 1959) two volumes

MASONIC, ROSICRUCIAN AND HERMETIC STUDIES

Ambelain, Robert, *La Franc-Maçonnerie Occultiste et Mystique (1643-1943): Le Martinisme, histoire et doctrine* (Niclaus, Paris, 1946)
Barrett, Francis, *The Magus,* Introduction by Timothy d'Arch Smith (New York, 1967)

Barruel, Abbé, *The Rise of Jacobinism,* translated by Clifford (1797-98) four volumes

Blavatsky, H.P., *Isis Unveiled* (Theosophical Publishing House, New York, 1877) two volumes

Blavatsky, H.P., *The Secret Doctrine,* (Theosophical Publishing House, Adyar, India, 1888) six volumes

Churchward, A., *Origin and Antiquity of Freemasonry* (Sir J. Clauston & Sons, 1898)

Churchward, A., *Origin and Evolution of Freemasonry* (Allen and Unwin, 1920)

Dewar, James, *The Unlocked Secret, Freemasonry Examined* (Kimber, 1966)

Encausse, Gérard (Papus), *Traité Elementaire de Science Occulte* (Dangles, Paris, 1936)

French, Peter J., *John Dee, The World of an Elizabethan Magus* (Routledge, 1972)

Gould, Robert Freake, *The History of Freemasonry* (Jack, London, 1883) three volumes

Hamilton-Jones, J.A., *Bachstrom's Alchemical Anthology* (Watkins, 1960)

Hammond, William, *Masonic Emblems and Jewels* (Philip, 1917)

Holmyard, E.K., *Alchemy,* (Pelican, 1957)

Jones, Bernard E., *Freemason's Guide* (Harrap, 1950)

Knoop, Douglas, Jones, M.A. and Hamer, Douglas, *Early Masonic Pamphlets* (Manchester U.P., 1945)

Knoop, Douglas, Jones, M.A. and Hamer, Douglas, *The Genesis of Freemasonry, an account of the Rise and Development of Freemasonry in its Operative, Accepted and early Speculative Phases* (Manchester U.P., 1947)

Knoop, Douglas, Jones, M.A. and Hamer, Douglas, *Two Earliest Masonic Manuscripts* (Manchester U.P., 1938)

Levi, Eliphas, *History of Magic,* translated by Waite, Arthur Edward (Rider, 1913)

Levi, Eliphas, *Key to the Mysteries,* translated by Aleister Crowley (Rider, 1959)

Levi, Eliphas, *Transcendental Magic,* translated by Waite, Arthur Edward (Rider, 1896)

Leadbeater, C.W., *The Hidden Life in Freemasonry* (Theosophical Publishing House, Adyar, India, 1928)

Lilly, William, *Ancient and Modern Prophesies* (1645)

Lizerand, Georges, *Le Dossier de l'Affaire des Templiers, edité et traduit* (Paris, 1964)

Loiseleur, *La Doctrine Sécrète des Templiers* (Paris, 1872)

Mathers, S.L. (McGregor), *The Kabbalah Unveiled,* containing the following books of the Zohar, *The Book of Concealed Mystery, The Greater Holy Assembly, the Lesser Holy Assembly, translated into English from the Latin version of Knorr von Rosenroth, and collated with the original Chaldee and Hebrew text* (Routledge, 1957)

Mead, G.R.S., *Thrice Greatest Hermes, Studies in Hellenistic Theosophy and Gnosis, Being a Translation of the Extant Sermons and Fragments of the Trismegistic Literature, with Prolegomena, Commentaries and Notes* (Watkins, 1949) three volumes

Mead, G.R.S., *Pistis Sophia, A Gnostic Miscellany: being for the most part*

extracts from the Books of the Saviour, to which are added excerpts from a cognate literature (Watkins, 1963)
Oliver, G., *A Dictionary of Symbolic Masonry* (Spencer, 1853)
Rosicrucian manifestos, *Fama Fraternitatis* and *Confessio* (originally published, anonymously, at Kassel in 1614 and 1615 respectively), translated by Thomas Vaughan
Waite, Arthur Edward, *The Real History of the Rosicrucians, founded on their own manifestoes and on acts and documents collected from the writings of initiated brethren* (Redway, 1887)
Waite, Arthur Edward, *The Secret Tradition in Freemasonry* (Rebman, 1911) two volumes
Waite, Arthur Edward, *Emblematic Freemasonry* (Rider, 1925)
Westacott, E., *Roger Bacon in Life and Legend* (Rockliff, 1953)
Wittermans, Fr., *A New and Authentic History of the Rosicrucians* (Rider, 1938)
Yates, Frances, *Giordano Bruno and the Hermetic Tradition* (Routledge, 1964)
Yates, Frances, *The Rosicrucian Enlightenment* (Routledge, 1973)

VIRGINIA AND THE NEW WORLD

Bennis, Samuel, ed., *The Three Charters of the Virginia Company of London* (1913)
Kingsbury, G.M., ed., *Records of the Virginia Company of London* (Washington, D.C., 1915), IV
Griffiths, Sir Percival, *A Licence to Trade: the History of the English Chartered Companies* (1974)
Strachey, William, *Historie of the Travaile into Virginia Britannica* (1612)
Strachey, William, *A True Repertory of the Wrack and redemption of Sir Thomas Gates, knight, upon and from the islands of the Bermudas his coming to Virginia, and the estate of that colony,* in *Purchas his Pilgrimes* (1625)
Craven, Wesley Frank, *Dissolution of the Virginia Company* (OUP, 1932)
Neil, Edward D., *History of the Virginia Company of London, with letters to and from the first colony never before printed* (Albany, N.Y. Joel Munsell, 1856)
Smith, Captain John, *The Generall Historie of Virginia, New England and the Summer Isles* (1624)
Bradley, A.G., *Captain John Smith* (Macmillan, 1909)
Chatterton, E. Keble, *Captain John Smith* (John Lane, The Bodley Head, 1927)
Gayley, Charles Mills, *Shakespeare and the Founders of Liberty in America* (Macmillan, New York, 1917)
Ward, Sir A.W., *Shakespeare and the Makers of Virginia,* in *Proceedings of the British Academy, 1919-1920*

BACKGROUND BIOGRAPHIES AND RELATED STUDIES

Henry VIII and period
Chamberlain, Frederick, *The Private Character of Henry VIII* (John Lane, 1932)

Scarisbick, J.J., *Henry VIII* (Eyre & Spottiswoode, 1968)
Thomson, Patricia, *Sir Thomas Wyatt and his Background* (Routledge, 1964)

Elizabeth and period
Chamberlain, Frederick, *The Private Character of Queen Elizabeth* (John Lane, 1922)
Jenkins, Elizabeth, *Elizabeth the Great* (Gollancz, 1965)
Jenkins, Elizabeth, *Elizabeth and Leicester* (Gollancz, 1961)
Waldman, Milton, *Elizabeth and Leicester* (Collins, 1941)
Williams, Neville, *Elizabeth, Queen of England* (Weidenfeld, 1967)
Williams, Neville, *Thomas Howard, Fourth Duke of Norfolk* (Barrie & Rockcliffe, 1964)
Williams, Neville, *All the Queen's Men* (Weidenfeld, 1972)
Devereux, Walter Bouchier, *Lives and Letters of the Devereux, Earls of Essex* (Murray, 1853) two volumes
Strachey, Lytton, *Elizabeth and Essex* (Chatto, 1928)
Harrison, G.B., *Robert Devereux, Earl of Essex* (Cassell 1937)
Lacey, Robert, *Robert, Earl of Essex* (Weidenfeld, 1971)
Rowse, A.L., *Raleigh and the Throckmortons* (Macmillan, 1962)
Valois, Marguerite de, ed. André Mauléon, *Les Mémoires de la Reine Marguerite* (1626)
Maréjol, J.H., *A Daughter of the Medicis* (1929)
Haldane, Charlotte, *Queen of Hearts, Marguerite de Valois* (Constable, 1968)
Handover, P.M., *Arabella Stuart, Royal Lady of Hardwick and Cousin to King James* (Eyre & Spottiswoode, 1963)
McInnes, Ian, *The Life and Times of Lady Arabella Seymour, (1575-1615)* (W.H. Allen, 1968)

James I
Matthew, David, *James I* (Eyre & Spottiswoode, 1967)
Matthew, David, *Tobie Matthew* (Max Parrish, 1950)
Ashton, Robert, ed., *James I by his Contemporaries* (Hutchinson, 1969)
Oman, Carola, *Elizabeth of Bohemia* (Hodder, 1964)
Bowen, Catherine Drinker, *The Lion and the Throne, the Life and Times of Sir Edward Coke, 1552-1634* (Hamish Hamilton, 1957)
Amos, Andrew, *The Great Oyer of Poisoning* (Richard Bentley, 1846)
Parry, Edward H, *The Overbury Mystery . . .* (Fisher Unwib, 1925)
White, Beatrice, *Cast of Ravens, the Strange Case of Sir Thomas Overbury* (Murray, 1965)
Lawrence, T, *Giuliemi Harvii* (1766)
Gibb, M.A., *Buckingham* (Collins, 1925)
Cammell, Charles Richard, *The Great Duke of Buckingham* (Collins, 1939)
Williamson, Hugh Ross, *George Villiers, First Duke of Buckingham* (Duckworth, 1940)
Erlanger, Philippe, *George Villiers, Duc de Buckingham* (Gallimard, Paris, 1951)

GENERAL AND MISCELLANEOUS

Maitland, F.M., *The Constitutional History of England* (CUP, 1908)
Froude, J.A., *History of England from the Fall of Wolsey to the Defeat of the Spanish Armada* (Longman, 1865-70)
Cambridge Modern History, IV, (CUP, 1900)
Wedgwood, C.V., *The Thirty Years War* (Cape, 1938)
Howell and Corbett, *State Trials*, 14 (1805)
Neale, Sir John, *The Elizabethan House of Commons* (Cape, 1949)
Stowe, John, *The Annales of England, 1580* (1605)
Camden, William, *Remains Concerning Britaine* (1605)
Cox, J. Charles, *The Parish Registers of England* (Methuen, 1910)
Tate, W.E., *The Parish Chest, a Study of the Parochial Administration in England* (CUP, 1906)
Wilson, F.P., *The Plague in Shakespeare's London* (OUP, 1927)
Sprat, Thomas, *History of the Royal Society* (1667)
Purvor, Margery, *The Royal Society, Concept and Creation* (Routledge, 1967)
The Loseley Manuscripts, ed. Alfred John Kemp (John Murray, 1935)
Calendar of State Papers, Domestic
Calendar of State Papers, Spanish
Calendar of State Papers, Foreign
Calendar of State Papers, Venetian
Calendar of State Papers, Colonial

Index

acacia trees, 248-9
Adams, J.Q., 171
Addenbrook, John, 229
Adonis gardens, 77-8
Agrippina, 174-6
Akrigg, G.P.V., cited, 106, 151, 179
Alcibiades, 291-2
Alençon, Duc d', 45, 112, 114
Alexander, Peter, 308
Alford, Edward, 283
Allen, Francis, 53, 192, 208
Amboise, Pierre, 41, 190, 349
Ambros, M.V., cited, 216
Amos, Andrew, 255-6
Andreae, Johann Valentin, 246
Angel, Rosemary, 249
Anhalt, Christian of, 217, 268-9
Anne Boleyn, Queen of Henry VIII:
    appearance, 30, 32, 109; sister, 39n15;
    marriage, 111n2, 309; FB on, 196; trial
    216; represented in Larrey's *Histoire*, 349
Anne (of Denmark), Queen of James I,
    214-15
Annesley, Sir Brian, 191
Annesley, Cordell, 191, 213
Anthony, Marc, 197, 206
Antonio, Don (Portuguese Pretender), 66
Aristotle, 207, 306
Armadas (Spanish), 51, 60
Arundel, Thomas Howard, 14th Earl of,
    288, 310, 345
Asclepius, 218
Ashley, Catherine, 350
Ashley, John, 350
Ashmole, Elias, 247
Ashton, 254
Asmund and Cornelia, 75
astrology, 299
Aubrey, John, 28, 230, 233, 267, 290, 344
Augustus Caesar (Octavian), 100-102,
    197, 207, 212
Awbry, Christopher, 282, 287

Bacon family: motto, 86
Bacon, Alice, Viscountess St Albans (FB's
    wife; *née* Barnham): FB courts, 183;
    marriage, 190-91; infidelities, 191; and
    Sonnets, 213; intercedes with Prince of
    Wales, 295; and FB's will, 344; remarries
    (Underhill), 344-5
Bacon, Ann, Lady (Lord Keeper's wife; *née*
    Cooke): marriage and children, 25;

accomplishments, 26; portraits and
    appearance, 27, 32; husband's will, 44;
    fear of Catholics, 53; and son Anthony,
    53-5, 67-9, 192, 208; declines money to
    FB, 62-3; calls FB her 'ward', 63-4;
    concern for FB, 67; fear of bawdry, 68-9;
    on FB's Solicitorship, 130; relations with
    FB, 176; in old age, 192-3; and *King Lear,*
    192-3; death, 199
Bacon, Anthony (Lord Keeper's son):
    relations with FB, 25, 122, 139, 180;
    portrait bust and appearance, 27-8, 32;
    gout, 31; and father's will, 44;
    communicates with Walsingham, 53; and
    mother, 53-5, 67-9, 192, 208;
    homosexuality, 53, 143, 192, 208; shares
    rooms with FB, 53; and Essex, 55; financial
    help for FB, 62-4, 67-8, 143; and sale of
    Barly, 64; moves to Bishopsgate, 68; and
    Northumberland manuscript, 73, 75;
    Navarre passport name, 122; and FB's
    Solicitorship, 130; letters in Essex case,
    158-9, 166; death, 179-80
Bacon, Delia, 74, 202
Bacon, Sir Edmund, 29-30, 308
Bacon, Edward (Lord Keeper's son), 25
Bacon, Elizabeth (Lord Keeper's daughter),
    73
Bacon, Francis, Baron Verulam and Vis-
    count St Albans: birth, 25, 27n1, 36;
    horoscope, 26n2; portraits and appearance,
    27-31; question of parenthood, 30-31, 36,
    58, 113, 115, 127, 133-4, 181, 349-50;
    and father's will, 30, 44; genetic evidence
    of parentage, 31-2; childhood and
    education, 40-41, 233; early travels, 41-3,
    122-4; Sir Nicholas Bacon's death, 43; and
    Alençon's suit for Elizabeth's hand, 45; at
    Gray's Inn, 47; as MP for Melcombe, 48;
    advises Elizabeth, 49, 52, 54; as lawyer,
    52, 54, 65; MP for Taunton, 52; shares
    rooms with Anthony, 53; and Essex as
    patron, 55; opposes Burghley's triple
    subsidy request, 60-61; proposed as
    Attorney-General, 61-2, 64-5; debts
    62-3, 141, 183; relations with Lady Bacon,
    62-4, 176; and conspiracies against
    Elizabeth, 66-8; loses Solicitorship, 66-7,
    130-32; MA degree, 67; handwriting,
    74-5, 147; Marston on, 86-8; as Labeo,
    95-6; in Jonson's *Poetaster,* 102; and
    Great Instauration, 102; and Countess of